DE FACTO INTERNATIONAL PROSECUTORS IN A GLOBAL ERA

In the past decades, great strides have been made to ensure that crimes against humanity and state-sponsored organized violence are not committed with impunity. Alongside states, large international organizations such as the United Nations and forums such as the International Criminal Court, 'de facto international prosecutors' have emerged to address these crimes. Acting as investigators and evidence-gathers to identify individuals and officials engaged in serious human rights violations, these 'private' non-state actors, and state legal 'officials' in a foreign court, pursue criminal accountability for those most responsible for core international crimes. They do so when local options to investigate fail and an international criminal tribunal remains unavailable. This study outlines three case studies of witnesses and victims who pursue those most responsible, including former heads of state. It examines their practices and strategies, and shows how witnesses and victims of core crimes emerge as key leaders in the accountability process.

Melinda Rankin is Honorary Research Fellow at School of Political Science and International Studies at The University of Queensland, Australia. Prior to this, she was Postdoctoral Research Fellow at The University of Queensland, a Visiting Research Fellow at the Centre for Global Constitutionalism at WZB Berlin and a Lecturer at The University of Sydney. She is the author of *The Political Life of Mary Kaldor: Ideas and Action in International Relations* (2017).

De Facto International Prosecutors in a Global Era

WITH MY OWN EYES

MELINDA RANKIN
The University of Queensland

CAMBRIDGE
UNIVERSITY PRESS

CAMBRIDGE
UNIVERSITY PRESS

University Printing House, Cambridge CB2 8BS, United Kingdom

One Liberty Plaza, 20th Floor, New York, NY 10006, USA

477 Williamstown Road, Port Melbourne, VIC 3207, Australia

314–321, 3rd Floor, Plot 3, Splendor Forum, Jasola District Centre, New Delhi – 110025, India

103 Penang Road, #05–06/07, Visioncrest Commercial, Singapore 238467

Cambridge University Press is part of the University of Cambridge.

It furthers the University's mission by disseminating knowledge in the pursuit of education, learning, and research at the highest international levels of excellence.

www.cambridge.org
Information on this title: www.cambridge.org/9781108498166
DOI: 10.1017/9781108632546

First published 2022

A catalogue record for this publication is available from the British Library.

ISBN 978-1-108-49816-6 Hardback

For
Ashla Bott
and
de facto international prosecutors everywhere

Contents

Acknowledgements

From the very beginning, this project was envisaged as an interdisciplinary endeavour. In this respect, I was enormously fortunate to be guided by many generous, clever and innovative people who saw closing the accountability gap as an inherently interdisciplinary puzzle. They also viewed the roles of private non-State actors and State legal officials in a foreign court (what I describe as '*de facto* international prosecutors') as essential actors in the fight for justice and accountability – particularly when local options for accountability fail. Through their kindness and generosity, including through debates, field trips, interviews, text reviews and corrections, they have profoundly informed this project.

First and foremost, I would like to thank William Wiley, director of the Commission for International Justice and Accountability (CIJA). From the time I first contacted Wiley in 2016, he has remained characteristically honest, humble, open minded, keen to debate and intellectually curious. Throughout the duration, he has insisted that at the heart of the CIJA is the willingness of local Syrian investigators, who have remained in Syria, often under perilous conditions, to collect the type of material that would inform a future criminal prosecution.

Just as importantly, without Wiley, I would not have interviewed 'Chief Investigator 1 (Syria)'. My interview with Chief Investigator 1 (Syria) largely inspired the organisation of the study, including the focus on witnesses and victims of core international crimes. Chief Investigator 1 (Syria) also inspired the second part of the title of this book: 'With My Own Eyes'. It was his words 'with my own eyes' that sharpened the project's direction.

Following on from there, I am enormously grateful to Juan Garcés and Souleymane Guengueng, who have also fought long and hard for justice and inspired the other two biographical case studies in this book. Both

Garcés and Guengueng were enormously kind and generous in reviewing Chapters 2 and 3, respectively, providing much needed feedback and corrections.

Enormous gratitude also goes to John Berger, senior editor at Cambridge University Press. Berger immediately supported this project and understood from its inception the importance of focusing on private non-State actors as important in the global legal order. Thanks also to the two anonymous reviewers of the book proposal, who improved and sharpened key features of the project.

I am indebted also to Chris Reus-Smit, who gave me the opportunity to work with him as a postdoctoral research fellow at The University of Queensland. It was Reus-Smit's suggestion that I draw upon the 'community of practice' scholarship, and he strongly encouraged the interdisciplinary nature of the project. He also reviewed a number of drafts of this book in various forms and was a wonderful mentor for the project and my intellectual development.

Several others also reviewed sections, chapters or the entire manuscript, providing invaluable feedback and corrections: Tarik Abdulhak, Emanuel Adler, Katie Brennan, Benedetta Brevini, Reed Brody, Anthony Cassimatis, Robert Mullins, Paulo Sérgio Pinheiro, Stephen Rapp, Christian Ritscher, Kevin Walton and Christian Wenaweser.

Besides William Wiley and Chief Investigator 1, I am also grateful to many others who work with (or for) the CIJA, some named in the book but also many who remain anonymous. Just as significantly, I am immensely grateful to other witnesses, victims and survivors of core crimes whom I also interviewed for the project, and who continue to work as criminal law practitioners. Although they are not identified as 'witnesses', 'victims' or 'survivors' in this book, they have played a huge role in shaping my thinking.

I would like to thank the following who also supported this project, either intellectually or practically (or both): Sara Afshar, Lindy Baker, Alex Bellamy, Michelle Burgis-Kasthala, Sara Davies, Tobin Fonseca, Nicole George, Sassan Gholiagha, Robert Horvath, Richard Jefferson, John Keane, Mattias Kumm, Susan Lamb, Dirk Moses, Jacinta O'Hagan, Hilde Ottschofski, Andrew Phillips, Sarah Phillips, Gaj Premnath, Sabine Selchow, Colin Wight, and Shannon Zimmerman.

I am also grateful to the librarians at The University of Queensland, including Thomas Palmer and Debbie Martin, who worked tirelessly, searching for elusive texts and case material, and remained unfailingly patient and big hearted.

I am thankful for the feedback given through a number of workshops and colloquiums at The University of Queensland: History and IR Reading Group, International Law Reading Group, Futures of International Order Seminar Series, Food for the Mind POLSIS series; co-hosted by London School of Economics (LSE) and The University of Queensland: The Rules Based International Order workshop; at Humboldt University of Berlin: KFG Rise and Decline of International Law; at *Wissenschaftszentrum Berlin für Sozialforschung* (WZB): the Centre of Global Constitutionalism colloquium series; at Griffith University and The University of Melbourne: International Criminal Law conference; and at the Conference for the International Society of Public Law (ICON-S) in Chile.

I am also grateful for two grants received for this project: the Berlin Fellowship Award from the Sydney Democracy Network, The University of Sydney, and a POLSIS Travel Grant from The University of Queensland. In addition, I am immensely thankful for the intellectual and personal support of the Center for Global Constitutionalism at *Wissenschaftszentrum Berlin für Sozialforschung* (WZB), particularly as visiting research fellow.

Lastly, I am grateful to my loved ones for their generosity, kindness and encouragement.

Some of the chapters in this book draw upon material previously published but have since been developed further in this book. I gratefully acknowledge the following articles:

> M. Rankin (2019) '"Responsibility to Prosecute" Core International Crimes: German Universal Jurisdiction and Suspected Atrocities Committed by the Syrian Government'. *Global Responsibility to Protect*, 11, no. 4. (Chapter 5)
>
> M. Rankin (2018) 'The Future of International Criminal Evidence in New Wars? The Evolution of the Commission for International Justice and Accountability (CIJA)'. *Journal of Genocide Research*, 20, no. 3. (Introduction and Chapter 4)

While this project has benefitted from the generosity and kindness of many, all mistakes are my own.

Introduction

In the beginning, when I heard about the incidents taking part in Dara'a [in 2011, following the torture of schoolboys by the Syrian government for anti-government graffiti], I returned and then I saw with my own eyes what was happening ... as a lawyer I could see a lot of crimes happening, but nobody was documenting them.

CIJA Chief Investigator 1, 2017.[1]

Commission for International Justice and Accountability (CIJA)

[T]he jus cogens nature of the international crime of torture justifies states in taking universal jurisdiction over torture wherever committed ... in this case it is alleged that during the Pinochet regime torture was an official, although unacknowledged, weapon of government [against opposition]. ... If these allegations are true, the fact that the local court had jurisdiction to deal with the international crime of torture was nothing to the point so long as the totalitarian regime remained in power: a totalitarian regime will not permit adjudication by its own courts on its own shortcomings. ... The Torture Convention was agreed not in order to create an international crime which had not previously existed, but to provide an international system under which the international criminal – the torturer – could find no safe haven.

Lord Brown-Wilkinson (Pinochet 3), British House of Lords, 1999.[2]

International criminal justice has emerged as a central tenet of the United Nations (UN) system in the post–World War II era. The decision by Allied Forces to prosecute senior political and industrial leaders of Nazi Germany

---

[1] CIJA Chief Investigator 1 (with translator CIJA Liaison Officer 1), Interview with author, January 2017.
[2] R v. *Bow Street Metropolitan Stipendiary Magistrate*, ex parte Pinochet Ugarte (No 3) (Pinochet 3) [2000], 198–9.

1

ushered in a new era of international law.[3] As Crawford aptly argued, 'It is not too much of an exaggeration to say that the United Nations era began with a trial and a promise.'[4] The trial was the Nuremberg Tribunal, and the promise was that the principles underpinning the Nuremberg Charter were treated as international law.[5,6] By introducing a new body of international criminal law, the Nuremberg Charter 'reached deep' into traditional notions of State sovereignty, including the laws that governed immunity.[7] As Guénaël Mettraux argued, '[T]he Charter pierced through the concept of State sovereignty and inflicted much damage to the idea of absolute sovereignty under law ... the Charter literally retired vibrant legal symbols of the idea of State sovereignty – namely, the doctrine of "acts of State" – and caused official immunities to shrink, including those granted to heads of State.'[8] Such was the effect of the Nuremberg Charter. Despite this – or perhaps because of it – the newly established United Nations General Assembly (UNGA) *unanimously* adopted a resolution in 1946 affirming the principles of international law recognised by the Nuremberg Charter and the judgement of the Tribunal.[9] Yet, according to the majority of States in the international community, adopting the principles of the Nuremberg Charter into international law was not enough.

Numerous legal instruments and treaties followed that signalled justice and human rights were not minor characters cast to honour the horrifying effects of two world wars, but uncompromising principal actors charting the new global stage. In 1945, the Preamble of the UN Charter determined that justice was inextricably linked to the maintenance of obligations arising from international law, and that fundamental human rights applied to all.[10] The drafting of the Universal Declaration of Human Rights (UDHR), adopted by the UNGA in 1948 (including by many States of the so-called Global

---

3 Guénaël Mettraux, 'Trial at Nuremberg', in *Routledge Handbook of International Criminal Law*, ed. William Schabas and Nadia Bernaz (Oxford: Routledge, 2013), 5–16; James Crawford, *Brownlie's Principles of Public International Law*, 9th ed. (Oxford and New York: Oxford University Press, 2019).

4 Crawford, *Brownlie's Principles of Public International Law*, 645.

5 Crawford, *Brownlie's Principles of Public International Law*, 645.

6 Ian Brownlie and James Crawford, *Brownlie's Principles of Public International Law*, 8th ed. (Oxford: Oxford University Press, 2012), 671.

7 Mettraux, 'Trial at Nuremberg', 8. This is not to say that there was no international criminal law prior to this. See Crawford, *Brownlie's Principles of Public International Law*.

8 Mettraux, 'Trial at Nuremberg', 8.

9 United Nations General Assembly, 'General Assembly Resolution 95 (1), Affirmation of the Principles of International Law Recognised by the Charter of the Nurnberg Tribunal' (1946), 95, https://search-proquest-com.ezproxy.library.uq.edu.au/docview/1679073021?accountid=14723.

10 United Nations, 'The Charter of the United Nations' (1945).

South[11]), further enshrined fundamental human rights.[12] Indeed, the UDHR affirmed human rights as under the protection of the 'rule of law', which included protection from torture.[13] Add to this the 1946 Resolution for 'The Crime of Genocide' adopted by the UNGA, the 1949 Geneva Conventions for the protection of war victims, the 1966 International Covenant on Civil and Political Rights and the 1975 Resolution for 'Protection of All Persons from Being Subjected to Torture and Other Cruel, Inhuman or Degrading Treatment or Punishment)' adopted by the UNGA.[14] All cast justice and human rights as central features of the new international order. Many of these international resolutions and treaties have since been reflected in the domestic realm. By the time Senator Augusto Pinochet, former president of Chile, was indicted in the Madrid Courts in the 1990s, 110 States were party to the Convention Against Torture (CAT), including Chile.[15]

Further still, to reinforce the proliferation of treaties that enshrined justice and human rights, States began to establish other treaties that legally *obliged* State parties to hold those suspected of behaviours deemed so abhorrent, with no derogation, to account. For instance, treaties such as the Genocide Convention in 1948[16] and the CAT in 1984[17] were established by States not solely as tools of prohibition, as these behaviours were already deemed prohibited with the establishment of the Nuremberg Tribunal, and with the array of conventions adopted shortly after. Rather, these treaties also established an international regime whereby States were legally obliged to investigate and prosecute those suspected of genocide and/or torture, respectively, within their jurisdiction and whereby States were legally obliged to prosecute or *extradite* (*aut dedere aut judicare*) those suspected of torture or genocide, respectively, irrespective of where the crimes occurred or, at least initially, those party to the conventions.

Moreover, the establishment of the International Criminal Tribunal for the former Yugoslavia (ICTY) and International Criminal Tribunal for Rwanda (ICTR) in the 1990s signalled a recommitment by the international community

---

[11] Roland Burke, *Decolonization and the Evolution of International Human Rights* (Philadelphia: University of Pennsylvania Press, 2010), http://muse.jhu.edu/book/924.

[12] United Nations, 'The Charter of the United Nations'.

[13] United Nations, 'The Charter of the United Nations'.

[14] General Assembly Resolution 3452/30.

[15] R v. *Bow Street Metropolitan Stipendiary Magistrate*, ex parte Pinochet Ugarte (No 3) (Pinochet 3) [2000] (House of Lords, Great Britain (UK) March 24, 1999).

[16] United Nations, 'Convention on the Prevention and Punishment of the Crime of Genocide (Genocide Convention)', December 9, 1948.

[17] United Nations, 'Convention against Torture and Other Cruel, Inhuman or Degrading Treatment or Punishment (CAT)', Treaty Series, 1465 § (1984).

of States to prosecute those most responsible for core international crimes (also referred to as core crimes).[18] Furthering the expansion of the 'system' of international criminal law, a number of international criminal tribunals and hybrid tribunals followed and culminated in the adoption of the Rome Statute and establishment of the International Criminal Court (ICC), the world's first permanent international criminal tribunal.[19] In the post-Nuremberg era, international criminal law had emerged as a central feature of the international order and, with it, was the ascent of international criminal tribunals, including a permanent one.

ACCOUNTABILITY, INTERRUPTED?

Today, the future of international criminal justice appears bleak. As international criminal tribunals have continued to wind down and the ICC remains limited and fraught with difficulties,[20] optimism for the future of international criminal justice, as well as confidence in the ICC, appears on the decline.[21] A primary example of this sentiment is the case of Syria. Since 2011, notwithstanding allegations of crimes against humanity, including torture, international (State) institutions, such as the ICC and the United Nations Security Council (UNSC), have yet to receive or grant, respectively, the requisite permission to conduct a *criminal* investigation within Syria – either upon the invitation of Damascus or under a Chapter VII mandate set by

---

[18]   'Core international crimes' are defined in this book as war crimes, crimes against humanity and genocide (with torture and slavery as subsets of wars crimes and crimes against humanity). The terms 'core international crimes' and 'core crimes' are used interchangeably in this book.

[19]   Marlies Glasius, *The International Criminal Court: A Global Civil Society Achievement*, 1st ed. (London and New York: Routledge, 2006); Kenneth Pennington, *The Prince and the Law, 1200–1600: Sovereignty and Rights in the Western Legal Tradition* (Berkeley: University of California Press, 1993).

[20]   Kip Hale and Melinda Rankin, 'Extending the "System" of International Criminal Law? The ICC's Decision on Jurisdiction over Alleged Deportations of Rohingya People', *Australian Journal of International Affairs* 73, no. 1 (2 January 2019): 22–8, https://doi.org/10.1080/10357718.2018.1548565.

[21]   David Crane, '"Not Perfect Candidates" to Be the Next Prosecutor of the International Criminal Court', *Jurist* (blog), 10 July 2020, www.jurist.org/commentary/2020/07/david-crane-icc-prosecutor/; Kirsten Ainley, 'The International Criminal Court on Trial', *Cambridge Review of International Affairs* 24, no. 3 (2011): 309–33, https://doi.org/10.1080/09557571.2011.558051; Kirsten Ainley, 'The Responsibility to Protect and the International Criminal Court: Counteracting the Crisis', *International Affairs* 91, no. 1 (2015): 37–54, https://doi.org/10.1111/1468-2346.12185; Hovhannes Nikoghosyan, 'Government Failure, Atrocity Crimes and the Role of the International Criminal Court: Why Not Syria, but Libya', *The International Journal of Human Rights: R2P: Perspectives on the Concept's Meaning, Proper Application and Value* 19, no. 8 (2015): 1240–56, https://doi.org/10.1080/13642987.2015.1082838.

the UNSC. Widely criticised by both international law and international relations (IR) scholars alike,[22] the inability of the ICC to investigate in Syria has, some argue, reflected a broader crisis in the system of international criminal and humanitarian law. David Crane, a former international prosecutor, goes as far as to talk of a 'bruised and battered court', suggesting that the ICC is 'languishing', and whereby the 'age of accountability', which was once supported by the international community, has all but dissipated.[23] Indeed, these observations cast a bleak future for international criminal justice.

Nevertheless, while international and hybrid criminal tribunals have played an important role in international criminal justice, what is less noticed in IR and legal literature is the role of 'de facto international prosecutors', a term I define and develop further throughout this book. Briefly, de facto international prosecutors are private non-State actors, and State legal officials in *foreign* courts:[24] specifically, they pursue criminal accountability for those *most* responsible for core international crimes when local options to investigate fail and international or hybrid criminal tribunals remain unavailable. Instead, they prosecute in foreign courts that exercise universal jurisdiction.

While this book examines the role of both private non-State actors and State legal officials in *foreign* courts as de facto international prosecutors, it pays particular attention to the role of private non-State actors. To date, much has been written on the role of State legal officials in foreign courts, which prosecute exercising universal jurisdiction[25] (as well as the practice of States

---

[22] Ainley, 'The Responsibility to Protect and the International Criminal Court'; Nikoghosyan, 'Government Failure, Atrocity Crimes and the Role of the International Criminal Court'.

[23] Crane, '"Not Perfect Candidates" to Be the Next Prosecutor of the International Criminal Court'.

[24] In this book, I refer to private non-State actors and State legal officials for two broad audiences: international relations and legal scholars, including legal theorists. I draw upon aspects (although not all) of H. L. A. Hart's *The Concept of Law*. Hart refers to officials and private individuals as key actors in a legal system. He believed that in a legal system, rules confer legal powers to private actors and officials. In this study, I refer to private non-State actors as individuals that act in their private capacity (even if they may *also* at times be legal officials). In this study, I specifically refer to State legal officials as including police, public prosecutors and judges to make it clear to the reader. Yet only the judge can decide law in each case. Separately I may refer to government officials, who are separate from the judiciary (at least in principle). To make it clear to scholars and lay readers, I refer to them consistently as private non-State actors and State legal officials. See H. L. A. Hart, *The Concept of Law*, ed. Joseph Raz and Penelope A. Bulloch, 3rd ed., Clarendon Law Series (Oxford: Oxford University Press, 2012).

[25] Mitsue Inazumi, *Universal Jurisdiction in Modern International Law: Expansion of National Jurisdiction for Prosecuting Serious Crimes under International Law*, School of Human Rights Research Series, v. 19 (Antwerpen: Intersentia, 2005); Máximo Langer, 'Universal Jurisdiction Is Not Disappearing: The Shift from "Global Enforcer" to "No Safe Haven" Universal

and how they contribute to the body of international criminal law, more broadly).[26] Yet, the role of private non-State actors who adopt the tasks of international prosecutors to pursue criminal accountability in foreign courts remains curiously understudied.

This study aims to remedy this gap. It shines light on the role of de facto international prosecutors, as *an emerging phenomenon*. It illuminates how and why they adopt the practices implicitly or explicitly of the offices of international prosecutors. The practices they undertake include *inter alia* identifying key witnesses and victims, collecting evidence in accordance with international standards, writing case briefs and/or submitting private criminal complaints to foreign courts. Moreover, the study demonstrates how de facto international prosecutors play an essential role in the maintenance of the UN system and the international rule of law, specifically in establishing the conditions for justice and accountability for core crimes.

Furthermore, of particular focus in this study is the role of witnesses and victims of core crimes who act as de facto international prosecutors. To investigate this emerging phenomenon, the study outlines three biographical case studies to illuminate how individual witnesses and victims of core crimes adopt the practices of international prosecutors. They consist of three subjects: they are Juan Garcés, Souleymane Guengueng and Chief Investigator 1 (Syria) in relation to core crimes perpetrated in Chile, Chad and Syria, respectively. While Juan Garcés and Souleymane Guengueng constitute historical cases, Chief Investigator 1 (Syria) continues to investigate in Syria and is a founding member of the Commission for International Justice and Accountability (CIJA). In this way, it explores how and why individuals can play a key role in the pursuit of justice and accountability. By focusing initially on the role these individuals play, as Kathryn Sikkink explained in her seminal book *The Justice Cascade*,[27] the study attempts to show how 'early diffusion' of

Jurisdiction', *Journal of International Criminal Justice* 13, no. 2 (May 1, 2015): 245–56, https://doi.org/10.1093/jicj/mqv009; Luc Reydams, *Universal Jurisdiction: International and Municipal Legal Perspectives, Universal Jurisdiction* (Oxford: Oxford University Press, 2015); Thomas Beck and Christian Ritscher, "'Do Criminal Complaints Make Sense in (German) International Criminal Law? A Prosecutor's Perspective'," *Journal of International Criminal Justice* 13, no. 2 (May 1, 2015): 229–35, https://doi.org/10.1093/jicj/mqv010.

26 Ian Brownlie, *State Responsibility* (Oxford: Clarendon Press, 1983); Brownlie and Crawford, *Brownlie's Principles of Public International Law*; Michael Byers, *Custom, Power and the Power of Rules: International Relations and Customary International Law* (Cambridge and New York: Cambridge University Press, 1999).

27 Kathryn Sikkink, *The Justice Cascade: How Human Rights Prosecutions Are Changing World Politics*, 1st ed. (New York: W. W. Norton & Co., 2011).

practices and objectives 'happens through individuals'.[28] Furthermore, it reveals the need for, and interaction with, a community of practice 'in which individuals operate'.[29]

A study of these particular individuals also offers a counter narrative to the notion that witnesses and victims of core crimes remain solely passive actors in establishing justice and that only Western actors aspire towards criminal accountability (as a form of neocolonialism). Indeed, it shows how these witnesses and victims of core crimes – Juan Garcés, Souleymane Guengueng and Chief Investigator 1 – are key drivers in, and lead the practice of, justice and accountability in a number of important cases, including on behalf of thousands of victims. With others, they pursue justice in the face of what often appear to be claims of the legitimate use of force by sovereigns or rulers on behalf of the State against domestic opposition. By illuminating how former heads of State and senior leaders suspected of core international crimes are rendered equal under international law through criminal accountability for particular acts of violence deemed to be non-derogable, combined with how private non-State actors draw on the pre-existing instruments and conditions to establish this, this book invites a richer view of the practice of international law and its operation, historically and today.

To that end, the study argues that while the establishment of individual criminal liability for particular core crimes remains one of the most radical shifts to the contemporary international order, and to notions of State sovereignty and immunity, second to that is the role of private non-State actors as essential actors in the maintenance of international justice and to the protection of human rights. Moreover, how de facto international prosecutors – private non State actors and State legal officials in foreign courts – work together and adopt the practices of international prosecutors, as well as draw upon the legal obligations of States arising from treaties and other sources of international law, to ensure former heads of State or senior leaders are criminally liable, are two key interrelated concerns of this book. The study also highlights the extent that international criminal law increasingly reflects an array of actors, institutions and means that are perhaps little reflected in IR and legal literature to date. The role of private non-State actors in extending the reach of international criminal law further challenges the traditional nature of public international law as one primarily in the hands of States for the exclusive objectives of the sovereign. While States largely establish international criminal law, this project elucidates how it is increasingly being

---

[28] Sikkink, *The Justice Cascade*, 91.
[29] Sikkink, *The Justice Cascade*, 91.

practised by a multiplicity of actors, including private non-State actors, for core crimes. For those scholars interested in the future of international order and global criminal accountability at large, these actors should spark curiosity.

This book has two broad objectives. First, and the primary objective of this book, is to provide an empirical account to explain how and why de facto international prosecutors, with greater emphasis on private non-State actors, extend the reach of international criminal law to those most responsible for core international crimes, particularly when local efforts for criminal account-ability fail and an international or hybrid criminal tribunal remains unavail-able. Through biographical inquiry, the study illuminates what spurs particular witnesses and victims of core international crimes to pursue crim-inal accountability, despite the extraordinary challenges global criminal accountability poses. This book also takes an interdisciplinary approach to examining the role of de facto international prosecutors. Most particularly, it draws upon IR and international law as practice but also includes, to a lesser extent, legal theory.

Second, and less prominently, the book proposes two theoretical frame-works. The first outlines the conceptual and theoretical arguments of the book. It starts by defining de facto international prosecutors further, particu-larly in relation to the tasks and practices they adopt and the particular context within which they operate. It situates the role of de facto international pro-secutors in the broader context of a 'community practice'. Indeed, it illumin-ates the particular legal practices that govern international criminal law. In all three cases, de facto international prosecutors, including witnesses and victims of core crimes, are guided by the evidence they collect when writing legal briefs or submitting private criminal complaints. It also shows how and why individuals work together to identify sources of international law and pose complex legal arguments concerning the *jus cogens* nature of the crimes.

The second conceptual framework explains the way de facto international prosecutors, particularly private non-State actors, and to a lesser extent State legal officials, outlined in this book, implicitly and explicitly conceptualise international criminal law.

Before I detail the central arguments of the book in greater detail, I first briefly explain how this study extends current academic literature. In particu-lar, it shows how this study extends important work by scholars, such as Kathryn Sikkink, including her formative book *The Justice Cascade*,[30] with

---

[30]   Sikkink, *The Justice Cascade*; Veronica Michel-Luviano, 'Access to Justice, Victims' Rights, and Private Prosecution in Latin America: The Cases of Chile, Guatemala, and Mexico,' ed. Lisa Hilbink et al. (ProQuest Dissertations Publishing, 2012).

particular emphasis on private non-State actors, who pursue criminal accountability. I close with a high-level overview of the approach and structure of the book.

DEFINING DE FACTO INTERNATIONAL PROSECUTORS: AN EMERGING PHENOMENON?

Explaining What Is New: De Facto International Prosecutors as Private non-State Actors

Arguably, private non-State actors who engage in international law are not new subjects of IR or international law scholarship.[31] Through the years, the role of private non-State actors and how they engage with international law is well documented, including in international human rights, humanitarian and criminal law.

In terms of international human rights and humanitarian law, political and legal scholars have made many contributions. For example, scholars have explored the role of private non-State actors as activists who spur State action to establish human rights at the international level.[32] One example is the international abolition of slavery. The Anti-Slavery Society founded in 1839 is possibly the oldest international human rights group and is much studied.[33] Academic literature has also investigated private non-State actors who drafted the early rules for humanitarianism in armed conflict. In 1864, the International Committee of the Red Cross (ICRC) was instrumental in the development of the 'Geneva Convention for the Amelioration of the Condition of the Wounded in Armies in the Field',[34] followed by a number

[31] Math Noortmann et al., *Non-State Actors in International Law* (Oxford, UK and Portland, OR: Hart Publishing, 2015); Ramses A. Wessel et al., *International Governmental Organizations as Non-State Actors* (Oxford: Hart Publishing, 2015); A. Claire Cutler, 'The Judicialization of Private Transnational Power and Authority', *Indiana Journal of Global Legal Studies* 25, no. 1 (2018): 61–95, https://doi.org/10.2979/indjglolegstu.25.1.0061; A. Claire Cutler, *Private Power and Global Authority : Transnational Merchant Law in the Global Political Economy*, *Private Power & Global Authority* (Cambridge: Cambridge University Press, 2003); A. Claire Cutler, Virginia Haufler, and Tony Porter, *Private Authority and International Affairs* (Albany: State University of New York Press, 1999).

[32] Margaret E. Keck and Kathryn Sikkink, *Activists beyond Borders : Advocacy Networks in International Politics* (Ithaca, NY: Cornell University Press, 2014).

[33] Glasius, *The International Criminal Court*; Pennington, *The Prince and the Law, 1200–1600 Sovereignty and Rights in the Western Legal Tradition.*

[34] Glasius, *The International Criminal Court*; International Committee of the Red Cross (ICRC), 'Convention for the Amelioration of the Condition of the Wounded in Armies in the Field,' 22 August 1864.

of other conventions, which later formed the basis of the Geneva and Hague Conventions.[35] Moreover, scholars, such as Martha Finnemore have examined how private non-State actors interact with the rules of war in relation to humanitarian relief in the midst of large-scale conflict and atrocity crimes, such as the ICRC,[36] amongst others. Scholars have also detailed the role of Bernard Kouchner and *Médecins Sans Frontières* (MSF) in the 'duty to intervene' when providing humanitarian medical relief, including operating without relying upon the permission of the relevant State.[37] Sikkink has explored how private non-State actors bring important human rights cases to regional and international tribunals.[38] While not criminal prosecution cases, these cases can have a powerful effects on the respective State.

In addition to international human rights and humanitarian law, IR and legal scholar have also investigated how private non-State actors have engaged in international *criminal* law. For example, scholars have investigated broader notions of international criminal tribunals from the viewpoint of both structural and sociological considerations[39] as well as questions of legitimacy.[40] IR and legal scholars have also investigated how private non-State actors have played other practical roles. For instance, Marlies Glasius examined civil society actors who contributed to advocacy and advisory roles in the establishment of the International Criminal Court (ICC).[41] Williams, Woolaver and Palmer explore how they can contribute to *amicus curiae*

[35]   Brownlie and Crawford, *Brownlie's Principles of Public International Law.*
[36]   Martha J. Finnemore, 'Rules of War and Wars of Rules: The International Red Cross and the Restraint of State Violence', in *Constructing World Culture: International Nongovernmental Organisations Since 1873* (Stanford, CA: Stanford University Press, 1999), 149–65.
[37]   Tim Allen and David Styan, 'A Right to Interfere? Bernard Kouchner and the New Humanitarianism,' *Journal of International Development*; Chichester 12, no. 6 (August 2000): 825–42.
[38]   Kathryn Sikkink, 'Human Rights: Advancing the Frontier of Emancipation', *Development* 61, no. 1–4 (2018): 14–20, https://doi.org/10.1057/s41301-018-0186-1; Keck and Sikkink, *Activists beyond Borders*; Kathryn Sikkink, *Amnesty in the Age of Human Rights Accountability: Comparative and International Perspectives* (New York: Cambridge University Press, 2012); Kathryn Sikkink, *The Persistent Power of Human Rights: From Commitment to Compliance* (Cambridge: Cambridge University Press, 2013).
[39]   Mikkel Jarle Christensen, 'From Symbolic Surge to Closing Courts: The Transformation of International Criminal Justice and Its Professional Practices', *International Journal of Law, Crime and Justice* 43, no. 4 (1 December 2015): 609–25, https://doi.org/10.1016/j.ijlcj.2015.02.001.
[40]   Joanna Nicholson, 'The Role Played by External Case Law in Promoting the Legitimacy of International Criminal Court Decisions', *Nordic Journal of International Law* 87, no. 2 (2018): 189, https://doi.org/10.1163/15718107-08702005; Nienke Grossman et al., eds., *Legitimacy and International Courts, Studies on International Courts and Tribunals* (Cambridge: Cambridge University Press, 2018), https://doi.org/10.1017/9781108529570.
[41]   Glasius, *The International Criminal Court.*

(friend of the court) legal assistance to international criminal tribunals.[42] Other scholars have also examined how private non-State actors play an *activist* role encouraging and lobbying States (and interstate institutions) to establish the mechanisms to prosecute those responsible for core international crimes.[43] Further still, Sikkink's work has focused on how private non-State actors are instrumental in establishing human rights accountability in *local* courts in the jurisdiction where the human rights violations occurred.[44] Similarly, Veronica Michel-Luviano has illuminated how private non-State actors have collected material that contributed to *private* prosecutions for *inter alia* human rights violations or other crimes perpetrated by officials or civilians – once again, using *local* courts, such as in Europe and Latin America, in the jurisdiction where crimes are perpetrated.[45] Most important to this study, Sikkink's scholarship highlights the role of private non-State actors who investigate crimes committed in their local jurisdictions but must pursue criminal accountability abroad in a foreign court when options for prosecution are limited in their home State. It is this last category that is of primary focus of this study.

In short, this study centres on private non-State actors who pursue criminal accountability for those most responsible (purposely and intentionally) in *foreign* courts, when local options for accountability fail or are not possible and when an international criminal tribunal remains unavailable.

Witnesses and Victims at the Heart of the Community of Practice

In particular, it focuses on witnesses and victims of core crimes who adopt the tasks and practices of offices of international prosecutors to extend the reach of international criminal law when others cannot or will not. As stated earlier, to do this I narrow my focus to three key actors who are witnesses and victims of core crimes. Previous studies have individually examined the roles of these actors, including Juan Garcés,[46] Souleymane Guengueng[47]

---

[42] Sarah Williams, Hannah Woolaver and Emma Palmer, *The Amicus Curiae in International Criminal Justice*, 1st ed. (Oxford: Hart Publishing, 2020).

[43] Sikkink, *The Justice Cascade*.

[44] Sikkink, *The Justice Cascade*; Michel-Luviano, 'Access to Justice, Victims' Rights, and Private Prosecution in Latin America'.

[45] Sikkink, *The Justice Cascade*; Michel-Luviano, 'Access to Justice, Victims' Rights, and Private Prosecution in Latin America'.

[46] Naomi Roht-Arriaza, *The Pinochet Effect: Transnational Justice in the Age of Human Rights* (Philadelphia: University of Pennsylvania Press, 2005).

[47] Celeste Hicks, *The Trial of Hissène Habré: How the People of Chad Brought a Tyrant to Justice* (London: Zed Books Ltd., 2018).

and Chief Investigator 1.[48] Nevertheless, all three studies addressed their subjects separately as isolated incidents. I extend these previous studies to identify them as (what I term) de facto international prosecutors. Rather than isolated incidents, I seek to bring the study of the three subjects together to illustrate how private non-State actors who act as de facto international prosecutors are *an emerging phenomenon*. By comparing and contrasting them, this book serves to extend our understanding of how these actors adopt practices that lead to criminal accountability for those most responsible for core crimes, as well as what practices they must adopt, and the interaction between private non-State actors and State legal officials in foreign courts. Moreover, it identities the connections between the actors and cases, and the lessons learned among the three. It illustrates how they become anchored and established within a broader community of practice, and must do so to achieve their goals.

To do this, I adopt Kathryn Sikkink's classification for *local, foreign* or *international* courts for human rights and criminal prosecution.[49] *Local* courts are those whose States allow prosecution of core crimes committed within their geographical jurisdiction. *International* criminal courts can be established by the UNSC (such as the ICTY), or with the consent of the relevant State on whose territory core international crimes were perpetrated – usually by treaty (such as the ICC), or by a combination of a treaty and implementing domestic legislation (such as the ECCC).[50] As stated earlier, in each of the three biographical case studies, prosecutions before local and international criminal courts remain unavailable. However, *foreign* court cases involve situations where the core crimes are perpetrated in another State that is unable or unwilling to prosecute, and a case is brought before a court in a third State exercising 'universal jurisdiction'. It is the nature of the crime, such as torture and genocide (as well as other international crimes), which grants foreign courts in third States universal jurisdiction.[51] In all three biographical case studies, the international crime of torture, which is an accepted and

---

[48] Melinda Rankin, 'Investigating Crimes against Humanity in Syria and Iraq: The Commission for International Justice and Accountability', *Global Responsibility to Protect* 9, no. 4 (2017): 395–421, https://doi.org/10.1163/1875984X-00904004; Melinda Rankin, 'The Future of International Criminal Evidence in New Wars? The Evolution of the Commission for International Justice and Accountability (CIJA)', *Journal of Genocide Research* 20, no. 3 (2018): 392–411, https://doi.org/10.1080/14623528.2018.1445435.

[49] Sikkink, *The Justice Cascade*, 4–5.

[50] Sikkink, *The Justice Cascade*. It is difficult to capture all the ways in which the ICC can derive jurisdiction. Nevertheless, one key way is UNSC conferral of jurisdiction on the ICC, as was the case for the Darfur region and Libya.

[51] *Attorney General of Israel v. Eichmann*, Supreme Court of Israel 36 ILR 277 (1962).

recognised peremptory norm (*jus cogens*) of international law, enables courts to exercise jurisdiction over the crime. Once universal jurisdiction is established over the crime, its investigation and prosecution before the foreign court follows the criminal codes and procedures embedded in the legal system of the respective third State.[52] Unlike ordinary crimes, however, suspects are often beyond the reach of foreign courts and authorities. A viable prosecution may depend on the suspect travelling abroad, which may oblige a State under international or domestic law (or both) to investigate and prosecute, or for foreign courts to successfully extradite the suspect.

Increasingly, universal jurisdiction of core international crimes has been limited by foreign governments only recognising universal jurisdiction when a suspect or victim of the relevant core crime has a relationship with them (for example, either must be a citizen of the investigating foreign State). Since the prosecution of Pinochet and Habré, both Spain and Belgium have increasingly limited the courts' ability to enforce universal jurisdiction in this way. Conversely, Germany exemplifies one of the broadest approaches to universal jurisdiction in the world, insofar as it does not require either the alleged perpetrator or victim to be a German citizen, or the crime to have been perpetrated in German jurisdiction (Chapter 5).

Nevertheless, for foreign courts to prosecute crimes that occur in another State on the basis of universal jurisdiction, as noted earlier, the crime must be an established core international crime. In two of the biographical case studies concerning Pinochet and Habré, an essential role of de facto international prosecutors was to argue their case before courts and, drawing upon international laws that govern core international crimes, to establish that a foreign court had jurisdiction over such crimes. Conversely, this study also provides a brief overview of the German legal context which allows a broad exercise of universal jurisdiction, combined with the powers State legal officials are conferred in relation to investigating and prosecuting core crimes. In this instance, it was not necessary for Chief Investigator 1 or other de facto international prosecutors to argue that Germany had jurisdiction of the cases of the two Syrian suspects, Anwar R. and Eyad A.

What other practices must de facto international prosecutors adopt to close the accountability gap left by local and international criminal courts? Moreover, what practices do they need to adopt to show senior leaders are responsible for core international crimes in a criminal prosecution? What sets

---

[52] Luc Reydams, 'The Rise and Fall of Universal Jurisdiction,' in *Routledge Handbook of International Criminal Law*, ed. William Schabas and Nadia Bernaz (Oxford: Routledge, 2013), 337–54; Inazumi, *Universal Jurisdiction in Modern International Law*.

them apart from the offices of the international prosecutors? How do de facto international prosecutors work together to pursue criminal accountability given the complex nature of international criminal justice?

In Chapter 1, I define and conceptualise de facto international prosecutors in further detail. I explain how and why I've labelled them as 'de facto international prosecutors', as well as compare and contrast their practices to those of the offices of the international prosecutor. Throughout the book, I broaden my arguments concerning how and why de facto international prosecutors implicitly or explicitly draw upon the practices of previous offices of the international prosecutor, such as the Nuremberg Tribunal and other international criminal tribunals, but adapt them with the intention of initiating a public criminal prosecution in a foreign court exercising universal jurisdiction.

I now turn to provide a brief overview of the central arguments. Thereafter, I provide an overview of the approach and the structure of the book.

CENTRAL ARGUMENTS

This study poses four key, but interrelated, arguments. First, I argue that de facto international prosecutors are an emerging phenomenon. As private non-State actors, as well as State legal officials in foreign courts, they aim to close the accountability gap when local authorities in the respective jurisdiction fail to investigate and prosecute those suspected of core international crimes. I argue that witnesses or victims of core international crimes remain at the heart of the communities of practice,[53] including in the broader context of international law.[54] The experiences of Juan Garcés (Chile), Souleymane Guengueng (Chad) and Chief Investigator 1 (Syria) also allow us to focus on the role of individuals, which further illuminates our understanding of the actors, institutions and means that contribute to criminal accountability.

Although they are not the only witnesses or victims who play a role in each of the three cases, a focus on three key individuals reveals how witnesses and victims feel personally obligated to investigate core crimes, why and how they extend the reach of international criminal law, and how they view international law as the means to hold those most responsible to account. While de facto international prosecutors are not appointed *de jure* by an international

---

[53]   Emanuel Adler, 'The Spread of Security Communities: Communities of Practice, Self-Restraint, and NATO's Post–Cold War Transformation,' *European Journal of International Relations* 14, no. 2 (2008): 195–230, https://doi.org/10.1177/1354066108089241.

[54]   Jutta Brunnée and Stephen J. Toope, 'Interactional International Law and the Practice of Legality,' in *International Practices* (Cambridge: Cambridge University Press, 2011), 108–36.

criminal tribunal, they do – 'as a matter of fact' (de facto) – adopt the investigative and prosecutorial practices of the offices of international prosecutors, *because* local efforts are ineffective or not available. They are informed by the practices of previous offices of the international prosecutor but adjust these practices with a view of initiating a public criminal prosecution in a foreign court (Chapter 1).

Second, while private non-State actors, particularly witnesses and victims of core crimes, are essential to the accountability process, they cannot, and do not seek to, work alone. Instead, they adopt many of the practical tasks of offices of international prosecutors, either implicitly or explicitly, with the intention of handing over their material to officials in foreign public criminal courts exercising universal jurisdiction. To do this, they must draw upon a broader community of practise and expertise – including drawing upon other private non-State actors, as well as State legal officials in foreign courts.

Moreover, as de facto international prosecutors increasingly engage and define a community of practice, I argue that sharing knowledge, learning from previous attempts and adapting practices further informs the knowledge-based system of international criminal law. Similarly, it shows how communities of practice invent new ways of applying standard practices as international criminal law continues to evolve over the duration of the three biographical case studies. Together, witnesses, victims and other private non-State actors initiate (and, in some cases, lead) the investigation and/or criminal complaint and adopt some or many of the practices of a criminal investigator or prosecutor, whereby material collected and prepared has the effect of informing future legal cases or criminal prosecution. Initially witnesses or victims form a community of practice with one another and with other private non-State actors, but over time this extends to include State legal officials in foreign courts.

While de facto international prosecutors rely on adaption and innovation and apply it to an evolving system of international criminal law, I argue that they do not attempt to act as norm entrepreneurs whereby their goal is to invent new laws. They go to great lengths to demonstrate how crimes, such as torture, are accepted and recognised peremptory norms (*jus cogens*) of international law created and established by States. I highlight how de facto international prosecutors, and the cooperative-criminal accountability community they rely upon, adapt and innovate practices in a particular context. In this way, I attempt to explain the context in which these actors are situated to understand further the realm they draw upon for 'situated learning'.[55] Rather,

---

[55]   Lave and Wenger, *Situated Learning*.

de facto international prosecutors draw upon standard practices used and accepted in international criminal law, such as rules governing evidence and admissibility, but apply them in ways that States and other actors may not, due to political and other considerations.

Third, I argue that de facto international prosecutors must work *cooperatively* to achieve justice in a third jurisdiction, in what I call a cooperative 'criminal accountability community'. Given the complexity of the criminal accountability process, they must do more than engage in and form a community of practice: they must also form a cooperative community of practices or cooperative criminal accountability communities. For example, they must work cooperatively to collect and develop evidence, as well as devise a coherent case strategy, amongst other things. Together, they must also draw upon the sources of international and domestic law and thereafter pose complex legal interpretations and legal arguments to explain how the respective foreign courts exercise jurisdiction over the respective international crimes, and how senior actors, such as Pinochet and Habré, are subjects of international criminal law (and do not enjoy immunity). The importance of cooperation extends from the start of the criminal accountability process to the end: from the collection and production of admissible evidence to the practice of posing legal arguments in particular domestic appeal courts (the British House of Lords) and an international court (International Court of Justice), to the prosecution in foreign courts. Similarly, they must employ cooperation to ensure that States adhere to their legal obligation to prosecute or extradite (*aut dedere aut judicare*) in the international legal system, and in the context of particular core crimes, such as torture and genocide, which are accepted and recognised as peremptory norms (*jus cogens*) of international law. Indeed, this may require that States recognise their obligations 'owed to all' (*erga omnes*) in pursing criminal accountability. It also demonstrates that some States that employ active universal jurisdiction, such as Germany, as well judicial bodies such as the International Court of Justice, increasingly view their role as not just settling disputes between other States but also upholding the norms governing core international crimes.[56] These cooperative elements underpin the cooperative criminal accountability community's ability to pursue criminal accountability for those most responsible.

---

[56] This is an idea I've taken from Vaughan Lowe, QC. Although two ICJ decisions remain that can be viewed as making it difficult to uphold this entirely: the 2002 *Arrest Warrant* decision (on the immunity of an incumbent foreign minister from the court processes of third States) and the 2012 *Jurisdictional Immunities* case (on the Immunity of Germany from national court proceedings related to war time atrocities).

Lastly, I argue that private non-State actors who act as de facto international prosecutors conduct probationary acts of recognition, whereby they identify the sources of international law on an interim basis, with the aim of having these acts validated by State legal officials in a future domestic or international criminal court.

APPROACH TO THE STUDY

This book advances the study of de facto international prosecutors in an interdisciplinary manner, which includes international relations and international law as practice, as well as, to a lesser extent, legal theory. It also draws on three approaches to the study: political biography, political and legal analysis, and case analysis. It does not intend to apply the approaches in whole or separately. Rather, aspects of the three approaches are applied and are deliberately blended or combined in many of the chapters. Together they serve as a particular lens to the study of de facto international prosecutors.

Political Biography

Historically, international law and international relations seldom explore the significance of individuals and the context of their political, social and legal thought. Nonetheless, an examination of the history of ideas contributes to how we frame action, and therefore how we interpret history contributes to our understanding of international legal history.[57] As Duncan Bell argued: 'History, in its various manifestations, plays an essential, constitutive, role in shaping the present: in mainstream IR this has often been disregarded.'[58] This study seeks to address this problem by illuminating how individual private non-State actors,[59] including witnesses and victims of core crimes, have contributed to key international criminal cases – and, whereby, one of the outcomes of the cases was to set benchmarks in international law.

In particular, the study highlights the role of individuals who are witnesses to and victims of the related crimes, including Juan Garcés (Chile), Souleymane Guengueng (Chad) and Chief Investigator 1 (Syria). The case

---

[57] Duncan S. A. Bell, 'International Relations: The Dawn of a Historiographical Turn?,' *British Journal of Politics & International Relations* 3, no. 1 (2001): 115–26, https://doi.org/10.1111/1467-856X.00053.

[58] Bell, 'International Relations', 116.

[59] Melinda Rankin, *The Political Life of Mary Kaldor: Ideas and Action in International Relations* (Boulder, CO: Lynne Rienner, 2017).

studies attempt to explain the political and social context in which these individuals respond to the brutal suppression of actual and alleged opposition and decide to adopt the practices of international investigators and prosecutors as a means to close the 'accountability gap'. The organisation of the case studies is largely historio-chronological (and to some extent thematic) in approach[60] to explore how context and character informed their response to the accountability gap for core international crimes. It also explores how they adapt and innovate the use of particular practices over time.

While character and context are key features of political and social biography,[61] the focus of the case studies is predominantly context. As political biographer Robert Skidelsky argued, biography 'is above all about character and context, not about propositions'.[62] To that end, the focus on Garcés, Guengueng and Chief Investigator 1 reflects upon key problems and experiences relating to the accountability gap and traces the particular strategies and practices, both failures and successes, that contribute to their respective prosecutions of former senior leaders.[63] This does not mean that all three biographical case studies result in successful prosecution. In the case of Pinochet, for example, while the prosecution process begins in the Madrid Courts and the British House of Lords decided that Pinochet was not immune to the crime of torture, Jack Straw, then British home secretary, decided to allow Pinochet to return to Chile on health grounds – a decision challenged by a number of States, including Spain. Nevertheless, the Pinochet case was important to victims and witnesses of Pinochet's Chile. It also remains one of the most important cases in international criminal law[64] and inspired those working on the Chad and Syrian cases.

In this way, political and social biography acts as a unique analytical lens. As stated earlier, unlike previous forms of analysis, it places the study of Garcés, Guengueng and Chief Investigator 1 together, and it shows how individuals who are witnesses to and victims of core international crimes can act as de facto international prosecutors. Rather than isolated incidents, they are placed together to demonstrate they are an emerging phenomenon. In doing so, this lens contributes to legal history by demonstrating that witnesses and victims of core crimes and other de facto international prosecutors, who

---

[60]   Rankin, *The Political Life of Mary Kaldor*.
[61]   Rankin, *The Political Life of Mary Kaldor*.
[62]   Robert Skidelsky, 'Essay: Confessions of a Long-Distance Biographer', *Independent on Sunday*, 29 November 2003, www.skidelskyr.com/site/article/a-writer-at-large-confessions-of-a-long-distance-biographer/; Rankin, *The Political Life of Mary Kaldor*.
[63]   Skidelsky, 'Essay: Confessions of a Long-Distance Biographer'.
[64]   Roht-Arriaza, *The Pinochet Effect*.

adopt the tasks of the offices of international prosecutors, are not anomalies but are, in fact, a key feature of the accountability process, when local accountability fails.

A political and social biography of Garcés, Guengueng and Chief Investigator 1 also sheds some light on the relationship between ideas and practice in international politics. A focus on these individuals as subjects of research not only reveals the practices and tasks that non-State actors adopt to achieve accountability, but also how they might implicitly view international law in particular ways. On the surface, they are all different actors with different experiences. Yet ultimately they all adapt their approach to processes and practices that explicitly seek to achieve criminal accountability for those most responsible for core crimes in a criminal prosecution. To do this, they adapt and learn from previous attempts, and from the expertise and practices of others, most notably the Nuremberg Trials. This study attempts to highlight the interplay between character, context, ideas and practices.

In this way, the biographical aspects of the book intentionally seek to understand accountability and the practices they adopt from *their point of view*. It aims to understand how and why they – Garcés, Guengueng and Chief Investigator 1 – engage in law and legal practices, and also how and why they engage with the wider criminal accountability community to achieve common goals. Moreover, it explores political violence perpetrated by government actors through the eyes of three individuals spanning three continents – Chile, Chad and Syria, respectively. In all three cases, they draw upon lessons learned in the Nuremberg Trials, which were established in response to the extraordinary atrocities of the German Third Reich.[65]

Political and Legal Analysis

In addition to biographical aspects, this study also draws on political and legal theoretical concepts as a series of lenses to investigate the role of private non-State actors and, to a lesser extent, State legal officials, as de facto international prosecutors. As noted earlier, it draws on conceptual tools, such as a community of practice (Emanuel Adler,[66] Etienne

---

[65] Philippe Sands, *East West Street: On the Origins of 'Genocide' and 'Crimes Against Humanity'* (London: Knopf Doubleday, 2016).

[66] Adler, 'The Spread of Security Communities'; Emanuel Adler and Vincent Pouliot, eds., *International Practices* (Cambridge: Cambridge University Press, 2012); Emanuel Adler and Vincent Pouliot, 'International Practices', *International Theory* 3, no. 1 (2011): 1–36, https://doi .org/10.1017/S175297191000031X.

Wegner[67] and Jean Lave[68]), and applies them to the context of an evolving system of international law (Martha Finnemore, Stephen Toope and Jutta Brunnée).[69] It also attempts to adapt concepts, such as Adler's cooperative security communities, to highlight what I refer to as cooperative criminal accountability communities (see Chapter 1).

To enrich the study, the book also draws on the work of a number of legal scholars and practitioners to illuminate the dynamics of international law (Hugh Thirlway, Samantha Besson and Jean d'Aspremont),[70] as well as highlighting the unique nature of international criminal law (Antonio Cassese, M. Cherif Basiouni, James Crawford and Ian Brownlie),[71] particularly in relation to customary international law (Noora Arajärvi).[72] The final component of this book in Chapter 6 draws on these concepts, as well as legal

[67] Etienne Wenger, 'Communities of Practice and Social Learning Systems', *Organization* 7, no. 2 (May 1, 2000): 225–46, https://doi.org/10.1177/135050840072002; Etienne Wenger, 'A Social Theory of Learning', in *Contemporary Theories of Learning: Learning Theorists ... in Their Own Words*, ed. Knud Illeris (London: Taylor & Francis Group, 2018), 219–28; Etienne Wenger, Richard A. McDermott and William Snyder, *Cultivating Communities of Practice: A Guide to Managing Knowledge* (Boston, MA: Harvard Business Review Press, 2002).

[68] Lave and Wenger, *Situated Learning*.

[69] Adler, 'The Spread of Security Communities'; Adler and Pouliot, 'International Practices', 2011; Adler and Pouliot, *International Practices*, 2012; Martha Finnemore, 'Fights about Rules: The Role of Efficacy and Power in Changing Multilateralism', *Review of International Studies* 31, no. S1 (2005): 187–206, https://doi.org/10.1017/S0260210505006856; Jutta Brunnée and Stephen J. Toope, *Legitimacy and Legality in International Law: An Interactional Account* (Cambridge, UK and New York: Cambridge University Press, 2010); Jutta Brunnée and Stephen J. Toope, 'Interactional International Law: An Introduction,' *International Theory* 3, no. 2 (2011): 307–18, https://doi.org/10.1017/S1752971911000030; Brunnée and Toope, 'Interactional International Law and the Practice of Legality'.

[70] H. W. A. Thirlway, *The Sources of International Law*, 2nd ed., Oxford Public International Law (Oxford: University Press, 2019); Samantha Besson and Jean d'Aspremont, *The Oxford Handbook of the Sources of International Law* (Oxford: Oxford University Press, 2017), https://doi.org/10.1093/law/9780198745365.001.0001.

[71] Antonio Cassese, *Cassese's International Criminal Law*, 3rd ed./revised by Antonio Cassese et al. (Oxford: Oxford University Press, 2013); Antonio Cassese, *International Law*, 2nd ed. (Oxford and New York: Oxford University Press, 2005); M. Cherif Bassiouni and Edward M. Wise, *Aut Dedere Aut Judicare: The Duty to Extradite or Prosecute in International Law* (Dordrecht: Martinus Nijhoff, 1995); M. Cherif Bassiouni, 'International Crimes: Jus Cogens and Obligations Erga Omnes', *Law and Contemporary Problems* 59, no. 4 (1996); M. Cherif Bassiouni and William Schabas, *The Legislative History of the International Criminal Court*, 2nd rev. and exp. ed. (Leiden and Boston, MA: Brill Nijhoff, 2016); M. Cherif Bassiouni, 'Statement at the Ceremony for the Opening for Signature of the Convention on the Establishment of an International Criminal Court', Rome, 18 July 1998, http://mcherifbas siouni.com/wp-content/uploads/MCB-Rome-Speech-18_July_1998.pdf.

[72] Noora Arajärvi, *The Changing Nature of Customary International Law: Methods of Interpreting the Concept of Custom in International Criminal Tribunals* (London and New York: Routledge, 2014); Brian D. Lepard, ed., *Reexamining Customary International*

theory (H. L. A. Hart),[73] to propose a conceptual framework for understanding the larger system of justice that the work of private non-State actors and State legal officials informs. In this book, I reflect upon a narrow and particular component of international law, specifically international criminal law, to provide conceptual clarity and facilitate operationalisation of the concepts I outline in this book.

Case Analysis

Unlike previous studies in international law and international relations that focus mainly on State compliance, such as in the case of torture,[74] I attempt to investigate international law beyond compliance[75] and focus on how de facto international prosecutors engage in criminal accountability processes with the aim of establishing individual criminal responsibility in a public criminal court. For this reason, I focus on the legal cases and judicial decisions that result from their attempts to close the accountability gap.

While not the primary objective of this book, some high-level analysis of relevant legal cases is provided, including in Part I. For example, in Chapter 1, I explore the cases of *Pinochet* 3 in the British House of Lords (Pinochet, Chile) and *Belgium v. Senegal* in the ICJ (Habré, Chad). I also briefly note the case against former members of the Syrian government, Anwar R. and Eyad A., in the German courts for crimes against humanity. Although the case against Anwar R., formerly a tertiary-level figure of the Assad government, is ongoing at the time of writing and will be decided in early 2022, Eyad A. was convicted in February 2021 for aiding and abetting crimes against humanity including torture. It represents the first conviction of a former member of the Assad government for crimes against humanity since 2011 (also see Chapters 4 and 5). To a far lesser extent, I also provide a brief analysis of the recent diplomatic note sent by the Netherlands to Syria concerning their obligations under the Convention Against Torture.

Law, ASIL Studies in International Legal Theory (Cambridge: Cambridge University Press, 2017), https://doi.org/10.1017/9781316544624; Monica Hakimi, 'Making Sense of Customary International Law', *Michigan Law Review*, no. 118.8 (2020): 1487–1538, https://doi.org/10.36644/mlr.118.8.making.

73 Hart, *The Concept of Law*.

74 Brunnée and Stephen J. Toope, *Legitimacy and Legality in International Law*. Specifically see the chapter on 'Torture', 220–70.

75 Ian Clark et al., 'Crisis in the Laws of War? Beyond Compliance and Effectiveness', *European Journal of International Relations* 24, no. 2 (1 June 2018): 319–43, https://doi.org/10.1177/1354066117714528.

By providing some basic case analysis, the study seeks to explore the particular legal dynamics of the relevant three case studies and how they might relate to one another. In doing so, it illuminates how de facto international prosecutors extend the reach of international criminal law.

Structure of the Book

This book consists of three sections. Part I, composed of Chapter 1, outlines a theoretical framework to further define and understand de facto international prosecutors. It contributes to the conceptual and theoretical aspects of the book and further elucidates key arguments for the study of de facto international prosecutors in the context of a community of practice. It lays down the basis for some of the main conceptual argument to explain how and why de facto international prosecutors extend the reaches of international criminal law. It also seeks to answer the following: how (or when) do particular interpretations of international law 'win out' over others in particular legal arguments? What mechanisms can we observe and theorize as effective or not (beyond these actors' own legal interpretive work) in pursuing accountability? The conceptual framework provides a conceptual lens to understand the historio-chronological examination of the biographical case studies that follow and reveals how innovation, imagination and adaptation are vital.

Part II of this book consists of four chapters, which are empirical in nature. Chapters 2 and 3 explore two historical biographical studies of witnesses and a victim. Chapter 2 investigates Juan Garcés as a witness to the early crimes of then-General Augusto Pinochet in Chile (and as victim of the military siege of the Moneda Palace the day that Pinochet staged the coup). Chapter 3 examines Souleymane Guengueng as witness and victim of crimes under Hissène Habré, then dictator of Chad, including torture.

In contrast to the historical studies, Chapter 4 examines a current and ongoing biographical study. Chapter 4 starts with Syrian investigator, Chief Investigator 1, as a witness to core crimes perpetrated by the Assad government since 2011. Chief Investigator 1 remains anonymous throughout the book to protect his identity, as he continues to investigate in the field. The chapter explores how Chief Investigator 1 increasingly adopted the practices of an international criminal investigator and became an early and essential member of what is now called the Commission for International Justice and Accountability (CIJA). Unlike the previous two cases, the criminal investigation and prosecution processes have begun while the alleged crimes are continuing and before the head of State has retired or been ousted. It shows how CIJA worked with State legal officials in Germany to facilitate the arrest of Anwar R., as well as the prosecution of Anwar R. and co-defendant Eyad A.[76]

To provide greater detail on the role of State legal officials, Chapter 5 examines the German legal system. Specifically, it investigates how Germany provides for a unique and broad interpretation of universal jurisdiction. Indeed, German legal officials have acted not only as de facto international prosecutors but also increasingly as *de jure* international prosecutors, including in their pursuit of those most responsible for core international crimes in Syria. The chapter focuses on how private non-State actors, such as Chief Investigator 1 and the CIJA, as well as others, have supported State legal officials in Germany, and elsewhere, to pursue criminal accountability for alleged core crimes perpetrated in Syria. Furthermore, as stated earlier, at the time of writing this book, the case of Anwar R. was continuing in the Higher Regional Court of Koblenz in Germany. Nonetheless, Chapter 5 briefly details the verdict of co-defendant Eyad A. On the 24 February 2021, the Higher Regional Court of Koblenz convicted Eyad A. for aiding and abetting crimes against humanity, including torture.[77] The chapter seeks to explain what role the CIJA played in the prosecution.

In Part III, consisting of Chapter 6, I propose a second theoretical framework. The purpose of the framework is to explain how de facto international prosecutors implicitly conceptualise international criminal law. The book concludes with a brief overview of the basic tools available to de facto international prosecutors to aid their practices and sharpen their ability to innovate.[78]

---

[76] To comply with German privacy laws, only the defendants' first name and the initial of their surname are made public.

[77] Oberlandesgericht Koblenz, 'Urteil Gegen Einen Mutmaßlichen Mitarbeiter Des Syrischen Geheimdienstes Wegen Beihilfe Zu Einem Verbrechen Gegen Die Menschlichkei', Landesregierung Rheinland-Pfalz, 24 February 2021, https://justiz.rlp.de/de/service-informa tionen/aktuelles/detail/news/News/detail/urteil-gegen-einen-mutmasslichen-mitarbeiter-des-syrischen-geheimdienstes-wegen-beihilfe-zu-einem-ver/.

[78] For example, refer to the 'Basic Toolbox' for de facto international prosecutors at www .defactointernationalprosecutors.org 16 May 2021.

FRAMEWORK I: CONCEPTUALISING DE FACTO INTERNATIONAL PROSECUTORS IN A GLOBAL ERA

1

Extending the Reach of International Criminal Law (ICL)

In contrast to the *practical* focus of Part II of this book, Part I, composed of this chapter, proposes a theoretical framework for how de facto international prosecutors extend the reaches of international criminal law. Part II provides the empirical account of how and why de facto international prosecutors, particularly witnesses and victims of core international crimes, adopt the practical tasks required to hold a senior leader suspected of core crimes accountable in foreign or international courts. The theoretical framework outlined in this chapter is an attempt to answer the following questions: what dynamics and mechanisms can we observe and theorise as effective or not (beyond these actors' own legal interpretive work) in pursuing accountability? How (or when) do particular interpretations of international law 'win out' over others in court judgements? The chapter also serves to further define and conceptualise de facto international prosecutors and the international legal order within which they operate.

To that end, the proposed theoretical framework, which seeks to explain how we should view de facto international prosecutors and to illuminate how they extend the reaches of international criminal law, consists of four elements. First, I compare and contrast de facto international prosecutors with the offices of international prosecutors to further elucidate how they are similar and what sets them apart. I give particular attention to the types of practices they adopt. I argue that de facto international prosecutors implicitly or explicitly adopt the practices of the offices of international prosecutors to fill an accountability gap initially left by the local judiciary, and when international criminal tribunals remain unavailable.

Second, and following on from the first, I draw upon the practices defined, and I position de facto international prosecutors within a broader study of a 'community of practice'. Innovation, imagination and adaption are key to extending the reaches of international criminal law in the context of a community of practice. I argue that de facto international prosecutors do not seek to invent new laws or norms; rather, they attempt to show that they are drawing on pre-existing and established sources of international law. I also argue that private non-State actors and State legal officials in foreign courts must work together as 'cooperative criminal accountability communities' to pursue criminal justice in foreign or international courts. This can include engaging State actors, such as the Belgian government, to take formal disputes to the International Court of Justice (ICJ), which ensures foreign States fulfil their obligations to prosecute those suspected of core crimes.

Third, I explore the practice of drawing on sources of international law and posing legal arguments in important court cases. Aside from identifying victims and witnesses, collecting 'linkage material' and writing criminal case briefs and private complaints, amongst other things, one of the most important practices of the cooperative criminal accountability community is to pose complex legal arguments in courts to establish that, *inter alia*, the relevant foreign court has jurisdiction over the respective core international crime and to show how the suspect in question is subject to international criminal law rather than enjoying immunity.

Following on from this, the cooperative criminal accountability community must show that particular core crimes, such as torture and genocide, are accepted and recognised as peremptory norms (*jus cogens*) of international law, which infers a unique hierarchy of rules or sources of law. This unique rule in international law serves to invalidate or override other domestic and international laws, including immunity for former heads of States, although it does not extend to incumbent heads of State, incumbent heads of government and incumbent foreign ministers. As will be explored in the Syrian case, international criminal law can extend to other incumbent ministers. These arguments are largely and increasingly accepted by official judges in the respective courts, particularly in relation to the *jus cogens* crimes of torture and genocide. Moreover, de facto international prosecutors argued that States not only have a legal 'obligation to prosecute or extradite' (*aut dedere aut judicare*) for crimes such as torture and genocide but also obligations 'owed to all' (*erga omnes*)[1] in relation to the prosecution of torture and other such

---

[1] Later, I distinguish further between obligations *erga omnes partes* (i.e. owed by *Obligation to Prosecute or Extradite* (*Belgium v. Senegal*) case at the ICJ, in relation to the Convention Against Torture) and obligations *erga omnes* (i.e. obligations owed to the international community as a whole – as in the *East Timor* (*Portugal v. Australia*) case at the ICJ. These two types of *erga omnes* obligations are set out in Article 48 of the Draft Articles on Responsibility of States for Internationally Wrongful Acts in the traditional context of standing to bring international legal claims. See, Draft Articles on Responsibility of States for Internationally Wrongful Acts, in

crimes. In the cases outlined later, this includes peremptory norms (*jus cogens*) of international law and the obligation to prosecute or extradite (*aut dedere aut judicare*) being applied to those suspected of torture at the most senior level of government – as was the case of Pinochet and Habré, as former heads of state.

Lastly, I highlight how de facto international prosecutors, and the cooperative criminal accountability community more broadly, adapt and innovate in a particular context. Moreover I attempt to explain the context these actors are situated in to understand further the realm they draw upon for 'situated learning'. The conceptual framework proposes that international criminal law has emerged as a unique and distinct system of public international law in the post-Nuremberg era. While de facto international prosecutors draw on previous legal case judgements in domestic and international courts as evidence of international criminal law, invariably the decisions made by courts have the effect of filling legal gaps or clarifying points of law. What emerges is something that resembles 'precedents', whereby the unique nature of international criminal law is increasingly akin to a case law or common law system. Although there are great debates among international relations and legal scholars as to what extent customary international law overrides a State's domestic laws, and whether precedents are a key feature of international law (if at all), the case studies here provide some further illustration for how a particular crime is classed (as a *jus cogens*) has the effect of overriding other rules in domestic and international legal orders and systems, and how decisions from previous cases are drawn upon to inform others.

The chapter is structured as follows. First, it further sharpens our understanding of de facto international prosecutors in contrast with official and *de jure* offices of the international prosecutors. Second, it contextualises de facto international prosecutors within the broader context of the theory of community of practice. It draws upon existing notions of community of practice canvassed by international relations (IR) scholars,[2] as well as in the field of

---

Report of the International Law Commission on the Work of Its Fifty-third Session, UN GAOR, 56th Sess., Supp. No. 10, at 43, UN Doc. A/56/10 (2001), *available at* www.un.or/a/lc. The final text with commentary and apparatus is in James Crawford, The International Law Commission's Articles on State Responsibility: Introduction, Text and Commentaries (2002).

[2] Emanuel Adler, 'The Spread of Security Communities: Communities of Practice, Self-Restraint, and NATO's Post–Cold War Transformation', *European Journal of International Relations* 14, no. 2 (2008): 195–230, https://doi.org/10.1177/1354066108089241; Emanuel Adler and Vincent Pouliot, eds., *International Practices* (Cambridge: Cambridge University Press, 2012); Emanuel Adler and Vincent Pouliot, 'International Practices', *International Theory* 3, no. 1 (2011): 1–36, https://doi.org/10.1017/S175297191000031X.

international law.[3] In this way, this chapter attempts to extend the field of enquiry to include de facto international prosecutors. Third, while Lon Fuller's interactional approaches are important to the study of international law,[4] this chapter challenges the notion that a hierarchy of rules or sources of international law is absent when posing legal arguments and interpretations of international criminal law, specifically with respect to *jus cogens* crimes such as torture. The study demonstrates how a cooperative criminal accountability community poses legal arguments to establish torture as a peremptory norm (*jus cogens*) of international law, which produces a hierarchy of rules or serves to void others. It also explores how a cooperative criminal accountability community can argue for the notion of a legal obligation to prosecute or extradite (*aut dedere aut judicare*) for crimes such as torture. Moreover, over time, the cooperative criminal accountability community poses legal arguments establishing torture not only as a peremptory norm (*jus cogens*) of international law but also as imbuing obligations owed to all (*erga omnes*) in the international system of law. Lastly, I outline the unique nature of customary international law as a source of international criminal law. Unlike previous studies that examine the nature of customary international law in relation to the International Criminal Tribunal for the former Yugoslavia (ICTY),[5] this study focuses on decisions made in the exercise of universal jurisdictions and the International Court of Justice relevant to the three case studies – Chile, Chad and Syria.

I now turn to briefly explore the similarities and differences that private non-State actors and state legal officials in foreign courts, as de facto international prosecutors, exhibit in view of the role of the offices of international prosecutors.

DE FACTO INTERNATIONAL PROSECUTORS AND THE OFFICES OF INTERNATIONAL PROSECUTORS

For all its importance, the role of international prosecutors and their offices is little examined in IR and legal literature. As Luc Reydams observed, 'International criminal justice involves a multitude of actors but none are more identified with the undertaking than the prosecutors. It is surprising,

---

[3] Jutta Brunnée and Stephen J. Toope, 'Interactional International Law and the Practice of Legality', in *International Practices*, ed. Emanuel Adler and Vincent Pouliot (Cambridge: Cambridge University Press, 2012), 108–35.

[4] Brunnée and Toope, 'Interactional International Law and the Practice of Legality'.

[5] Larissa van Den Herik, 'The Decline of Customary International Law as a Source of International Criminal Law', in *Custom's Future: International Law in a Changing World*, ed. Curtis A Bradley (Cambridge: Cambridge University Press, 2016), 230.

therefore, that there are very few texts on the subject.'[6] This goes someway to explain how other actors that emulate the tasks and practices of the '*offices* of international prosecutors' may also be missed or misunderstood. With this in mind, Reydams argues that a number of characteristics are unique to the role of the 'offices of international prosecutors',[7] as well as the international prosecutors who occupy them. Here I compare and contrast what they share with de facto international prosecutors.

First, the international prosecutor is the *principal architect* or *strategist* whose practices and decisions shape the work of international criminal institutions and international criminal justice more broadly.[8] Private non-State actors can and do play an essential role as principal architect or strategist for a criminal case. While offices of international prosecutors may have narrow and internalised decision-making processes shaping their strategy, it is rarely the prosecutor alone. Similarly, as will be explored further in this book, private non-State actors often work as a community of practice, not alone. Nevertheless, in the case of Pinochet, Judge Baltasar Garzón, the investigating judge in the Madrid Courts, described Juan Garcés, a private non-State actor and witness to Pinochet's earliest crimes, as the principal architect of the Pinochet case.[9] Garcés largely modelled his approach with that taken at the Nuremberg Trials. The Pinochet case remains of great significance to the practice of international criminal law.[10]

Second, the role of the offices of international prosecutors includes international investigations and prosecutions.[11] While the international prosecutor as an individual may be the most publicly visible official, the term 'offices' denotes independent organs shouldered with the responsibility of investigating and prosecuting. It often reflects a diverse array of expertise and practices aside from those of the prosecutor. These often include investigators, legal advisors, subject matter experts and analysts. In addition to these roles, the Office of the Prosecutor (OTP) at the International Criminal Court (ICC) includes diplomatic and public relations roles.

---

[6]   Luc Reydams, 'The Rise and Fall of Universal Jurisdiction', in *Routledge Handbook of International Criminal Law*, ed. William Schabas and Nadia Bernaz (Oxford: Routledge, 2013), 1.

[7]   Reydams, 'The Rise and Fall of Universal Jurisdiction', 1.

[8]   Reydams, 'The Rise and Fall of Universal Jurisdiction', 1.

[9]   Baltasar Garzón, 'Spanish Judge Baltasar Garzón Tells the Story of the Arrest of Chile's Augusto Pinochet (Transcript)', Democracy Now! 11 September 2013, www.democracynow.org/blog/2013/9/11/spanish_judge_baltasar_garzn_tells_the_story_of_the_arrest_of_chiles_augusto_pinochet.

[10]   Naomi Roht-Arriaza, *The Pinochet Effect: Transnational Justice in the Age of Human Rights* (Philadelphia: University of Pennsylvania Press, 2005).

[11]   Luc Reydams, Jan Wouters and Cedric Ryngaert, 'Introduction', in *International Prosecutors*, ed. Luc Reydams, Jan Wouters and Cedric Ryngaert (Oxford: Oxford University Press, 2012), 1.

As noted earlier, all offices of international prosecutors include the investi-gation and prosecution function.[12] Of necessity, this means that, like de facto international prosecutors, appointed international prosecutors do not work alone. They must work within the context of a particular system of inter-national criminal law, and one that continues to evolve as States adopt additional conventions and practices. Navigating that changing landscape of substantive and procedural rules and principles requires a range of skills and expertise in criminal and international law.

Further to this is the particular nature of a criminal investigation in establish-ing individual criminal liability, which must ultimately be proven beyond reasonable doubt. Unlike the practice of human rights, where *States* can be held responsible for breaches of international law, *individuals* are held crimin-ally responsible for core international crimes.[13] Traditionally States were the primary actors of public international law.[14] Yet, since the Nuremberg Trials, individuals have emerged as the focus of international criminal law.[15] Moreover, as a legacy of the Nuremberg Trials, international law has included an emphasis on holding those *most* responsible to account.[16] As is often the case in organised crime investigations in domestic jurisdictions, the focus of international investi-gations is on the 'big fish', including those at the very top of an alleged criminal organisation, plan or enterprise.[17] Yet, establishing individual criminal respon-sibility, particularly for those most responsible in local, foreign or international courts[18] for core international crimes, is particularly difficult, as it requires

[12]   Reydams, 'The Rise and Fall of Universal Jurisdiction', 1.
[13]   Antonio Cassese, *Cassese's International Criminal Law*, 3rd ed./revised by Antonio Cassese et al. (Oxford: Oxford University Press, 2013).
[14]   Arthur Watts, 'The Importance of International Law', in *The Role of Law in International Politics: Essays in International Relations and International Law*, ed. Michael Byers (Oxford: Oxford University Press, 2001), 5–16.
[15]   Guénaël Mettraux, 'Trial at Nuremberg', in *Routledge Handbook of International Criminal Law*, ed. William Schabas and Nadia Bernaz (Oxford: Routledge, 2013), 5–16.
[16]   David Scheffer, 'Staying the Course with the International Criminal Court', *Cornell International Law Journal* 35, no. 1 (2002): 47, 69–87; David Scheffer, 'The United States and the International Criminal Court. (Developments in International Criminal Law)', *American Journal of International Law* 93, no. 1 (1999): 12–22, https://doi.org/10.2307/2997953 ; Ian Brownlie and James Crawford, *Brownlie's Principles of Public International Law*, 8th ed., Principles of Public International Law (Oxford: Oxford University Press, 2012), 673, 675.
[17]   Robert H. Jackson, 'Second Day, Wednesday, 11/21/1945, Part 04', in *Trial of the Major War Criminals before the International Military Tribunal. Volume II. Proceedings: 11/14/1945–11/30/ 1945. [Official Text in the English Language.]* Nuremberg: International Military Tribunal, 1945, 98–102.
[18]   Kathryn Sikkink, *The Justice Cascade: How Human Rights Prosecutions Are Changing World Politics*, 1st ed. (New York: W. W. Norton & Co., 2011), 4–5. As stated earlier, I adopt Kathryn Sikkink's classification: for 'local', 'foreign' or 'international' courts for human rights prosecu-tion and apply them to the prosecution of core international crimes.

prosecutors to locate material that *links* (linkage material) senior actors to the underlying crimes. As in the Nuremberg model, documents produced by the perpetrator[19] or materials that can be attributed to them (or, more recently, intercepted verbal communications) serve to link underlying crimes to those most responsible. Both the underlying crimes and an accused person's responsibility for them must be proved by admissible evidence, beyond reasonable doubt. This standard of proof lies at the heart of both domestic and international criminal prosecutions, which are governed by legal rules concerning criminal procedure and admissibility of evidence.[20] While material collected in a fact-finding process or observer missions may contribute to proving a grave breach of international human rights and humanitarian law (and/or to crime-based evidence, such as forensic material collected at a crime scene), these types of missions often fail to identify or collect evidentiary material (or material at the standard required for a domestic or international criminal prosecution) that links senior leaders suspected of core crimes to the underlying crimes in a criminal prosecution (i.e. to those carrying out the crime).[21] Furthermore, the evidentiary standard in criminal cases is far more onerous than that applicable to civil litigation or in a case that seeks to establish State responsibility in a domestic or international tribunal. This stems from the symbolic nature of establishing particular behaviours as criminal and is justified by the severity of punitive measures which can be imposed on an individual, if found guilty.[22]

Therefore, investigation and prosecution remain in themselves complex and notoriously difficult practices, especially so at the international level. Establishing criminal liability by one or more modes of liability,[23] particularly at the senior level,[24] is especially challenging – including for

---

[19] Whitney R. Harris, *Tyranny on Trial: The Evidence at Nuremberg* (New York: Barnes and Noble Books, 1954).

[20] Nancy A. Combs, *Fact-Finding without Facts: The Uncertain Evidentiary Foundations of International Criminal Convictions* (New York and Cambridge: Cambridge University Press, 2010); Nancy Amoury Combs, 'Grave Crimes and Weak Evidence: A Fact-Finding Evolution in International Criminal Law', *Harvard International Law Journal* 47–58, no. 1 (2017): 125; Nancy Amoury Combs, 'Evidence', in *Routledge Handbook of International Criminal Law*, ed. William Schabas and Nadia Bernaz (Oxford and New York: Routledge, 2013), 323–34.

[21] Combs, *Fact-Finding without Facts*; Combs, 'Grave Crimes and Weak Evidence'.

[22] Karim A. A. Khan, Caroline Buisman and Christopher Gosnell, *Principles of Evidence in International Criminal Justice* (Oxford: Oxford University Press, 2015).

[23] Marjolein Cupido, Manuel J. Ventura and Lachezar Yanev, eds., *Modes of Liability in International Criminal Law* (Cambridge: Cambridge University Press, 2019), https://doi.org/10.1017/9781108678957.

[24] Carla Del Ponte, 'Prosecuting the Individuals Bearing the Highest Level of Responsibility', *Journal of International Criminal Justice* 2, no. 2 (1 June 2004): 516–19, https://doi.org/10.1093/jicj/2.2.516.

well-resourced international criminal tribunals – a fact the practice of the ICC exemplifies. From its inception, prosecutions at the ICC have had a bumpy ride and, on occasion, the OTP has struggled to secure convictions against senior leaders for core international crimes. Although the ICC was established in 2003, it was not until 2009 that it prosecuted its first suspect, Thomas Lubanga Dyilo, a founding member and senior leader of the Union of Congolese Patriots (UCP), for war crimes. The Lubanga case was controversial for several reasons, including accusations that Luis Gabriel Moreno Ocampo, the ICC's first prosecutor, used unethical methods and *inter alia* refused to disclose possibly exculpatory evidence, which was said to be in breach of the defendant's right to a fair trial. To this day, the issue of ICC's efficacy remains a point of contention. Over the past seventeen years, the court has issued thirty-six arrest warrants. There have been twenty-two completed proceedings. In six of those, the charges were dismissed; two cases resulted in acquittals; in two cases charges were withdrawn; and in one instance the court declared the case inadmissible. The collection and analysis of evidence that establishes criminal responsibility to the requisite standard remains a considerable challenge for the ICC.

Notwithstanding these challenges, private non-State actors have adopted the investigative and prosecutorial models and practices of offices of international prosecutors – either intentionally or unintentionally. In all three cases examined in this book, they collected evidence (including linkage material), identified key witnesses and victims, conducted case analysis and evidence management, drafted criminal case briefs and/or submitted those briefs and/or evidence to foreign courts. In terms of investigations, all three biographical case studies reflect instances where private non- State actors were the first to initiate international criminal investigations, before State legal officials in either local or foreign courts. Indeed, in the three case studies, private non-State actors fulfil Article 6, paragraph 2, of the Convention Against Torture, often before State legal officials are able or willing to investigate. Paragraphs 1 and 2 of Article 6 state the following:

> (1.) Upon being satisfied, after an examination of information available to it, that the circumstances so warrant, any State Party in whose territory a person alleged to have committed any offence referred to in article 4 is present shall take him into custody or take other legal measures to ensure his presence. The custody and other legal measures shall be as provided in the law of that State but may be continued only for such time as is necessary to enable any criminal or extradition proceedings to be instituted.

(2.) Such State shall immediately make a preliminary inquiry into the facts.[25]

In all three case studies, private non-State actors attempt to follow the Nuremberg model by focusing on those most responsible for core crimes. Moreover, in all three cases, private non-State actors viewed documents produced by the perpetrators (or co-perpetrators) as an essential means to link the underlying crimes to those most responsible, as was the case with the Nuremberg Trial. In terms of initiating the official public prosecutions in foreign courts, the cases of Pinochet and Habré are two instances where private non-State actors submitted private criminal complaints to foreign courts, which resulted in an official investigation by State legal officials. In the case of Syria, Germany's criminal code and procedures obliged federal investigators and prosecutors to initiate an investigation into senior leaders of the Syrian government. Nevertheless, they relied upon private non-State actors for witness statements and materials produced by or linked to the alleged perpetrator in Syria. In all three of the case studies, investigative judges or prosecutors worked with private non-State actors to continue to investigate the allegations and initiate the official prosecution process. Also in all three instances, this cooperative relationship enabled an arrest of a former senior leader (and two former heads of State) who were physically located in a third jurisdiction or in the jurisdiction where officials in foreign prosecutorial/ judicial institutions were able and willing to investigate.

Moreover, the three case studies show how private non-State actors in particular are directly shaped and informed by the practices of the offices of international prosecutors of international tribunals. Juan Garcés adapted lessons learned from the international prosecutors of the Nuremberg Tribunal, as did Souleymane Guengueng and Reed Brody. Conversely, Chief Investigator 1 and the CIJA were not only informed by the Nuremberg Tribunal but also by their more recent experiences of the offices of the international prosecutors, including the International Criminal Tribunal for the former Yugoslavia (ICTY), International Criminal Tribunal for Rwanda (ICTR), International Criminal Court (ICC) and the Extraordinary Chambers in the Courts of Cambodia (ECCC), amongst others. In fact, the CIJA, in many respects, is composed of those with experiences in these

---

[25] United Nations, 'Convention against Torture and Other Cruel, Inhuman or Degrading Treatment or Punishment (CAT)', Treaty Series, 1465 § (1984); J. Herman Burgers and Hans Danelius, *The United Nations Convention against Torture: A Handbook on the Convention against Torture and Other Cruel, Inhuman, or Degrading Treatment or Punishment* (Dordrecht and Boston, MA: Nijhoff, 1988).

international tribunals. Furthermore, in large part, the CIJA has developed as a more formal institution that features many of the components of the modern office of the international prosecutor (Chapter 4).

This may lead some observers to point out that the primary role of the international or domestic prosecutor is to *prosecute*, and should be conducted by legal officials alone. Nonetheless, this view does not account for the role private non-State actors play in some domestic criminal processes, as reflected in the three case studies. For example, national criminal systems permit private non-State actors to bring criminal prosecutions directly. Spain's and Belgium's universal jurisdiction laws originally allowed for this, and to some extent Spain's still does. Having said this, private non-State actors cannot completely replace the offices of international or domestic prosecutors, nor do they try to do so. Each case study shows how they have attempted to bring cases to a position where State legal officials in public foreign courts are obliged and willing to investigate and initiate a public criminal prosecution. However, it also highlights the importance of the practices and efforts required to enable successful prosecution, often little discussed in academic literature on offices of international prosecutors or more widely. It highlights the need for a wider debate on the role of the offices of international prosecutors and international prosecution, at least the practices and efforts required to complete a successful criminal investigation and prosecution of those most responsible for humanity's greatest crimes.

Yet, it is also fair to say that international prosecutors are not always just prosecuting, and not all investigations lead to prosecution. For example, the prosecutor at the ICC may be required to take a case to the pretrial chamber to ascertain jurisdiction over a crime, and to confirm that those suspected of the alleged crimes come within the court's remit. The recent proceedings involving investigations of Myanmar officials for the forced deportation of the Rohingya people are a case in point.[26] Similarly, some of the important cases outlined in the biographical case studies involve domestic appeal court or international court rulings – Pinochet in the British House of Lords and Habré in the International Court of Justice, respectively – concerning jurisdiction and/or the extent to which the suspect is subject to international criminal law (or enjoys immunity), before they can be extradited or prosecuted.

---

[26]   Kip Hale and Melinda Rankin, 'Extending the "System" of International Criminal Law? The ICC's Decision on Jurisdiction over Alleged Deportations of Rohingya People', *Australian Journal of International Affairs* 73, no. 1 (January 2, 2019): 22–28, https://doi.org/10.1080/10357 718.2018.1548565.

While the case studies throughout the book show how these practical tasks are adopted in a different context to international criminal tribunals, it serves to reiterate that de facto international prosecutors intend to fill the accountability gap first posed by local legal officials in the country in which the crime occurred, with the hope that an *international* criminal tribunal or *foreign* court would, at some point, be willing and able to investigate and hear the case. In the case of Anwar R., the Syrian senior leader of suspected core crimes, the German judiciary is obliged to prosecute core international crimes under domestic law and has the suspect within its jurisdiction.

Third, to assist with investigations and prosecutions, an international prosecutor is sometimes required to shoulder *political functions*.[27] They liaise with various state actors and international organizations whose cooperation is needed in the process of investigation and gathering of relevant material. In other instances, they ask states to use their leverage to achieve objectives in jurisdictions they cannot access,[28] such as to collect evidence or to effect arrests. According to one former prosecutor, international prosecutors must incorporate 'diplomacy and politics into a prosecutorial strategy'.[29] They may also become the *'public face* of international criminal justice'.[30] As Reydams argued, this range of 'outside-the-courtroom' activities 'sets international prosecutors apart from the bench and the defence', and in this way the offices of international prosecutors are 'players like no other in the administration of international criminal justice'.[31]

Aside from Reydams's points, I make two further points to explain the distinct nature of de facto international prosecutors in this context. First, I describe them as de facto international prosecutors because, as stated earlier, the international community has established that certain core crimes have the status of peremptory norms (*jus cogens*) of international law, from which there can be no derogation. *This point is central to defining and understanding* de facto *international prosecutors*. All three biographical cases relate to the international crime of torture, which is an accepted and recognised peremptory norm (*jus cogens*) of international law. In other words, torture, like

---

[27] Luc Reydams, Jan Wouters and Cedric Ryngaert, *International Prosecutors* (Oxford: Oxford University Press, 2012); David Crane, '"NotPerfect Candidates" to Be the Next Prosecutor of the International Criminal Court', *Jurist* (blog), July 10, 2020, hwww.jurist.org/commentary/2020/07/david-crane-icc-prosecutor/.

[28] Reydams, Wouters and Ryngaert,; Crane, '"Not Perfect Candidates" to Be the Next Prosecutor of the International Criminal Court'.

[29] Crane, '"Not Perfect Candidates" to Be the Next Prosecutor of the International Criminal Court'

[30] Reydams, Wouters and Ryngaert, *International Prosecutors*, 'Introduction', 1.

[31] Reydams, Wouters, and Ryngaert, *International Prosecutors*, 'Introduction', 1

genocide, is a breach of international law and is extraterritorial in nature. The nature of the core crime is what permits states to exercise universal jurisdiction and enables de facto international prosecutors to pursue criminal prosecution in foreign courts. Unlike private non-State actors who are able to pursue public[32] or private[33] criminal prosecution in local courts (in the geographical jurisdiction where the crimes are perpetrated), private non-State actors are unable to do either. For this reason, they pursue criminal prosecutions in the foreign courts and in all three biographical case studies, they do so in *public* criminal prosecutions. In this way, de facto international prosecutors must draw on an array of complex sources of international law to argue that the crimes are international in character, and that the foreign courts have jurisdiction to prosecute or extradite suspects for such crimes. As stated earlier, both the Convention Against Torture (CAT) and the Genocide Convention establish international regimes whereby State Parties are legally *obliged* to prosecute or extradite (*aut dedere aut judicare*) those suspected of the relevant crimes, within their jurisdiction, irrespective of where the crimes occurred.[34] As the *Eichmann* judgment recognised,[35] where individuals were prosecuted for Nazi war crimes in foreign courts that exercised universal jurisdiction, those crimes were treated as breaches of international law. Similarly, as Crawford has aptly explained, 'universal jurisdiction is defined by the character of the crime concerned, rather than by the presence of some kind of nexus with the prescribing state. The prosecution of crimes under customary international law is often expressed as an acceptance of the principle of universality, but this is not strictly correct, since what is punished is the breach of international law.'[36]

---

[32] Sikkink, *The Justice Cascade*.

[33] Sikkink, *The Justice Cascade*; Veronica Michel-Luviano, 'Access to Justice, Victims' Rights, and Private Prosecution in Latin America: The Cases of Chile, Guatemala, and Mexico', ed. Lisa Hilbink et al. (Ann Arbor, MI: ProQuest Dissertations Publishing, 2012).

[34] A general customary obligation to extradite or prosecute may still remain controversial even for genocide, war crimes and crimes against humanity. See The ILC's 2019 draft articles on Prevention and Punishment of Crimes Against Humanity which addresses the obligation *aut dedere aut judicare* in Article 10, See International Law Commission, 'Report of the International Law Commission on the Work of Its Sixty-Ninth Session UN Doc. A/74/10' (New York: Office of Legal Affairs, United Nations, 2019); Michael P. Scharf, *Aut Dedere Aut Iudicare: Max Planck Encyclopedia of Public International Law [MPEPIL]*, Oxford Public International Law (Oxford: Oxford University Press, 2008); International Law Commission, 'Report of the International Law Commission on the Work of Its Sixty-Sixth Session, UN GAOR, 69th Sess, Supp No 10, UN Doc A/69/10' (New York: Office of Legal Affairs, United Nations, 5 August 2014).

[35] *Attorney General of Israel* v. *Eichmann*, Supreme Court of Israel 36 ILR 277 (1962).

[36] James Crawford, *Brownlie's Principles of Public International Law*, 9th ed. (Oxford and New York: Oxford University Press, 2019), 451.

Nevertheless, not all states observe the international laws that should, in principle, guide the work of their domestic criminal institutions. As will be outlined in the cases against Pinochet (Chapter 2) and Habré (Chapter 3), this can mean that while private non-State actors may be informed by the criminal evidence and principles of international law, they must consider which crimes a particular jurisdiction will recognise to bring a former head of state or senior leader who is suspected of core international crimes within the jurisdiction of the foreign court. For example, Pinochet was suspected of committing an array of crimes, including the torture of 200,000 people. When Juan Garcés submitted the complaint against Pinochet in the Spanish courts, he had included in the complaint a number of crimes, including genocide, terrorism and torture. The initial extradition request to the United Kingdom characterised the alleged crimes against Pinochet as genocide. Although the UK government had signed the Genocide Convention, it had not yet introduced the crime into its domestic criminal laws. However, the United Kingdom had signed the Convention Against Torture and had enacted legislation introducing torture into its domestic law. For this reason, Juan Garcés amended the crime on the second extradition request (developed with Garzón, the Spanish investigating judge) to include torture, before it was sent to the UK authorities. This served to justify the continuation of Pinochet's arrest. The British House of Lords decided that Pinochet was subject to the crime of torture, in line with its domestic and international legal obligations.

Second, and following on from this, de facto international prosecutors must establish that the senior actors, including former heads of state, do not enjoy immunity from particular crimes. To do this, de facto international prosecutors must draw upon the sources of international law, and international precedents, to demonstrate before the relevant courts that particular crimes, such as genocide and torture, are recognised as peremptory norms of international law. They must then present compelling arguments and evidence to show that the particular alleged conduct falls within the *jus cogens* crimes. All this is to establish a route to accountability by relying on a hierarchical arrangement of international principles, where peremptory norms take precedence over domestic and international rules governing immunity.[37]

---

[37] Having said this, the 2002 decision of the ICJ in the *Arrest Warrant* (*Congo* v. *Belgium*) case held that incumbent heads of State, incumbent heads of government and incumbent foreign ministers still enjoy immunity for *jus cogens* crimes. In other words, criminal accountability of *jus cogens* crimes do not extend to alleged perpetrators to these three particular actors while they remain in office.

In short, de facto international prosecutors navigate a complex array of international laws, principles and practices in foreign jurisdictions to pursue criminal accountability for those most responsible for core crimes. While international institutions do not appoint de facto international prosecutors *de jure*, they do – 'as a matter of fact' (de facto) – adopt the investigative and prosecutorial practices of the offices of international prosecutors, *because* local and international courts are ineffective or not available.

This leads to an explanation of the next component of how de facto international prosecutors function. As stated earlier, de facto international prosecutors are both private non-State actors as well as state legal officials in foreign courts. While private non-State actors, including witnesses and victims of core crimes, play an essential role by adopting the practices of the offices of international prosecutors, they cannot (and do not intend to) act alone. Rather, they work with officials in foreign courts to complete all of the tasks necessary to prosecute a person suspected of core crimes. Together, de facto international prosecutors may also rely upon State government actors in a third State to raise the issue as a dispute in the ICJ, where such a route is available – for example, under an international treaty. I now turn to explain how de facto international prosecutors work together in the context of a community of practice, and what I describe as cooperative criminal accountability communities and cooperative criminal accountability practices.

COMMUNITY OF PRACTICE: DE FACTO INTERNATIONAL PROSECUTORS AS PRACTITIONERS

As noted earlier, the three biographical case studies begin with a focus on an individual witness and/or victim of core crimes – Juan Garcés (Chapter 2), Souleymane Guengueng (Chapter 3), and Chief Investigator 1 (Chapter 4) respectively. Each chapter illustrates how individuals play an essential role in the pursuit of justice. Like Kathryn Skikkink aptly explained, a focus on individuals shows how 'early diffusion' of practices and objectives 'happens through individuals'.[38] Yet, witnesses and victims of core crimes do not seek to work alone. Indeed, the biographical case studies reveal how these individuals engage with and/or establish communities of practice in which these 'individuals operate' effectively to achieve their goal.[39] In studying de facto international prosecutors as communities of practice, this study reveals how

---

[38] Sikkink, *The Justice Cascade*, 91.
[39] Sikkink, *The Justice Cascade*, 91.

particular individuals, such as witnesses and victims of core international crimes,[40] partner with or team up with other practitioners to become more than simply a network. Here, I draw largely on the work of Emanuel Adler,[41] Jean Lave[42] and Etienne Wegner,[43] whereby members of a community of practice are specifically and intentionally *practitioners*.[44] Adler maintained that practices are 'knowledge-constituted, meaningful patterns of socially recognised activity embedded in communities, routines and organisations that structure experience'.[45] An exploration of the role of de facto international prosecutors highlights how and why their role extends past a function that could be described as a 'network'.[46]

That is to say, while de facto international prosecutors could be described as a network, I argue they are more than this. By focusing on their practices, and how they develop practices within a community to pursue criminal accountability for those most responsible for core crimes, this study illuminates the tasks, expertise and knowledge required to ensure powerful actors are subject to international law, including former heads of state. As a relatively specialised area of public international law, the particular nature of international criminal law reflects a distinct realm of '"collective knowledge" or set of shared understandings'.[47] As noted earlier, it relies on particular and formalised practices that govern international criminal law, including rules that govern evidence and admissibility. These practices also include identifying appropriate sources of domestic and international criminal law when drafting criminal

---

[40]   In this article, core international crimes are defined as war crimes, crimes against humanity and genocide.

[41]   Adler, 'The Spread of Security Communities'; Adler and Pouliot, *International Practices*, 2012; Adler and Pouliot, 'International Practices', 2011.

[42]   Jean Lave and Etienne Wenger, *Situated Learning: Legitimate Peripheral Participation* (Cambridge: Cambridge University Press, 1991).

[43]   Etienne Wenger, 'Communities of Practice and Social Learning Systems', *Organization* 7, no. 2 (1 May 2000): 225–46, https://doi.org/10.1177/135050840072002; Etienne Wenger, 'A Social Theory of Learning', in *Contemporary Theories of Learning: Learning Theorists . . . in Their Own Words*, ed. Knud Illeris (London: Taylor & Francis Group, 2018), 219–28; Etienne Wenger, Richard A. McDermott and William Snyder, *Cultivating Communities of Practice: A Guide to Managing Knowledge* (Boston, MA: Harvard Business Review Press, 2002).

[44]   Wenger, 'Communities of Practice and Social Learning Systems'; Adler, 'The Spread of Security Communities'.

[45]   Adler, 'The Spread of Security Communities', 198.

[46]   Manuel Castells, *The Rise of the Network Society* (Oxford: Wiley-Blackwell, 2009); Margaret E. Keck and Kathryn Sikkink, *Activists beyond Borders: Advocacy Networks in International Politics* (Ithaca, NY: Cornell University Press, 2014).

[47]   Michael Byers, *Custom, Power and the Power of Rules: International Relations and Customary International Law* (Cambridge and New York: Cambridge University Press, 1999), 148.

complaints or posing complex legal arguments in courts. Practices normally associated with the offices of international prosecutors involve very specific practical tasks, as well as a diverse range of expert knowledge. As will be explained further later in this chapter and in the succeeding chapters, this knowledge and expertise must be shared and recognised across the community. It also relies on innovation, imagination and adaption within the community of practice to pursue complex legal actions. Moreover, it depends upon individuals in the community of practice to form a cooperative criminal accountability community.

Specialised Knowledge and Practices

As stated earlier, the practice of international criminal law highlights the importance of knowledge and the realm of *specialised* knowledge.[48] This includes, amongst other things, material collected to link (linkage material) senior leaders to the underlying crimes; rules concerning evidence and admissibility; identification of complex sources of international law; and discernment of how the particular nature of some international crimes, such as torture, will have the effect of overriding other sources of domestic and international law.[49] As Entienne Wenger maintained, 'Even though the topic of Communities of Practice covers mostly things that everybody knows in some ways, having a systematic vocabulary to talk about it does makes a difference. An adequate vocabulary is important because the concepts we use to make sense of the world direct both our perception and our actions.'[50] Knowledge surrounding how and why criminal accountability has emerged as a key feature of the UN system and norms governing the complex system of international criminal law also informs how de facto international prosecutors, particularly private non-State actors, adopt specific practices and how they conceptualise international criminal law, and the institutions that serve it (see also Chapter 6).

In particular, they not only identify sources of international law but also draw on previous international criminal cases as important models that inform their practice.[51] One of the most important is the Nuremberg Tribunal.[52] As stated earlier, it informed private non-State actors in both

---

[48]   Wenger, McDermott and Snyder, *Cultivating Communities of Practice*.
[49]   H. W. A. Thirlway, *The Sources of International Law*, 2nd ed., Oxford Public International Law (Oxford: Oxford University Press, 2019).
[50]   Wenger, 'A Social Theory of Learning', 224.
[51]   Wenger, 'Communities of Practice and Social Learning Systems'.
[52]   Roht-Arriaza, *The Pinochet Effect*; Celeste Hicks, *The Trial of Hissène Habré: How the People of Chad Brought a Tyrant to Justice* (London: Zed Books, 2018).

the Pinochet and Habré cases. Indeed, the case strategy was adapted from Nuremberg to include investigating a small group of those *most* responsible, with an emphasis on locating linkage material – that is, material that links those most responsible for the alleged crime to those who perpetrated the underlying crimes. Similarly, it informed how Chief Investigator 1 and CIJA collected linkage material and focused building cases on a small group of those most responsible. In all three cases, as in Nuremberg, the linkage material emphasised collecting documents produced by the perpetrators (or co-perpetrator). As will be demonstrated, de facto international prosecutors are adept at particular practices, and the knowledge associated with them. Given the complexity between the rules that govern international criminal law and other laws, no one person can be expected to hold all the knowledge relevant to all the practices required in the criminal accountability process. Rather, they rely on a community of practitioners to bridge the gap in knowledge and expertise,[53] including the interplay between domestic law, international conventions and customary international law. Indeed, they endeavour to cooperate and share knowledge and concepts required to ensure criminal accountability,[54] which leads me to my next point.

Cooperative Criminal Accountability Practices and Communities

Each of the three case studies reveals the importance of what I term cooperative criminal accountability practices and cooperative criminal accountability communities. Here, I adapt Adler's notion of cooperative security practices and communities[55] to examine the formation of cooperative criminal accountability communities. While they may debate and disagree, de facto international prosecutors must also work together to pursue those suspected of core crimes through explicit cooperation within a particular community of practitioners. As mentioned earlier, they adopt practices that share, amongst other things, a defined common objective, a coordinated investigation and case strategy, as well as knowledge of and expertise in international law (including how it intersects with domestic law).[56] They must also cooperate to pose complex legal arguments in particular court cases. For example, in the cases of Chile and Chad, not all criminal accountability communities or

---

53 Wenger, 'Communities of Practice and Social Learning Systems'.
54 Wenger, 'Communities of Practice and Social Learning Systems'; Wenger, 'A Social Theory of Learning'.
55 Adler, 'The Spread of Security Communities'.
56 Roht-Arriaza, *The Pinochet Effect*, *The Trial of Hissène Habré*; Wenger, 'Communities of Practice and Social Learning Systems'.

communities of practice cooperated effectively. For example, Juan Garcés, a witness to Pinochet's earliest crimes, was a private non-State actor working on the Pinochet case in the Madrid courts. With colleagues, Garcés represented *all* the victims of the Chilean government under Pinochet in the complaint submitted to the Madrid courts, irrespective of their nationality or political leanings. Moreover, he adopted the Nuremberg approach by focusing on a small group of those most responsible, with the mode of liability being criminal conspiracy (as in Nuremberg Trial).[57] Although he was described as the 'architect' of the Pinochet case by the investigating judge in the Madrid courts,[58] he also worked cooperatively with an extensive community of victims, witnesses and practitioners. In contrast, those private non-State actors working together on the related Argentine case in the Madrid courts were characterised by infighting and a lack of cooperation and persisted with an inconsistent or unclear strategy.[59] In the case of Hissène Habré, larger NGOs, such as Amnesty International and Human Rights Watch (HRW) were described as 'rivals' in pursuing Habré's accountability.[60] Yet, Souleymane Guengueng, a victim of torture under the Habré government, formed a cooperative coalition of groups, including with HRW, which coherently and cooperatively worked together.[61]

Moreover, de facto international prosecutors can also show they can work cooperatively with State government actors to pursue accountability in international (State) institutions as part of cooperative criminal accountability communities. For instance, as a State actor, Belgium filed the ongoing dispute between the Belgium State legal officials and Senegal in the ICJ. In *Questions relating to the Obligation to Prosecute or Extradite* (*Belgium* v. *Senegal*), Belgium state legal officials filed an extradition request to Senegal via INTERPOL to fulfil its international legal obligation according to the CAT to extradite Habré.[62]

In this respect, communities of practice that pursue criminal accountability in a foreign or international court are responding to, and grounded in, the social and material world.[63] The lack of local measures for accountability

---

[57]   Roht-Arriaza, *The Pinochet Effects*.
[58]   Garzón, 'Spanish Judge Baltasar Garzón Tells the Story of the Arrest of Chile's Augusto Pinochet (Transcript)'.
[59]   Roht-Arriaza, *The Pinochet Effect*.
[60]   Reydams, 'The Rise and Fall of Universal Jurisdiction', 349.
[61]   Hicks, *The Trial of Hissène Habré*.
[62]   Questions relating to the Obligation to Prosecute or Extradite (*Belgium* v. *Senegal*), Judgment, I.C.J. Reports (2012).
[63]   Saskia Sassen, 'New Frontiers Facing Urban Sociology at the Millennium', *The British Journal of Sociology* 51, no. 1 (2000): 143–59, https://doi.org/10.1111/j.1468-4446.2000.00143.x.

meant that Juan Garcés, Souleymane Guengueng and Chief Investigator 1, as victim and witnesses, looked to international law to close the gap, as well as to the knowledge and practices of the wider community of practice to prosecute former heads of state in a third state.

A Richer View of International Law's Operation

As a further lens to the study of de facto international prosecutors as a community of practice, the three biographical case studies illuminate the need for a fuller and deeper appreciation of what international law *is*. Indeed, the study of de facto international prosecutors invokes a greater understanding for how international law can influence behaviour, and the nature of legal obligation in international criminal law from both a political and legal standpoint. International relations (IR), as a discipline, often limits its study of States to conventions and treaties while overlooking the role of customary international law,[64] including the role of universal jurisdiction. As Martha Finnemore and Stephen Toope maintained: 'International legal scholars have long understood international law as more than the formal, treaty based law. ... Law is a broad social phenomenon deeply embedded in the practices, beliefs and traditions of societies, and shaped by intersections among societies. Customary international law displays this richer understanding of law's operations.'[65] Such an analytical lens serves to clarify how the evolving nature of international criminal law, including customary international law as a key source, reflects upon different subjects of international law and similarly confers duties and *obligations* on states and individuals.[66] As will be demonstrated, legal obligations can also be explained as 'resulting from the work of communities of legal practice that uphold specific criteria of legality.'[67] The three biographical case studies reveal how international law enables and mobilises particular actors[68] to adopt particular practices as the means to hold senior leaders to account for humanity's greatest crimes. In doing so,

---

[64] Martha J. Finnemore and Stephen Toope, 'Alternatives to "Legalization": Richer Views of Law and Politics', *International Organization* 55, no. 3 (2001): 1, https://doi.org/10.1162/00208180152507614.

[65] Finnemore and Toope, 'Alternatives to "Legalization"', 1.

[66] Mettraux, 'Trial at Nuremberg'; Noora Arajärvi, *The Changing Nature of Customary International Law: Methods of Interpreting the Concept of Custom in International Criminal Tribunals* (London and New York: Routledge, 2014).

[67] Brunnée and Toope, 'Interactional International Law and the Practice of Legality', 108.

[68] Brunnée and Toope, 'Interactional International Law and the Practice of Legality'; Finnemore and Toope, 'Alternatives to "Legalization"'.

cooperative criminal accountability communities also play a role in upholding human rights and justice norms at the heart of the UN-System.

Adaptation and Innovation

The three biographical case studies – in Chile, Chad and Syria – illuminate the role of imagination, adaption and innovation as key features to overcoming the criminal accountability gap for those most responsible for core international crimes. Again, I draw on Adler's understanding of communities of practice as innovators.[69] As Adler maintained, '[b]y facilitating both the innovation and stabilisation of practices, communities structure consciousness and intention, constitute agency, and encourage the evolution or spread of structure.'[70] Efforts by de facto international prosecutors to pursue criminal accountability do not always result in successful prosecution. The three cases studies demonstrate how de facto international prosecutors draw upon lessons learned in previous failed attempts, and how this acts as a key driver to later success. In this respect, attempts matter and failure is an important means of gaining knowledge and understanding of legal orders and systems.

I also draw upon Wenger's notions of community of practice to show the ability of cooperative criminal accountability communities to understand and design processes that allow them to adapt and learn.[71] In turn, this shapes their identity implicitly as practitioners of law and justice but also as witnesses and victims of core crimes. That is to say, they identify with common objectives and practices that aim to extend the reach of international criminal law to those most responsible. Furthermore, an integral part of the investigation and prosecution process is the influence and shaping of an individual's identity: for example, it requires witnesses and victims to make formal statements, which serve as vital evidence. Within the community of practice, individuals can also constitute a multiplicity of identities: they can be at once a witness *and* victim of core international crimes, *as well as* a practitioner in international criminal law, such as an international prosecutor or investigator. Indeed, the biographical studies illustrate this, including in relation to Garcés, Guengueng and Chief Investigator 1, amongst others (including those not explicitly identified as such in the study). This multiplicity of identities can shape agency, as well as the broader community of practice and its willingness to cooperate. For

---

[69] Adler, 'The Spread of Security Communities', 196.
[70] Adler, 'The Spread of Security Communities', 196.
[71] Wenger, 'Communities of Practice and Social Learning Systems'; Wenger, 'A Social Theory of Learning'.

instance, the fact that Garcés was a witness and a victim of the early atrocities of the Pinochet government and had escaped the morning of the coup meant that as a prosecutor, other Chilean victims and witnesses trusted him. As a consequence, victims and witnesses became willing to provide formal statements in the Pinochet case. Perhaps the role that is most scrutinised in terms of identity is the role of the deciding judge, who must be seen at all times to be independent and impartial. In the case of *Pinochet 2*, for instance, it was claimed that one of the judges in the British House of Lords was linked to Amnesty International, which, it was argued, served to discredit the decision.[72]

While these actors strive to innovate when barriers are presented, they also go to great lengths to argue that they are drawing on pre-existing and established international laws. By innovate, I do not mean radical changes in the law or indeed the system of international criminal law. Nor do I attempt to associate de facto international prosecutors as norm entrepreneurs whereby their goal is to innovate new laws or legal norms. Here I draw on Finnemore and Sikkink's definition of norm entrepreneurs, whereby 'Norm entrepreneurs attempt to convince a critical mass of states (norm leaders) to embrace new norms.'[73] Rather, I argue that when posing legal arguments and interpretations relating to the *jus cogens* nature of crimes in court cases, de facto international prosecutors seek to establish that these international laws *already exist*, including a State's obligation to prosecute or extradite those suspected of torture and genocide. Therefore, in this study, 'innovation' consists of small adaptations or shifts in standard practices to pursue accountability on a practical level, and within the current system of international criminal law. Through subtle adaptations and practices in simple and nuanced ways, de facto international prosecutors seek to innovate and extend the reaches of international criminal law, often in ways that others, including powerful State actors, cannot or will not.

Furthermore, the three biographical case studies show the extent that de facto international prosecutors are adapting in a unique and particular international criminal law context, which continues to evolve. With it, they are informed by particularities of the international criminal legal system through 'situated learning'.[74] According to Lave and Wenger, practitioners learn by immersing themselves in the emerging or new community, and by absorbing and adapting modes of action and practice as the means to become a part of

---

[72] Roht-Arriaza, *The Pinochet Effect*.

[73] Martha Finnemore and Kathryn Sikkink, 'International Norm Dynamics and Political Change', *International Organization* 52, no. 4 (1998): 895, https://doi.org/10.1162/002081898550789.

[74] Lave and Wenger, *Situated Learning*.

the community, and also to understand norms and principles that govern international criminal law:

> Learning viewed as situated activity has as its central defining characteristic a process that we call legitimate peripheral participation. By this we mean to draw attention to the point that learners inevitably participate in communities of practitioners and that the mastery of knowledge requires newcomers to move toward full participation in the sociocultural practices of a community. 'Legitimate peripheral participation' provides a way to speak about the relations between newcomers and old timers, and about activities, identities, artifacts and communities of knowledge and practice.[75]

Witnesses and victims of core crimes have been just that, witness and victims, which also lends them the trust necessary to enable other witnesses and victims of core crimes (as well as other private non-State actors) to cooperate in the enormous effort and complex practices required to achieve criminal accountability. Witnesses and victims must then adapt their learning and knowledge to the complexities of the evolving system of international criminal law, as well as the domestic laws that govern foreign courts. One could argue that as international criminal law has evolved as a unique system of international law, it also aids these actors in drawing upon it in ways that States cannot or may not expect. I examine this context in a later section, titled 'ICL as a Unique and Distinct System of International Law'.

Cooperative Practices: Interpreting the Sources of Law and Innovation

Lastly, as stated earlier, a vital practice of the cooperative criminal accountability community is identifying the existing sources of laws – including local, foreign and international laws.[76] With this, it must pose complex legal arguments in the domestic appeal courts (as in the British Supreme Court, formerly known as the House of Lords) and international courts (as in the International Court of Justice) to establish that foreign courts have jurisdiction over the international crime and that the suspect does not enjoy immunity. As in domestic legal systems, in international criminal law, the '[l]aw's role in mobilising different groups is much more profound than mere provision of information',[77] as might be

---

[75]   Lave and Wenger *Situated Learning*.

[76]   H. L. A. Hart, *The Concept of Law*, ed. Joseph Raz and Penelope A. Bulloch, 3rd ed., Clarendon Law Series (Oxford: Oxford University Press, 2012); Brunnée and Toope, 'Interactional International Law and the Practice of Legality'; Finnemore and Toope, 'Alternatives to "Legalization"'.

[77]   Finnemore and Toope, 'Alternatives to "Legalization"', 1.

associated with a network. A study of de facto international prosecutors not only illuminates another sub-area of the study of community of practice, it offers a richer view of law's operations, as well as how these actors interact with different sources of law as a cooperative criminal accountability community. In the cases of Chile and Chad, not only are de facto international prosecutors the first to initiate an investigation, as per Article 6, paragraph 2, of the Convention Against Torture and to submit criminal complaints to foreign courts, they also work with a cooperative criminal accountability community to pose complex legal arguments in a number of important legal cases.

With that in mind, I now discuss how de facto international prosecutors worked as a cooperative criminal accountability community to practise *interpreting* complex sources of international law. Thereafter, they *posed complex legal arguments* in court, which reflected an important practice (and step) in the accountability process for core crimes in foreign courts. Specifically, I focus on the earlier cases of Chile and Chad: in a domestic appeal court case concerning Pinochet (in the British House of Lords) and an international court case concerning Habré (in the International Court of Justice), respectively. In each case, they argued that the crime of torture was an accepted and recognised peremptory norm *(jus cogens)* of international law. Peremptory norms of international law, they argued, provided for a unique hierarchy in international law, whereby the crimes trumped other rules governing international and domestic norms, including the rules that govern immunity. The section that follows allows us to further understand the complex array of practices de facto international prosecutors must adopt and understand, as well as their reliance on the wider cooperative criminal accountability community to both cooperate and bridge knowledge of particular legal practices. It also aids in answering the question: how (or when) do particular interpretations of international law 'win out' over others in court judgments? With a focus on the two historical case studies, Chile and Chad, I provide the means to understand how Syrian cases may be shaped in the future. Although it is too early to draw on Syria as a comparable study (particularly given that alleged core crimes remain ongoing in Syria), I provide some initial analysis on Syria before I conclude this chapter.

ESSENTIAL PRACTICES: INTERPRETING LAW AND POSING COMPLEX LEGAL ARGUMENTS

Arguably, some IR and international legal scholars maintain that there is an absence of a hierarchy of rules in international law. For instance, Brunnee and Toope draw inspiration from Lon Fuller's legal theory to propose an interactional theory of international law and legal obligation. They argue that law is 'not grounded in the will of the sovereign or of the Parliament; it is not simply the fiat of the state, nor is it rooted in a hierarchy of rules'.[78] While this study concurs with the earlier points made in this chapter, it is on this latter point concerning a hierarchy of rules in international law that this theoretical framework attempts to address. Furthermore, rather than focus on compliance, as Brunnee and Toope have,[79] the case studies attempt to move beyond compliance,[80] to focus on the key court decisions.

While many aspects of their interactional theory illuminate the role of different actors, including de facto international prosecutors, in contributing to international law and legal obligation, I argue that the particular nature of international criminal law reflects the emergence of a hierarchy.[81] I argue that both private non-state actors and state legal officials pose legal arguments and interpretations of law in relation to particular crimes, such as torture, crimes against humanity and genocide, that win out over other international and domestic laws.

The Hierarchical Nature of Peremptory Norms (Jus Cogens)

Unlike many domestic legal systems, a hierarchy of the rules or sources of international law did not emerge historically.[82] Indeed, the two main sources of law, international conventions and customary international law, emerged with equal rank.[83] Neither established a hierarchy of rules within a particular source of law, such as within customary international law.[84] More recently,

---

[78] Jutta Brunnée and Stephen J. Toope, *Legitimacy and Legality in International Law: An Interactional Account*, Legitimacy & Legality in International Law (Cambridge and New York: Cambridge University Press, 2010), 23.

[79] Brunnée and Toope, *Legitimacy and Legality in International Law: An Interactional Account*.

[80] Ian Clark et al., 'Crisis in the Laws of War? Beyond Compliance and Effectiveness,' *European Journal of International Relations* 24, no. 2 (1 June 2018): 319–43, https://doi.org/10.1177/1354066117714528.

[81] Most international lawyers accept that there exists a rudimentary hierarchy of rules in relation to peremptory norms. As will be noted below, this hierarchical character is expressly acknowledged in Articles 53 and 64 of the Vienna Convention on the Law of Treaties. It has also been acknowledged by the International Law Commission (ILC) and the ICJ. For a discussion these issues of hierarchy, see International Law Commission, 'Fragmentation of International Law: Difficulties Arising from the Diversification and Expansion of International Law: Report of the Study Group of the International Law Commission, Fifty-Eighth Session, A/CN.4/L.682' (New York: United National General Assembly, 2006) Para. 324–409.

[82] Brownlie and Crawford, *Brownlie's Principles of Public International Law*.

[83] Antonio Cassese, *International Law*, 2nd ed. (Oxford and New York: Oxford University Press, 2005), 198.

[84] Cassese, *International Law*, 198–99.

Article 103 of the Charter of the United Nations created a form of hierarchy in favour of obligations under the UN Charter: 'In the event of a conflict between the obligations of the Members of the United Nations under the present Charter and their obligations under any other international agreement, their obligations under the present Charter shall prevail.'[85] The Statute of the Permanent Court of International Justice, established in 1945 under the Charter of the United Nations, listed the sources of international law under Article 38 without specifying a hierarchical arrangement.[86] While in practice international conventions and customary international law remain the main sources of law, Crawford argues, 'we can explain the priority of (a) by the fact that it refers to a source of obligation which will ordinarily prevail as being more specific'. Nevertheless, he emphasised that the statute refrained from explicitly referring to a hierarchy of sources or rules.[87]

Nevertheless, although traditionally international law did not evolve as a hierarchy of rules and sources of law,[88] peremptory norms (*jus cogens*) of international law represent a unique feature of the international legal order. Most legal scholars recognise that peremptory norms (*jus cogens*) of international law create a hierarchy in international law. For example, Crawford[89] refers more generally to peremptory norms (*jus cogens*) of international law as outlined in the Vienna Convention on the Law of Treaties[90] (in Articles 53 and 64) as having the effect of *voiding* a treaty.[91] Article 53 states,

> A treaty is void if, at the time of its conclusion, it conflicts with a peremptory norm of general international law. For the purposes of the present Convention, a peremptory norm of general international law is a norm accepted and recognized by the international community of States as a whole as a norm from which no derogation is permitted and which can be modified only by a subsequent norm of general international law having the same character.

---

[85] United Nations, 'The Charter of the United Nations' (1945).
[86] United Nations, 'Statute of the International Court of Justice', 18 April 1945, Article 38.
[87] Crawford, *Brownlie's Principles of Public International Law*. It is important to separate the issue of whether a hierarchy exists between the sources set out in Article 38(1)(a), (b) and (c) (for example between ordinary treaties, ordinary custom and ordinary general principles of law where there is no general hierarchy between such sources) and with Art 103 of the UN Charter and peremptory norms which are not ordinary rules.
[88] Cassese, *International Law*; Brownlie and Crawford, *Brownlie's Principles of Public International Law*.
[89] Brownlie and Crawford, *Brownlie's Principles of Public International Law*.
[90] United Nations, 'Vienna Convention on the Law of Treaties (VCLT)', 23 May 1969.
[91] Crawford, *Brownlie's Principles of Public International Law*.

Article 64, titled 'Emergence of a new peremptory norm of general international law ("jus cogens")' states, 'If a new peremptory norm of general international law emerges, any existing treaty which is in conflict with that norm becomes void and terminates.' Added to this is the role legal interpretation plays in relation to peremptory norms. For instance, in his separate opinion of the 2003 ICJ decision *Case Concerning Oil Platforms (Islamic Republic of Iran v. United States of America)*, Judge Bruno Simma argued, 'If these general rules of international law are of a peremptory nature ... then the principle of interpretation ... turns into a legally insurmountable limit to permissible treaty interpretation.'[92] Crawford also refers to the necessary role interpretation plays in determining treaty obligations and the interrelationship between treaty and customary international law, in relation to peremptory norms (*jus cogens*) of international law:

> Source (a) [of Article 38 of the Statute of the International Court of Justice] relates to *obligations*; in some circumstances a treaty does not give rise to a corresponding obligation of a state party, notably when it is contrary to a peremptory norm of international law; and in all cases the *content* of the treaty obligation depends on the interpretation of the treaty, a process governed by international law. A treaty may even be displaced by a subsequent rule of customary international law, at least where its effects are recognised in the subsequent conduct of the parties.[93]

Most international lawyers view peremptory norms (*jus cogens*) of international law as a clear hierarchy of rules, particularly in relation to international criminal law. Klabbers, Peters and Ulfstein go one step further to describe it as type of verticalisation, particularly in relation to its application to international criminal law: 'Verticalization, by definition, carries a sense of hierarchy with it, and the argument can increasingly be heard that international law is moving in this direction. This is symbolized not least by the emergence of international criminal law as a branch of international law.'[94] Antonio Cassese was more specific and confident of the role peremptory norms (*jus cogens*) played in international law. He argued that although no hierarchy was created between the two key sources of international law –

---

[92] Case Concerning Oil Platforms (*Islamic Republic of Iran* v. *United States of America*), Judgment, merits, ICJ Reports (separate opinion of Judge Simma) (2003), para. 9.
[93] Crawford, *Brownlie's Principles of Public International Law*, 20.
[94] Jan Klabbers, Anne Peters and Geir Ulfstein, *The Constitutionalization of International Law* (Oxford: Oxford University Press, 2009), 15. As noted before, some peremptory norms are not part of international criminal law. The right to self-defence, for example, has been recognised by the ILC to be a peremptory norm.

conventions and customary international law – peremptory norms (*jus cogens*) of international law have emerged to reflect 'special class' status:

> Rather, a special class of *general rules* made by custom has been endowed with a *special legal force*: they are peremptory in nature and make up the so-called *jus cogens*, in that they may not be derogated from by treaty (or by ordinary customary process); if they are, the derogating rules may be declared null and void. Thus these peremptory norms have a rank and status superior to those of all the other rules of the international community.[95]

A key area of international criminal law that peremptory norms are in tension with is that of laws governing immunity. As will be shown in relation to Pinochet and Habré, de facto international prosecutors who worked as a cooperative criminal accountability community worked together to pose complex legal arguments that implicitly and explicitly interpret *jus cogens* in relation to core crimes as superior or supreme to other international laws. To do this, they drew on a number of codified laws, such as the Vienna Convention on the Law of Treaties (VCLT),[96] which defined the nature of peremptory norms (*jus cogens*) of international law, as well as other UN conventions concerning crimes against humanity, torture and genocide. They also drew on customary international law and previous case judgements as evidence of law. As Hugh Thirlway observed, unlike other aspects of customary international law, which are accepted as already 'known' by courts (see section titled 'The Role of Jus Cogens in the Cases of Pinochet and Habré') the sources of peremptory norms are less straightforward.[97] According to the International Law Commission, *jus cogens* 'found its way into positive international law' through the VCLT in the 1960s.[98] In this way, *jus cogens* provides for a (relatively new) rule of hierarchy for particular behaviours (*senso stricu*)[99] – those deemed to be non-derogable by the international community. It is this fidelity to positive law[100] that de facto international prosecutors draw upon as the basis for their legal arguments concerning *jus cogens* crimes. However, they must establish that *jus cogens* of international law has evolved to include particular behaviours under customary international law where no derogation is permitted, such as *inter alia* torture, genocide and slavery

---

95   Cassese, *International Law*, 199.
96   United Nations, 'Vienna Convention on the Law of Treaties (VCLT)'.
97   Thirlway, *The Sources of International Law*, 40.
98   International Law Commission, 'Fragmentation of International Law: Difficulties Arising from the Diversification and Expansion of International Law: Report of the Study Group of the International Law Commission, Fifty-Eighth Session, A/CN.4/L.682', 183 (para. 362).
99   International Law Commission, 184 (para. 365).
100 Arajärvi, *The Changing Nature of Customary International Law.*

(although not all *jus cogens* are necessarily crimes).[101] It is this rule that explains how and why interpretations of torture as a *jus cogens* crime win out or void other obligations or laws.

I now turn to explain how peremptory norms, as a unique type of rule of international law, were drawn upon to pose complex legal arguments in a domestic appeals court and an international court concerning Pinochet and Habré, respectively. While the cooperative criminal accountability community aimed to prosecute Pinochet and Habré, it was challenged by them in courts arguing that they *inter alia* enjoyed immunity for the crime of torture and therefore could not be prosecuted or extradited. Pinochet appealed the extradition order issued from Spain in the British courts, and Habré in the Senegal courts. Crucially, in both cases, all relevant states were State Parties to the Convention Against Torture (CAT). In the case of Pinochet, Chile, Spain and the United Kingdom were State Parties; in the case of Habré, Senegal and Belgium were also.[102] This enabled the cooperative criminal accountability community working together to pose complex legal arguments to the British House of Lords and the International Court of Justice respectively, explaining how international criminal law applied to Pinochet and Habré, respectively.

The Role of Jus Cogens in the Cases of Pinochet and Habré

How did the cooperative criminal accountability community explain the nature of *jus cogens* crimes as superior to other rules and sources of international law? During the Pinochet (*Pinochet 3*) case in London (R v . *Bow Street Metropolitan Stipendiary Magistrate*, ex parte Pinochet Ugarte (No 3) (Pinochet III)), Christopher Greenwood, representing the UK Crown Prosecution Services acting on behalf of Spain, argued that in the drafting of the CAT, there was no head of state exception and states could already exercise universal jurisdiction for the crimes of torture. Greenwood argued as follows:

---

[101]   The ILC Fragmentation Study Group reported that the following are ranked as *jus cogens*:

> (a) 'The prohibition of aggressive use of force; (b) the right to self-defence; (c) the prohibition of genocide; (d) the prohibition of torture; (e) crimes against humanity; (f) the prohibition of slavery and the slave trade; (g) the prohibition of piracy; (h) the prohibition of racial discrimination and apartheid; and (i) the prohibition of hostilities directed at civilian populations ('basic rules of international humanitarian law')'. See International Law Commission, 'Fragmentation of International Law', 189, para. 374.

[102]   Although Chad was not at that time a State Party to the Convention Against Torture, it was accepted that torture was an international crime. Chad also referred to the Universal Declaration of Human Rights in its constitution, which did not permit torture. Conversely, both Senegal and Belgium were State Parties to the Convention Against Torture, at the time Habré resided in Senegal (see Chapter 3).

Torture Convention codified existing law norms prohibiting torture, but added a duty to exercise the jurisdiction which existed under customary international law. . . . Accordingly, either the Torture Convention established that the applicant can have no immunity from prosecution for acts of torture or alternatively the prohibition against torture has the status of *jus cogens* and he can be prosecuted under customary international law.[103]

Similarly, Peter Duffy QC, who acted on behalf of private non-State actors, such as Amnesty International et al. (who were interveners on the Pinochet hearing), argued as follows:

Under customary international law heads of state are responsible internationally for grave crimes against humanity including torture. . . . To recognise a *ratione materiae* immunity in respect of complicity in torture would be to contradict the very scheme of the Torture Convention. . . . To regard the rule against torture as *jus cogens* and *erga omnes* underlines its fundamental place in the public policy of international law.[104]

During the trial, even the Republic of Chile accepted that by the time Pinochet seized power in 1973, torture was prohibited under international law. It also acknowledged that the 'prohibition of torture by international law has the character of *jus cogens* or obligation *erga omnes*'.[105] Nevertheless, they argued it still did not impose upon the question of immunity, particularly personal responsibility of heads of state before international criminal tribunals.[106]

In response to these arguments, the House of Lords held that torture was an accepted and recognised peremptory norm (*jus cogens*) of customary international law, placed above all domestic and international laws, including laws governing immunity for a former head of state. The headnote to the judgement records that a majority of the House of Lords (*Pinochet 3*) held that

(2) . . . a former head of state had immunity from the criminal jurisdiction of the United Kingdom for acts done in official capacity as head of state pursuant to section 20 of the State Immunity Act 1978 when read with article 39(2) of Schedule 1 to the Diplomatic Privileges Act 1964; *but that torture was an international crime against humanity and jus cogens* and after the coming into effect of the International Convention against Torture and other Cruel, Inhuman or Degrading Treatment or Punishment 1984 there had been

---

[103] Christopher Greenwood, *R* v. *Bow Street Metropolitan Stipendiary Magistrate*, ex parte Pinochet Ugarte (Pinochet 3), 156.

[104] Peter Duffey QC, *Pinochet 3*, 163–5.

[105] Collins, *Pinochet 3*, 174

[106] Collins, *Pinochet 3*, 174

a universal jurisdiction in all the Convention state parties to either extradite or punish a public official who committed torture. . . . The systematic use of torture was an international crime for which there could be no immunity even before the Convention came into effect and consequently there is no immunity under customary international law for the offences relating to torture alleged against the applicant.[107]

Pinochet was the first former head of State to be subject to international criminal law since Nuremberg and upon a successful extradition hearing, he would be sent to Spain to be prosecuted in the Madrid courts for the crime of torture. The highest domestic court of a State held that as torture was an accepted and recognised peremptory norm (*jus cogens*) of international law, it trumped the immunity of a former head of State. Nonetheless, this was not the first time a court had recognised torture as a peremptory norm (*jus cogens*) of international law. A fact recognised by Lord Brown-Wilkinson in the British House of Lords in the Pinochet case (*Pinochet 3*). Lord Brown-Wilkinson referred to the recent *Furundzia* case judgment at the International Criminal Tribunal for the former Yugoslavia (ICTY) in December 1998, whereby torture was not only considered a crime under customary international law but also a *jus cogens* in the ICTY (TC, section 162) decision.[108] Lord Brown-Wilkinson quoted paragraphs 153 and 154 of the ICTY judgment in his own judgment:

> Because of the importance of the values it protects, [the prohibition of torture] has evolved into a peremptory norm or *jus cogens*, that is, a norm that enjoys *a higher rank in the international hierarchy* than treaty law and even 'ordinary' customary rules. The most conspicuous consequences of this higher rank is that the principle at issue cannot be derogated from by states through international treaties or local or special customs or even general customary rules not endowed with the same normative force.[109]

This view of customary international law is difficult but not impossible to reconcile with the 2002 decision by the ICJ in the case of *Arrest Warrant*

---

[107] *Pinochet 3*, 149, emphasis added.

[108] The Convention Against Torture was codified in 1984 and today there are 170 Parties to the Convention. Unlike other conventions, it is not necessary to ratify the CAT. Once signed, States are State Parties to the convention. While the CAT was signed in 1984, torture was identified as a crime under international law, particularly under customary international law, for far longer. See *Filártiga* v. *Peña-Irala*, 630 F.2d 876, United States Court of Appeals for the Second Circuit (2d Cir. 1980), which stated that 'the torturer has become like the pirate or the slave trader before him, *hostis humani generis*, an enemy of all mankind' (at 980).

[109] *Prosecutor* v. *Furundzia*, Judgment, ICTY, quoted in Lord Brown-Wilkinson, *Pinochet 3*, 198, emphasis added.

(*Congo* v. *Belgium*). An important difference between the Pinochet decision and the 2002 *Arrest Warrant* decision was that Pinochet was a *former* head of state, whereas the 2002 ICJ decision dealt with the immunity of an *incumbent* foreign minister.[110] Furthermore, the distinction between the decision of the British House of Lords and the International Criminal Tribunal for the former Yugoslavia is important, as it goes to the heart of how we understand State practice in international law, and also how judges may draw upon other cases to make decisions about law.[111]

Much later, when Belgium acted on behalf of de facto international prosecutors in taking their case of Hissène Habré, as a former head of State, to the ICJ, the court reflected customary international law; by doing so, it echoed a judgement in line with the *Pinochet 3* in the British House of Lords. In *Questions relating to the Obligation to Prosecute or Extradite* (*Belgium* v. *Senegal*), Belgium made a case to the ICJ that *inter alia* crimes against humanity, with torture being a constituent part of the offence, had

---

[110]   Paragraph 61 of the *Arrest Warrant* judgment may allow the two decisions to stand together. Paragraph 61 reads as follows:

> 61. Accordingly, the immunities enjoyed under international law by an incumbent or former Minister for Foreign Affairs do not represent a bar to criminal prosecution in certain circumstances.
>
> First, such persons enjoy no criminal immunity under international law in their own countries, and may thus be tried by those countries' courts in accordance with the relevant rules of domestic law.
>
> Secondly, they will cease to enjoy immunity from foreign jurisdiction if the State which they represent or have represented decides to waive that immunity.
>
> Thirdly, after a person ceases to hold the office of Minister for Foreign Affairs, he or she will no longer enjoy all of the immunities accorded by international law in other States. Provided that it has jurisdiction under international law, a court of one State may try a former Minister for Foreign Affairs of another State in respect of acts committed prior or subsequent to his or her period of office, as well as in respect of acts committed during that period of office in a private capacity.
>
> Fourthly, an incumbent or former Minister for Foreign Affairs may be subject to criminal proceedings before certain international criminal courts, where they have jurisdiction. Examples include the International Criminal Tribunal for the former Yugoslavia, and the International Criminal Tribunal for Rwanda, established pursuant to Security Council resolutions under Chapter VII of the United Nations Charter, and the future International Criminal Court created by the 1998 Rome Convention. The latter's Statute expressly provides, in Article 27, paragraph 2, that 'immunities or special procedural rules' which may attach to the [p 26] official capacity of a person, whether under national or international law, shall not bar the Court from exercising its jurisdiction over such a person.

Arrest Warrant of 11 April 2000 (Democratic Republic of the Congo v. Belgium), Judgment, ICJ Reports. (2002).

[111]   Ian Brownlie, *State Responsibility* (Oxford: Clarendon Press, 1983).

long been prohibited under customary international law and an accepted and recognised *jus cogens* of international law. In Belgium's application to the ICJ, it made a number of key arguments surrounding the interplay between jurisdiction, immunity and peremptory norms. It also attempted to outline the evolving nature of international law. First, their application emphasised the effects of the Pinochet case in recognising crimes against humanity as offences under customary international law, and that this had been incorporated into domestic Belgian law. Second, Belgium argued that *Nullum crimen, nulla poena sine lege* (no penalty without law) could not be applied in this case, as crimes against humanity had clearly been outlawed: 'there are grounds for considering that, before being codified in treaties or laws, crimes against humanity are established by international custom and as such form part of the international *jus cogens* which is binding in the internal legal system and applies *erga omnes*'.[112] Third, Belgium argued that despite the ICJ 2002 *Arrest Warrant* ruling (*Congo v. Belgium*), international law applied to former heads of state for crimes against humanity, including torture, and referenced *inter alia* the Pinochet ruling by the British House of Lords as evidence of the acceptance under international law. Besides this, Belgium argued, Chad had already lifted Habré's immunity.[113]

In its judgment, the ICJ acknowledged Chad had officially lifted the immunity on Hissène Habré, but it also recognised that torture was prohibited under customary international law and classed as *jus cogens*.[114]:

> In the Court's opinion, the prohibition of torture is part of customary international law and it has become a peremptory norm (*jus cogens*).
>
> That prohibition is grounded in a widespread international practice and on the *opinio juris* of States. It appears in numerous international instruments of

[112] Application Instituting Proceedings filed in the Registry of the Court on 19 February 2009, *Questions Relating to the Obligation to Prosecute or Extradite (Belgium v. Senegal)*, International Court of Justice, 78–79.

[113] In a letter to the Belgium Minister of Justice, that was shared with the court, Chad confirmed that 'The Sovereign National Conference held in N'Djamena from 15 January to 7 April 1993 officially lifted all immunity from legal process from Mr. Hissein Habré. That position was reinforced by Law No. 010/pR/95 of 9 June 1995, which granted amnesty to political prisoners and exiles and to persons engaged in armed opposition, with the exception of 'the former president of the Republic, Hissein Habré, his co-perpetrators and/or accomplices'. See Application Instituting Proceedings filed in the Registry of the Court on 19 February 2009, *Questions Relating to the Obligation to Prosecute or Extradite (Belgium v. Senegal)*, International Court of Justice, Annex 4 Letter of 7 October 2002 From the Minister of Justice of Chad Lifting Any Immunity which Might be Claimed by Mr. H. Habré.

[114] ICJ did not refer to the notion of peremptory norms (*jus cogens*) until 2006, see *Armed Activities (DRC v. Rwanda)*, ICJ Reports 2006, 6, 31–2.

universal application (in particular the Universal Declaration of Human Rights of 1948, the 1949 Geneva Conventions for the protection of war victims; the International Covenant on Civil and Political Rights of 1966; General Assembly resolution 3452/30 of 9 December 1975 on the Protection of All Persons from Being Subjected to Torture and Other Cruel, Inhuman or Degrading Treatment or Punishment), and it has been introduced into the domestic law of almost all States; finally, acts of torture are regularly denounced within national and international fora.[115]

Possibly what is most revealing about peremptory norms is that States do not disagree on *what* is classed or categorised as a peremptory norm.[116] As stated earlier, during the trial of *Pinochet* 3 before the British House of Lords, the Chilean representative acknowledged that torture was an accepted and recognised *jus cogens* of customary international law.[117] The issue was to what extent *jus cogens* overrode long-held historical notions of immunity for incumbent and former heads of State. Yet, in the *Pinochet* 3 appeals case in the British House of Lords and the *Belgium* v. *Senegal* dispute before the ICJ, both courts held that *jus cogens* superseded concerns such as immunity for former heads of state. In this way, the cooperative criminal accountability community had sufficiently and necessarily practised the interpretation of international law and from that posed complex legal arguments explaining how former heads of State were subject to international criminal law.

Added to the notion of *jus cogens*, other sources of law may contribute to a hierarchical view of rules or sources of international law. In national systems which are monist in orientation, a hierarchy of sources of law between domestic laws that govern states and international law (with respect to conventions and customary international law) is present.[118] The more monist a national legal system, the more important peremptory norms will be. For example, the German Constitution ('Basic Law for the Federal Republic of Germany', *Grundgesetz für die Bundesrepublik Deutschland*) (see Chapter 5)[119] favours a monist national system. The converse is true for

---

[115] Questions relating to the Obligation to Prosecute or Extradite (*Belgium* v. *Senegal*), Judgment, ICJ Reports.

[116] Crawford, *Brownlie's Principles of Public International Law*.

[117] Collins *Pinochet* 3, 174.

[118] For example, the High Court of Australia has accepted that the Australian Parliament can legislate in a manner that violates Australia's international human rights obligations.

[119] 'Grundgesetz Für Die Bundesrepublik Deutschland (Basic Law for the Federal Republic of Germany) in the Revised Version Published in the Federal Law Gazette Part III, Classification Number 100–1, as Last Amended by Article 1 of the Act of 28 March 2019 (Federal Law Gazette I, 404)' (n.d.), www.gesetze-im-internet.de/englisch_gg/englisch_gg .html.

more dualist national systems, which raises a major challenge for dualist states, such as Australia, Canada, New Zealand and the United Kingdom, in that national law and international law can diverge. The executive branch of government may enter into treaties on behalf of the State, but the parliaments in those States control what forms part of national law, and the executive branch is not able to legislate independently. This creates the potential for unresolved conflict between national law and the international obligations of these States. This was evident in the case of Senegal. Although a State Party to the CAT, it remained hesitant to prosecute Habré. Yet, the Vienna Convention on the Law of Treaties informed the way the CAT was interpreted in the ICJ decision in relation to the legal obligations of Senegal to prosecute or extradite Habré. Article 27 of the Vienna Convention, titled 'Internal Law and Observance of Treaties', states: 'A party may not invoke the provisions of its internal law as justifications for its failure to perform its treaty.'[120] In the case of *Belgium* v. *Senegal*, the ICJ held that the fact that Senegal had not amended its domestic legal jurisdiction as required by the CAT to prosecute Habré was not an acceptable excuse, and it must conform to the CAT, amend its internal laws and prosecute Hissène Habré as per the CAT.[121]

I now turn to explain how legal obligation rests upon States in relation to the crimes of torture and genocide. This also goes some way to explaining how the cooperative criminal accountability community extended the reach of international criminal law, particularly in the context of universal jurisdiction, and the means by which some states could and do pursue extradition.

The Nature of Obligation in Relation to the Crime of Torture

As is reflected in the three biographical case studies, torture is deemed a *jus cogens* crime under customary international law. Some scholars may argue that while powerful States, such as the United States, continue to practise torture, they undermine the anti-torture norm.[122] Of course, it is disappointing when democratic states initially at the forefront of establishing the Convention Against Torture are suspected of practising torture on an unofficial basis. Yet, the continued unofficial practice of torture by States in itself does not necessarily produce another rule.[123] This is reflected in the decision of *Military and Paramilitary in and against Nicaragua Activities (Nicaragua v. United*

---

[120]   United Nations, 'Vienna Convention on the Law of Treaties (VCLT)'.
[121]   Questions relating to the Obligation to Prosecute or Extradite (*Belgium* v. *Senegal*), Judgment, ICJ Reports.
[122]   Brunnée and Toope, *Legitimacy and Legality in International Law*, 17.
[123]   Thirlway, *The Sources of International Law*.

States).[124] In its judgment, the ICJ did not view that 'for a rule to be established as customary, the corresponding practice must be in absolute rigorous conformity with the rule'.[125] Moreover, the ICJ observed that '[i]n order to deduce the existence of customary rules, the Court deems it sufficient that the conduct of States should, in general, be consistent with such rules, and that instances of State conduct inconsistent with a given rule should generally have been treated as breaches of that rule, not as indications of the recognition of a new rule'.[126]

Although state actors may continue to perpetrate torture unofficially, the drafting of the CAT was the *means* by which to address this. States may continue to practice torture in breach of customary international law, but the task of the CAT was to establish an international regime whereby there was no safe haven for suspects of torture in foreign jurisdictions. As Lord Brown-Wilkinson observed in his *Pinochet 3* judgment in the British House of Lords in 1999, while

> Over 110 states (including Chile, Spain and the United Kingdom [the States related to the *Pinochet 3* case in the House of Lords]) became state parties to the Torture Convention . . . it is far from clear that none of them practised state torture. What was needed therefore was an international system which could punish those who were guilty of torture moving from one state to another.[127]

In this way, a large part of establishing the CAT was not to outlaw the act, for that had already been established under customary international law. Rather it was to create an international regime whereby there would be 'no safe haven' for those suspected of torture.[128]

More specifically, States are obliged in two particular ways. In addition to torture and genocide being recognised as *jus cogens* crimes under customary international law, the first legal obligation resting upon State Parties in either or both the Convention Against Torture and the Genocide Convention was the obligation to extradite or prosecute (*aut dedere aut judicare*) those suspected of torture or genocide, respectively. This obligation is explicitly enshrined in both conventions. Second, customary international law has established a broader obligation 'owed to all' (*erga omnes*) whereby States as

---

[124]   Military and Paramilitary Activities in and against Nicaragua (*Nicaragua v. United States of America*). Merits, Judgment. ICJ Reports (1986).
[125]   Military and Paramilitary Activities in and against Nicaragua (*Nicaragua v. United States of America*). Merits, Judgment. ICJ Reports at 186.
[126]   Military and Paramilitary Activities in and against Nicaragua (*Nicaragua v. United States of America*). Merits, Judgment. ICJ Reports at 186.
[127]   Lord Brown-Wilkinson, *Pinochet 3*, 199.
[128]   Lord Brown-Wilkinson, *Pinochet 3*.

a party to the convention (or as a part of the international community) have an obligation to all to hold to account those suspected of particular crimes. While Crawford has noted that obligations *erga omnes* are a relatively recent notion, he maintains that 'few today would question the notion of obligation *erga omnes*'.[129] The first time the concept of the *erga omnes* norm was referenced was in the *Barcelona Traction* case (*Belgium* v. *Spain*, second phase) at the ICJ in 1970. In its judgment, the ICJ held the following:

> In view of the importance of the rights involved, all States can be held to have a legal interest in their protection; they are obligations *erga omnes*. [at 34] Such obligations derive, for example, in contemporary international law, from the outlawing of acts of aggression, and of genocide, as also from the principles and rules concerning the basic rights of the human person, including protection from slavery and racial discrimination.[130]

Further still, some have argued that *jus cogens* and obligation *erga omnes* are inextricably linked. Indeed, M. Cherif Bassiouni, international law scholar and practitioner, viewed *jus cogens* and obligations *erga omnes* as two sides of the same coin: 'International crimes that rise to the level of *jus cogens* constitute obligation *erga omnes* which are inderogable.'[131] For crimes such as torture, crimes against humanity, and genocide, Bassiouni explicitly linked these notions to 'the duty to extradite or prosecute in international law' (*aut dedere aut judicare or aut dedere aut punire*).[132]

---

[129] Crawford, *Brownlie's Principles of Public International Law*, 564.

[130] *Barcelona Traction* case (*Belgium* v. *Spain*, second phase) at the International Court of Justice in 1970. In their judgment, the ICJ held that

> [at 33] ... an essential distinction should be drawn between the obligations of a State towards the international community as a whole, and those arising vis-à-vis another State in the field of diplomatic protection. By their very nature, the former are the concern of all States. In view of the importance of the rights involved, all States can be held to have a legal interest in their protection; they are obligations *erga omnes*. [at 34] Such obligations derive, for example, in contemporary international law, from the outlawing of acts of aggression, and of genocide, as also from the principles and rules concerning the basic rights of the human person, including protection from slavery and racial discrimination. Some of the corresponding rights of protection have entered into the body of general international law (*Reservations to the Convention on the Prevention and Punishment of the Crime of Genocide, Advisory Opinion, I.C.J. Reports 1951, 23*); others are conferred by international instruments of a universal or quasi-universal character.

[131] M. Cherif Bassiouni, 'International Crimes: Jus Cogens and Obligations Erga Omnes', *Law and Contemporary Problems* 59, no. 4 (1996): 63.

[132] Bassiouni, 'International Crimes: Jus Cogens and Obligations Erga Omnes'; M. Cherif Bassiouni and Edward M. Wise, *Aut Dedere Aut Judicare: The Duty to Extradite or Prosecute in International Law* (Dordrecht: Martinus Nijhoff, 1995).

The Role of Obligation in the Cases of Pinochet and Habré

In the cases of Chile and Chad, private non-State actors submitted complaints to State legal officials in foreign courts, with the understanding that the respective State had an international obligation to prosecute or extradite those in their jurisdiction for the crime of torture, including former heads of state.

These interpretations of international law were accepted in the British House of Lords in the case of *Pinochet 3*, and at the ICJ in the case of *Belgium v. Senegal* in relation to Habré. In the *Pinochet 3* case, the British House of Lords linked *jus cogens* to obligation. In separate judgments made by the British House of Lords, explicit reference was given to the terms 'extradite or prosecute in international law' (*aut dedere aut judicare*) and an obligation *erga omnes*. For instance, Lord Goff of Chieveley maintained that provision Article 7 (1) of the CAT 'reflects the principle *aut dedere aut punire* [a duty to prosecute] designed to ensure that torturers do not escape by going to another country'.[133] Furthermore, Lord Hope of Craighead,[134] Lord Millet[135] and Lord Phillips of Worth Matravers[136] refer to *erga omnes* obligations explicitly. Brown-Wilkinson stated in his decision that given the *jus cogens* nature of the crime, it was of legal interest to all states to punish perpetrators:

> [T]he **jus cogens** nature of the international crime of torture justifies states in taking universal jurisdiction over torture wherever committed. International law provides that offences jus cogens may be punished by any state because the offenders are 'common enemies of all mankind and all nations have an equal interest in their apprehension and prosecution'. *Demjanjuk v. Petrovsky* (1985) 603 F.Supp. 1486: 77F2d 571.[137]

In the case of *Belgium v. Senegal* at the ICJ in relation to Habré, legal arguments pertaining to 'the duty to extradite or prosecute in international law' (*aut dedere aut judicare*) were central to the dispute. Indeed, the title of the dispute was *Questions relating to the Obligation to Prosecute or Extradite (Belgium v. Senegal)*.[138] Given the interpretation of obligations 'owed to all' (*erga omnes*), the cooperative criminal accountability community increasingly

---

[133] Lord Goff of Chieveley, *Pinochet 3*, 212.
[134] Lord Hope of Craighead, *Pinochet 3*, at 242 and 247
[135] Lord Millet, *Pinochet 3*, at 275
[136] Lord Phillips of Worth Matravers, *Pinochet 3*, at 290
[137] Lord Brown-Wilkinson, *Pinochet 3*,
[138] Questions relating to the Obligation to Prosecute or Extradite (*Belgium v. Senegal*), Judgment, ICJ Reports.

widened the interpretation of a State Party's responsibility to prosecute or extradite even when the suspect was not residing or visiting the respective jurisdiction (such as Belgium), and when another State Party to the Convention Against Torture refused to prosecute (such as Senegal) – thus reflecting an obligation 'owed to all' (*erga omnes*). Unlike the Pinochet case, and perhaps reflecting the nature of the International Court of Justice as a dispute settlement body between states,[139] arguments posed to the ICJ concerning obligations *erga omnes* were tied closely to obligations of State Parties to CAT, rather than more broadly. In its submission to the ICJ, Belgium argued that while it did not have the alleged perpetrator physically located within its jurisdiction, as torture was an 'obligations *erga omnes partes*', it was not required that Belgium be a direct party impacted by the dispute. Rather there was a vested interest by all parties to the CAT that *each State party ensure compliance*, and therefore Belgium could take the dispute to the ICJ to compel Senegal to prosecute or extradite Habré.[140]

In their judgment, the ICJ held that the crime of torture was indeed an 'obligations *erga omnes partes*' and could be compared to the crime of genocide in this respect. The ICJ judgment held as follows:

> [at 68] As stated in its Preamble, the object and purpose of the Convention is 'to make more effective the struggle against torture . . . throughout the world'. The States parties to the Convention have a common interest to ensure, in view of their shared values, that acts of torture are prevented and that, if they occur, their authors do not enjoy impunity. The obligations of a State party to conduct a preliminary inquiry into the facts and to submit the case to its competent authorities for prosecution are triggered by the presence of the alleged offender in its territory, regardless of the nationality of the offender or the victims, or of the place where the alleged offences occurred. All the other States parties have a common interest in compliance with these obligations by the State in whose territory the alleged offender is present. That common interest implies that the obligations in question are owed by any State party to all the other state parties to the Convention. All the States parties 'have a legal interest' in the protection of the rights involved (*Barcelona Traction, Light and Power Company, Limited (Belgium v. Spain), Second Phase, Judgment, I. C.J. Reports 1970*, p. 32, para. 33). These obligations may be defined as '**obligations *erga omnes partes***' in the sense that each State party has an

---

[139] Belgium did pose a claim based on customary international law, the court decided that it had not jurisdiction in this respect. Also see Thirlway, *The Sources of International Law*, 172.

[140] Questions relating to the Obligation to Prosecute or Extradite (*Belgium* v. *Senegal*), Judgment, ICJ Reports.

interest in compliance with them in any given case. In this respect, the relevant provisions of the Convention against Torture are similar to those of the Convention on the Prevention and Punishment of the Crime of Genocide, with regard to which the Court observed that

'In such a convention the contracting States do not have any interests of their own; they merely have, one and all, a common interest, namely, the accomplishment of those high purposes which are the *raison d'être* of the Convention.' (*Reservations to the Convention on the Prevention and Punishment of the Crime of Genocide, Advisory Opinion, ICJ Reports 1951,* p. 23.)

[at 69] The common interest in compliance with the relevant obligations under the Convention against Torture implies the entitlement of each State party to the Convention to make a claim concerning the cessation of an alleged breach by another State party. If a special interest were required for that purpose, in many cases no State would be in the position to make such a claim. It follows that any State party to the Convention may invoke the responsibility of another State party with a view to ascertaining the alleged failure to comply with its obligations *erga omnes partes*, such as those under Article 6, paragraph 2, and Article 7, paragraph 1, of the Convention, and to bring that failure to an end. [at 70] For these reasons, the Court concludes that Belgium, as a State party to the Convention against Torture, has standing to invoke the responsibility of Senegal for the alleged breaches of its obligations under Article 6, paragraph 2, and Article 7, paragraph 1, of the Convention in the present proceedings.[141]

Nonetheless, some argue that the ICJ judgment is not consistent in some respects. As Thirlway observed, the judgment may have reflected obligations *omnium* (an obligation shared by all), rather than an obligation *erga omnes* (owed to all) or to each treaty party.[142] Notwithstanding this, it demonstrated that the ICJ increasingly views its role as not just settling disputes between states but also upholding the international norms governing core international crimes.[143] Today, the concept of *erga omnes* remains relevant. For example, the concept of *erga omnes partes* was revisited by the ICJ in *Application of the Convention on the Prevention and Punishment of the Crime of Genocide (The Gambia* v. *Myanmar).* In its 2020 Myanmar provisional measures order, the ICJ referred to the *Belgium* v. *Senegal* case recognising The Gambia's obligations *erga omnes partes*:

---

[141] Questions relating to the Obligation to Prosecute or Extradite (*Belgium* v. *Senegal),* Judgment, ICJ Reports.
[142] Thirlway, *The Sources of International Law,* 172.
[143] This is an idea I have taken from Vaughan Lowe, QC.

[41] … In view of their shared values, all the States parties to the Genocide Convention have a common interest to ensure that acts of genocide are prevented and that, if they occur, their authors do not enjoy impunity. That common interest implies that the obligations in question are owed by any State party to all the other States parties to the Convention. In its Judgment in the case concerning Questions relating to the Obligation to Prosecute or Extradite (Belgium v. Senegal), the Court observed that the relevant provisions in the Convention against Torture were 'similar' to those in the Genocide Convention. The Court held that these provisions generated 'obligations [which] may be defined as "obligations erga omnes partes" in the sense that each State party has an interest in compliance with them in any given case' (Judgment, ICJ Reports 2012 (II), p. 449, para. 68). It follows that any State party to the Genocide Convention, and not only a specially affected State, may invoke the responsibility of another State party with a view to ascertaining the alleged failure to comply with its obligations erga omnes partes, and to bring that failure to an end.

[42] The Court concludes that The Gambia has prima facie standing to submit to it the dispute with Myanmar on the basis of alleged violations of obligations under the Genocide Convention.

The Case of the Syrian Government and Allegations of Ongoing Crimes

While it is perhaps too early to comment on criminal accountability for the situation in Syria, as the war remains ongoing, a few important developments should be mentioned. At the start of 2019, material collected by CIJA Syrian investigators contributed to the first arrest and public criminal prosecution of a senior government official of the Syrian government. Arrested in German jurisdiction, Anwar R. is considered to be a tertiary-level figure in the chain of command from Assad. The German Federal Police Office (*Bundeskriminalamt, BKA*) arrested him for crimes against humanity, specifically in relation to the illegal detention and torture of Syrian demonstrators in the early days of the Arab Spring.[144] In achieving an arrest, both CIJA and the German Federal Police Office revealed a cooperative criminal accountability community. At the time of writing, the case against Anwar R. remained ongoing in the Higher Regional Court of Koblenz. However, his co-defendant Eyad A., of lesser rank, was convicted on 24 February 2021[145] for aiding and abetting crimes against humanity,

---

[144]   Melinda Rankin, 'The "Responsibility to Prosecute" Core International Crimes? The Case of German Universal Jurisdiction and the Syrian Government', *Global Responsibility to Protect* 11, no. 4 (2019): 394–410, https://doi.org/10.1163/1875984X-01104003.

[145]   Oberlandesgericht Koblenz, 'Urteil Gegen Einen Mutmaßlichen Mitarbeiter Des Syrischen Geheimdienstes Wegen Beihilfe Zu Einem Verbrechen Gegen Die Menschlichkeit', Landesregierung Rheinland-Pfalz, 24 February 2021, https://justiz.rlp.de/de/service-

including torture. The conviction against Eyad A. acts as a test case for core international crimes committed in Syria by the Syrian government (see Chapters 4 and 5).

One could argue that Germany reflected an obligation to extradite or prosecute (*aut dedere aut judicare*) when it arrested Anwar R. and Eyad A. within German jurisdiction. Furthermore, in 2018 German legal officials issued an arrest warrant against Jamil Hassan, then incumbent head of Syrian Air Force Intelligence for core international crimes, including *inter alia* torture. Syria has been a State Party to the CAT since 2004. As Hassan still remained in Syrian jurisdiction at the time the arrest warrant was issued, and thus not in German jurisdiction, one could argue that Germany was exercising a broader legal responsibility. It reflected the *jus cogens* nature of torture, as well as its broader legal obligation: obligations *erga omnes partes*, obligations *omnium* (an obligation shared by all) or an obligation *erga omnes* (owed to all) – or an obligation that reflected all of these at once. In both cases, German legal officials demonstrated a capacity to work within cooperative criminal accountability communities, which included private non-State actors, such as the CIJA and the European Center for Constitutional and Human Rights (ECCHR) (Chapters 4 and 5), amongst others.

Added to this, the government of the Netherlands has also pursued accountability for Syrian core international crimes, specifically for the *jus cogens* crime of torture. On 18 September 2020, the Netherlands government released a public statement outlining its decision to hold the Syrian government accountable for grave breaches to international law. In the statement titled 'The Netherlands decides to hold Syria responsible for gross human rights violations',[146] the Netherlands Ministry for Foreign Affairs maintained that the Netherlands had communicated with the Syrian government by diplomatic note of its wish to ensure accountability. Stef Blok, the Netherlands minister for foreign affairs, emphasised its obligation towards victims of Syrian crimes, maintaining that '[t]he victims of these serious crimes must obtain justice, and we are pursuing that end by calling the perpetrators to account'.[147]

informationen/aktuelles/detail/news/News/detail/urteil-gegen-einen-mutmasslichen-mitarbeiter-des-syrischen-geheimdienstes-wegen-beihilfe-zu-einem-ver/.

[146] Ministry of Foreign Affairs, 'The Netherlands Holds Syria Responsible for Gross Human Rights Violations', Government of the Netherlands, 19 September 2020, www.government.nl/latest/news/2020/09/18/the-netherlands-holds-syria-responsible-for-gross-human-rights-violations.

[147] Ministry of Foreign Affairs, 'The Netherlands Holds Syria Responsible for Gross Human Rights Violations'. Government of the Netherlands, 19 September 2020, www.government.nl/latest/news/2020/09/18/the-netherlands-holds-syria-responsible-for-gross-human-rights-violations.

Specifically, the Netherlands highlighted the role of the CAT and the obligations under international law for the Syrian government to investigate and
prosecute those suspected of perpetrating torture. The Netherlands warned
that if the matter could not be resolved within six months, the Netherlands
could take the matter as a dispute to arbitration, or the ICJ, which would
follow in the same vein as *Belgium* v. *Senegal* outlined earlier. According to
the statement:

> The Netherlands has invoked Syria's responsibility for human rights viola-
> tions under international law, specifically holding Syria responsible for
> torture under the UN Convention against Torture. In the diplomatic note,
> the Netherlands reminded Syria of its international obligations to cease the
> violations and offer victims full reparation. The diplomatic note asked Syria
> to enter into negotiations, which is a necessary first step in dispute settlement.
> Should the two states be unable to resolve the dispute, the Netherlands can
> propose to submit the case to arbitration. If no agreement can be reached on
> this issue, the Netherlands will submit the case to an international court.[148]

Moreover, to support the victims' claims, the Netherlands pointed to overwhelming evidence. As Blok maintained, 'The Assad regime has committed
horrific crimes time after time' and the 'evidence is overwhelming'.[149]
Advising the Netherlands government on the issue of accountability for torture
in Syria, Guernica 37, an emerging group of international lawyers, has worked
with a number of Syrian civil society groups, which have supported the
diplomatic note. One of the co-founders of Guernica 37, Toby Cadman,
also sits on the Advisory Panel of the Commission for International Justice
and Accountability (CIJA), which has collected more than 1 million pages of
government documents from Syria. It is possible for the Netherlands to draw
upon the evidence collected by Syrian investigators in the field, including
Chief Investigator 1, as well as German federal prosecutors, ECCHR and the
IIIM for Syria. It can also draw upon jurisprudence stemming from the
Pinochet case in the British House of Lords and the case of *Belgium*
v. *Senegal* in the ICJ. In particular, the Netherlands could draw upon the
jus cogens nature of the crime of torture and *erga omnes* legal obligation to
request the prosecution or extradition of those most responsible in Syria.

---

[148]   Ministry of Foreign Affairs, 'The Netherlands Holds Syria Responsible for Gross Human
Rights Violations'. Government of the Netherlands, 19 September 2020, www.government.nl
/latest/news/2020/09/18/the-netherlands-holds-syria-responsible-for-gross-human-rights-
violations.

[149]   Ministry of Foreign Affairs, 'The Netherlands Holds Syria Responsible for Gross Human
Rights Violations'.

With the emergence of *jus cogens* in public international law, particularly international criminal law, it begs the question: does this reflect an 'emerging system of multilateral public order' as Crawford has posited.[150] Similarly, as Klabbers, Peters and Ulfstein argued, 'Criminal law, after all, in presupposing the existence of a public order and someone to speak for that public order, presupposes a strong notion of hierarchy to begin with.'[151] This also begs the question: to what extent is international criminal law a distinct and unique system of public international law?

Next I highlight how de facto international prosecutors, and the cooperative criminal accountability community more broadly, adapt and innovate in a particular social, political and legal context. In other words, I attempt to explain the context these actors are situated in to understand further the realm they draw upon for 'situated learning'. I argue international criminal law has emerged as a distinct and unique system of public international law, and this uniqueness also explains conceptually why de facto international prosecutors can extend the reaches of international criminal law.

ICL AS A UNIQUE AND DISTINCT SYSTEM OF INTERNATIONAL LAW?

The Legacy of Nuremberg

Arguably, international criminal law has emerged as a distinct form of public international law. As noted, the decision by Allied Forces to prosecute senior political and industrial leaders of Nazi Germany forged a new era of international law. While a number of well-founded criticisms of the Nuremberg Charter and Nuremberg Trials have been canvassed,[152] two remain. The first is that the possible retrograde nature of the Nuremberg Trials undermined the principle of *nullum crimen sine lege* (no punishment without law).[153] Second, while the Nuremberg Trial was established, for the most part, by the four allied powers as victors of the Second World War, the fact that allied forces were never held to account for war crimes, such as the bombing of Dresden,

---

[150]   Crawford, *Brownlie's Principles of Public International Law*, 587.
[151]   Klabbers, Peters and Ulfstein, *The Constitutionalization of International Law*, 15.
[152]   For a more details analysis of the criticisms of the Nuremberg Charter and the Nuremberg Trials, see the issue of sixty years after: 'The Nuremberg Legacy', *Journal of International Criminal Justice*, 2006.
[153]   Brownlie and Crawford, *Brownlie's Principles of Public International Law*; Mettraux, 'Trial at Nuremberg'.

represents a significant blight.[154] As Crawford has argued, both continue to inform and shape the legacy of Nuremberg in different ways. Moreover, while the Nuremberg Tribunal established the foundations of modern international criminal law, establishing what counts as core international crimes today remains a key area of debate, particularly in relation to what counts as State practice and what crimes can be prosecuted by States that exercise universal jurisdiction.

Despite its failures, Nuremberg was notable for its innovation and experimentation. When Robert H. Jackson, chief US prosecutor, presented his opening speech at Nuremberg, he described the tribunal as 'novel and experimental'.[155] Indeed, the legacy of the Nuremberg Charter and Nuremberg Trials has formed the basis for modern international criminal law and shaped this particular subsection of public international law in a number of important ways.

First, as stated earlier, the Nuremberg Charter and Nuremberg Trials cut deep into traditional notions of national *sovereignty*. As Mettraux argued, the Nuremberg Charter not only added or removed aspects of existing international law, it also caused a radical shift in international law more broadly and made state political decisions on particular forms of organised violence of international concern and with punitive repercussions.[156] The Nuremberg legacy was to *criminalise* grave breaches to international law under the label *inter alia* of 'crimes against humanity'. It included those crimes commissioned by individuals on behalf of the State against its own people. By creating this new era of international criminal law, the 'Charter reached deep into the sovereign territory of states'.[157] While the Nuremberg Trial was established, for the most part, by the four allied powers as victors of the Second World War, the principles established in the Nuremberg judgment were later accepted by the United Nations General Assembly. Indeed, as noted in the Introduction, Resolution 95(1) was adopted by the United Nation General Assembly *unanimously*, and it reaffirmed the principles outlined in the Nuremberg Tribunal Charter and judgment under international law.[158]

---

[154]   Guénaël Mettraux, *Perspectives on the Nuremberg Trial* (Oxford and New York: Oxford University Press, 2008).

[155]   International Military Tribunal (IMT) (1946) *The Trial of German Major War Criminal by the International Military Tribunal Sitting at Nuremberg, Germany* (Commencing 20 November 1945): Opening Speeches of the Chief Prosecutors for the United States of America, the French Republic, the United Kingdom of Great Britain and Northern Ireland and the Union of Soviet Socialist Republics, London: HMSO.

[156]   Mettraux, 'Trial at Nuremberg', 8.

[157]   Mettraux, 'Trial at Nuremberg', 8.

[158]   United Nations General Assembly, 'General Assembly Resolution 95 (1), Affirmation of the Principles of International Law Recognised by the Charter of the Nurnberg Tribunal' (1946),

Although the international community as a whole explicitly adopted the Nuremberg Principles as international law,[159] there remained some ambivalence as to their legality for some time. By the 1990s, however, the international community, particularly through the UN Security Council, reaffirmed 'crimes against humanity' as core international crimes upon the establishment of the ICTY and ICTR.[160]

Second, and following on from the first, the Nuremberg Charter and Nuremberg Trials challenged the principle of *immunity*, including for a head of state. Indeed, the Nuremberg Tribunal held the following: 'He who violates the laws of war cannot obtain immunity while acting in pursuance of the authority of the state if the state in authorising action moves outside its competence under international law.'[161] In particular, this assault on immunity included notions of *functional immunity*, such as obligations to follow an order by superior command of a military or political body: 'Individuals have international duties which transcend the obligations of obedience imposed by the individual state.'[162]

Today, scholars are still undecided on the issue of immunity for some positions of government, including for crimes considered *jus cogens* of international law.[163] On the one hand, scholars envisioned a system whereby incumbent heads of state and foreign ministers must enjoy immunity to ensure the smooth operation of diplomatic cooperation between states, unimpeded.[164] On the other hand, Bassiouni and others argued that immunity for crimes classed as *jus cogens* of international law do not enjoy immunity

95, https://search-proquest-com.ezproxy.library.uq.edu.au/docview/1679073021?accountid=14723.

[159] United Nations General Assembly, 'General Assembly Resolution 95 (1)', 95.

[160] Cassese, *Cassese's International Criminal Law*; William Schabas, *The UN International Criminal Tribunals: The Former Yugoslavia*, Rwanda and Sierra Leone (Cambridge: Cambridge University Press, 2006); Antonio Cassese, *International Criminal Law: Cases and Commentary* (Oxford and New York: Oxford University Press, 2011); Brownlie and Crawford, *Brownlie's Principles of Public International Law*.

[161] IMT (1946) *The Trial of German Major War Criminal by the International Military Tribunal Sitting at Nuremberg, Germany, 20 November, 1945 to 1 December, 1945 –. Taken from the Official Transcript*. 21 vols, London: HMSO, Judgment of the International Military Tribunal, 223.

[162] IMT (1946) *The Trial of German Major War Criminal by the International Military Tribunal*, 223.

[163] Rémy Prouvèze, 'Immunities', in *Routledge Handbook of International Criminal Law*, ed. William A. Schabas and Nadia Bernaz (London and New York: Routledge, 2011), 355–68; Brownlie and Crawford, *Brownlie's Principles of Public International Law*.

[164] Steffen Wirth, 'Immunity for Core Crimes? The ICJ's Judgment in the Congo v. Belgium Case', *European Journal of International Law* 13, no. 4 (September 1, 2002): 877–93, https://doi.org/10.1093/ejil/13.4.877.

under international criminal law, including for an incumbent head of state.[165] As stated earlier, this was a view shared in the judgment of the Nuremberg Trial.[166] However, as Rain Liivoja aptly observes, under domestic and international law, rather than binary notions of immunity, increasingly, the question posed is '*to what extent* are they immune (if at all)?'[167] While immunity for core international crimes is still contentious in scholarship and legal judgements, including those considered *jus cogens*, courts have played a role in clarifying the issue of immunity in relation to core international crimes. For example, the *Pinochet 3* judgment in the British House of Lords in 1999 held that a *former* head of state did not enjoy immunity for the crime of torture, *because* torture was an accepted and recognised peremptory norm of international law.[168] Going one step further, Lord Millett and Lord Phillips of Worth Matravers in *Pinochet 3* observed: 'The systematic use of torture was an international crime for which there could be no immunity even before the Convention [Against Torture] came into effect and consequently there was no immunity under customary international law for the offences relating to torture alleged against the applicant.'[169]

Yet, the position of an incumbent head of state, head of government or foreign minister still remains one of immunity in public international law. The 2002 *Congo v. Belgium* case in the ICJ held that incumbent ministers of foreign affairs enjoyed immunity in foreign courts exercising universal judication.[170] While some scholars applauded the decision,[171] others criticised it for being out of step with customary international law,[172] including one judge on the *Congo v. Belgium* case. As Judge Van den Wyngaert explained in her dissenting opinion:

[165] Bassiouni, 'International Crimes: Jus Cogens and Obligations Erga Omnes', 63.
[166] Trial of the Major War Criminals before the International Military Tribunal. Nuremberg: IMT (1945).
[167] Rain Liivoja, *Criminal Jurisdiction over Armed Forces Abroad* (Cambridge: Cambridge University Press, 2017), 79, https://doi.org/10.1017/9781139600392.
[168] *R v. Bow Street Metropolitan Stipendiary Magistrate*, ex parte Pinochet Ugarte (No 3) (Pinochet 3) [2000] (House of Lords, Great Britain (UK) 24 March 1999).
[169] *R v. Bow Street Metropolitan Stipendiary Magistrate*, ex parte Pinochet Ugarte (No 3) (Pinochet 3) [2000] at 149.
[170] International Court of Justice, *Case Concerning the Arrest Warrant of 11 April 2000 (Democratic Republic of the Congo v. Belgium)*, 14 February 2002; Steffen Wirth, 'Immunity for Core Crimes? The ICJs Judgement in the Congo v. Belgium case'. *European Journal of International Law* 13, no. 4 (2002): 877–93.
[171] Wirth, 'Immunity for Core Crimes?'
[172] Adam Day, 'Crimes against Humanity as a Nexus of Individual and State Responsibility: Why the ICJ Got Belgium v. Congo Wrong'. *Berkeley Journal of International Law* 22, no. 3 (2004): 489–512, https://doi.org/10.15779/Z38GH1Z.

There is no rule of customary international law granting immunities to incumbent Foreign Ministers. . . . I disagree with the proposition that incumbent Foreign Ministers enjoy immunities on the basis of customary international law for the simple reason that there is no evidence in support of this proposition . . . identifying a common raison d'être for a protective rule is one thing, evaluating this protective rule to the status of customary international law is quite another thing.[173]

Nevertheless, once they leave office, former heads of state are subject to international criminal law. In the Habré case of *Belgium* v. *Senegal* in the ICJ in 2012, the court reflected a decision consistent with the British House of Lords in *Pinochet 3*, whereby former heads of state did not enjoy immunity under customary international law for the *jus cogens* crime of torture.

In short, while it is broadly accepted that former heads of States do not enjoy immunity for *jus cogens* crimes, what is less clear is a consensus on the legal standing of immunity for incumbent heads of State and foreign ministers. This is a debate that is considered the 'last bastion' of sovereign protection of the State.[174] While incumbent heads of State, heads of government and foreign ministers may remain protected under international law, it seems it does not extend to other incumbent roles. As stated earlier, in 2018, the Office of the German Federal Public Prosecutor General (*Generalbundesanwalt*, GBA) issued an arrest warrant for Jamil Hassan, then incumbent head of Syrian Airforce Intelligence, while the crimes were suspected to be ongoing in Syrian detention centres. Similarly, a French investigating magistrate has been appointed to aid in the investigation of Mohammed bin Zayed Al-Nahyan, the crown prince of Abu Dhabi and de facto ruler of the United Arab Emirates (UAE). The crown prince is suspected of being responsible for torture committed in detention centres controlled by the United Arab Emirates in Yemen, after private non-State actors submitted a number of private criminal complaints to a court in Paris.[175] The immunity *ratione materiae* (i.e. functional immunity) of lower officials does not protect them from prosecution for war crimes, crimes against humanity and genocide.

---

[173] Dissenting opinion of Judge Van den Wyngaert (English Original Text), *Arrest Warrant* of 11 April 2000 (*Democratic Republic of the Congo* v. *Belgium*), 143.

[174] Jeremy Ostrander, 'The Last Bastion of Sovereign Immunity: A Comparative Look at Immunity from Execution of Judgments', *Berkeley Journal of International Law* 22, no. 3 (2004): 541–82, https://doi.org/10.15779/Z38706X; James Crawford, 'Execution of Judgments and Foreign Sovereign Immunity', *The American Journal of International Law* 75, no. 4 (1981): 820–69, https://doi.org/10.2307/2201355.

[175] 'France Investigates Crown Prince of Abu Dhabi on Torture Charges', France 24 News, 17 July 2020, www.fr24news.com/a/2020/07/france-investigates-crown-prince-of-abu-dhabi-on-torture-charges.html.

Third, the Nuremberg Charter and Nuremberg Trials established *individuals* as key subjects of international criminal law. The charter not only appeared to limit the use of force by states, it also had the profound effect of recognising a broader array of *individuals* as *subjects* of international criminal law, with particular legal rights and obligations.[176] For example, the Nuremberg Charter (Article 6) stipulated that '[l]eaders, organises[sic], instigators and accomplices participating in the formulation or execution of a common plan or conspiracy to commit any of [the crimes listed in the charter] are responsible for all acts performed by any persons in execution of such a plan'. Liability was therefore *individual* and penal in character and arose directly from international law."[177] Indeed, this was a point reiterated in the British House of Lords in the *Pinochet 3* decision. As Lord Brown-Wilkinson observed: 'The traditional subjects of international law are states not human beings. But the consequence upon the war crimes trials after 1939–45 World War, the international community came to recognise that there could be criminal liability under international law for a class of crimes such as war crimes and crimes against humanity."[178] The effect of this is that while States can be held to account for grave breaches of international law, such as human rights and humanitarian law, in international criminal law only *individuals* could be held *criminally* responsible.[179] As the famous judgment defined in the first Nuremberg Trial states: 'Crimes against international law are committed by men, not by abstract entities, and only by punishing individuals who commit such crimes can the provisions of international law be enforced."[180]

Fourth, the Nuremberg Tribunal focused on those *most* responsible for 'crimes against humanity', 'war crimes' and 'crimes against peace'. Given that alleged crimes committed by Nazi Germany were characteristically systematic and widespread, the prosecution focused on holding a few senior individuals in the highest ranks of political and industrial Nazi leadership as a 'common plan' or 'conspiracy' to account. This emphasis on prosecuting the *most* responsible for core international crimes was adopted by other international criminal tribunals since Nuremberg, starting with the ICTY.[181] As will be noted, this emphasis was also adopted as a lesson learned by the de facto

---

[176]   Mettraux, 'Trial at Nuremberg', 8.
[177]   Mettraux, 'Trial at Nuremberg', 8.
[178]   Lord Brown-Wilkinson, *Pinochet 3*, 197
[179]   Cassese, *Cassese's International Criminal Law*.
[180]   Trial of the Major War Criminals before the International Military Tribunal. Nuremberg: IMT.
[181]   Del Ponte, 'Prosecuting the Individuals Bearing the Highest Level of Responsibility'.

international prosecutor in each of the three cases studies – Chile, Chad and Syria. Moreover, in the case of Syria, Chief Investigator 1 and other local Syrian investigators in CIJA collected this material in the midst of abject insecurity, and as Syria slid into war with multiple participants with shifting alliances (see Chapter 4). To establish a criminal link between the most senior leaders of Nazi Germany and their underlying crimes, including crimes against humanity, Chief US Prosecutor Roberts relied upon documents produced by the perpetrators.[182] This linkage material played an important role in establishing the facts and was drawn upon to set out the forms of participation by individuals in a 'common plan' or 'conspiracy'.

Lastly, the legacy of the Nuremberg Charter and the Nuremberg Tribunal also includes the enduring and evolving role of how international criminal law has informed universal jurisdiction, as well as the nature of customary international law as a source of international criminal law more broadly. According to Crawford, universal jurisdiction, put simply, 'amounts to the assertion of criminal jurisdiction by a state in the absence of any other generally recognised head of prescriptive jurisdiction'.[183] And while many States ratified conventions, such as the Convention Against Torture which requires that States introduce torture as a crime in the domestic criminal legal system and to prosecute suspects, customary international law also informs the character of universal jurisdiction and the *jus cogens* nature of the crime of torture.

The Changing Character of Customary International Law

Added to this is the changing nature of customary international law as a source of law for international criminal law.[184] As in other areas of public international law, customary international law is a key source of international criminal law and relies on notions of state practice and *opinio*

---

[182] Robert H. Jackson, *The Nurnberg Case* (New York: Cooper Square Publishers, 1971); Robert H. Jackson, *Report of Robert H. Jackson, United States Representative to the International Conference on Military Trials, London, 1945: A Documentary Record of Negotiations of the Representatives of the United States of America, the Provisional Government of the French Republic, the United Kingdom of Great Britain and Northern Ireland, and the Union of the Soviet Socialist Republics, Culminating in the Agreement and Charter of the International Military Tribunal* (Washington, DC: United States Government Printing Office, 1949); Jackson, *Second Day, Wednesday, 11/21/1945, Part 04', in Trial of the Major War Criminals before the International Military Tribunal. Volume II. Proceedings: 11/14/1945–11/30/1945. [Official Text in the English Language.]* Nuremberg: IMT; Harris, *Tyranny on Trial: The Evidence at Nuremberg.*

[183] Brownlie and Crawford, *Brownlie's Principles of Public International Law*, 467.

[184] Arajärvi, *The Changing Nature of Customary International Law.*

juris.[185] Unlike treaties, as Thirlway argued, 'in principle customary law is applicable to all States without exception'.[186] Moreover, it applies to States even when the party does not explicitly accept or practice the law:

> A State which relies in a dispute on a rule of treaty-law has to establish that the other party to the dispute is bound by the treaty; whereas if a claim is based on general customary law, it is in principle sufficient to establish that the rule exists in customary law, and there is no need to show that the other party has expressly accepted it, or participated in the practice.[187]

Similarly, Crawford has maintained, it is not necessary to show complete consistency to reflect generality of practice, and '[s]ilence may denote either tacit agreement or a simple lack of interest in the issue'.[188]

With this in mind, it could be argued that two factors increasingly inform the customary form of international criminal law. First, it relies upon, in large part, what Noora Arajärvi describes as 'tacit' acceptance by States of the particular way customary international law has evolved as a source of international criminal law.[189] Second, the uniqueness of international criminal law highlights what Arajärvi posed as a 'new type of law-making'.[190] Moreover, it resembles what Chester Brown described as the common law 'system' of international law, whereby judgements made in international tribunals and domestic courts act as precedents.[191] Alas, this latter point remains contentious in public international law. Traditionally, customary international law, it is argued, is not premised on court decisions. For example, Crawford argues that '[j]udicial decisions are not strictly a formal source of international law, but in many instances they are regarded as evidence of the law. A coherent body of previous jurisprudence will have important consequences in any given case. Its value, however, stops short of precedent as it is understood in the common law tradition.'[192] Similarly, Thirlway argued that 'customary law may be found stated in opinions of scholars, or in decisions of international (or indeed national) tribunals, but these are not themselves sources'.[193] Moreover,

---

[185] Brownlie and Crawford, *Brownlie's Principles of Public International Law*; Arajärvi, *The Changing Nature of Customary International Law*; Cassese, *International Criminal Law: Cases and Commentary*.

[186] Thirlway, *The Sources of International Law*, 63.

[187] Thirlway, *The Sources of International Law*, 63.

[188] Crawford, *Brownlie's Principles of Public International Law*, 451.

[189] Arajärvi, *The Changing Nature of Customary International Law*.

[190] Arajärvi, *The Changing Nature of Customary International Law*, 2.

[191] Chester Brown, *A Common Law of International Adjudication* (Oxford: Oxford University Press, 2007).

[192] Crawford, *Brownlie's Principles of Public International Law*, 35.

[193] Thirlway, *The Sources of International Law*, 14–15.

although Article 38 of the ICJ Statute identified the sources of law as judicial decisions and the teachings of the most highly qualified publicists of the various nations, as subsidiary means for the determination of rules of law, it also refrained from describing international court decisions, including the International Court of Justice, as 'precedent'. According to Article 59 of the ICJ Statute: 'The decision of the Court has no binding force except between the parties and in respect of that particular case.'[194] Yet, as Thirlway observed, while judges do not make law, the 'paradox is, of course, that the ICJ will probably only be turning to the judge or the scholar because the Court has not succeeded in finding authority in one of the other sources'.[195] Judges may, through arguments and interpretations, fill in the gaps of law or clarify essential legal points or principles of law within the particular context. Furthermore, when it comes to the notion of *jus cogens*, Thirlway argued, 'Only a court decision could authoritatively invalidate an agreement between States as contrary to jus cogens, and thus demonstrate that the category of *jus cogens* exists.'[196] Throughout the three studies, de facto international prosecutors worked hard following accepted practices to identify sources of international law, including identifying prior judgments as evidence of customary international law. For example, they did so to establish that because the senior leaders in question were suspected of *jus cogens* crimes, including torture, they therefore did not enjoy immunity. Yet, it was only the courts that could provide the authority to confirm or establish this in international law.

Others continue to argue that a 'common law' system or a common international law system has emerged – not just in international criminal law but also in other areas of public international law. For example, Chester Brown argued that a common law system exists in the area of international adjudication,[197] whereby 'international courts often adopt common approaches to questions of procedure and remedies. These common approaches lead in turn to increasing commonality in the case law of international courts.'[198] This approach is reflected in the courts themselves. For example, in *Pinochet 3*, arguments posed by Greenwood for the Crown prosecution referred to the *Tadic* and *Furundzija* cases at the ICTY on matters of substantive law.[199] In his decision in the British House of Lords, Lord

---

[194] United Nations, 'Statute of the International Court of Justice,' Article 59.
[195] Thirlway, *The Sources of International Law*, 12.
[196] Thirlway, *The Sources of International Law*, 173–4.
[197] Brown, *A Common Law of International Adjudication*.
[198] Brown, *A Common Law of International Adjudication*, 3.
[199] *R v. Bow Street Metropolitan Stipendiary Magistrate*, ex parte Pinochet Ugarte (No 3) (Pinochet 3) [2000] at 157.

Wilkinson-Brown referenced decisions and opinions of previous ICTY judgments, although ICTY decisions were not evidence of State practice or strictly reflecting State practice or *opinio juris*. In its Application Instituting Proceedings to the ICJ, dated 19 February 2009, the state of Belgium posed its legal arguments in reference to the *Pinochet 3* case as evidence that customary international law recognised and accepted that *jus cogens* crimes invalided rules governing immunity.

Further still, the uniqueness of international criminal law as a sub-area of public international law is reflected in a broader debate on the fragmentation and diversification of international law. In the report of the work of the fifty-fourth session (2002), the International Law Commission canvassed this point,[200] following questions raised in United Nations General Assembly Resolution 56 (82).[201] The International Law Commission noted '[t]here was agreement that fragmentation' of international law 'was not a new phenomenon'.[202] Indeed, it argued that the 'view was expressed that international law was inherently a law of a fragmented world' with some members explaining that 'fragmentation was also a natural consequence of the expansion of international law'.[203]

Having said this, I argue that fragmentation does not mean a split or separation from other systems of law. Rather, I argue that international criminal law resembles a unique and distinct system of law – one that resembles a common law or case law system but overlaps or coexists with other international and domestic systems of law.[204] Indeed, international criminal law has a history of necessarily being in tension with other systems of law, including laws that govern sovereignty and immunity. That international criminal law has emerged as a specialised and distinct area of public international law means de facto international prosecutors must share knowledge and practices and develop cooperative criminal accountability communities. The specialised and distinct nature of international criminal law also means it is an enabler. It empowers de facto international prosecutors to engage in accountability practices and processes and build on shared knowledge and prior

---

[200] International Law Commission, 'Report on the Work of the Fifty-Fourth Session (2002)' (New York: Office of Legal Affairs, United Nations, 2002).

[201] United Nations General Assembly, 'Resolution 56 (82) Report of the International Law Commission on the Work of Its Fifty-Third Session' (2002).

[202] United Nations, *Yearbook of the International Law Commission 2002: Report of the Commission to the General Assembly on the Work of Its Fifty-Fourth Session*. Vol. 2, Part 2 (New York and Geneva: United Nations, 2009), 97 (para 497).

[203] United Nations, *Yearbook of the International Law Commission 2002*, 97 (para 497).

[204] Keith Culver and Michael Giudice, *Legality's Borders: An Essay in General Jurisprudence* (Oxford: Oxford University Press, 2010).

learnings in their communities to adapt lessons learned (including failures), and to move forward by using practices and lessons learned in novel and innovative ways. As Condorelli observed, the 'relentless expansion and diversification of international law are increasingly leading to specialization'.[205] The three biographical case studies act to highlight the rapid expansion, change and diversification of international criminal law, and how international criminal law has become a unique area of international law, whereby a multiplicity of actors (including de facto international prosecutors), institutions and means are engaged to hold those *most* responsible for humanity's greatest crimes to account.

Lastly, although de facto international prosecutors draw upon the law developed in the post-Nuremberg era, through their applied practices they unavoidably challenge traditional notions of international order, whereby the former head of State is inseparable or inextricably linked to the State and therefore protected by long-held notions of State immunity. Specifically, de facto international prosecutors interpret international criminal law in what they view as its current form, which has the effect of testing classical views rooted in previous international orders.[206] As Phillips and Reus-Smit argued, 'Today's global sovereign order dates only from the 1970s – prior to that, the modern order was a sovereign-imperial hybrid.'[207] This shift is also reflected in how we understand contemporary international law. Yet, Thirlway understands this shift as the weakening of natural law, which dates prior to the 1970s. Positivism that replaced natural law explanations of international law is generally seen as becoming ascendant around the 1920s. Both natural law and positivism were capable of accommodating sovereign-imperial hybrids. As Thirlway argues, 'Historically, at an international level, once the authority of natural law, in the sense of what was given by God or imposed by the nature of an international society made up of independent princes, had weakened, it was natural to derive legal obligations from the legitimate expectations created in others by conduct.'[208] It is this modern international legal order, one that has also enshrined human rights and justice as central tenets, that empowers

---

[205] Luigi Condorelli, 'Customary International Law: The Yesterday, Today, and Tomorrow of General International Law', in *Realizing Utopia: The Future of International Law*, ed. Antonio Cassese (Oxford: Oxford University Press, 2012), 147–57.

[206] Andrew Phillips and Christian Reus-Smit, eds., *Culture and Order in World Politics*, LSE International Studies (Cambridge: Cambridge University Press, 2020), https://doi.org/10.1017/9781108754613.

[207] Phillips and Reus-Smit, *Culture and Order in World Politics*, 25.

[208] Thirlway, *The Sources of International Law*, 61. The Nuremberg trials and human rights in the 1940s and onwards are seen by some as inspired by a natural law resurgence against the positivism embodied in Nazi Germany.

de facto international prosecutors with the means to pursue accountability and by doing so enables that them to maintain the UN-System.

CONCLUSION

This study investigates how and why de facto international prosecutors extend the reaches of international criminal law. In particular, it examines the practices adopted by de facto international prosecutors to pursue criminal accountability in a third jurisdiction. It examines how private non-State actors and, to a lesser extent, State legal officials work cooperatively to close the accountability gap first left by local State legal officials. Like other studies which explore theories of community of practice, criminal accountability communities are a social phenomenon. One of the enduring points that the three case studies show is how cooperative criminal accountability communities respond to a particular social context and place in response to the accountability gap for core international crimes. In this respect, criminal accountability communities are situated in and responding to a particular social context.

In the next part of the book, each chapter begins by demonstrating how individual witnesses and victims of core crimes respond to the accountability gap in greater detail. Part II explores how they evolve to develop competency in some or many of the practices and tasks of offices of international prosecutors, as well as link up with a community of international practitioners. These case studies pose a challenge to some who view the system of international criminal law as primarily centred on international (State) institutions, such as the ICC. Recently, some arguments posed by international relations and international law scholars, as well as legal practitioners, suggest that international criminal tribunals are the primary institutions responsible – and the only institutions increasingly left – to address core international crimes. Similarly, some view NGOs as filling the gaps left by the closing of international criminal tribunals. As David Crane argued:

> In a 'third wave' of accountability ... grass-root organizations, NGOs, mechanisms, and domestic prosecutions are filling in the gaps created by the shutting down of the international tribunals in Yugoslavia, Rwanda, and Sierra Leone. Those courts are done with their work. Accountability has shifted from international efforts (the first and second waves) to domestic efforts. Only the ICC stands as a permanent international bastion to the beast of impunity as it feeds on the edges of humanity and civilization.[209]

---

[209] Crane, '"Not Perfect Candidates" to Be the Next Prosecutor of the International Criminal Court'.

As will be investigated in Part II, private non-State actors attempted to fill the gap before the ICC was up and running, at a time when international criminal tribunals, such as the ICTY and ICTR, were established, as well as after the ICC was established. For these private non-State actors, international criminal tribunals were not available for a variety of reasons. In fact, the Convention Against Torture had already established an international regime that went beyond these international (State) institutions. Rather de facto international prosecutors interpreted international legal obligations for *jus cogens* crimes, such as torture and genocide, as first and foremost residing with States, whereby States are legally obliged to prosecute those suspected of torture as either the obligation to prosecute or extradite or the obligation owed to all (*erga onmes*). These interpretations of international law, which were accepted by courts in the case studies outlined in this book, show that foreign courts exercising universal jurisdiction are an essential means to pursue criminal accountability for *jus cogens* crimes, and an essential feature to the international legal order. In Chapter 5, the final chapter of Part II, I focus on Germany as a unique example of universal jurisdiction. Chapter 5 also raises the question: to what extent are State legal officials emerging beyond de facto international prosecutors to become *de jure* international prosecutors – not only for *jus cogens* crimes but also for an array of other core international crimes.

THREE BIOGRAPHICAL CASE STUDIES

De Facto International Prosecutors in Practice

2

De Facto International Prosecutors and Prosecuting Pinochet (Chile)

This chapter investigates how de facto international prosecutors, particularly private non-State actors, played an essential role in extending the reach of international criminal law to Augusto Pinochet, former president of Chile. The chapter starts by introducing Juan Garcés, a private non-State actor and witness to the earliest crimes of the Pinochet government in Chile. On 11 September 1973, General Augusto Pinochet launched his US-back coup against the Allende government and, with it, a campaign to brutally suppress democratic opposition. As a presidential advisor, Garcés was in the presidential palace with Salvador Allende, incumbent president of Chile, the day Pinochet attacked the palace. Much later, when Garcés had returned to his native Spain, he began an investigation into Pinochet for crimes against humanity as a private non-State actor and on behalf of Pinochet's victims. In 1996, Garcés and others submitted a private complaint against Pinochet to the Madrid Courts for crimes against humanity exercising universal jurisdiction, triggering a public investigation by Spanish legal officials.

This chapter explores how and why Garcés felt compelled to hold Pinochet to account in a public criminal prosecution, and the practical tasks he adopted to do so. Baltasar Garzón, then investigative judge in the Central Court of Criminal Proceedings No. 5 in Madrid, is often referred to as the 'super-judge' who issued the extradition request against Pinochet for *inter alia* genocide and torture. Yet, later Garzón insisted that Juan Garcés, in his capacity as private non-State actor, was the 'great architect' of the Pinochet case.

While Garcés played an essential role in the Pinochet case, as a private non-State actor and witness to Pinochet's earliest crimes, he also relied upon a broader community of practice. Indeed, Garcés was formative in developing and engaging with a cooperative criminal accountability community that initially consisted of private non-State actors, both in Spain and aboard, and increasingly with State legal officials in Madrid, including Garzón, and abroad. When Pinochet was visiting London for a back operation, it was Garcés who insisted that Garzón make his request to the UK authorities to question Pinochet. After the arrest, this cooperative criminal accountability community broadened to include State legal officials in the United Kingdom.

This chapter does the following. First, it provides the empirical account for how and why Garcés and the broader community of practice adopted the practical tasks of the offices of international prosecutors. It shows how they attempted to collect and organise credible linkage material that linked Pinochet to the underlying crimes, locate and record witness statements, write and submit private complaints and contribute to legal arguments and interpretations in important legal hearings. To a lesser extent, it investigates why and how the broader cooperative criminal accountability community posed complex legal arguments and interpretations in the Madrid courts (twice), in the British House of Lords (twice) and the UK extradition case to establish that Pinochet was subject to international criminal law. In particular, these complex legal arguments and interpretations of the sources of international law were key to establishing in the British House of Lords the *jus cogens* crimes of torture, which trumped other rules and sources of international law, and the United Kingdom's obligation to prosecute or extradite to Spain (see Chapter 1).

Second, the chapter illuminates how unsuccessful attempts and failures matter. It probes how de facto international prosecutors draw upon previous attempts, as well as the interplay between imagination, adaption and innovation in understanding how they contribute to the criminal accountability processes for those most responsible for core international crimes. That is to say, the prosecution of Pinochet demonstrated how practical adaptions and innovations in criminal accountability might be preceded by numerous failed attempts by de facto international prosecutors to hold a senior leader to account. Garcés's attempt to hold Pinochet to account was not the first. Attempts had been made in Chile and the United Kingdom previously, amongst others. Yet, the case study shows how 'failed' attempts nonetheless allowed private non-State actors to learn and adapt the types of actors, institutions and means they employed to pursue criminal accountability for Pinochet. Failure lends itself to increased background knowledge and expertise across the wider criminal accountability community. Conversely, while Jack Straw, then UK home secretary, allowed Pinochet to return to his native Chile on health grounds, averting the possibility of a successful criminal prosecution in the Madrid courts, this was not considered a failure by some de facto international prosecutors. Indeed, Juan Garcés believed the fact the

British House of Lords and Madrid courts had held that Pinochet was not immune, namely because torture was an accepted and recognised peremptory norm (*jus cogens*) of international law, meant he was subject to individual criminal responsibility – and that in itself was significant. Indeed, the judgment in the British House of Lords concerning Pinochet remains one of the most important cases in international criminal law today.[1] Furthermore, as will be seen in the next chapter, it also informed other cases, such as the prosecution of Hissène Habré, former president of Chad.

Lastly, Garcés and the broader cooperative criminal accountability community were keen to argue that they were not attempting to establish new laws within the system of international criminal law. Rather, they worked hard to make the case that the international laws governing Pinochet were well established.

JUAN GARCÉS AS WITNESS

Although Juan Garcés studied law in Spain, it was his passion for Chilean politics and its democratic aspirations that first led him to Chile. Born in Lliria, Valencia, Spain, in 1944, Garcés graduated from the University Complutense of Madrid in law in 1967. His interest in politics led to his being awarded doctorates from the University of Madrid in 1967 and the Sorbonne and SciencesPo in 1970, both in political science.[2] While on a study trip to Chile, he met Allende who was then president of the Senate. At that point, he had run for the Chilean presidency three times unsuccessfully. Garcés's thesis had predicted that Allende would win the elections if the electorate divided into three groups – centre, right and left. They became friends. Much later Garcés stated: 'I shared Salvador Allende's goals of moving towards 'a socialism in democracy, pluralism and freedom'.[3] After Garcés had finished his dissertation, Allende asked him to return to Chile and work with him on his fourth presidential campaign, which he won.[4] Thereafter, Allende

---

[1] Naomi Roht-Arriaza, *The Pinochet Effect: Transnational Justice in the Age of Human Rights* (Philadelphia: University of Pennsylvania Press, 2005); Antonio Cassese, *Cassese's International Criminal Law*, 3rd ed./revised by Antonio Cassese et al. (Oxford: Oxford University Press, 2013).

[2] 'Juan Garcés – The Right Livelihood Award', The Right Livelihood Foundation, 1999, www .rightlivelihoodaward.org/laureates/juan-garcs/.

[3] Garcés quoted in, Isabel Hilton, Geoffrey Bindman and Juan Garcés, 'Justice in the World's Light', openDemocracy, 15 June 2001, www.opendemocracy.net/en/justice-in-worlds-light/.

[4] Karen DeYoung, 'The Prosecutor Who Never Rested', *Washington Post*, 8 October 1999, www .washingtonpost.com/archive/lifestyle/1999/10/08/the-prosecutor-who-never-rested/64047db5- 0991-4b43-8907-38251ff16bf7/; Isabel Hilton, Geoffrey Bindman and Juan Garcés, 'Justice in the

asked Garcés to become his personal political adviser.[5] As Garcés stated later, 'My interest in Chile always was an intellectual interest in its political evolution'.[6] Specifically, Garcés was curious about Chile's evolving democratic model. At the time, Garcés believed Chile was the most democratic country of the Spanish-speaking world. Almost three years after Allende was elected, he believed that Chile was transformed. As Garcés later maintained, 'Chile was the most developed, democratic country in the Spanish-speaking world, with a robust Parliament and robust political parties, effective freedom of the press, providence in the society to different opinions and worships. And suddenly, in one day, all [that] changed'.[7] In the early morning of 11 September 1973, General Augusto Pinochet led a US-backed military coup against the Allende government, with the knowledge and support of President Richard Nixon and Secretary of State Henry Kissinger, and with the aid of the US intelligence services.[8]

In this way, Garcés described himself as a witness to Pinochet's earliest crimes, and this experience would serve to inform him for the rest of his life. The evening before 11 September 1973, Allende and Garcés had been working together in preparation for officially proposing a referendum the following day. Working late, Garcés stayed over at Allende's home, and together they went to the presidential palace the following day. Just as Allende was about to address the nation, General Pinochet launched his military coup by surrounding and shelling the La Moneda presidential palace. As Garcés later maintained:

> And, well, this was a political fight. At 9:00 a.m., I asked the president . . . 'Do you have some regiment, [on] your side?' And the answer was, 'No, no regiment'. So, . . . in military terms, the outcome was very clear: There [was no] capability of military resistance . . . . The land infantry and artillery attack began around 9:00 until 11:00. Then, the silence [suggested] that the airplanes will bomb in a matter of 15 minutes. In this moment, his assistants, all civil assistants, his staff, around 15 people, were with him . . . . [Allende] offered them, each one, to have freedom to [leave] the palace and save their

World's Light', openDemocracy, 15 June 2001, www.opendemocracy.net/en/justice-in-worlds-light/.

5   Adela Gooch, 'The Lawyer Who Wouldn't Forget', *The Guardian*, 2 February 1999, www.theguardian.com/world/1999/feb/02/law.theguardian.

6   DeYoung, 'The Prosecutor Who Never Rested'.

7   Garcés quoted in, Amy Goodman and Juan Garcés, '40 Years After Chilean Coup, Allende Aide Juan Garcés on How He Brought Pinochet to Justice (Transcript)', Democracy Now! 10 September 2013, www.democracynow.org/2013/9/10/40_years_after_chilean_coup_allende.

8   Peter Kornbluh, *The Pinochet File: A Declassified Dossier on Atrocity and Accountability* (New York: The New Press, 2013).

life, because for him it was very clear that he will resist until the last moment, because he considered [it] ... his duty as a president, elected by the people and with the legitimacy of the republic institutions. And nobody accepted to leave him alone.[9]

Nevertheless, Allende looked to Garcés and entrusted him with an extraordinary task. While there was an interim break in the shelling, Allende urged Garcés to leave the presidential palace and to tell the story of Chile. According to Garcés, he argued vehemently with Allende to remain in the presidential palace. But Allende insisted. In the end, Allende wrestled Garcés's briefcase out of his hands so that, if captured, the documents inside could not incriminate Garcés and physically pushed Garcés out of the palace.[10] It seemed Allende had made Garcés an exception for a reason.

Allende had encumbered Garcés with the task of explaining to the world what had really happened to Chile: 'Someone has to recount what happened here and only you can do it', Garcés recalled later.[11] While Chile had been a temporary experiment in social democracy, rare in the Spanish-speaking world at the time, its sudden military upheaval threatened to cloud that. Given Garcés's close contact with Allende, Garcés was in a good position to explain the nature of the government over the past three years, as well as its goals and objectives: 'And so, he considered that I was the person that could explain better [than anyone] what was the real meaning of this government'.[12]

While less obvious at the time, as Garcés would later understand, the experience had left him with two personal obligations. The first was an obligation to Allende and to the history of Chile's short-lived democratic experiment: to explain the political nature of Chile's rise to social democracy. As Garcés maintained later, 'I had a very strong sense of duty to contribute to the understanding of the period that came to an end on September 11'.[13] Moreover, when Garcés left the presidential palace that day, he soon realised he was the only person from the palace to escape that day, and to survive.[14] The second was a different type of obligation and not immediately apparent. Garcés had also been a 'witness' to what he considered the earliest 'crimes' of Pinochet. As Garcés later recalled, 'I was a witness to [Pinochet's] crimes . . . .

---

[9] Garcés quoted in Goodman and Garcés, '40 Years After Chilean Coup, Allende Aide Juan Garcés on How He Brought Pinochet to Justice (Transcript)'.

[10] Gooch, 'The Lawyer Who Wouldn't Forget'.

[11] Gooch, 'The Lawyer Who Wouldn't Forget'.

[12] Garcés quoted in Goodman and Garcés, '40 Years After Chilean Coup, Allende Aide Juan Garcés on How He Brought Pinochet to Justice (Transcript)'.

[13] Garcés quoted in Gooch, 'The Lawyer Who Wouldn't Forget'.

[14] 'Juan Garcés – The Right Livelihood Award'; Gooch, 'The Lawyer Who Wouldn't Forget'.

I was there when they were committed, [at] the beginning of the crimes'.[15] Immediately, Garcés fled Chile, with the assistance of fellow Spaniard, Joaquin Leguina. As General Francisco Franco was still dictator of Spain, Garcés preferred to return to Paris, initially pouring his efforts into fulfilling his first obligation to Allende. For several years, Garcés wrote prolifically about the crucial period of Chilean politics that preceded Pinochet's brutal crackdown. While working as a consultant to the director general of UNESCO and later investigator at the National Foundation of Political Science, he wrote extensively on the subject of the Allende government, including 'Allende and the Chilean Experience' (1976) and 'Democracy and Counterrevolution' (1975), amongst other articles, which were published widely and in a number of languages.[16] While the first obligation had been to Allende, the second was a more abstract personal obligation. It was a personal obligation as a witness to the crime, and to the knowledge that the Pinochet government had continued to commit crimes once in power against actual and alleged opposition. It was this second obligation that imbibed him with the greatest burden and later proved the toughest.

GARCÉS AS DE FACTO INTERNATIONAL PROSECUTOR

Garcés's evolution to become a de facto international prosecutor came much later. After Franco's death, Garcés returned to his native Spain with his Chilean-born wife to practice civil and criminal law. By 1982, Garcés had become a member of the Madrid Bar Association and had set up his own law firm in Madrid. For the next twenty years, Garcés studied and practiced criminal and international humanitarian law.[17] He became particularly expert at defending clients wanted for extradition.[18] Although he was involved in politics with the Spanish left after Franco's death, he made a point of not being involved in any political activity against the Pinochet regime and not becoming a member of any political party in Chile.[19] Nonetheless, Garcés continued to reflect upon how Chile's democracy and human rights had radically changed following the 1973 coup. For many years, Garcés continued to follow events in Chile under the Pinochet regime.[20] He also followed the criminal

---

[15] Garcés quoted in, Rosemary Church et al., 'The Death of Augusto Pinochet' (CNN Insight, 11 December 2006).
[16] 'Juan Garcés – The Right Livelihood Award'.
[17] DeYoung, 'The Prosecutor Who Never Rested'.
[18] Roht-Arriaza, *The Pinochet Effect*, 4.
[19] Gooch, 'The Lawyer Who Wouldn't Forget'.
[20] Roht-Arriaza, *The Pinochet Effect*, 4.

and civil cases concerning the assassination of Orlando Letelier, former foreign minister of Chile during the Allende presidency, and Ronnie Moffit, his aide. Both were killed by a car bomb in 1976 in Washington, DC, by Chilean secret police, the Dirección de Inteligencia Nacional (DINA). In the civil case *De Letelier* v. *Republic of Chile*,[21] the families were represented by lawyers Sam Buffone and Michael Tigar, both of whom would become members of Garcés's legal team in the Pinochet case in the Madrid courts years later. Similarly, Larry Barcella, the US attorney in Washington, DC, was also later a witness in the Pinochet case in Madrid.

Throughout the years, Garcés remained troubled by how a socialist democracy in Chile had been replaced in one morning by a regime wherein systematic torture, extrajudicial killings, kidnappings and extraordinary rendition became normalised, as well as what he called a pervasive 'habeas corpus ineffectiveness'.[22] It seemed the local Chilean judiciary continually failed to address crimes committed by the Pinochet government, or to effect a rule of law that protected ordinary people from arbitrary power.

Even after Pinochet's presidency, holding Pinochet to account seemed unlikely. When Pinochet retired as president, his new role as 'senator for life' provided him with indefinite domestic immunity, and local State legal officials remained reticent to challenge him. As redress in Chilean courts remained limited, victims of the Pinochet government grew impatient and looked elsewhere. Similarly, international options for criminal accountability seemed equally scarce. As stated in the previous chapter, while Nuremberg was instrumental in establishing the basis of international criminal law, the Cold War saw States less inclined to cooperate on the subject of criminal accountability and international criminal prosecution.

Yet, the thawing of the Cold War opened the possibility of greater international criminal accountability. In the 1990s, the United Nations Security Council (UNSC) reengaged to establish several international criminal tribunals, such as the Criminal Tribunal for the Former Yugoslavia (ICTY) and the International Criminal Tribunal for Rwanda (ICTR). The thawing of the Cold War also impacted universal jurisdiction. While prosecution in a Chilean domestic court or the establishment of an international criminal tribunal for Chilean crimes still seemed improbable, private non-State actors had started considering

---

[21] *De Letelier* v. *Republic of Chile*, 567 F. Supp. 1490 (SDNY) US District Court for the Southern District of New York – 567 F. Supp. 1490 (SDNY 1983) (28 July 1983). Also see *Letelier* v. *Republic of Chile*, 502 F.Supp. 259 (DDC 1980); *Letelier* v. *Republic of Chile*, 488 F.Supp 665 (DDC1980).

[22] Garcés quoted in Goodman and Garcés, '40 Years After Chilean Coup, Allende Aide Juan Garcés on How He Brought Pinochet to Justice (Transcript)'.

universal jurisdiction in a foreign court as a third means to close the accountability gap. Likewise, Garcés had kept abreast of the changes in universal jurisdiction in Spain. In July 1985, Spain had passed Article 23.4 of the Judicial Power Organisation Act (LOPJ). Spain established the National Court following Franco's death to prosecute grave breaches of international law perpetrated both within Spain and abroad, irrespective of whether the crimes were perpetrated against a Spaniard or non-Spaniard.[23] This meant that the Act established Spanish courts with jurisdiction for crimes perpetrated by Spanish nationals or foreign citizens outside of Spain as per the principles of universal jurisdiction. In particular, it established that courts had jurisdiction over the crimes of torture, genocide and terrorism.[24] At the time, the Act was considered wide-ranging and permitted both victims and their families to pursue accountability. As Garcés stated later, '[d]uring the cold war no one was willing to apply laws against crimes of this type';[25] the post–Cold War era opened up the possibilities.

Further still, the uniqueness of the Spanish legal system enabled private non-State actors to be involved in a criminal prosecution in several distinct ways. It permitted counsel for the plaintiffs to adopt the role of prosecutor at public criminal trial.[26] It allowed for criminal complaints to be filed by ordinary citizens, not just the public prosecutor's office, including victims and non-government organisations.[27] Unlike the US and UK legal systems, victims could bring a complaint to an investigating magistrate directly and ask for an investigation.[28] The victim could also become a party to the case and was permitted to follow the investigative process and any related trials. While the public prosecutor could oppose the investigation, the victim could persuade the investigating magistrate of the validity of a case. Moreover, victims were not required as complainants to initiate a case; others could also initiate an investigation on their behalf. The investigating judge could make requests abroad, and officials in the Spanish foreign ministry were obliged to forward them to corresponding officials in foreign governments.[29] Despite the distinct nature of the Spanish legal system, and the thawing of the Cold War, Garcés and many others believed that the possibility of indicting Pinochet in Spanish courts still appeared rather slim.[30]

---

[23]   Gooch, 'The Lawyer Who Wouldn't Forget'.
[24]   'Juan Garcés – The Right Livelihood Award'.
[25]   Garcés quoted in Gooch, 'The Lawyer Who Wouldn't Forget'.
[26]   DeYoung, 'The Prosecutor Who Never Rested'.
[27]   Roht-Arriaza, *The Pinochet Effect*.
[28]   Roht-Arriaza, *The Pinochet Effect*; Hilton, Bindman and Garcés, 'Justice in the World's Light'.
[29]   Roht-Arriaza, *The Pinochet Effect*, 6.
[30]   Gooch, 'The Lawyer Who Wouldn't Forget'.

That is, until a criminal complaint was filed in the Madrid courts for allegations of torture by the Argentine government. In March 1996, on his own volition, Carlos Castresana, a Spanish anti-corruption prosecutor, filed a criminal complaint in his private capacity to the Audiencia National in Madrid, a centralised Spanish court with jurisdiction over all Spain. In a case that seemed surprisingly similar to that of Chile, the complaint was against a number of well-known torturers in the Argentine military following the coup in Argentina, and it also listed thirty-eight victims of the related crimes. The charges included *inter alia* genocide, terrorism, illegal detention and disappearances. By chance, the case was assigned by lottery to Baltasar Garzón, an ambitious young judge in the Fifth Chamber (No. 5) of the Central Court of Criminal Proceedings in Madrid. Even at the time, Garzón was considered a super-judge. Garzón had investigated well-publicised organised crime cases and required constant security protection.[31] Once the case was filed, a number of Argentine human rights groups, which were based in Spain, contacted Castresana and helped him develop the case further, thus forming an informal criminal accountability community of practitioners.[32]

For Garcés, the Argentine case was a type of test for Spanish universal jurisdiction – one that posed the question: would the courts accept a similar case in relation to neighbouring Chile?[33] Garcés had read about the filing of the Argentine case, which was featured obscurely in a domestic newspaper, and contacted the Union of Progressive Prosecutors for advice. Miguel Miravet, then president of the Union of Progressive Prosecutors, and Garcés agreed to wait to see if Garzón believed he had jurisdiction over the case in accordance with Spanish law.[34] In July 1996, days after Judge Garzón had formally decided he had jurisdiction over the Argentine case, Garcés and his colleagues from the Association of Progressive Prosecutors in Valencia, along with victims of Pinochet as co-complainants, filed a criminal complaint against Pinochet and other senior Chilean junta leaders in the Madrid courts,[35] specifically for the crimes of genocide, torture and terrorism. The case was assigned by lot to Judge Manuel García Castellón. In large part at his own personal financial cost, Garcés instigated the criminal complaint, which would bear substantial costs as he continued to develop the case over the next several years.[36] As he maintained later: 'It was an honour to do so – free of

---

[31] Roht-Arriaza, *The Pinochet Effect*, 2.
[32] Roht-Arriaza, *The Pinochet Effect*, 8–11.
[33] DeYoung, 'The Prosecutor Who Never Rested'.
[34] Roht-Arriaza, *The Pinochet Effect*, 5.
[35] 'Juan Garcés – The Right Livelihood Award'.
[36] 'Juan Garcés – The Right Livelihood Award'.

charge, of course . . . . Many are people of modest means, who have suffered enough'.[37]At the same time the criminal case was filed, a civil suit was also submitted on behalf of the families of victims of the Chilean dictatorship. Garcés organised and directed the lawyers of the civil case. Eventually, the Spanish courts accepted both the criminal and civil cases.[38]

Over several years, Garcés worked with the victims and witnesses of Chile's dictatorship, as well as with other Spanish lawyers to form a community of practice. According the Roht-Arriaza, the two leading strategists on the case were Garcés and Manuel Murillo, a Spanish lawyer who represented the President Allende Foundation, an organisation based in Spain. Increasingly, Garcés and Murillo developed expertise and extensive knowledge on the proposed case. They also adopted a 'Nuremberg-type strategy'. Like Nuremberg, they developed a case against a small number of Pinochet's military and political elite, who they alleged were *most* responsible for the crimes.[39] Similarly, in terms of criminal participation, Garcés also developed the case against Pinochet and those most responsible as a 'conspiracy'. The case that Garcés and his associates developed concerned around thirty former Chilean government leaders and military personnel, including Pinochet. In this respect, the Chilean case was markedly different from the Argentine case, which had by contrast more perpetrators and included those at a low level. As Garcés later explained:

> The Chilean case from the start was different from the Argentine, in a few ways. First, we had far fewer suspects, never more than thirty. The Argentine case at one point had over a hundred suspects. That's because we focused on a Nuremberg-type strategy. We wanted to get the guys at the top, not the shooters, and we figured that since the court had limited resources to put into investigations, we shouldn't dissipate its energy. Second, we were far less public with the legal documents [instead sharing them only with state legal officials]. We issued summaries, but not the actual documents [to the public]. The investigating judge also had a far lower profile, and seemed to like it that way.[40]

There was also a third difference. The Chilean legal team was considerable more unified and cooperative, which reflected a cooperative criminal accountability community. As Roht-Arriaza argued, the emphasis was on a *cooperative* approach of the practitioners, working with victims and

[37] Garcés quoted in Gooch, 'The Lawyer Who Wouldn't Forget'.
[38] 'Juan Garcés – The Right Livelihood Award'.
[39] Roht-Arriaza, *The Pinochet Effect*, 13.
[40] Garcés quoted in Roht-Arriaza,*The Pinochet Effect*, 13.

witnesses.[41] Conversely, practitioners working on the Argentine case were known for disagreements, antagonism and sniping, which led to an inability to develop a coherent, shared case strategy or plan. Together, Garcés and Murillo represented all the individuals and organisations in the case filed in the Madrid courts, irrespective of their political persuasion or nationality (they represented Chilean and Spanish victims), and included those who had initially sided with Pinochet. As the Chilean legal team, they could focus energy in developing a coherent legal case and case theory,[42] and one largely drawn from the Nuremberg approach. As Garcés later stated,

> It was very important for me that I was applying the principles of international law, according to which there is no distinction in terms of nationality or ideologies with respect to fundamental crimes. I filed my original complaint in Spain on 4 July 1996, on behalf of *all* the victims of the genocide, terrorism and torture that had been committed by officers under the command of Pinochet.[43]

This included acting on behalf of relatives of Carmelo Soria, a Spanish-Chilean UN diplomat who was assassinated by Chilean secret police, the Dirección de Inteligencia Nacional (DINA), as well as the priests Antoni Llidó and Joan Alsina. Eventually, Garcés and Murillo were acting on behalf of about 4,000 victims[44] or family members,[45] as plaintiffs. In this way, Garcés played an important role in developing a cooperative criminal accountability community *between* Spain and Chile. As Roht-Azziaza argued, practitioners such as Garcés played an important 'bridging' role between the victims and witnesses in Chile and the Spanish legal system. Veronica Reyes, of the legal aid organization Foundatón de Ayuda Social de las Iglesias Cristianas (FASIC), later stated:

> We heard from Garcés, who some people knew had managed to escape after the coup through the Spanish Embassy. We thought it was a bit crazy, when he started sending us lists of things he needed, among them things that were impossible to find. But the Association of Family Members of the Disappeared began to believe in him. They started going to the Spanish embassy in Santiago to give their statements for transmission to Madrid.[46]

[41] Roht-Arriaza, *The Pinochet Effect*.
[42] Roht-Arriaza, *The Pinochet Effect*.
[43] Garcés quoted in Hilton, Bindman and Garcés, 'Justice in the World's Light'.
[44] Francesc Relea, 'Un Grupo Especial Del FBI Colabora Con El Juez García Castellón Para Investigar a Pinochet (An FBI Special Group Collaborates with Judge Garcia Castellon to Investigate Pinochet)', *El Pais*, 19 October 1997, www.elpais.es.
[45] Gooch, 'The Lawyer Who Wouldn't Forget'.
[46] Reyes quoted in Roht-Arriaza, *The Pinochet Effect*, 25.

Lastly, and following on from the previous discussion, Garcés also had extensive knowledge of Chilean history, society and politics,[47] as well as a sense of Chilean political and military structures. For Garcés, a significant component of studying the case involved mapping criminal responsibility between the victims of underlying crimes to the senior leadership. As in the Nuremberg Trials, Garcés set out to draw the relationship between the different key actors in the Pinochet government: 'What [was] the link between these persons?'[48] In fact, the Pinochet government had established a clear hierarchy and chain of command, which lent itself to a Nuremberg model. Later, when describing the case against Pinochet to a journalist, Garcés referred to the principles of responsibility of chain of command, in the same way that criminal responsibility had been linked to the senior leadership structure of Nazi Germany in the Nuremburg Tribunal.[49] Garcés stated it was not difficult to establish the workings of the Pinochet regime, as it maintained a strict hierarchical model. Moreover, as a matter of public record, Roht-Arriaza maintained, 'The head of the [Chilean secret police, the Dirección de Inteligencia Nacional] (DINA), Manuel Contreras, had boasted that he breakfasted every day with Pinochet to keep him abreast of progress in the fight against subversion, and Pinochet himself had remarked that not a leaf moved in Chile without his knowledge'.[50] Nonetheless, Garcés explained that it took several years to build the case theory and to establish the evidence and facts linking senior leaders as suspected perpetrators to the underlying crimes committed against particular victims.[51]

Despite these efforts, the possibility of prosecuting Pinochet in the Spanish courts still appeared distant. Notwithstanding significant strides in Spanish jurisdictional reach, universal jurisdiction still seemed a tough terrain to pursue accountability. In fact, several attempts to hold Pinochet to account had been made in several other States exercising universal jurisdiction, including in the United Kingdom. And so the broader cooperative criminal accountability community continued to consider its options.

AN ENDURING AND EXTRAORDINARY CRIMINAL INVESTIGATION

Added to jurisdictional difficulties were many other practical challenges for the case against Pinochet. The first was locating linking material that could

---

47 Roht-Arriaza, *The Pinochet Effect*, 173.
48 Garcés quoted in DeYoung, 'The Prosecutor Who Never Rested'.
49 DeYoung, 'The Prosecutor Who Never Rested'.
50 Roht-Arriaza, *The Pinochet Effect*, 13.
51 DeYoung, 'The Prosecutor Who Never Rested'.

later inform evidence linking Pinochet to the underlying crimes. On the one hand, Garcés had conducted much of the analytical work in relation to the political and military organisation of the Pinochet government. As a political advisor to Allende during his three years of government, his intimate knowledge of how political organisation in Chile had worked combined with some knowledge of the inner workings of Chile's military had proved useful. This insight provided political and military analytical expertise in terms of understanding the structure of the organisation, which could contribute to his case theory of a conspiracy (or common plan). Garcés had also reached out to human rights groups to identify other victims who could provide statements via the Spanish Embassy in Chile. On the other hand, Garcés knew that organisational analysis and witness statements would not be enough in a future criminal court. He considered the type of linkage material required to establish criminal responsibility, beyond reasonable doubt in a criminal prosecution. On the latter, Garcés decided that, like Nuremberg, documentation produced by the perpetrator would be key. Given that accessing material in Chile would be difficult, he considered accessing material elsewhere, although initially the source was not expected to lead to the door of the White House and the Clinton administration.

During their investigation, a link between the Argentine and Chilean cases became apparent – namely through the US-backed Operation Condor. Increasingly, as Garcés, Judge Manuel García Castellón and Judge Garzón were conducting their investigations into kidnappings in Argentina and Chile, they began to discover reports of cross-border disappearances and kidnappings. Interviews conducted with a number of victims and their families opened the investigation to covert operations that stretched across Latin America and included an alliance among Argentina, Bolivia, Brazil, Chile, Paraguay, and Uruguay to suppress opposition, starting in 1973. At the heart of Operation Condor was Chile. The investigation revealed that the primary strategist behind the plan was Pinochet, with the key coordinator of operations being Maunel Contreras, then head of the Chilean secret police, the DINA.[52] Much later, it also became clear that the precursor of Operation Condor was the US-backed Operation FUBELT, the alleged US plan to overthrow Allende, and that the United States had played an important role supporting Pinochet's Operations Condor. This meant that Judge Garzón's case on Argentina and Judge García Castellón's case on Chile were not only similar but were in fact related crimes. Later, Garcés recalled his alarm when through the

---

[52]   Roht-Arriaza, *The Pinochet Effect*, 29–31.

investigation he realised these crimes 'were applied in Chile with the knowledge and the backing of the Nixon-Kissinger administration in this period'.[53]

Yet, this also offered an opportunity. Accessing documentation on these
covert operations in Chile and across much of Latin America, where Pinochet
was still a powerful figure in Chilean politics and where many perpetrators still
held positions in government or military seemed unlikely. However, accessing
covert intelligence documentation from the United States, under the Clinton
administration, was considered a more feasible option and could demonstrate
the extent of the alleged criminal plan. In 1997, Garcés made a request to the
US government to release material to assist with the investigation. He began
travelling to the United States to meet with various officials to release documents pertaining to the Pinochet era, starting with the overthrow of the
Allende government, which he increasingly viewed as the beginning of the
crime as a conspiracy and continued with the brutal crackdown on actual and
alleged opposition. Moreover, in 1997, Judge García Castellón also sent an
official request to the United States to cooperate with the official investigation,
and Janet Reno, then US attorney general agreed and began working with the
Central Intelligence Agency (CIA) and the Federal Bureau of Investigation
(FBI) to release files to send to Spain.[54] This was to be a long and arduous affair
with initially piecemeal documents being released. Finally, after several years
the United States released more than 20,000 documents. Moreover, several
US congress members, as well as other insider witnesses from Chile, also
began travelling to Spain to provide testimony.[55] By 13 March 1998, Garcés
and Murillo made a request to Judge García Castellón to issue an arrest
warrant for Pinochet as well as thirty-nine of the most senior military and
political leaders of the Pinochet regime.[56]

The second challenge was the difficulty in successfully extraditing Pinochet
and senior leaders from Chile to Spanish courts. Chile remained unwilling to
cooperate with the investigations. Similarly, States that Pinochet travelled
through were also apprehensive to prosecute. A number of failed attempts
had been made in the past. Indeed, other private non-State actors had made
attempts in other jurisdictions with little success. It seemed an extraordinary
feat. As Geoffrey Bindman, a human rights solicitor, later explained, he had
attempted to have Pinochet arrested before in the United Kingdom:

---

[53] Garcés quoted in Goodman and Garcés, '40 Years After Chilean Coup, Allende Aide Juan
      Garcés on How He Brought Pinochet to Justice (Transcript)'.
[54] Roht-Arriaza, *The Pinochet Effects*, 26.
[55] Roht-Arriaza, *The Pinochet Effects*, 26.
[56] Roht-Arriaza, *The Pinochet Effects*, 26–27.

Augusto Pinochet visited London on several occasions. On two of them I tried
to have him arrested. I was representing Amnesty International UK. On one
occasion we went to Bow Street to ask for a warrant for Pinochet's arrest – he
was attending an arms fair in Birmingham. The magistrate was reluctant, and
adjourned the case. The following day Pinochet returned to Chile.[57]

Nonetheless, Garcés and the cooperative criminal accountability community
had laid the groundwork and preconditions for an extradition request, should
a likely opportunity arise. They had conducted extensive investigations, completed large-scale analytical work on the Pinochet government as an organisation, collected numerous witnesses' and victims' statements (including insider
witness statements) and started receiving some documents from the United
States. In this respect, Geoffrey Bindman argued that Garcés was key to laying
the groundwork. He maintained that Garcés was 'in many ways the architect of
this whole affair', namely because he 'prepared well in advance for the
moment Pinochet came to a country where [Garcés] could take a legal
initiative', and secondly, the procedure that Garcés initiated through Judge
Garzón for the extradition request from the United Kingdom was a standard
process of extradition, and one with which the 'police and courts were
familiar'.[58] While the UK magistrate was reluctant to make an arrest for crimes
against humanity, including torture, within the United Kingdom, the procedures
governing extradition requests from their European partners were a well-oiled
machine. Although the United Kingdom did not have the same inquisitorial
system as in Spain, it did recognise the State legal officials in the Spanish courts
and, just as importantly, extradition requests issued by the Spanish judiciary.[59]
Similarly, Garcés agreed that the practical nature of investigation combined with
the familiar procedures of extradition governing the United Kingdom and Spain
had contributed significantly to Pinochet's later arrest. Added to this is the
particular nature of the Spanish legal system whereby private non-State actors
could engage in an active (rather than passive) manner with the investigating
judge:

> First, the importance of collecting the evidence. Without two years of previ-
> ous investigation and gathering documentation, no Spanish judge would
> dare to order an warrant of arrest. Second, the network of interstate judicial
> and police cooperation [between Spain and the United Kingdom] .... The
> European Convention on Extradition meant you could put a case of geno-
> cide, torture and terrorism into the network of routine daily cooperation. We

[57] Bindman quoted in Hilton, Bindman and Garcés, 'Justice in the World's Light'.
[58] Garcés quoted in Hilton, Bindman and Garcés, 'Justice in the World's Light'.
[59] Hilton, Bindman and Garcés, 'Justice in the World's Light'.

did this. The Spanish public prosecutor was absolutely passive and against our case, probably following government instructions. But Spanish law gives the lawyers representing victims the power to file a motion. So we asked the judge to interrogate Pinochet as a defendant, according to the European Convention on Extradition.[60]

By the time Pinochet arrived in London again, a dynamic cooperative criminal accountability community had developed. Garcés and Murillo, as private non-State actors, and Judge García Castellón and Judge Garzón (as the two cases were now understood to be linked), as State legal officials, had developed a cooperative criminal accountability community in the development of case briefs and evidence (including sourcing some initial linkage evidence through the US administration) for alleged core crimes.

Yet, some may argue that the interplay between Garcés and Murillo and the two Spanish judges blurred the lines between officials and private actors within the cooperative criminal accountability community, which could result in a conflict of interest at the trial. Moreover, some may question the role of a judge intervening in the collection of evidence. Yet in the Spanish legal system, the functions of the pretrial investigating judge and the trial judge passing the respective judgments are separated. In other words, they are different judges. In this way, the pretrial investigating judge can intervene in the production of evidence, while the judge passing judgment remains judicially impartial and assesses the trial independently on the basis of what evidence has been produced that proves criminal liability.[61] Eventually, this cooperative criminal accountability community also extended more profoundly to the State legal officials and political actors in the US Clinton administration, as well as witnesses and victims in Argentina, Chile and Spain.

PINOCHET TRAVELS TO LONDON

Although Pinochet was aware of the criminal complaint filed against him and senior Chilean leaders in Madrid, he travelled to London nonetheless. In fact, the Chilean press had reported on the ongoing investigation since its inception in 1996. Two lawyers – the lawyer for the Foreign Ministry and his own personal lawyer – warned Pinochet not to travel to London, in light of the Spanish investigations. Disregarding both of them, Pinochet arrived in London on 23 September 1998 and was invited to tea with Baroness

---

[60]   Garcés quoted in Hilton, Bindman and Garcés, 'Justice in the World's Light'.
[61]   Naomi Roht-Arriaza, *Prosecuting Heads of State* (Cambridge: Cambridge University Press, 2009); Roht-Arriaza, *The Pinochet Effect: Transnational Justice in the Age of Human Rights*.

Margaret Thatcher, former British prime minister, before undergoing a medical operation for a herniated disk in his back. He would remain there for 503 days.[62]

It was Garcés who raised Pinochet's arrival in London with Judge Garzón. In early October 1998, Garcés received a call from Andy McEntee, chair of Amnesty International's (AI's) UK section, and Federico Andreu, of AI's International Secretariat, that Pinochet was in London for a medical procedure. As McEntee latter recalled, 'We were thinking about domestic prosecution at the time. Then we started thinking that if the Spanish courts requested judicial cooperation on their investigation, we might get the courts involved and get over the hurdle of the police having complete discretion whether to act.'[63] According to Enrique Santiago, a lawyer working on the Argentine case, he and Garcés decided to submit a request to Judge Garzón that he ask the British to assist in a 'letter rogatory' on Pinochet with a list of questions drawn up by Garcés, requesting information relevant to the Operation Condor investigation. On Tuesday 13 October, Santiago and Garcés sent briefs to Judge García Castellón and Judge Garzón, which referred to evidence of Pinochet's role as central to Operation Condor, as well as details of the crimes perpetrated. The following day and in response to the briefs, both Judge García Castellón and Judge Garzón issued requests, via INTERPOL to London, for British authorities to permit them to question Pinochet directly following his surgery.[64]

Yet, to increase the odds of the request to London, Garcés had also visited Judge Garzón, personally. As Judge Garzón later recalled:

> To make a long story short, a week before . . . October 16th, Juan Garcés came and saw me. He was not defending the Argentine case. And he asked me – he informed me that Pinochet was in fact in London. I told him, 'OK, very good. What do you want?' 'Well, I want you to know that he's in London. What can we do?'[65]

Garzón maintained that once British authorities confirmed Pinochet was in London, they asked, 'What are you accusing him of?'[66] According to Judge Garzón, he went to Garcés for information relating to the Chilean case: 'I had

[62] Roht-Arriaza, *The Pinochet Effect*, 1–2, 34.

[63] McEntee quoted in Roht-Arriaza, *The Pinochet Effect*, 33.

[64] Roht-Arriaza, *The Pinochet Effect*, 34.

[65] Baltasar Garzón, 'Spanish Judge Baltasar Garzón Tells the Story of the Arrest of Chile's Augusto Pinochet (Transcript)', Democracy Now! 11 September 2013, www.democracynow.org/blog/2013/9/11/spanish_judge_baltasar_garzn_tells_the_story_of_the_arrest_of_chiles_augusto_pinochet.

[66] Garzón, 'Spanish Judge Baltasar Garzón Tells the Story of the Arrest of Chile's Augusto Pinochet (Transcript)'.

an open [related] case, which was the Condor Operation, so I told Juan, "Here we can proceed with this case." And, in fact, that's what I did.'[67] Given the investigative developments of the Argentine and Chilean cases, Garzón agreed to increasingly play a larger role in the requests to London. Two types of requests were sent to UK authorities: the first was made by both Judge García Castellón and Judge Garzón to simply question Pinochet to record his testimony. However, the second type of request was to issue an arrest warrant via INTERPOL, which was far more controversial in nature and was made by Judge Garzón. As he later explained:

> On October 16 of 1998, [the UK authorities] had said that Pinochet had wanted to leave. I had asked for the possibility to send an interrogatory with the questions for Pinochet, in order to get the testimony from Pinochet. I had asked Juan to prepare the questions. And that's how everything finished that day, by 1:00 p.m. on a Friday. And around 2:00, I received a message from the British police telling me, 'Pinochet leaves tomorrow. We won't be able to take this testimony from him. You have to make the decision you need to make, because he's going to leave.' That's when there was no one left in the court. There was only one person there. I made the decision, first, to hold back this office worker to not ... leave, because she was about to leave. And when I gave her the request by hand, this person came back to my office, and [said, 'Are you sure about this?' And I told [her], 'Just write and be quiet' [so as not to alert the media or Pinochet]. And that's how the arrest warrant was issued. I asked the Spanish police to also be quiet, because the judge may do so if he decides. The request was placed, filed.[68]

At first, Judge Garzón was unsure if the UK authorities would make the unprecedented arrest, given it was for a former head of State. To Garzón's surprise, they did. Nonetheless, the initial arrest order Judge Garzón had attached was insufficient. Once Judge Garzón discovered that the UK authorities had arrested Pinochet while still in the hospital that same evening, and fearing that one case would not be enough, he and Garcés finished the second arrest order together, adding a further 104 cases. Judge Garzón had relied upon Garcés for the particulars of each case. As Judge Garzón later recalled:

> [T]he truth is, the day after, I called Juan Garcés. I told him, 'Juan, Pinochet knows he's arrested. We need to reaffirm and complete the arrest order,' ... and then we added 104 more cases. So we had to finish up the case. And thanks to

---

[67] Garzón, 'Spanish Judge Baltasar Garzón Tells the Story of the Arrest of Chile's Augusto Pinochet (Transcript)'.

[68] Garzón, 'Spanish Judge Baltasar Garzón Tells the Story of the Arrest of Chile's Augusto Pinochet (Transcript)'.

Juan [Garcés], we consolidated in 24 hours, with 18 translators, without sleeping, there in the court, eating sandwiches there, finished up the order. The order was issued. Thanks to that order, Pinochet remained arrested.[69]

COOPERATIVE CRIMINAL ACCOUNTABILITY COMMUNITY AND THE TRIAL OF PINOCHET

While in many respects Garcés is considered the architect of the Pinochet case, he could never go it alone. From the beginning, Garcés relied upon the broader cooperative criminal accountability community – in Spain and Chile. Arguably, Garcés relied upon guidance from his Chilean victims and survivors, whom he represented *pro bono*. And increasingly Garcés drew upon the expertise of a broader international community across both cases in the Madrid and London courts.[70] This cooperative criminal accountability community also worked on identifying *local* sources of law. To date, Garcés had developed the Chilean case against Pinochet and the senior leaders based on the charges of torture, genocide, and terrorism. In the Madrid courts, Spain had limited universal jurisdiction to particular crimes such as genocide and terrorism. At the time, Spain's interpretation of genocide in law was also unique.[71] Nevertheless, the English courts did not recognise the crime of genocide at that stage, as it had not yet been introduced in UK domestic law, although the United Kingdom had signed the Genocide Convention. As Andy McEntee at Amnesty International recalled later,

> I talked to Juan Garcés and he kept insisting that Pinochet be charged with genocide. I kept trying to explain that, even though the UK is a party to the Genocide Convention, Genocide was never defined in our penal code, so our judges won't use it as the basis of a prosecution. The only option was to rely on section 134, which translated the Torture Convention into domestic law.[72]

It was this advice that informed Garcés and Judge Garzón in writing the second arrest warrant, which saw them extend the cases to focus on those relating to torture and terrorism, while the first arrest warrant had related to genocide.[73] In

---

[69] Garzón, 'Spanish Judge Baltasar Garzón Tells the Story of the Arrest of Chile's Augusto Pinochet (Transcript)'.

[70] Roht-Arriaza, *The Pinochet Effect*.

[71] Roht-Arriaza, *The Pinochet Effect*, 47.

[72] McEntee quoted in Roht-Arriaza, *The Pinochet Effect*, 42–43.

[73] This community also developed arguments concerning constitutional laws and criminal codes governing Chile at the time Pinochet's military junta took over, as well as signing international conventions, such as the Convention Against Torture in 1985. Roht-Arriaza, *The*

short, the cooperative criminal accountability community was important in identifying sources of law that already governed UK, Spanish, and Chilean domestic law, as well as international criminal law.[74]

In the English courts, this cooperative criminal accountability community also worked to further identify and clarify the complex sources of *international* law. In the first case in the High Court, private non-State actors had resisted being involved. But when the first appeals judgment in the High Court, *Pinochet (No. 1)*, decided that Pinochet enjoyed immunity and prosecutors requested an appeal to the British House of Lords, private non-State actors attempted to engage more formally in the case. They did this mainly because they were disappointed in what they considered to be a disregard for international law in the legal arguments. To do this, Geoffrey Bindman, a human rights lawyer, petitioned for leave to intervene on behalf of Amnesty International, two other human rights groups and three individuals as victims (and/or family of victims). These groups included the Medical Foundation for the Care of Victims of Torture and the Redress Trust and the Association of the Relatives of the Disappeared Detainees. This meant they were granted leave to provide oral submissions in the British House of Lords. Human Rights Watch (HRW) was also permitted to provide a written submission.[75] A committee consisting of Lord Nicholls, Lord Slynn and Lord Steyn granted their leave to intervene without protest from other parties. That private non-State actors were granted leave to intervene had occurred only on one separate occasion – when the Society for the Protection of Children intervened in a previous case.[76] Thus, this was the first human rights case where private non-State actors were granted leave to intervene.

At the hearings of the appeals, they not only submitted several written submissions but were represented by experts in the fields of *inter alia*

Pinochet Effect; R v. Bow Street Metropolitan Stipendiary Magistrate, ex parte Pinochet Ugarte (No 3) (Pinochet 3) [2000] (House of Lords, Great Britain (UK) 24 March 1999).

[74] In the United Kingdom, a cooperative criminal accountability community also worked to develop a broad two-track strategy from the start of the Pinochet extradition procedures. The first, which was also the priority for the community, was the extradition to Spain where they believed the evidence and case were the most developed, and the odds of the case reaching a trial most achievable. They also considered a domestic prosecution in the United Kingdom. Should the extradition processes fail for any reason, they wanted to be ready for with case in the UK courts. Roht-Arriaza, *The Pinochet Effect*, 40.

[75] Christine Chinkin and Alan Boyle, *The Making of International Law* (Oxford: Oxford University Press, 2007); Roht-Arriaza, *The Pinochet Effect*, 50.

[76] *R v. Bow Street Metropolitan Stipendiary Magistrate*, ex parte Pinochet Ugarte (No 3) (Pinochet 3) [2000]; Hilton, Bindman and Garcés, 'Justice in the World's Light'.

extradition, common law, human rights and international law as counsel.[77] In the Second Appeals (*Pinochet 2*) trial, counsel for private non-State actors included Professor Ian Brownlie QC, Peter Duffy QC, Michael Fordham, Owen Davies, Frances Webber and David Scorey for Amnesty International. Brownlie, a world expert in public international law, had played a role in a number of important international cases, including winning the landmark Nicaragua case against the United States (*Nicaragua v. United State of America*) at the ICJ.[78] As a broader cooperative criminal accountability community, they worked alongside the Crown Prosecution Service, which also brought in a number of international lawyers.[79] The Second Appeals (*Pinochet 2*) trial counsel also included Alun Jones QC, Christopher Greenwood, James Lewis and Campaspe Lloyd-Jacob. As Bindman later stated, the result of including counsel with knowledge of international law shifted the case from one focused on domestic law in the High Court to one with greater inclusion of international law in the two cases in the British House of Lords (*Pinochet 2* and *Pinochet 3*).[80] In fact, in *Pinochet 3*, this point was acknowledged in the British House of Lords by those less familiar with international criminal law, and particularly customary international law. As Lord Browne-Wilkinson stated, 'you are going to have to tell me when things do become part of international law and when they do not. It is a point I have never understood since I was at Oxford.'[81]

Moreover, engagement between UK and Spanish officials and private non-State actors was also a key feature of the Pinochet extradition for the crime of torture. For instance, prior to the second case in the British House of Lords (*Pinochet 3*) hearing, Alun Jones, from the UK Crown Prosecutor Services, travelled to Spain to meet with Judge Garzón, as well as Garcés. Together, Jones, Garzón and Garcés refined their arguments on the question of Pinochet's immunity for the crime of torture.[82] As a cooperative criminal accountability community – a UK legal official, a Spanish official judge and Garcés as a private non-State actor – it showed that the distinction between the international and domestic between the two States, as well as officials and private non-State actors, was increasingly bridged through the various cases.

---

[77] *R v. Bow Street Metropolitan Stipendiary Magistrate*, ex parte Pinochet Ugarte (No 3) (Pinochet 3) [2000].

[78] Military and Paramilitary Activities in and against Nicaragua (*Nicaragua v. United States of America*). Merits, Judgment. ICJ Reports (1986).

[79] Hilton, Bindman and Garcés, 'Justice in the World's Light'.

[80] Hilton, Bindman and Garcés, 'Justice in the World's Light'.

[81] Lord Browne-Wilkinson, transcript of the hearings, *Pinochet 3*, day 2, Tuesday, 19 January 1999, p. 52.

[82] Roht-Arriaza, *The Pinochet Effect*, 56.

Added to this was that they were playing the role of de facto international prosecutors for international crimes committed in a third State, Chile. Most particularly, in the UK context, their legal arguments pertained to challenging Pinochet's immunity as a former head of State, as well as the obligations that each State had in holding senior actors to account, which had not been brought upon a former head of State since Nuremberg (see Chapter 1).

This cooperative criminal accountability community also extended to those in the US Clinton administration. As stated earlier, linkage material was formally requested by Judge García Castellón and Judge Garzón but also informally by Garcés. While in 1997 the United States had agreed to cooperate officially, efforts were largely piecemeal in the beginning, with a few documents sent along. When Pinochet was arrested in the United Kingdom, it flung the international spotlight on the Pinochet era and pressure on the US government to explain its role. During this time, Garcés had continued to travel to the United States several times to persuade government officials to release key documents relating to the case. By 28 January 1999, Clinton ordered a large-scale declassification of documents relating to Pinochet and his regime,[83] before the final appeals judgment (Pinochet 3) was made in the British House of Lords in March 1999. The Declassification Project was the greatest discretionary executive branch release of documents on a foreign policy issue or any country. It is estimated that more than 20,000 documents were eventually released by the United States.[84] Documents revealed the extent of the Pinochet regime's suppression on opposition, as well as the role of the United States in the plan. The Chile Declassification Project yielded some 2,200 CIA records. Further still, approximately 3,800 White House, National Security Council, Pentagon and FBI records were released, along with 18,000 State Department documents that shed considerable light on Pinochet's rule between 1973 and 1990.[85] The documentation revealed recordings that included the private commentary of several US presidents, including Richard Nixon, Gerald Ford, Jimmy Carter and Ronald Reagan, along with those of their aides. It also extended to records of covert action planning meetings chaired by Henry Kissinger, as well as intelligence reports provided by informants inside the Pinochet regime. It showed communications between CIA Directorate of Operations and agents based in Santiago Station, including details of covert actions to change the Allende

---

[83] www.rightlivelihoodaward.org/laureates/juan-garcs/
[84] Abdul Quader Chowdhury, 'Trial of Former Chilean Dictator General Pinochet', *The Independent*, 10 September 2000, www.independent.co.uk.
[85] Kornbluh, *The Pinochet File*.

government.[86] It reflected the nature of the US-supported Operation Condor campaign to suppress opposition in six South American countries, including Chile, which included *inter alia* State terrorism, kidnapping, torture, disappearances and assassinations.[87] According to Peter Kornbluh, director of the National Security Archive's Chile Documentation Project, Garcés played an essential role in the release of the documents. As Kornbluh later maintained, without Garcés's 'quest to hold the perpetrators' in Chile accountable for crimes against humanity, 'Pinochet would never have been arrested in London, and the Clinton Administration would never have been forced to declassify the US documents on Chile'.[88] Later, Garcés would also request Henry Kissinger, former US secretary of state, to explain his involvement and knowledge in Operations FUBELT and Condor.[89]

Throughout the late 1990s and after, the cooperative criminal accountability community, particularly Garcés, was accused of a politically motivated vendetta against Pinochet and his legacy. Pinochet called the trial a 'show trial in a foreign land', which was the result of 'spurious attempts by foreign prosecutors to convict me on unproven charges'.[90] He concluded that it was 'certainly not British justice'.[91] Conversely, Garcés argued that there was no political discrimination in his case against Pinochet. To demonstrate this, he argued, he represented *all* the victims and their families, irrespective of their position or political sympathies – including representing those senior leaders who fell out of favour with Pinochet.[92] For Garcés, the primary motivator was to show that no one was above international law – no matter how politically important they were. As Garcés later stated 'There is no question of revenge. What we are involved in is a thoroughly honourable enterprise to create a precedent for judging crimes against humanity through international cooperation.'[93]

Characteristically, Garcés remained notoriously private through the investigation and trials. He was less engaged with the media, often only speaking in relation to the case and what it meant for the victims and international law. Over the years, he had increasingly resisted being involved in Spanish politics

[86]   Kornbluh, *The Pinochet File*.
[87]   Kornbluh, *The Pinochet File*.
[88]   Kornbluh, *The Pinochet File*.
[89]   'Garzón Solicita Interrogar a Kissinger El 24 de Abril En Londres Por El Caso Pinochet', *Europa Press*, 17 April 2002, Factiva edition.
[90]   Raymond Whitaker, 'Pinochet Denounces "Show Trial"', *The Independent*, 18 November 1998, www.independent.co.uk/news/uk/crime/pinochet-denounces-show-trial-739580.html.
[91]   Whitaker, 'Pinochet Denounces "Show Trial"'.
[92]   DeYoung, 'The Prosecutor Who Never Rested'.
[93]   Garcés quoted in DeYoung, 'The Prosecutor Who Never Rested'.

and had persuaded Spain's political parties not to get involved in the case, even to support it, emphasising that they leave it to Spain's independent judiciary to decide. In 1999, a journalist described Garcés's keenness to separate himself from the political parties and his propensity to shy away from any media celebrity status at the time: Garcés 'left the hurly-burly of politics a long time ago (though his brother is a socialist MP) and he has studiously avoided the publicity so eagerly courted by investigating magistrate Baltasar Garzón, who last October put in the request for Britain to detain Pinochet'.[94] Garcés had also been careful not to include political groups or parties in the application or prosecution: 'it was so important that our case be conducted on strictly legal grounds without a political element. We do not involve any political institutions or State bodies and have asked political parties not to take part in any way'.[95] Likewise, political leaders in both Spain and the United Kingdom were keen to separate themselves, insisting that the question of Pinochet's immunity be left to their respective courts to decide.[96]

JUDGEMENT AND LEGACY OF PINOCHET

On 24 March 1999, the British House of Lords decided (in *Pinochet No. 3*) that Pinochet did not enjoy immunity for the *jus cogens* crime of torture and therefore could be extradited to Madrid to face prosecution. Although, the Lords did not agree on all legal points and stuck to a very narrow view of international law, the majority recognised that torture was an accepted and recognised *jus cogens* of international law, which had the effect of overriding Pinochet's claims for immunity.[97] While the judgments in the British House of Lords illustrated the complexity of decisions concerning immunity, the principle *nullum crimen sine lege* and the application of universal jurisdiction, the extradition hearing in late September was comparably simpler. The final Extradition Hearing in Bow Street Court Central London, whereby Judge Ronald Bartle heard the conditions of Pinochet's extradition, was formative. While *Pinochet 3* in the British House of Lords had, on the whole, only

---

[94]   Quoted in Gooch, 'The Lawyer Who Wouldn't Forget'.
[95]   Garcés quoted in Gooch, 'The Lawyer Who Wouldn't Forget'.
[96]   Roht-Arriaza, *The Pinochet Effect*.
[97]   Ian Brownlie and James Crawford, *Brownlie's Principles of Public International Law*, 8th ed. (Oxford: Oxford University Press, 2012), 687; Roht-Arriaza, *The Pinochet Effect*. While the previous appeals case in the House of Lords (*Pinochet No. 2*) was more engaged with the principles of international law, *Pinochet No. 3* held a far more narrow view of international law.

accepted jurisdiction for crimes after the signing of the Convention Against Torture (CAT), the Extradition Hearing accepted the mode of liability as conspiracy and therefore the nature of conspiracy could include crimes perpetrated prior to the signing the CAT.[98] Judge Bartle decided that the requirements for extradition were met, allowed new charges that had been developed by the prosecution to be included in the hearing and held they were extraditable offences.

Judge Bartle added two further points crucial for de facto international prosecutors in preparation for Pinochet's prosecution in the Madrid courts. Bartle argued that, first, 'information relating to the allegation of conspiracy prior to 8th December 1988 can be considered by the court, as conspiracy is a continuing offence';[99] and, secondly, 'whether the disappearances amount to torture; the effect on the families of those who disappeared can amount to mental torture. Whether or not this was intended by the regime of Senator Pinochet is in my view a matter of fact for the trial court.'[100] In this way, Garcés's initial architecture of the case, in borrowing key aspects from the Nuremberg Model and applying them to Pinochet, particularly in relation to the nature of the crimes as 'conspiracy' had been instructive. As Roht-Arriaza argued, it meant that the Madrid courts could consider all the material collected, not just that from post-1998 when the United Kingdom had ratified the CAT, in making decisions concerning jurisdiction over the alleged crimes.[101] This was important because jurisdiction over the crimes could therefore start from the date that the coup was launched and led by Pinochet, as well as subsequent crimes conducted thereafter as part of a wider plan to suppress actual and alleged opposition, including acts of torture, and for which they had a greater number of documents and witness statements that could inform evidence.[102]

Meanwhile in Spain, prosecutors had challenged jurisdiction over the Pinochet's crimes, including two cases in the Madrid courts.[103] In each of the cases, the judges decided Spain had jurisdiction over the alleged crimes of genocide, terrorism and torture conducted in Chile, exercising universal jurisdiction. During the Spanish investigation, it was estimated that while in

---

[98] Roht-Arriaza, *The Pinochet Effect*.
[99] Bartle quoted in Roht-Arriaza, *The Pinochet Effect*, 61.
[100] Bartle quoted in Roht-Arriaza, *The Pinochet Effect*, 61.
[101] Roht-Arriaza, *The Pinochet Effect*, 61–62.
[102] Roht-Arriaza, *The Pinochet Effect*, 61, rather than the relatively small number of crimes conducted at the end of the 1980s when the CAT was signed
[103] For documents on the respective cases, see Caso Pinochet, www.elclarin.cl https://www.elclarin.cl /clarin_joomla_old_2020/fpa/pinochet.html?phpMyAdmin=cf9bca0ef760364025bb da1263ac199f.

power in Chile from 1973 to 1990, Pinochet was responsible for the torture of around 200,000 people; the assassination and disappearance of 3,000 and 1,000, respectively; and a further 5,000 to 6,000 were buried in unmarked graves.[104]

Despite the decisions in the British House of Lords and the Extradition Hearing, Pinochet never made it to Madrid's courts. Instead, Jack Straw, then UK home secretary, granted Pinochet permission to return to his native Chile on medical grounds, a decision met with protest. By the time of Pinochet's extradition hearing, ten countries were engaged and had cooperated in the large-scale investigation of Pinochet. They had also contributed to the prosecution with evidence and assisted with witness statements. Furthermore, the European Parliament had passed legislation to show solidarity for the investigations.[105] The United States, amongst other countries, was considering extradition requests, had Britain recognised Pinochet's immunity.[106] Yet, before States could arrange for their case to be heard at the ICJ, Straw had allowed Pinochet to take a flight home to his native Chile.

While Pinochet arrived a free man in Chile in March 2000, the political landscape had altered significantly. The ensuing series of legal processes in Spain and the United Kingdom had opened up domestic debate in Chile concerning the legacy of the Pinochet era. Over time, a series of legal battles in the courts ensued. By December 2000, Judge Juan Guzman, a Chilean judge, had ordered Pinochet's arrest for the murder of 77 activists who were victims of 'Death Caravans', and Pinochet was arrested in 2001. Moreover, important documents started to be released concerning the Pinochet era. For example, in September 2000, the Chilean College of Medicine had held a cache of documentation that suggested that the Chilean military had tortured approximately 200,000 people.[107] By 2004, Chile's Supreme Court held that Pinochet no longer enjoyed immunity from criminal prosecution. Although Pinochet died before a criminal case was concluded, it showed Chile was finally willing to address its past injustices. It also encouraged other Latin American States involved in Operation Condor to also face their pasts.

Aside from the Pinochet case, Juan Garcés assisted in a number of other steps towards accountability. As stated earlier, when Garcés filed the complaint against Pinochet in the Madrid courts, it was as part of a two-part process: in the Spanish legal system criminal and civil complaints are filed

---

[104]   Gooch, 'The Lawyer Who Wouldn't Forget'.
[105]   Roht-Arriaza, *The Pinochet Effect* 25.
[106]   Whitaker, 'Pinochet Denounces "Show Trial"'.
[107]   Chowdhury, 'Trial of Former Chilean Dictator General Pinochet'.

at the same time on behalf of the victims, the latter regarding civil compensation. While it was not possible to criminally prosecute Pinochet in the Madrid courts, Garcés continued to pursue the civil component of the case. As Garcés explained: 'Pinochet "one" was about torture and crimes against humanity', while 'Pinochet "two" is about the money the criminal made and hid. It's the same case, in two facets, and in both, the key is international judicial cooperation.'[108] To do this, Garcés had located some of Pinochet's personal assets in a bank in the United States, the Riggs Bank, then based in Washington, DC. As part of the civil legal proceedings, an order was enacted to freeze Pinochet's assets in 1999, when criminal proceedings against Pinochet had already begun in the Madrid courts. Nevertheless, Riggs Bank appeared hesitant to respond. In July 2004, the US Senate's Permanent Subcommittee on Investigations published a report titled 'Money Laundering and Foreign Corruption: Enforcement and Effectiveness of the Patriot Act', which addressed Pinochet's relationship with Riggs Bank.[109] It found that Riggs Bank had held Pinochet's assets from 1994 to 2002, which were estimated between US$4 million and US$8 million. The US Senate report maintained the bank had 'resisted' regulating Pinochet's accounts: 'Riggs Bank assisted Augusto Pinochet, former president of Chile, to evade legal proceedings related to his Riggs bank account and resisted OCC [Office of the Comptroller of the Currency] oversight of these accounts, despite red flags involving the source of Mr Pinochet's wealth, pending legal proceedings to freeze his assets and public allegations of serious wrongdoing by this client.'[110] Once the Senate committee published its report, Garcés filed a request to seize the assets of Riggs Bank on behalf of the victims of the Pinochet government in the Madrid courts, and in September 2004, Judge Baltasar Garzón issued a court order requesting that the United States freeze approximately USD$10.3 million at Riggs Bank. Judge Garzón asked the US authorities to file criminal charges against seven senior executives of the bank for concealing Pinochet's assets. By January 2005, executives of Riggs Bank had pled guilty to US charges of money laundering and agreed to pay US$8 million to Pinochet's victims for damages for acts of terrorism, torture

---

[108] Al Goodman, 'Pinochet: U.S. Urged to Charge Bank', CNN.com, 16 September 2004, https://edition.cnn.com/2004/WORLD/europe/09/16/spain.riggs/.

[109] Minority Staff of the Permanent Subcommittee on Investigations, 'Money Laundering and Foreign Corruption: Enforcement and Effectiveness of the Patriot Act – Case Study Involving Riggs Bank Report' (Washington, DC: United States Senate, Permanent Subcommittee on Investigations, Committee on Government Affairs, 15 July 2004).

[110] Minority Staff of the Permanent Subcommittee on Investigations, 'Money Laundering and Foreign Corruption', 7.

and genocide.[111] Shortly after, Riggs Bank was acquired. Over the course of 2006, 2007 and 2008, the funds received from Riggs Bank were distributed as compensation to 22,073 victims of Pinochet, throughout Chile and across fifty countries, via the President Allende Foundation. While the amount received by victims was not a great sum, it sent a powerful message to those who had assisted in hiding Pinochet's funds.[112]

In Spain, Garzón and Garcés continued to pursue accountability. This included issuing a request via INTERPOL to question Henry Kissinger, former US secretary of state, while he was on a visit to London, in relation to his role in Operation Condor.[113] One of the requests, signed by Juan Garcés, was, he argued, necessary 'given the direct and broad knowledge Mr Kissinger has of the international terrorist activities carried out in the framework of the "Condor Plan"'.[114] Similarly, Garzón's interest extended to questioning Kissinger for his alleged involvement in crimes committed in association with Operation Condor.[115] In 2009, Garcés also began working with Spanish courts to investigate crimes committed under the Franco dictatorship from 1936 to 1975.[116]

More recently, Juan Garcés assisted the President Allende Foundation in the ongoing case in the Madrid courts against those *civilians* who aided the Pinochet regime in crimes against humanity to be held criminally responsible. While individual senior leaders in the Chilean *military* junta have since been indicted in Chile, local courts have remained reluctant to prosecute civilians who assisted the Pinochet government as it perpetrated crimes against humanity, such as torture and disappearance of opposition, and/or aided in hiding assets acquired by the regime. In January 2021, the appeals court in Madrid held that the case could be prosecuted in Spanish courts exercising universal jurisdiction, as one of the victims was a Spanish citizen.[117] Similarly, the President Allende Foundation has assisted in the ongoing *El Carin* newspaper

[111] 'Riggs Bank to Pay Millions to Pinochet Victims: Press Release from Spanish Legal Team', Transnational Institute (TNI), 25 February 2005, www.tni.org/es/node/13586.
[112] 'Fondo de Ayuda a Las Víctimas Del Alzamiento de Bienes y Blanqueo de Capitales de Augusto Pinochet', El Clarin.cl, 12 February 2008, www.elclarin.cl/fpa/indemnizaciones .html?phpMyAdmin=cf9bca0ef760364025bbda1263ac199f.
[113] Mar Roman, 'Spanish Judge Seeks Permission from Britain to Question Kissinger over South American Dictatorship Links', Associated Press Newswires (Factiva), 17 April 2002.
[114] Garcés quoted in 'Garzón Solicita Interrogar a Kissinger El 24 de Abril En Londres Por El Caso Pinochet'.
[115] John Innes, 'Permission Sought to Question Kissinger', *The Scotsman* (Factiva), 18 April 2002.
[116] 'Juan Garcés – The Right Livelihood Award'.
[117] Audiencia Nacional Sala de lo Penal Sección Cuarta Rollo 206/20 Juzgado Central de Instrucción No 5 Diligencias Previas 40/50, Auto n 15/2021.

confiscation case.[118] Owned by Victor Pey Casadeo during the Allende government, it was the largest newspaper at the time and was confiscated by the Pinochet government.

The Pinochet Precedent?

While, Garcés' never saw a successful indictment against Pinochet in Spanish courts, he believed it marked a turning point not only for Pinochet, but for the practice of international law more broadly. Garcés reiterated that while Pinochet was free to return home, it was not because the law had not applied to him: 'He will become a free person in his own country but he would be a fugitive from international justice with several detention orders against him. The case would continue'.[119] That the British House of Lords had decided that Pinochet did not enjoy immunity for the *jus cogens* crime of torture and should, according to domestic and international law, be extradited to Spain to be prosecuted was nothing short of groundbreaking. Both the London and Madrid courts had established an important legal principle, namely that in exercising universal jurisdiction in foreign courts, international criminal law had applied to Pinochet, as a former head of State. For Garcés, this was enough: 'The essential dimension of this case for the future is already a reality … it has become a normal legal case. A normal extradition, used for the first time against a former head of State.'[120] While the cooperative criminal accountability community was keen to show they were not proposing new international law in relation to Pinochet in the Spanish or English court, the effect of the judgment for some resembled a 'precedent' in nature. Indeed, Garcés referred to the judgment in the British House of Lords as a precedent, whereby the Pinochet case needed 'to become one of many'.[121] To this day, the Pinochet case remains one of the most important legal cases in the history of international criminal law (ICL).[122]

Garcés had worked with a cooperative criminal accountability community to achieve something that had not been done before in international criminal law. Yet, ultimately his motivation had stemmed from what he viewed as a personal and moral obligation, as a witness to the early crimes of Pinochet: 'I was an involuntary witness to a crime. When "la barbarie

---

[118]   *Víctor Pey Casado and President Allende Foundation v. Republic of Chile*, ICSID Case No. ARB/98/2.
[119]   Garcés quoted in Gooch, 'The Lawyer Who Wouldn't Forget'.
[120]   Chowdhury, 'Trial of Former Chilean Dictator General Pinochet'.
[121]   Garcés quoted in, Hilton, Bindman and Garcés, 'Justice in the World's Light'.
[122]   Roht-Arriaza, *The Pinochet Effect*.

hecho poder" ... when savagery created power. That is an experience I don't wish on anyone. But when you have the opportunity to help bring justice, it is a moral obligation."[123] In this respect, Garcés believed he was bestowed with 'great professional responsibility for the victims', who he noted showed 'enormous courage when testifying'.[124] It was this sense of personal and moral obligation as a witness which saw him later represent the victims and his unrelenting efforts to build a case against a powerful dictator, and the person most responsible for core crimes in Chile. As John Muller, a Chilean journalist then based in Madrid, stated '[Garcés] has been the hammer that knocked away at the anvil.'[125] The tenacity by the cooperative criminal accountability community to build a case based on evidence, combined with some serendipity whereby Pinochet's hubris to evade justice saw him travel to London, paved the way for Pinochet's indictment in the Madrid courts and arrest in London, respectively.

CONCLUSION

Attempts to bring Pinochet to account through a criminal prosecution reflects how the process of trial and error played a critical role not only in innovations in the types of actors, institutions and means to achieve accountability of former heads of State for core international crimes but also in terms of producing new jurisprudence. Attempts made by private non-State actors, such as Juan Garcés, to bring Pinochet to trial tell us something about the way private non-State actors adapted the institutions and means to close the impunity gap, particularly when Chile, as the home State where the respective core international crimes occurred, was unwilling or unable to pursue criminal accountability of powerful actors. It also shows Garcés in the context of a broader cooperative criminal accountability community, whereby they showed a willingness to use international criminal law to bring those most responsible to account through a criminal prosecution exercising universal jurisdiction. Over time, they conducted extensive research of the law, demonstrated an ability to identify primary sources of domestic and international law, collected witnesses' and victims' statements, as well as identifying linkage material, which could link Pinochet with the underlying crimes.

While the Pinochet case did not result in a successful indictment in the Spanish courts, it did set one of the most important precedents or events in

---

[123]   Garcés quoted in DeYoung, 'The Prosecutor Who Never Rested'.
[124]   Garcés quoted in Gooch, 'The Lawyer Who Wouldn't Forget'.
[125]   Muller quoted in Gooch, 'The Lawyer Who Wouldn't Forget'.

international criminal law in the post-Nuremberg era, still to this day. Not only because a former head of State could potentially be indicted for ordering the torture of his own citizens but also the Pinochet case reiterated how the domestic system of law within foreign courts could act as a site of accountability under international law, as it was designed in the Convention Against Torture. On the one hand, it appeared that international law was momentarily taken out of the hands of State leaders and international (State) institutions, and instead directed by private non-State actors, namely lawyers and victims, and State legal officials, such as Garzón. On the other hand, one could argue that it also illustrated how private non-State actors and State legal officials worked together to adapt and innovate practical tasks and processes to ensure that the CAT was functioning as designed and that States fulfilled their international obligations under international law to hold senior actors, suspected of the *jus cogens* crime of torture, to account.

Lastly, the Pinochet case demonstrated the merits of two States, the United Kingdom and Spain, supported by a strong, independent judiciary, which were willing to cooperate. Initially, both the United Kingdom's and Spain's political leaders were reticent to interfere in the judicial proceedings of their respective States. It also showed that while the United Kingdom enjoyed a common law system, and Spain a civil law legal system, they both recognised international laws and processes, such as laws concerning extradition, immunity and torture – albeit sometimes for different reasons. Nevertheless, the United Kingdom and Spanish States also showed the ability to cooperate in the extradition request of Senator Pinochet.

As a wider community of practice, many of the practitioners working with Garcés were influenced by the Pinochet case and continued to extend the 'Pinochet Jurisprudence' to other former heads of State. This includes Reed Brody, a lawyer from Human Rights Watch (HRW). Brody would later work on the indictment of Hissène Habré, former president of Chad in the Extraordinary African Chambers.

The next chapter explores the role of private non-State actors in relation to the Hissène Habré case. While a number of actors contributed, this chapter will initially focus on the role of Souleymane Guengueng, a witness and victim of torture in Chad during the 1980s. It examines how Guengueng eventually teamed up with Reed Brody, who was directly influenced by the Pinochet case. Together, they worked with a broader cooperative criminal accountability community to bring Hissane Habré to criminal prosecution. Along with an extensive community of practice, including other victims and human rights practitioners, they collected witnesses' and victims' statements and linkage material for a future criminal prosecution against Habré. This chapter also shows how Brody and Guengueng worked with various actors and institutions, including the Belgium government and Stephen Rapp, who was chief prosecutor of the Special Court for Sierra Leone and later US Ambassador for War Crimes.

3

De Facto International Prosecutors and a Verdict for Habré (Chad)

This chapter investigates how de facto international prosecutors, including those inspired by the indictment against Pinochet, played an essential role in extending the reaches of international criminal law to Hissène Habré, former president of Chad. Indeed, Habré was later referred to as the 'African Pinochet'.[1] Both local and international private non-State actors drew upon the lessons learned from the 'Pinochet precedent',[2] as well as the Nuremberg Tribunal, and implicitly attempted to adapt and innovate practical tasks and processes ordinarily associated with offices of international prosecutors. As in the previous chapter, witnesses and victims of cores crimes played an essential role as de facto international prosecutors. This chapter begins with Souleymane Guengueng, a victim and witness to core crimes perpetrated under Habré's dictatorship. It explores how and why Guengueng, and other victims of Habré's violent repression were instrumental in initiating an investigation into Habré. Unlike Juan Garcés, Souleymane Guengueng never studied law or politics. In the 1980s, when Habré was president of Chad, Guengueng was an accountant and was neither political nor a practitioner in the field of human rights or criminal law. That all changed when Guengueng was arbitrarily arrested, tortured and illegally detained for several years, despite arguing his innocence. Over the years, Guengueng saw his fellow inmates die in prison. If he should live, he promised before God that he would fight for justice and truth. Guengueng was convinced that if God

[1] Reed Brody, 'The Prosecution of Hissène Habré – An "African Pinochet"', *New England Law Review* 35, no. 2 (2001): 321–36.
[2] Human Rights Watch (HRW), 'The Pinochet Precedent: How Victims Can Pursue Human Rights Criminals Abroad', March 2000, www.hrw.org/legacy/campaigns/chile98/precedent.htm; Reed Brody, 'Bringing a Dictator to Justice: The Case of Hissène Habré', *Journal of International Criminal Justice* 13, no. 2 (1 May 2015): 209–17, https://doi.org/10.1093/jicj/mqv005.

preserved his life, he would seek justice for those who died and disappeared and, above all, so that Chad would never know such injustice ever again. Finally, when Habré was overthrown and fled to Senegal in 1990, Guengueng was released. With little recourse or opportunity for redress within Chad's domestic legal system, Guengueng began to adopt the tasks of a criminal investigator.

To do this, he initially developed a local cooperative criminal accountability community within Chad, which worked towards identifying and collecting material that could be developed as evidence. Initially, Guengueng focused on the crimes he had seen with his own eyes, which included systematic arbitrary detention, torture and murder. He started by finding other victims of the Habré government and by founding the Association of Victims of Political Repression and Crime (*Association des victimes des crimes et de répression politique de Chad*, AVCRP).[3] One of the first practices Guengueng adopted was to record witnesses' and victims' statements in meticulous detail.[4] Of equal importance was the role of other local private non-State actors, particularly female lawyers who rose up to address human rights and criminal accountability for former members of the Habré government. Jacqueline Moudenia, later president of the Chadian Association for the Promotion and Defence of Human Rights (APTDH), and Delphine Djiraibe, co-founder of APTDH. Both were part of the 'first wave' of female lawyers in Chad, and both played vital roles in contributing knowledge and expertise to the case. Djiraibe played an essential role in initially approaching Human Rights Watch (HRW), and arranged for it to meet with Guengueng. Djiraibe also helped Guengueng and others file the initial complaint in the Senegal courts against Habré, amongst other local and international private non-State actors. Over time, the AVCRP and APTDH decided to coordinate their efforts, which broadened to include international NGOs.[5]

A critical shift occurred when Guengueng handed copies of his material to an international group of private non-State actors, which served to bridge the relationship between local and international practitioners. Reed Brody, a lawyer from HRW, was looking for another 'Pinochet' after working with lawyers in London on the Pinochet extradition case. Brody considered Hissène Habré as a possible post-Pinochet candidate. Upon receiving copies

---

[3]   Celeste Hicks, *The Trial of Hissène Habré: How the People of Chad Brought a Tyrant to Justice* (London: Zed Books Ltd., 2018), 55; 'Victim to Victor: The Story of Souleymane Guengueng', Office of the High Commissioner for Human Rights OHCHR, 19 January 2017, www .ohchr.org/EN/NewsEvents/Pages/VictimToVictor.aspx.

[4]   Hicks, *The Trial of Hissène Habré*.

[5]   Hicks, *The Trial of Hissène Habré*.

of Guengueng's files, Brody believed he had some essential facts that could serve as the basis for a criminal case. It was also members of HRW who identified and located the requisite linkage material that would later form evidence linking Habré to the underlying crimes in the Extraordinary African Chamber held in Senegal. Like those engaged in the criminal accountability of Pinochet, de facto international prosecutors who pursued those most responsible in the Habré dictatorship for core crimes were also influenced by the Nuremberg Trials. Indeed, the prosecution of Habré at the Extraordinary African Chambers was later described as 'Chad's Nuremberg'.[6] Together, this broader cooperative criminal accountability community influenced the strategy and ensured Habré was held to account for torture, an accepted and recognised *jus cogens* of international law in Senegal, amongst other crimes.

This chapter is structured as follows. First it explores the role of Souleymane Guengueng as a victim and witness to large-scale crimes in Chad in the criminal accountability process. Although *not* trained in criminal or civil law, he nonetheless commenced an investigation into Habré when local options for criminal accountability remained limited or non-existent. It explores how Guengueng formed and engaged initially with a local cooperative criminal accountability community. At the beginning, he worked with fellow former prisoners and torture survivors, as well as the orphans and the widows of the dead and missing persons. Together, Guengueng and his organisation collaborated with other local human rights groups.

Second, the chapter investigates how this local criminal accountability community widened to include an international community of practitioners, which also drew on knowledge and lessons learned from the Pinochet case. It illuminates how this criminal accountability community evolved and submitted private criminal complaints to foreign courts exercising universal jurisdiction in both Senegal and Belgium, which later led to the establishment of the Extraordinary African Chambers (EAC). Described as an 'unprecedented trial in Africa' by one investigative judge of the EAC,[7] Habré was the first African former head of State, prosecuted in the foreign court of another African State exercising universal jurisdiction. Third, it explores how Guengueng and others in the broader cooperative criminal accountability community engaged

---

[6] Nako Madjiasra and Emma Farge, 'Chad Tries Habre-Era Security Agents', IOL, 15 November 2014, www.iol.co.za/news/africa/chad-tries-habre-era-security-agents-1780743.

[7] Judge Jean Kandé, 'Investigations in Senegal and Chad: Cooperation and Challenges', in *The President on Trial: Prosecuting Hissène Habré*, ed. Sharon Weill, Kim Thuy Seelinger and Kerstin Bree Carlson (Oxford: Oxford University Press, 2020), 89.

with State and interstate government actors, in a number of jurisdictions, in an effort to pursue criminal accountability for Habré.

GUENGUENG AS VICTIM AND WITNESS

From the very beginning, Souleymane Guengueng was careful to avoid politics in Chad. Although, during the 1980s, this offered little guarantee of avoiding the violent effects of Chad's secret police, the Directorate of Documentation and Security (*Direction de la Documentation et de la Sécurité*, DDS). In 1982, Hissène Habré led a coup against Goukouni Oueddei, then Chad's president. For more than eight years, Habré was known for his brutal suppression of actual and alleged opposition, including conducting campaigns of torture and murder, as well as targeting particular ethnic groups. Under the Habré government, arbitrary detention was not considered unusual in Chad. Indeed, the DDS was renowned for rounding up political opposition and anti-Habré forces with a wide net, which often included those not involved in either.[8] To add to this, options for legal redress were limited.[9] Some argued that they were completely absent.[10] Throughout the 1980s, diplomats residing in Chad sent reports to their governments detailing eye-witness accounts of bodies on the road side, rumours of disappearances, torture and extra-judicial killings.[11] Despite this, Habré was backed by the US and French governments and viewed as an important counter-force to Muammar Gadhafi, then leader of neighbouring Libya. One of Habré's most powerful allies was Ronald Reagan, then US president.[12]

---

[8] Commissions of Inquiry (Chad), 'Chad: Report of the Commission of Inquiry into the Crimes and Misappropriations Committed by Ex-President Habré, His Accomplices and/or Accessories – Investigation of Crimes Against the Physical and Mental Integrity of Persons and Their Possessions' (N'DJamena, 7 May 1992), www.usip.org/sites/default/files/file/resour ces/collections/commissions/Chad-Report.pdf.

[9] Commissions of Inquiry (Chad).

[10] Hicks, *The Trial of Hissène Habré*, 54.

[11] Hicks, *The Trial of Hissène Habré*.

[12] United States, Executive Office of the President, 'U.S. Interests and Policy in Chad [Attached to Cover Memorandum] Secret, National Security Decision Directive. DNSA Collection: Presidential Directives, Part II. Signator: Reagan, Ronald W. PR01643. NSDD 322', 14 December 1988; Commissions of Inquiry (Chad), 'Chad: Report of the Commission of Inquiry into the Crimes and Misappropriations Committed by Ex-President Habré, His Accomplices and/or Accessories – Investigation of Crimes Against the Physical and Mental Integrity of Persons and Their Possessions'; Reed Brody, 'Enabling a Dictator', Human Rights Watch, 28 June 2016, www.hrw.org/report/2016/06/28/enabling-dictator/united-states-and-chads-Hissène-Habré-1982–1990.

During this period, Guengueng worked as an accountant and official in the Lake Chad Basin Commission in N'Djamena. On 3 August 1988,[13] Guengueng's wife arrived at his office crying, stating that the DDS had arrived at his home to question him. Before Guengueng had the chance to leave his office, he was arrested. They detained him at the DDS offices for questioning and accused him of sheltering an anti-Habré group in Cameroon when the Lake Chad Basin Commission had been located there temporarily – an accusation he denied. Despite this, Guengueng remained imprisoned until December 1990.[14]

While in detention, Guengueng was a witness and victim to what he considered to be the crimes of the Habré government. He was, at times, subjected to solitary confinement, at others, overcrowded incarceration. While in detention, it was not unusual for a number of detainees to share a cell designed for one person,[15] which sometimes held up to ten other men.[16] While imprisoned for more than two years, Guengueng suffered a number of medical conditions, including dengue fever, hepatitis and malaria.[17] On occasion he was left in cells that were completely dark or in cells with intense lighting. His sight was significantly impaired for being incarcerated in these conditions for protracted periods of time. Guards managed the prisoners in different ways. Some allowed detainees to wash; others would not allow them to wash for weeks. Sometimes guards would serve detainees rotten rice or poured water from a plastic pipe into the cells forcing detainees to lick the water from the floor.[18] As Guengueng recalled latter, the 'drops of water that fell, the prisoners had to lick themselves like dogs or lick the water from the floor. ... They even tried to stop us from praying to our God. When we prayed, Christians or Muslims, they thought we were asking God to kill Hissène Habré.'[19] Guengueng also maintained that while incarcerated, prison guards perpetrated acts of torture against detainees systematically, as well as sexual assault against women detainees. He was routinely beaten and starved; when he was caught leading others in

---

[13] Norimitsu Onishi, 'He Bore Up Under Torture. Now He Bears Witness', *New York Times*, 31 March 2001, www.nytimes.com/2001/03/31/world/he-bore-up-under-torture-now-he-bears-witness.html.

[14] Souleymane Guengueng, 'Documenting Crimes and Organizing Victims in Chad', in *The President on Trial: Prosecuting Hissène Habré*, 31–38.

[15] Hicks, *The Trial of Hissène Habré*, 54.

[16] Onishi, 'He Bore Up Under Torture. Now He Bears Witness'.

[17] Hicks, *The Trial of Hissène Habré*, 54.

[18] Onishi, 'He Bore Up Under Torture. Now He Bears Witness'; Guengueng, Communication with author.

[19] Guengueng quoted in Onishi, 'He Bore Up Under Torture. Now He Bears Witness'.

prayer, the guards kicked his testicles.[20] Moreover, Guengueng was witness to the death of numerous prisoners while incarcerated. One of the rules enforced by some guards was that corpses would only be removed from a cell when ten had died in that cell.[21]

Over time, Guengueng was certain he would die in detention. But he pledged to himself that should he ever survive, he would make sure the world knew the truth about the prisons under the Habré government.[22] Indeed, he vowed he would never stop until he achieved justice and accountability for those responsible.[23] Much later, Guengueng explained what sparked a sense of personal obligation to achieve justice: 'I survived two years of near-starvation, beatings and dengue fever, but dozens of cell-mates died in my arms. From the depths of that madness, I took an oath that if I ever got out, I would fight for justice.'[24] Finally, Idriss Déby, a former ally, overthrew Habré and Habré fled west to Senegal. With that, Guengueng was released in December 1990.

IN SEARCH OF LOCAL ACCOUNTABILITY

In response to pressure, Chad's new government initially appeared committed to local options for justice and accountability. In 1990, with Idriss Déby in power, a Truth Commission was established headed by Chad's Chief Prosecutor Mahamat Hassan Abakar,[25] titled 'The Commission of Inquiry into the Crimes and Misappropriations Committed by Ex-President Habré, His Accomplices and/or Accessories' (*Commission d'Enquête du Ministère Chadien de la Justice sur les Crimes du Régime de Hissène Habré*).[26] Initially, no witnesses or victims came forward. Decades of tyranny which had extended before Habré's dictatorship had instilled fear into Chadian society, including witnesses and victims. Nevertheless, after attending a meeting, one of the first to sign up as a witness and victim was Guengueng. As Guengueng later recalled: 'Mr Abakar informed me' that the commission 'had not been able

---

20   Hicks, *The Trial of Hissène Habré*, 54.
21   Hicks, *The Trial of Hissène Habré*, 54.
22   'Victim to Victor: The Story of Souleymane Guengueng'.
23   'Victim to Victor: The Story of Souleymane Guengueng'.
24   Souleymane Guengueng, 'Send Habré to Belgium for Trial,' *New York Times*, 16 January 2006, www.nytimes.com/2006/01/16/opinion/send-habr-to-belgium-for-trial.html.
25   Mahamat Hassan Abakar, 'The Making of Chad's Truth Commission', in *The President on Trial*, 24–30.
26   The President of the Council of State, Chief of State, 'Chad: Decree Creating the Commission of Inquiry into the Crimes and Misappropriations Committed by Ex-President Habré, His Accomplices and/or Accessories, Decree No. 014/P.CE/CJ/90' (1990), www.usip.org/sites/default/files/file/resources/collections/commissions/Chad-Charter.pdf.

to begin its work because the victims refused to sign up on the commission's register, which would allow them to be heard. So, I was the very first to sign up, under number 00001'.[27] According to Guengueng, 'This broke the fear and allowed other colleagues – all of them former DDS prisoners – to register as well'.[28]

The Truth Commission's report condemned Habré's brutal crackdown on actual and alleged opposition. In 1992, the Truth Commission published its findings,[29] which included *inter alia* that the Habré government was responsible for killing approximately 40,000 people and conducting widespread, systematic torture. The report also highlighted the role foreign governments had played in funding and training those responsible for orchestrating the alleged crimes. Notably, two key recommendations of the report were as follows: first, that Chad fast-track the establishment of an independent judiciary and institute widespread reforms of the security forces, and second, the acts of those most responsible for the allegations of genocide and crimes against humanity, including torture, should be investigated and prosecuted.[30] While the report spoke to the difficulty of establishing the truth about every aspect of Habré's violent regime, it also stressed the importance of holding to account not only those who perpetrated the crimes alongside Habré but also those who benefitted from his time in power. In conclusion, the Truth Commission offered an unflinching assessment of Habré's presidency:

> The record of Habré's 8-year reign is terrifying. The Commission still wonders how a citizen, a child of the country, could have committed so much evil, so much cruelty, against his own people. The stereotype of the hard-core revolutionary idealist quickly gave way to that of a shabby and sanguinary tyrant. .... In seeking power and taking it, Habré was satisfying a personal and selfish ambition. Today, after his fall, only his tribe, which he elevated above all others, misses him. And a handful of cynical profiteers who encouraged and applauded him while he shed the blood of innocents for no reason.[31]

Despite stark findings and instructive recommendations, very little of the report was implemented. Indeed, in 1995 an HRW report maintained that

[27] Guengueng, 'Documenting Crimes and Organizing Victims in Chad', 33.
[28] Guengueng, 'Documenting Crimes and Organizing Victims in Chad'.
[29] Commissions of Inquiry (Chad), 'Chad: Report of the Commission of Inquiry into the Crimes and Misappropriations Committed by Ex-President Habre'.
[30] Commissions of Inquiry (Chad), 'Chad: Report of the Commission of Inquiry into the Crimes and Misappropriations Committed by Ex-President Habre', 93.
[31] Commissions of Inquiry (Chad), 'Chad: Report of the Commission of Inquiry into the Crimes and Misappropriations Committed by Ex-President Habre', 92.

very little of the report's key recommendations had been accomplished.[32] There were several reasons for this. Déby, now president of Chad, had been an ally of Habré. Many of those at the top of the Chadian government and military under Habré still held key or powerful positions in Chadian society. As the HRW report concluded, almost forty-one DDS officials', ranging from the mid to senior levels, still maintained important official roles in government or the security services, persisted under the new Chadian government.[33] Irrespective of the reason, the fact remained that many in the Chadian leadership were reluctant to implement the findings of the Truth Commission.

FORMING A COOPERATIVE CRIMINAL ACCOUNTABILITY COMMUNITY

While Guengueng was one of the first witnesses to be interviewed by the Truth Commission, he remained unconvinced that the Truth Commissions findings would be implemented. A year after his release, he began to adopt the tasks of a criminal investigator. In 1991, Guengueng set up the Chadian Association of Victims of Political Repression and Crime (*Association des victimes des crimes et de répression politique de Chad*, AVCRP),[34] and he began to record statements in relation to those imprisoned by the DDS, including from witnesses, victims and family members. According to one journalist, Guengueng applied an 'accountant's meticulousness' to the process of recording these statements.[35] Guengueng would later remark, 'When the regime fell there was no justice, there was no reason for the arrests. The purpose of being in prison was to let you die, so it was a miracle to be released'.[36] To help him document the statements, Clement Abaifouta, also a former prisoner in the DDS prison system, joined Guengueng in the mandate for holding those most responsible of core crimes through criminal prosecution. For Abaifouta, the motivations also included understanding the truth about *why* he had been detained. As Abaifouta would later explain: 'My motivation for carrying on this fight for justice . . . at the expense of everything in my personal life was just to

---

[32] Reed Brody, 'Chad: The Victims of Hissène Habré Still Awaiting Justice' *Human Rights Watch* 17, no. 10 (A) (July 2005). In particular, refer to the Annex I: List of Former DDS Directors and Agents Now in Leadership or Security Positions in Chad, 35.

[33] Brody, 'Chad: The Victims of Hissène Habré Still Awaiting Justice'. In particular, refer to the Annex I: List of Former DDS Directors and Agents Now in Leadership or Security Positions in Chad, 35.

[34] 'Victim to Victor: The Story of Souleymane Guengueng'.

[35] Onishi, 'He Bore Up Under Torture. Now He Bears Witness'.

[36] 'Victim to Victor: The Story of Souleymane Guengueng'.

answer that one question: why was I arrested?'[37] Electing Guengueng as president of the group, AVCRP formalised statutory texts and outlined six key objectives for the group. They were as follows:

1. Identify victims of political crimes and repression in Chad;
2. Identify property that has been looted or unfairly confiscated;
3. Initiate national and/or international legal proceedings against the perpetrators of these crimes and political repressions;
4. Demand compensation for victims who were physically or mentally harmed, or whose property had been unjustly expropriated;
5. Inform national and international opinion on the methods and means used to commit crimes and political repression; and
6. Prevent, denounce, and combat by all possible means all forms of political crimes and repression.[38]

Over several years, the AVCRP interviewed thousands of witnesses, victims and their families but narrowed the files to those that they could verify thoroughly. As Guengueng maintained, 'We interviewed more than a thousand people, but we had 712 very good files, with testimony and photos.'[39] Curiously, Guengueng found that those who had been victims were more willing to come forward than family members who still feared certain officials.[40] Guengueng divided the groups into two: direct victims and indirect victims; he noted, 'It was much easier to get the survivors of torture to share their stories but the families of those taken were afraid of the repercussions.'[41] This process would later inform a significant component of the crime base material that would contribute to Habré's indictment in Senegal fifteen years later.[42] Moreover, prosecutors could select particular witnesses and victims according to their experiences and submit crime-based evidence to the Extraordinary African Chambers. By 2000, Souleymane Guengueng's AVCRP group represented 792 people. With this material, Guengueng and AVCRP continued to engage a wider Chadian community of practitioners to explore options for accountability within Chad, including Delphine Djiraibe, one of the first female lawyers in Chad and co-founder of the Chadian Association for the Promotion and Defence of Human Rights

---

[37] Hicks, *The Trial of Hissène Habré*, 56.
[38] Guengueng, 'Documenting Crimes and Organizing Victims in Chad', 33.
[39] Onishi, 'He Bore Up Under Torture. Now He Bears Witness'.
[40] Guengueng, 'Documenting Crimes and Organizing Victims in Chad'; Guengueng, correspondence with author.
[41] Guengueng quoted in,'Victim to Victor: The Story of Souleymane Guengueng'.
[42] Hicks, *The Trial of Hissène Habré*, 55.

(APTDH). In 2000, Djiraibe began to advise witnesses and victims of the Chadian DDS, including assisting in the filing of the initial compliant against Habré in 2000 in the Senegal courts, and in the Belgium courts not long after.

While AVCRP had formally established a victims' group consisting of private non-State actors to pursue accountability, Guengueng had no clear plan for how the statements could be used, particularly as options for accountability remained limited within Chad. Increasingly, Guengueng and Abaifouta, as well as those working with them, endured harassment and threats to their lives by former DDS officers, which included their offices being raided. Abaifouta was arrested five times.[43] To safeguard the files, Guengueng hid the handwritten witnesses' and victims' statements in his home over a number of years, desperate to protect all the investigative efforts they had achieved to date. Despite enormous domestic efforts by local private non-State actors to support the prosecution of Habré, and those most responsible, State legal officials showed very little enthusiasm to have Habré extradited from his new home in Senegal or towards pursuing criminal accountability for those who remained in senior positions in Chad. This proved a challenging time for Guengueng and those witnesses and victims who cared deeply about justice and accountability. As Guengueng would later explain: 'Although a Truth Commission estimated that Habré's regime had killed 40,000 Chadians, the new government kept most of our tormentors in office and never sought Habré's extradition from Senegal, where he was exiled.'[44] In fact, for another twenty years, local and State legal officials within Chad were averse to criminal accountability for those most responsible for core crimes under the Habré government.

A critical shift occurred when Guengueng handed copies of his material to private non-State actors of an international organisation, HRW. After nine years of attempting accountability within Chad, the local cooperative criminal accountability community saw an opportunity to radically change its strategy.[45] This connection with HRW served to bridge local and international practitioners, and shifted steps towards criminal accountability to the international domain.

During the Pinochet case, the British House of Lords had granted leave for HRW to submit a brief for the Pinochet case, a task with which Reed Brody, a lawyer at HRW, had been involved.[46] Brody, as well as a number of other

43 Hicks, *The Trial of Hissène Habré*, 56.
44 Guengueng, 'Send Habré to Belgium for Trial'.
45 'Victim to Victor: The Story of Souleymane Guengueng'.
46 Human Rights Watch (HRW), 'The Pinochet Precedent'.

groups including the International Federation for Human Rights (*Fédération Internationale des Ligues des Droits de l'Homme*, FIDH) amongst others, was looking for a case like Pinochet's. Specifically, HRW had criteria for choosing its next 'Pinochet': 'a request from national NGOs; the availability of evidence; the absence of legal barriers such as immunity; the independence of the judiciary and respect for human rights in the forum country; and the likelihood of success'.[47] While Brody was at Harvard, a colleague suggested that he look into Hissène Habré as a possible post-Pinochet candidate. On Brody's behalf, two students from Harvard made the trip to Chad to investigate the case. Once in Chad, Djiraibe approached HRW and suggested it meet with Guengueng. As domestic efforts for accountability within Chad had remained futile, Guengueng agreed to hand over copies of all his files to HRW.[48] When Brody read Guengueng's files, he decided he had the beginnings of a case against Habré. Just as importantly, all the criteria appeared to be fulfilled. As Brody explained later: 'When the Chadian Association for the Promotion and Defence of Human Rights (ATPDH) asked Human Rights Watch to help Habré's victims bring him to justice in his Senegalese exile, all these criteria seemed to be fulfilled.'[49]

Unlike Guengueng, Brody's motivation for pursing a case against Habré was more abstract and more aligned with ideological and philosophical principles. More strikingly, Brody was inspired by the Pinochet case, and by Juan Garcés. As he later explained, 'My motivation was ideological. We wanted to create other Pinochets. It is hard to overestimate the impact of this case on the international human rights movement. It was like a moment of effervescence.'[50] As an evolving and broadening cooperative criminal accountability community, local Chadians began to work alongside international private non-State actors, such as HRW, which linked Chadian victims and witnesses to a larger international community of practitioners, resources and expertise. The importance of the cooperation between these individuals and groups cannot be overestimated. Local actors in Chad remained limited in pursuing a case through the local Chadian judiciary. The advantage of working with international practitioners shifted the case from one based on domestic law and the discretion of the local judiciary to one based on international law, and ultimately prosecution through foreign courts exercising universal jurisdiction. Increasingly, Chadians who had attempted

---

47 Human Rights Watch (HRW), 'The Pinochet Precedent'.
48 Hicks, *The Trial of Hissène Habré*, 58.
49 Brody quoted in Hicks, *The Trial of Hissène Habré*, 58.
50 Brody quoted in Hicks, *The Trial of Hissène Habré*, 58.

to fill the gap left by local police and prosecutors were evolving as de facto international prosecutors.

PROSECUTING HABRÉ IN FOREIGN COURTS

Several months after Brody received Guengueng's files, local and international private non-State actors cooperated to file a criminal complaint in the Dakar courts in Senegal. It seemed Habré had been left undisturbed by the Senegalese authorities, residing comfortably in a middle-class neighbourhood in Dakar. Like the Spanish civil law system whereby Garcés and others were permitted to file a complaint as private non-State actors in the Madrid courts, Senegal's legal system also permitted private non-State actors to file complaints in the Regional Court of Dakar.[51] On 25 January 2000, the complaint was filed as 'Souleymane GUENGUENG and others', which consisted of Guengueng and six others. The AVCRP and APTDH decided to coordinate their efforts.[52] The complaint was drafted with the expert assistance of Chadian lawyers, such as Delphine Djiraibe, as well as the expertise and the financial support of several international NGOs, such as HRW and FIDH. With this international support, Guengueng was able to travel to Dakar and play an active role in Habré's prosecution. Moreover, a broader coalition was formalised, titled the 'International Committee for the Fair Trial of Hissène Habré (the 'Coalition'), representing both local and international private non-State actors.

In addition, the complaint in Senegal also saw the expansion of the cooperative criminal accountability community to Senegal. It now included a number of lawyers from Senegal with knowledge of the local Senegalese criminal law system.[53] This included Boucounta Diallo,[54] representing Chadian victims. Similarly, local Senegalese lawyers assisted with filing the complaint against Habré. Just as importantly, it included State legal officials in Senegal, including Demba Kandji, the investigating judge who was assigned

---

[51] Jaqueline Moudeïna, 'From Victim to Witness and the Challenges of Sexual Violence Testimony', in *The President on Trial: Prosecuting Hissene Habre* (Oxford: Oxford University Press, 2020), 118–24.

[52] Public sitting held on Monday 6 April 2009, at 10 a.m., at the Peace Palace, President Owada presiding, in the case concerning Questions Relating to the Obligation to Prosecute or Extradite (*Belgium v. Senegal*), Verbatim record 2009/8, 10.

[53] Hicks, *The Trial of Hissène Habré*, 59.

[54] *Souleymane Guengueng et Autres C/Senegal, Communication Presentee au Comite Contre la Torture (Article 22 de la Convention), pour violation des Articles 5 et 7 de la Convention*, (submission to the Committee against Torture) (accessed 8 June 2020), www.hrw.org/legacy/french/themes/habre-cat.html

the complaint against Habré in the Dakar courts. In response to the complaint, Judge Kandji began investigating Habré and on 3 February 2000, to everyone's surprise, Habré was charged for *inter alia* complicity to torture[55] in violation of Articles 45, 46 and 294 *bis* and 288 of the Criminal Code of Senegal. Thereafter, Habré was placed under house arrest. It seemed that private non-State actors and state legal officials in a foreign court, acting together as de facto international prosecutors, had set the course for Habré's imminent prosecution.

In submitting the complaint to Dakar courts, de facto international pro-secutors drew on lessons learned from the Pinochet case.[56] Indeed, Habré was considered the 'African Pinochet'.[57] Similarly, they identified local and inter-national sources of law in filing the case, accusing Habré of crimes against humanity, in particular the *jus cogens* crime of torture. They argued that Senegal had ratified the Convention Against Torture (CAT) in 1987, and that as a State Party, Senegal was legally obligated to investigate and prosecute Habré.[58] As Guengueng later recalled:

> In 2000, inspired by the arrest in London of Chile's former dictator Augusto Pinochet, we flew from Chad to Senegal, with the help of Human Rights Watch, to file suit against Habré. Even we were surprised when a bold young Senegalese judge [Demba Kandji] listened to our testimony. After 10 years we were finally able to tell our horrifying story to a judge, and when he indicted Habré for crimes against humanity, all of Chad celebrated with me.[59]

While initially hopeful that justice would prevail in Dakar courts, Senegalese political elites were demonstratively less impressed. During this time, the Senegalese State was actively engaged in developing the Rome Statute which established the International Criminal Court (ICC) and, as stated earlier, was an early signatory to the CAT in 1985. They appeared, at least in principle, to champion the notion of international criminal justice for core international crimes. On 18 February, Habré's lawyers appealed the charges, filing an appeal before the Dakar Court of Appeal (*Cour d'appel de Dakar*) on the ground that Senegalese courts lacked jurisdiction over the crimes. On 4 July 2000, countering Kanji's indictment and efforts to investigate, the Dakar

---

55 Hissène Habré case, Dakar Court of Appeal, Judgement, 4 July 2000, Cour d'appel de Dakar, (ch. acc.), Hissène Habré, Arrêt No 135, 4 Juillet 2000.
56 Hicks, *The Trial of Hissène Habré*, 59.
57 Mia Swart, 'The African Pinochet? Universal Jurisdiction and the Habré Case', in *The President on Trial*, 406–14.
58 Hicks, *The Trial of Hissène Habré*, 59.
59 Guengueng, 'Send Habré to Belgium for Trial'.

Court of Appeal (*Cour d'appel de Dakar*) rejected charges against Habré on the basis that the crimes had not occurred in Senegal and, in accordance with domestic law, held Dakar courts did not enjoy jurisdictional reach over the crimes:

> The Senegalese courts can not take cognizance of acts of torture committed by a foreigner outside the Senegalese territory irrespective [of] the nationality of the victims. The wording of Article 669 of the Criminal Procedure Code excludes the jurisdiction of the Senegalese Courts. … [T]hat by indicting Hissène Habré of complicity in crimes against humanity and acts of torture and barbarity, the investigating judge manifestly violated the rules of material and territorial jurisdiction.[60]

Abdoulaye Wade, then president of Senegal, had Judge Kandji, the investigating judge, transferred soon after. Some accused Wade of stymieing Senegal's international legal obligation and the judiciary.[61] In response, private non-State actors attempted to raise the matter with the highest court in Senegal, the Court of Cassation (*Cour de cassation*). Nevertheless, the Court of Cassation upheld the decision of the Appeals Court and barred any further prosecution against Habré. The Court held that it

> Dismisses the appeal founded by Souleymane GUENGUENG and others against the judgment rendered on July 4, 2000 by the Dakar Indictment Chamber. … That no procedural text recognizes universal jurisdiction in the Senegalese courts with a view to prosecuting and judging, if they are found on the territory of the Republic, the alleged perpetrators or accomplices of acts [of torture] … when these acts were committed outside Senegal by foreigners; that the presence in Senegal of Hissène Habré cannot in itself justify the proceedings brought against him.[62]

It seemed a significant blow for de facto international prosecutors. Yet, despite this initial failure, these efforts would later inform, in large part, important arguments outlined in Belgium's application submitted to the International Court of Justice (ICJ) to show that despite efforts by private non-State actors (and Kandji, the Senegalese investigating judge) to hold Habré to account in Senegalese jurisdiction, Senegal's unwillingness to recognise its obligations under the CAT had represented a broader political unwillingness of the

---

[60] Hissène Habré case, Dakar Court of Appeal, Judgement, 4 July 2000, Cour d'appel de Dakar, (ch. acc.), Hissène Habré, Arrêt No 135, 4 Juillet 2000.

[61] Hicks, *The Trial of Hissène Habré*.

[62] *Cour de Cassation, Première chambre statuant en matière pénale. Aff. Habré, Arrêt n° 14 du 20.03.2001.*

Senegalese State to oblige its courts to practice universal jurisdiction, particularly with respect to the crime of torture,[63] a point that the ICJ recognised. Indeed, it later held that Senegal had failed in its obligation to prosecute Habré since the application of 'Souleymane GUENGUENG and others' in 2000 as obligated under the CAT.[64]

Meanwhile, the cooperative criminal accountability community had also made another attempt to file a compliant in Chad. Inspired by the complaint in Senegal, and upon meeting with Déby, then president of Chad, local private non-State actors filed a complaint in the Chad courts. Indeed, Déby had initially showed support for criminal accountability for Habré and others. Like Garcés, their complaint followed the Nuremberg model, which attempted to identify a small number of people *most* responsible, including Habré, to account. In October 2000, a complaint was filed against Habré's senior leaders, including the DDS, in Chadian courts. Jacqueline Moudenia, another important Chadian lawyer, cooperated with the community of practice a few months after they filed the complaint in the Senegalese courts. Moudenia was later president of APTDH. In 2001, she survived an assassination attempt by a former Habré aide, who was later indicted in Chad.[65] She would also represent victims as a lawyer acting as a civil party to the Extraordinary African Chambers, years later.[66]

Still, very little came of the complaint in Chadian courts. And it seemed that both Senegal and Chad were to remain unwilling to pursue criminal accountability for quite some time.

STUMBLING ON LINKAGE MATERIAL IN CHAD

Although criminal accountability seemed once again insurmountable, things took a remarkable shift. A few months after filing the complaint in Chadian courts, a group of international practitioners located a cache of critical documents that would contribute towards Habré's later indictment. On a trip to Chad in 2001, Reed Brody and colleague, Oliver Bercault, also a member of HRW, stumbled upon around 40,000 documents at the

---

[63] Public sitting held on Monday 6 April 2009, at 10 a.m., at the Peace Palace, President Owada presiding, in the case concerning Questions relating to the Obligation to Prosecute or Extradite (*Belgium* v. *Senegal*), Verbatim record 2009/8, 10.

[64] Questions relating to the Obligation to Prosecute or Extradite (*Belgium* v. *Senegal*), Judgment, ICJ Reports (2012).

[65] Brody, 'Bringing a Dictator to Justice'.

[66] Moudeïna, 'From Victim to Witness and the Challenges of Sexual Violence Testimony'; Alain Werner and Emmanuelle Marchand, 'Supporting Victims at Trial: Civil Parties' Perspective', in *The President on Trial*, 125–33.

abandoned former headquarters of the Chadian secret police, the DDS.[67] They had visited the former DDS building out of curiosity and were surprised to discover the floor was covered in a mass of papers. Later, Brody described what he saw that day as 'meticulously' detailed individual files on the treatment of hundreds of Chadian victims, which appeared to relate to alleged core international crimes. The papers included lists of former prisoners, identity cards, interrogation reports and death certificates.[68] Just as importantly, the material also explained Habré's relationship with the DDS[69] and therefore represented the necessary linkage material that could potentially link Habré with the underlying crimes including torture. In one memo, the DDS director maintained that 'thanks to the spider's web it has spun over the whole length of the national territory, keeps exceptional watch over the security of the State, as the 'eyes and ears of the President of the Republic whose control it is under and to whom it reports on its practices'.[70] Brody later explained that a team from Guengueng's group, the Chadian Association of Victims, Crimes and Political Repression in Chad (AVCRP), spent months organising the documents. By 2001, the team analysed the documents and identified more than 800 records verifying the communications between the DDS security force and Habré.[71] Much later, and just before Habré's indictment in the Extraordinary African Chambers in Senegal, Guengueng and Brody would send the files to the Human Rights Data Analysis Group at the Benetech Initiative, which provided the first statistical analysis of the crimes under Habré. According to its analysis, the documents mentioned 12,321 victims of abuse, which detailed 1,208 of them dying in detention. They also identified 1,265 communications from the DDS sent to Habré directly, and in particular the status of 898 detainees.[72] As Brody stated later: 'Equally important for the legal case, Benetech's study of the document flow revealed that there was a direct superior-subordinate relationship between Habré and his secret police. In short, there's no plausible deniability. Habré knew exactly what was going on.'[73] This meant that in addition to Guengueng's witness statements, these DDS documents, as well as later insider witness statements, would form the backbone of evidence

---

[67] Olivier Bercault, 'The "Archives of Terror"', in *The President on Trial*, 17–23.

[68] Reed Brody, 'Inside a Dictator's Secret Police', *Foreign Policy* (blog), 9 March 2010, https://foreignpolicy.com/2010/03/09/inside-a-dictators-secret-police/; Bercault, 'The "Archives of Terror"'; Kandé, 'Investigations in Senegal and Chad: Cooperation and Challenges'.

[69] Hicks, *The Trial of Hissène Habré*, 61.

[70] Brody, 'Inside a Dictator's Secret Police'.

[71] 'Victim to Victor: The Story of Souleymane Guengueng'.

[72] Brody, 'Inside a Dictator's Secret Police'.

[73] Brody, 'Inside a Dictator's Secret Police'.

(linkage material) linking Habré to the alleged crimes in his later prosecution. Together, the linkage material collected and Guengueng's witnesses' and victims' records provided powerful evidence for the role Habré and the DDS played in perpetrating crimes against humanity, including torture.

ACCOUNTABILITY THROUGH BELGIUM COURTS

With Senegal and Chad both unwilling to pursue criminal accountability, de facto international prosecutors began to consider other foreign courts. While the ICC was formally established in 2003, it was not a viable option for Habré. No doubt, Guengueng and Abaifouta were both clearly inspired by the ICC. In fact, according to one observer, both have named their much-loved dogs 'CPI' (*Cour Pénale Internationale* – International Criminal Court).[74] Although Chad had deposited its instrument of ratification to the Rome Statute on 1 November 2006, and the statute entered into force on 1 January 2007, the nature of the Rome Statute did not permit jurisdiction over crimes perpetrated under Habré's leadership in the 1980s. Moreover, the likelihood of a hybrid or international criminal tribunal being established with or by the UNSC was remote. There remained very few options for accountability left available to private non-State actors – with the exception of finding another foreign court willing and able to investigate.

Inspired by the complaint filed in Senegal, Chadian victims who had moved to Europe began to look there. Following Habré's appeals in the Senegalese courts, three victims of the Habré regime, some of whom were now citizens of Belgium, filed a complaint against Habré in the Belgium courts, with the help of the International Committee for the Fair Trial of Hissène Habré (the Coalition). This triggered an investigation by the Belgium authorities in November 2000, led by Daniel Fransen, an investigating judge.[75] By 2002, the judiciary in Belgium was ready to conduct its investigations in Chad. At the invitation of the Chadian government, Fransen, along with a Belgium federal prosecutor, four Belgian investigating officers (*officiers de police judiciaire*) and a clerk arrived in Chad.[76] Once in N'Djamena, they recorded witness statements with victims, as well as those who worked inside the DDS. They also inspected the former DDS facilities and archives, and

---

[74] Hicks, *The Trial of Hissène Habré*.
[75] Daniel Fransen, 'The Belgian Investigation of the Habré Regime', in *The President on Trial*, 54–59. This chapter is an excerpt of the testimony by Judge Fransen, answering questions by Habré's court-appointed lawyer, Mounir Ballal in Dakar, Senegal, at EAC Trial Chambers, 17 September 2015 – Minute 13:47'–51.
[76] Fransen, 'The Belgian Investigation of the Habré Regime', 55.

a number of sites suspected of being mass graves.[77] Fransen maintained that '[a]ll investigative acts were carried out by the Chadian investigative judge or Chadian investigating officers, with the presence and assistance of the Belgian staff.[78]

Guengueng and other victims had the opportunity to meet with Belgium's State legal officials, including the investigating judge. Indeed, local and international private non-State actors had the opportunity to explain to the investigating judge the nature of their investigation and what they had done so far.[79] Belgium's state legal officials also had the chance to make copies of the witnesses' and victims' records that Guengueng had collected, as well as the documents that Reed Brody and Human Rights Watch had discovered in the former DDS facility, which were submitted by the civil parties.[80] As Guengueng later recalled, that Belgium legal officials had arrived in Chad was nothing short of groundbreaking:

> When the judge arrived with a police team, it was as if justice itself had finally reached Chad. Victims lined up at the courthouse to tell their stories. I took the judge into the jail where I was imprisoned. The judge's team photocopied thousands of files kept by Habré's police, uncovered by Human Rights Watch, which detailed how Habré organized the repression of political opponents and listed 1,208 prisoners who died in detention.[81]

Despite the hope placed in Belgium's investigation, the path to accountability still remained long and arduous. At the same time the complaint was submitted to Belgium courts, some Chadian victims, including Guengueng, also submitted a communication to the UN Committee Against Torture.[82] In their communication to the UN, titled 'Suleymane Guengueng and others c/Senegal', they alleged that Senegal had violated Article 5, paragraph 2 and Article 7 of the CAT.[83] While their submission to the UN Committee Against Torture did not seem important immediately, it was critical when a year later, Wade, then president of Senegal,

---

77 Fransen, 'The Belgian Investigation of the Habré Regime'.
78 Fransen, 'The Belgian Investigation of the Habré Regime', 55.
79 Fransen, 'The Belgian Investigation of the Habré Regime', 58.
80 Fransen, 'The Belgian Investigation of the Habré Regime', 59.
81 Guengueng, 'Send Habré to Belgium for Trial'.
82 *Souleymane Guengueng et Autres C/Sénégal, Communication Présentée au Comite Contre la Torture (Article 22 de la Convention), pour violation des Articles 5 et 7 de la Convention*, available online at United Nations Committee Against Torture, 'Decisions of the Committee Against Torture under Article 22 of the Convention against Torture and Other Cruel, Inhuman or Degrading Treatment or Punishment, Communication No. 181/2001, CAT/C/36/D/181/2001', 19 May 2006, http://tbinternet.ohchr.org/_layouts/treatybodyexternal/Downlo ad.aspx?symbolno=CAT%2fC%2f36%2fD%2f181%2f2001&Lang=en.
83 *Suleymane Guengueng v. Senegal, Comm. 181/2001, U.N. Doc. A/61/44, at 160 (CAT 2006); Suleymane Guengueng and Autres c/Senegal Communication Presentee Au Contre la Torture (Article 22 de la Convention), pour violation des Article 5 et 7 de la Convention*, 18 April 2001.

demanded that Habré leave Senegal in a month, raising concerns from the criminal accountability community that Habré could flee to another African state, and one that would make extradition even more difficult for the Belgium judiciary. In April 2001, the UN Committee Against Torture wrote to Brody to confirm that it had issued an initial statement to Senegal requesting it 'take all necessary measures to prevent Mr. Hissène Habré from leaving the territory of Senegal except pursuant to an extradition demand'.[84] This was later followed by a plea by Kofi Annan, then UN secretary-general, to Senegal to observe the UN Committee Against Torture's request. Wade complied with the request. Finally, in May 2006 when the UN Committee Against Torture issued its statement in response to the 'Suleymane Guengueng and others c/Senegal' communication, it decided that Senegal was in violation of the Convention Against Torture because it had failed to introduce the requisite changes to its penal code that would allow its judiciary to have jurisdiction over suspected crimes of torture in Chad, thus making it possible to prosecute Habré. In reference to Article 7, the UN Committee Against Torture called upon Senegal to 'submit the present case to its competent authorities for the purpose of prosecution or to extradite them' and highlighted Senegal's duty to 'adopt the necessary measures, including legislative measures, to establish its jurisdiction' over alleged crimes perpetrated by Habré in Chad, in reference to Article 5 of the UN Convention Against Torture.[85]

At the same time, the cooperative criminal accountability community continued to engage Chad's political elite to pursue accountability crimes committed during the Habré era. Not wanting to leave anything to chance, they lobbied Chad to renounce Habré's immunity. In 2001/2002, the *Arrest Warrant* case[86] was raised by Congo against Belgium in the ICJ, which held that incumbent heads of State or ministers of foreign affairs held immunity for grave breaches of the Geneva Conventions and crimes against humanity, while acting in an official capacity.[87] At this time, this decision was criticised

---

[84] Letter from Chief of Support Services Branch, Office of the High Commissioner for Human Rights, to Reed Brody, HRW, 27 April 2001, available online at www.hrw.org/news/2015/02/17/legal-documents/documents-juridiques.

[85] United Nations Committee Against Torture, 'Decisions of the Committee Against Torture under Article 22 of the Convention against Torture and Other Cruel, Inhuman or Degrading Treatment or Punishment, Communication No. 181/2001, CAT/C/36/D/181/2001', 19 May 2006, http://tbinternet.ohchr.org/_layouts/treatybodyexternal/Download.aspx?symbol no=CAT%2fC%2f36%2fD%2f181%2f2001&Lang=en.

[86] Arrest Warrant of 11 April 2000 (*Democratic Republic of the Congo v. Belgium*), Judgment, ICJ Reports. (2002).

[87] Steffen Wirth, 'Immunity for Core Crimes? The ICJ's Judgment in the Congo v. Belgium Case', *European Journal of International Law* 13, no. 4 (1 September 2002): 877–93, https://doi.org/10.1093/ejil/13.4.877.

by some for not reflecting customary international law (see Chapter 1) and, in particular, the judgment in the Pinochet case. As Steffen Wirth argued:

> It seems that this statement (for which the Court gives no reasons) does not properly reflect the current state of customary international law. Rather, modern state practice and opinion juris deny immunities for core crimes to all former and incumbent state officials with the sole exception of the highest state representatives such as Heads of State or Ministers for Foreign Affairs; and even these persons are protected only while in office (as has been demonstrated in the Pinochet case).[88]

While the case was raised by Congo against Belgium in the ICJ, it triggered private non-State actors in Chad to appeal to the Déby government to officially renounce Habré's immunity, which the Déby government eventually did.

Another challenge presented itself when the US administration pressured Belgium to limit its universal jurisdiction. In 2003, the Bush administration warned Belgium to reverse its wide-ranging exercise of universal jurisdiction or face a boycott of NATO's headquarters in Brussels. Donald Rumsfeld, then US defence secretary, maintained that Belgium's current laws made it difficult for US officials to travel to Belgium, in light of the Bush administration's decision to intervene in Iraq without a UNSC resolution. As Rumsfeld maintained: 'It would obviously not be easy for US officials ... to come to Belgium. It would not make much sense to build a new [NATO] headquarters if they can't come here for meetings.'[89] While France and Germany supported Belgium's laws and were against the US intervention in Iraq, continued US political pressure saw Belgium repeal the more wide-reaching aspects of its universal jurisdiction. Would this impact the investigation into Habré's alleged crimes perpetrated in the 1980s? To ensure that the Belgium investigations would continue, the Coalition financially supported Chadian victims' travel to Belgium to argue their case with Belgium's political leaders, including key leaders from the major political parties and several ministers. Whether this made a difference is less clear. However, when the Belgian Parliament passed the bill to restrict universal jurisdiction, curiously it also introduced a 'grandfather' clause, which meant that several cases under investigation could continue. This included the case against Hissène Habré.[90]

---

[88] Wirth, 'Immunity for Core Crimes?'
[89] Rumsfeld quoted in, Ian Black and Ewen MacAskill, 'US Threatens NATO Boycott over Belgian War Crimes Law', *The Guardian*, 13 June 2003, www.theguardian.com/world/2003/jun/13/nato.warcrimes.
[90] Brody, 'Bringing a Dictator to Justice'.

After four long years of investigation, Belgium finally issued an extradition order against Habré. In September 2005, Judge Daniel Fransen commenced an indictment against Habré in the Belgium courts and issued an arrest warrant via INTERPOL to Senegal.

Nevertheless, Senegal still remained firmly wedged between two realities: while Senegal's leadership had appeared to intervene in its judiciary to protect Habré and continued to emphasis it did not have jurisdiction over Habré's crimes, it also showed aspirations to support an international human rights agenda, and indeed the mechanisms to support it, such as the International Criminal Court. Moreover, President Wade seemed to oscillate between statements that indicated his support for the prosecution of Habré, while harbouring constraints to Senegal's jurisdictional reach.

By this time, Guengueng was no longer based in Chad. While he and others had worked relentlessly for accountability for more than a decade in Chad, his work was not without costs. As concerns for his life increased and following a number of death threats, Guengueng moved with his family to the United States in 2004. There, he began working with the Bellevue/New York University Program for Survivors of Torture. The UN Voluntary Fund for Victims of Torture had funded the project, and this allowed Guengueng to receive important medical treatment for the effects on his eyes during Chadian detention. Working from the United States also allowed him to continue to pursue options for accountability in a safer environment.[91]

THE ROLE OF THE AFRICAN UNION

Under pressure from Belgium and perhaps keen to avoid criticism from his African neighbours, Wade remained reticent to cooperate with the Belgium courts. At the same time, he was unwilling to amend Senegalese laws to allow Dakar courts to exercise universal jurisdiction over Chadian crimes. Possibly for these reasons, he decided to refer Habré's case to the African Union (AU) – a step that deeply concerned the cooperative criminal accountability community. As Brody stated, this 'threatened to put the case in the hands of many rulers who themselves could be worried about human rights prosecutions'.[92] For many in the criminal accountability community, this continued to extend the political limbo, and many pleaded with those in the international community. For example, in January 2006, Guengueng wrote an article in the *New York Times*, insisting Habré should be prosecuted in a fair and

---

[91] 'Victim to Victor: The Story of Souleymane Guengueng'.
[92] Brody, 'Bringing a Dictator to Justice'.

independent court, and in Belgium if African states remained unwilling to do so. As Guengueng argued:

> But politics [has] intervened again.
>
> Habré's supporters [in Senegal] ... now argued that an African leader should not be sent for trial in Europe. Senegal's courts once again declined to act, and President Wade asked the African Union to recommend where Habré should be tried.
>
> I would also prefer to see Hissène Habré tried in Africa. But Senegal refused to prosecute him when it had the chance to do so, Chad could not guarantee him a fair trial, and no other African country has asked for his extradition ....
>
> Belgium is ready, willing and able to hear the case. That country has a regrettable colonial past, but it had nothing to do with Chad and it has an independent judiciary willing to give us – and Habré – a fair trial. After 15 years, surely Senegal and the African Union must allow us to have our day in court.[93]

International support for Habré's indictment grew, and it seemed the African Union was also reticent to decide. In an unexpected move, the African Union established a Committee of Eminent African Jurists to consider the options for accountability. Established in January 2006, the mandate of the Committee of Eminent African Jurists was to 'consider all aspects and implications of the Hissène Habré case as well as the options available for his trial'.[94]

In the meantime, international pressure continued to mount. On 17 March 2006, the European Union demanded that Senegal hand over Habré to be indicted in Belgium. Moreover, the UN Committee Against Torture finally issued its report in May 2006. As stated earlier, the report was in response to a communication submitted by Guengueng and other Chadian victims, but it appeared timely given the new role of the African Union in the Habré case. In short, the UN Committee Against Torture also emphasised in its decision of 17 May 2006 that Senegal was obligated to prosecute Habré:

> The State party cannot invoke the complexity of its judicial proceedings or other reasons stemming from domestic law to justify its failure to comply with these obligations under the Convention. [The committee] is of the opinion that the State party was obliged to prosecute Hissène Habré for alleged acts of

---

93 Guengueng, 'Send Habré to Belgium for Trial'.
94 Assembly of the African Union, 'Decision on the Hissène Habré Case and the African Union, Sixth Ordinary Session, Doc. Assembly/AU/Dec.103(VI)', 23 January 2006, www.au.int/en/si tes/default/files/ASSEMBLY_EN_23_24_JANUARY_2006_AUC_%20SIXTH%20_ORDINA RY_SESSION_DECISIONS_DECLARATIONS.pdf.

torture unless it could show that there was not sufficient evidence to prosecute, at least at the time when the complainants submitted their complaint in January 2000.[95]

To Wade's surprise, the establishment of the Committee of Eminent African Jurists had an unexpected outcome.[96] Several days after the UN Committee Against Torture issued its report, the Committee of Eminent African Jurists also issued a report. It outlined, amongst other things, its benchmark, which included the 'principle of total rejection of impunity', as well as the adherence to 'international fair trial standards including the independence of the judiciary and impartiality'.[97] In its conclusion, the report recommended that Senegal prosecute Habré. The report to the African Union also placed the Habré case in a broader historical light and firmly in the post-Nuremberg era. It recognised the jurisprudence of recent cases in international criminal law, including the case of Pinochet. More strikingly, it would go further than the later *Belgium* v. *Senegal* judgment by the ICJ:

> [12] The rejection of impunity was accepted in total by the Summit. The Committee sees no difficulty since this is a principle that has been recognised since World War II and is now upheld worldwide following the establishment of ICC. All need to understand that African States have to operate in a global environment and not in isolation. Africa must take account of recent developments in the international criminal law arena, such as the Pinochet, Taylor etc, cases have demonstrated. [13] The Committee considered that Hissène Habré cannot shield behind the immunity of a former Head of State to defeat the principle of total rejection of impunity that was adopted by the Assembly. [14] The Committee also considered that in view of the nature and gravity of the crimes alleged against him, Hissène Habré cannot benefit from any period of limitation (ie prescription).[98]

Furthermore, the African Union's response to the Committee's Report was equally extraordinary. In support of the recommendation, the African Union decided that Senegal should prosecute Habré 'on behalf of Africa'.[99]

---

95   United Nations Committee Against Torture, 'Decisions of the Committee Against Torture under Article 22 of the Convention against Torture and Other Cruel, Inhuman or Degrading Treatment or Punishment, Communication No. 181/2001, CAT/C/36/D/181/2001'.

96   Brody, 'Bringing a Dictator to Justice'.

97   African Union, 'Report of the Committee of Eminent African Jurists on the Case of Hissene Habre' (Addis Ababa, Ethiopia, 2006).

98   African Union, 'Report of the Committee of Eminent African Jurists on the Case of Hissene Habre', 3.

99   Assembly of the African Union, 'Decision on the Hissène Habré Case and the African Union, Sixth Ordinary Session, Doc. Assembly/AU/Dec.103(VI)', 5(ii).

Accepting the decision of the African Union, Wade initially amended some of Senegal's laws clearing the way for courts in Senegal to prosecute Habré, including amending Senegal's constitution. Nevertheless, despite these changes Senegal's progress remained a lacklustre affair. Wade posed an additional roadblock to Habré's trial. He claimed that the trial would be costly and would require external donors to pay US$36.5 million before the trial could begin. Over the duration of another three years, the broader cooperative criminal accountability community, including the Coalition, attempted to negotiate a budget for the trial with other States. Belgium continued to request the extradition of Habré and Wade continued to scrap Habré's chances of a prosecution in either Senegal or Belgium.

A ROADBLOCK TOO MANY?

By 2006, despite adopting a number of practices to hold Habré to account over a period of fifteen years, the cooperative criminal accountability community had, it seemed, reached its limit. What more could it do? Since Habré had lost power and gone into exile in Senegal in 1999, local private non-State actors had been the first to commence a criminal investigation. While the Chadian Truth Commission had conducted an investigation prior to Guengueng's involvement, it had not been mandated with a criminal investigation, although it had recommended one. Moreover, it had estimated that Habré was responsible for widespread torture, and for killing approximately 40,000 people. Guengueng and the local community had started their investigation by recording witnesses' and victims' statements in forensic detail, including for torture. Once local private non-State actors had linked up with international actors, they had written and submitted three private complaints to public prosecution courts in three countries: one included their home State, Chad. The other two were to foreign courts. At each time, both Belgium and Senegal were State Parties to the Convention Against Torture. The broader criminal accountability community had also recorded witnesses' and victims' statements and located the requisite linkage material in the form of DSS documents. They had made some progress on the task of preparing the material as evidence for a future criminal prosecution. This included conducting extensive analysis of the DSS material to show the link between Habré and the underlying crimes in relation to hundreds of victims, as well as the structure and organisation of senior suspects as a common plan or conspiracy.

Moreover, all this material was handed to Belgium legal officials investigating the case, including the investigating judge and prosecutor. The cooperative criminal accountability community had also sent a communication to the

UN Committee Against Torture in Habré's case. It had attempted to convince Belgium political leaders to allow the Habré investigation to continue in the Belgium public criminal courts, in the face of powerful US pressure to limit universal jurisdiction. Furthermore, it had also convinced Chadian leaders to formally strip Habré of immunity and had assisted in negotiating a budget for Senegal to prosecute Habré. More recently, it had begun to engage with Senegalese opposition leaders in an effort to convince them to prosecute Habré, should they come to power through democratic election. Despite all these efforts and practices, Habré had still not faced a day in a criminal court for crimes against humanity, including the *jus cogens* crime of torture. It seemed that de facto international prosecutors had taken the case as far as they could. Only one option appeared left: to convince the Belgium State to take the dispute with Senegal to the International Court of Justice.

BELGIUM AND SENEGAL AT THE ICJ

The next step was firmly in the hands of States. In 2009, Belgium submitted its ongoing extradition dispute with Senegal to the ICJ. Despite the earlier ICJ decision for *Arrest Warrant* raised by the Congo against Belgium, it appeared optimistic of its case. As stated earlier (Chapter 1), Belgium's application submitted to the ICJ showed that although Senegal was a State Party to the CAT, it remained unwilling to hold Habré to account, starting from the time the private complaint was submitted on behalf of Guengueng and the six other victims, as well as the Association of the Victims of Political Repression and Crime, in 2000. Since then, Belgium argued, Senegal had been outstanding on its legal obligations under the CAT. Belgium emphasised that the Senegalese judiciary had 'dismissed' the case on the grounds that 'crimes against humanity', including torture, did not form part of Senegal's system of criminal law, although one of the explicit conditions of the CAT was to amend domestic law to accommodate the crime of torture.[100] In addition to that, Belgium also argued that Chadians and Belgium nationals had filed a similar complaint in the Belgium courts. It explained in detail the attempts Belgium had made to request Habré's extradition, as Senegal continued unwilling to prosecute.[101] These facts and legal arguments contributed to ICJ accepting jurisdiction over the dispute.

---

[100] Public sitting held on Monday 6 April 2009, at 10 a.m., at the Peace Palace, President Owada presiding, in the case concerning Questions Relating to the Obligation to Prosecute or Extradite (*Belgium* v. *Senegal*), Verbatim record 2009/8, 10.

[101] Public sitting held on Monday 6 April 2009, at 10 a.m., at the Peace Palace, President Owada presiding, in the case concerning Questions Relating to the Obligation to Prosecute or Extradite (*Belgium* v. *Senegal*), Verbatim record 2009/8, 11.

While the ICJ considered the issue, to add to the complexity of the case, Habré filed a petition with the Court of Justice of the Economic Community of West African States (ECOWAS). Habré claimed that he could not be prosecuted on the principle of non-retroactivity of the law. On 18 November 2010, the Court of Justice of the ECOWAS ruled that Senegal was obliged to prosecute Habré through a 'special ad hoc procedure of an international character'.[102] Following this, in November 2010, Wade and the donor States settled on a budget for Habré's prosecution of US$11.4 million.[103] Yet, by January 2012, the Assembly of the Heads of State and Government of the African Union noted that Dakar courts had still not prosecuted Habré. It noted that Belgium had issued its fourth extradition request. In a striking act of African Unity solidarity, and perhaps in an attempt to rehabilitate the reputation of its judiciary in the eyes of the international community, Rwanda offered to arrange Habré's trial.[104] In the record of the eighteenth session of the African Union, Rwanda was ready to organise Habré's trial and had 'request[ed] the Commission [of the African Union] to continue consultations with partner countries and institutions and the Republic of Senegal[,] and subsequently with the Republic of Rwanda[,] with a view to ensuring the expeditious trial of Hissène Habré and to consider the practical modalities as well as the legal and financial implications of the trial'.[105] Since 2000, it seemed that President Wade was no closer to prosecuting Habré anytime soon.

Two events may have contributed to Senegal's eventual *volte face*. First, on 20 July 2012, the ICJ ruled in Belgium's favour, and the ICJ decided 'Senegal must, without further delay, submit the case of Mr. Hissène Habré to its competent authorities for the purpose of prosecution, if it does not extradite him',[106] a ruling that was in accordance with the UN Convention Against Torture (see Chapter 1). Second, a few months prior to the ICJ decision, Macky Sall was elected president of Senegal, defeating Wade. Perhaps more crucially, Sall was widely known to be sympathetic to Habré's prosecution. While in opposition, Sall had met with victims of Habré, and in 2009 had met with the wider cooperative criminal accountability community, including the Coalition. According to Reed Brody, Sall had conceded embarrassment for

---

[102]   https://ihl-databases.icrc.org/applic/ihl/ihl-nat.nsf/caseLaw.xsp?documentId=A59 DAF636BE1C348C12581BE003F356A&action=OpenDocument

[103]   Brody, 'Bringing a Dictator to Justice'.

[104]   Questions Relating to the Obligation to Prosecute or Extradite (*Belgium* v. *Senegal*), Judgment, ICJ Reports.

[105]   Questions Relating to the Obligation to Prosecute or Extradite (*Belgium* v. *Senegal*), Judgment, ICJ Reports at 5.

[106]   Questions Relating to the Obligation to Prosecute or Extradite (*Belgium* v. *Senegal*), Judgment, ICJ Reports at 422, § 122(6).

what he considered to be Senegal's mismanagement of the Habré case and was keen to make amends.[107] With this in mind, in December 2012, the Senegal Parliament passed a statute to establish an international criminal tribunal to prosecute Habré,[108] including amending its criminal code.

THE EXTRAORDINARY AFRICAN CHAMBERS AND THE LONG ROAD TO ACCOUNTABILITY

Following the decision of the ICJ and the ECOWAS court's judgment, Senegal and the African Union established a court. On 22 August 2012, Senegal and the African Union signed an agreement to establish the Extraordinary African Chambers. Essentially, the court was rooted in the Senegalese legal system, which was now permitted under Senegalese law to exercise universal jurisdiction over the international crimes committed in Chad. The mandate was to prosecute the 'person or persons' *most* responsible for core international crimes perpetrated in Chad from 1982 to 1990.[109] On 30 June 2013, Habré was arrested for the second time in Senegal.

The Extraordinary African Chambers consisted of four sections: Investigative Chamber, Indicting Chamber, Trial Chamber and an Appeals Chamber.[110] Under Article 3, the statute laid out the jurisdiction of the courts as clearly recognising the sources of international law, including customary international law, with an emphasis on those most responsible, as follows:

(1). The Extraordinary African Chambers shall have the power to prosecute and try the person or persons most responsible for crimes and serious viola-tions of international law, customary international law and international conventions ratified by Chad, committed in the territory of Chad during the period from 7 June 1982 to 1 December 1990 [and] (2). The Extraordinary African Chambers may choose to prosecute the most serious crimes within their jurisdiction.[111]

Moreover, Article 4 also outlined the crimes the Extraordinary African Chambers held jurisdiction: '(a) the crime of genocide; (b) crimes against

[107] Brody, 'Bringing a Dictator to Justice'.
[108] Art. Statute of the Extraordinary African Chambers (unofficial translation in English) avail-able at www.hrw.org/news/2013/09/02/statute-extraordinary-african-chambers
[109] https://ihl-databases.icrc.org/applic/ihl/ihl-nat.nsf/caseLaw.xsp?documentId=A59DAF6 36BE1C348C12581BE003F356A&action=OpenDocument
[110] Art. 3(1) Statute of the Extraordinary African Chambers (unofficial translation in English) available at www.hrw.org/news/2013/09/02/statute-extraordinary-african-chambers
[111] Art. 3 Statute of the Extraordinary African Chambers (unofficial translation in English) available at www.hrw.org/news/2013/09/02/statute-extraordinary-african-chambers

humanity; (c) war crimes; and (d) torture'.[112] Articles 5, 6, 7 and 8 also defined each of these crimes. Article 11 defined the composition of each of the chambers: the Trial Chamber consisted of two Senegalese judges, and the Appeals Chamber was composed of three Senegalese judges. Both the Trial and Appeals Chambers would include a president of the chamber who would be 'a non-Senegalese judge from another African Union Member State'.[113] Being a civil legal system, six investigative judges were appointed to the Investigative Chamber to investigate Habré, including Judge Jean Kandé.[114] As part of their training, seminars were conducted by the African Union and the International Committee of the Red Cross on international criminal law. They also travelled to the International Nuremberg Principles Academy in Germany.[115]

The evidence collected by de facto international prosecutors proved invaluable to the trial. As part of their investigation, *inter alia*, they arranged for experts to collect forensic evidence from mass graves, interviewed victims and witnesses and made certified copies of the DDS archives. Of the latter, Kandé maintained that '[d]espite their often deplorable condition, the archives were a precious mine of information on how the Habré regime functioned ... DDS documents that had been saved from destruction, making it even more credible. The archives made the Habré case probably one of the best-documented international trials.'[116] Unsurprisingly, there were limits to how much the Chadian government would cooperate with the Extraordinary African Chambers' (EAC) Investigative Chamber. Indeed, it failed to cooperate on two international arrest warrants. Moreover, Chadian President Déby and many other military and political leaders of the Habré era refused to be interviewed. Déby had maintained on Chadian radio that he was committed to the Senegalese prosecution: 'Let me say this clearly. I worked with Habré. If the judges want to hear me, I am available. . . . We have not excluded the possibility of testifying if it is deemed necessary and if the judges request it.'[117] Nevertheless, this promise was not fulfilled. Under domestic and international pressure, Chad eventually

[112] Art. 4 Statute of the Extraordinary African Chambers (unofficial translation in English) available at www.hrw.org/news/2013/09/02/statute-extraordinary-african-chambers
[113] Art. 11 Statute of the Extraordinary African Chambers (unofficial translation in English) available at www.hrw.org/news/2013/09/02/statute-extraordinary-african-chambers
[114] Kandé, 'Investigations in Senegal and Chad'.
[115] Kandé, 'Investigations in Senegal and Chad'.
[116] Kandé, 'Investigations in Senegal and Chad', 85.
[117] Deby quoted in Kandé, 'Investigations in Senegal and Chad', 86.

indicted its senior leaders – albeit, fifteen years after victims had filed a criminal complaint in the Chadian courts.[118]

HABRÉ'S JUDGMENT AND LEGACY

The Extraordinary African Chambers made it possible for private non-State actors to participate in the trial directly as civil parties. When Habré's trial started in July 2015, two legal teams were permitted to represent the victims, including Association of Victims of Political Repression and Crime (*Association des victimes des crimes et de répression politique de Chad*, AVCRP) and Association of the Victims of the Crimes of the Regime of Hissène Habré (AVCRHH), amongst others, as civil parties in the prosecution. While most of the chamber was represented by African lawyers, a small selection of European lawyers were also involved. Alain Werner and Emmanuelle Marchand, who represented one group of the civil parties, maintained that the 'value added by the Europeans lawyers was their knowledge and experience of international law and procedure'.[119] The civil parties also requested that sexual crimes be added to the charges against Habré.[120] By the time the Habré case was heard in the Extraordinary African Chambers, the cooperative criminal accountability community included a wide array of victims' groups and practitioners, including African Assembly for the Defense of Human Rights (RADDHO), one of the seven organizations (Senegalese, Chadian, French, British and American) that participated in the prosecution against Habré.[121]

On 30 May 2016, the Extraordinary African Chamber found Habré guilty of war crimes and crimes against humanity, including rape, torture, sexual slavery and ordering the killing of 40,000 people.[122] Like Garcés, Guengueng's journey to pursue criminal accountability for those most responsible was a long and arduous one. As Guengueng explained in 2017: 'Three years in prison. Nine years struggling in Chad without contact with the outside world. More than sixteen years of legal battles. Altogether, I have fought more than twenty-six years for justice.'[123]

---

[118] Hicks, *The Trial of Hissène Habré*, 61.
[119] Werner and Marchand, 'Supporting Victims at Trial', 128.
[120] Werner and Marchand, 'Supporting Victims at Trial'.
[121] Pierre Hazan. 2000. L'ex-dictateur tchadien Hissène Habré traqué par ses victimes jusque dans son refuge sénégalais. (Factvia)
[122] *Ministère Public v. Hissein Habré*, Extraordinary African Chambers, Judgment of 30 May 2016,' n.d., accessed 10 September 2020, https://ihl-databases.icrc.org/applic/ihl/ihl-nat.nsf/caseLaw.xsp?documentId=A59DAF636BE1C348C12581BE003F356A&action=openDocument&xp_countrySelected=SN&xp_topicSelected=GVAL-992BU6&from=state
[123] Guengueng quoted in 'Victim to Victor: The Story of Souleymane Guengueng'.

CONCLUSION

Once Habré was indicted, the cooperative criminal accountability community identified a long list of lessons learned. First, victims, as well as the broader cooperative criminal accountability community, had demonstrated tenacity and innovation in the way they adapted their practices as de facto international prosecutors. As Brody later argued:

> The Habré case shows that it is possible for a victim/NGO coalition, with tenacity and imagination, to create the political conditions for a successful universal jurisdiction prosecution, even against a former head of state .... Certainly one of the lessons therefore is persistence – and imagination .... Indeed, in a case which looked dead so many times, the victims and their supporters made it clear that they were just never going away. When the case was thrown out in Senegal, they went to Belgium. When Wade threatened to expel Habré, they used CAT to keep him in Senegal. When the Belgian law was repealed, they obtained a 'grandfather clause'. When Senegal went to the African Union, they improbably turned the AU into an ally which then helped them overcome the ECOWAS ruling. When Senegal stalled, they pressed Belgium to take the case to the ICJ.[124]

Second, the Habré case demonstrated the difficulties of prosecuting a former head of State for core international crimes when the political elite stymy local and foreign courts, as was the case in Chad and Senegal, respectively. On the one hand, the Pinochet case demonstrated the merits of two cooperative States, the United Kingdom and Spain – supported by a strong independent judiciary – which were willing to cooperate. Initially, both UK and Spanish political leaders were reticent to interfere in the judicial proceedings of their respective States. It also showed that while the United Kingdom enjoyed a common law system and Spain a civil law legal system, they both recognised the judiciary of each State as well as international laws governing extradition, immunity and the *jus cogens* crime of torture – albeit, sometimes for different reasons. On the other hand, the Habré case demonstrated the difficulties of prosecuting when State leaders blocked or limited the judiciary or would not empower it with jurisdictional reach, including in foreign courts. While the Senegalese court initially began prosecuting Habré, the judiciary's ability to exercise universal jurisdiction over the Habré case remained limited. Moreover, Senegal's political leaders were reluctant to empower courts by amending Senegal's law, including its constitution. Similarly, despite Senegal's obligation to adopt torture into the domestic legal system and

---

[124] Brody, 'Bringing a Dictator to Justice'.

prosecute or extradite under the CAT, Senegalese President Wade was hesitant to extradite Habré when Belgium courts issued an arrest warrant via INTERPOL four times. As Brody later stated, the Habré case 'highlighted many of the practical problems of litigating crimes far away from the territorial state without complete cooperation of that state's government'.[125]

International criminal prosecution in a foreign court was not a simple endeavour. Nonetheless, the Belgium government, following the advice of its judiciary and the concerns of the victims, stepped in and was willing to take Senegal to the ICJ. Many of the criminal accountability community had wanted other senior members of the Habré regime to also be criminally prosecuted at the Extraordinary African Chamber. In the end, only Habré was prosecuted in Senegal. Yet it opened the path to future accountability for other senior leaders in Chad. In this respect, Reed Brody described the prosecution of Habré at Extraordinary African Chamber as the beginning of 'Chad's Nuremberg'.[126]

Although some victims believed that the Habré prosecution had revealed the truth of the Habré's government and achieved justice, not all believed that a successful criminal prosecution established truth and reconciled victims with their past. On the one hand, some victims or witnesses, like Guengueng, held that justice equated to truth: 'Justice reflects the fact that there is truth.'[127] On the other hand, for victims such as Clement Abaifouta, who had worked with Guengueng from the beginning (and was incarcerated for four years in a DDS facility), the trial had not explained *why* he had been detained: 'Unfortunately even after the trial in Dakar I still don't know the answer. Hissène Habré refused to reveal anything. I still feel like a half man.'[128] It reflected the challenges of criminal prosecution for many victims to establish the truth about everything.

Yet, like Garcés, Guengueng trusted international law. Indeed, Guengueng believed that national and international courts played a critical role in upholding an international rule of law. When the case went to the Court of Appeal, Guengueng maintained, 'We believe that the Court of Appeal judges will only speak the law and especially international law.'[129] Moreover, like Garcés, Guengueng indicated justice was his motivation for the Habré's indictment, rather than retaliation: 'We did not seek

[125] Guengueng quoted in 'Victim to Victor: The Story of Souleymane Guengueng'.
[126] Nako Madjiasra and Emma Farge, 'Chad Tries Habre-Era Security Agents', IOL, 15 November 2014, www.iol.co.za/news/africa/chad-tries-habre-era-security-agents-1780743.
[127] Guengueng quoted in 'Victim to Victor: The Story of Souleymane Guengueng'.
[128] Abaifouta quoted in Hicks, *The Trial of Hissène Habré*, 56.
[129] Guengueng quoted in 'Victim to Victor: The Story of Souleymane Guengueng'.

revenge. We sought justice."[130] Today, Guengueng continues to work through his foundation with witnesses and victims of core crimes in other African states and elsewhere, in an effort to pursue criminal accountability for those most responsible.[131]

In the case of Hissène Habré, *interstate* legal officials also played an important role in transferring knowledge to State legal officials as a broader community of practice. For example, Stephen Rapp, while chief prosecutor for the Special Court for Sierra Leone (SCSL), provided organisational knowledge and capability from his team to the judiciary in Senegal, to assist with the establishment of the Extraordinary African Chambers.[132] Once the EAC was established, Rapp attended the Habré trial, in his new role as US ambassador-at-large for war crimes issues in the Office of Global Criminal Justice.

In this post, Rapp would also be instrumental in supporting Chief Investigator 1 and the Syrian local private non-State actors when they asked for his assistance in the establishment of an independent, non-government organisation for suspected Syrian regime crimes during the early days of the Arab Spring.[133] This organisation would later become the Commission of International Justice and Accountability (CIJA). Once Rapp resigned as US ambassador, he would become a commissioner for CIJA in a private *pro bono* capacity and continues to lend his expertise. This leads me to explore the third and final biographical case study focusing on Chief Investigator 1 (Syria). It illuminates Chief Investigator 1's role as one of the early members of what would later become the CIJA, and how he increasingly worked within a broader cooperative criminal accountability community.

---

[130] Guengueng quoted in 'Victim to Victor: The Story of Souleymane Guengueng'.

[131] See 'Souleymanu Guengueng Foundation', https://sggfblog.com/

[132] Stephen Rapp (Former Chief Prosecutor for the Special Court for Sierra Leone (SCSL) and former US ambassador-at-large for war crimes issues in the Office of Global Criminal Justice War, commissioner for CIJA), interview with author, 21 July 2018.

[133] Stephen Rapp, interview with author, 27 January 2017.

4

De Facto International Prosecutors and the Commission for International Justice and Accountability (CIJA) (Syria)

This chapter investigates how de facto international prosecutors attempted to extend the reaches of international criminal law to senior members of the Syrian government, as and while the alleged crimes were continuing. Unlike Garcés and Guengueng, in this case study, de facto international prosecutors started collecting material, which links suspected senior leaders to underlying crimes, during a period when the alleged crimes were being perpetrated. The chapter starts with the Chief Investigator for Syria (hereafter Chief Investigator 1),[1] a Syrian lawyer from the southern governorate of Dara'a.[2] Chief Investigator 1 would later become one of the founding members of the Commission for International Justice and Accountability (CIJA). Before the Arab Spring, Chief Investigator 1 had relocated abroad working in civil law. But after large-scale protests erupted all across Syria in March 2011, in response to the arrest and torture of schoolchildren from Dera'a, he returned to his home state. Chief Investigator 1 wanted to see for himself what was described as a violent crackdown by Syrian government forces against actual and alleged opposition. Upon his arrival, he witnessed crimes 'with my own eyes'.[3] Initially, Chief Investigator 1 worked with other Syrian journalists and lawyers to start 'documenting' the 'crimes' with, amongst other things, video footage.

It was not until Chief Investigator 1 and the other Syrian members of the informal group were trained by William Wiley, previously an analyst and investigator for a number of international criminal tribunals, that they

---

[1] Chief Investigator 1 continues to work in the field at the time of writing. To ensure his safety, the author has protected his identity, and so Chief Investigator 1 will remain anonymous.

[2] Melinda Rankin, 'The Future of International Criminal Evidence in New Wars? The Evolution of the Commission for International Justice and Accountability (CIJA)', *Journal of Genocide Research* 20, no. 3 (2018): 392–411, https://doi.org/10.1080/14623528.2018.1445435.

[3] CIJA Chief Investigator 1 (with translator CIJA Liaison Officer 1), interview with author, January 2017.

understood what practices were required, as well as what material was necessary, to establish individual criminal liability for those *most* responsible for core international crimes. In 2011 and again 2012, Chief Investigator 1 and a team of Syrian lawyers and journalists were trained by Wiley on how to collect the type of material that would inform a future international criminal prosecution, including 'linkage material'. Thereafter, Chief Investigator 1 and the initial Syrian investigators asked Wiley and Stephen Rapp, then US ambassador-at-large for Global Criminal Justice, to help them establish an independent commission to manage the material they began to collect. Eventually, the CIJA, itself and an international branch were established in an undisclosed location in Europe, with Wiley as director.[4]

As Chief Investigator 1 and the Syrian CIJA team began to collect thousands of documents from 2012, the CIJA expanded. In 2013, as it received funding, it included more Western-based international criminal analysts, investigators and ex-prosecutors with international experience. This served to extend the group of de facto international prosecutors, which increasingly established and engaged with a cooperative criminal accountability community. As the CIJA formalised organisationally and structurally, it began to add several practices to its remit, aside from investigation. Reflecting the increased knowledge in the group, it also began to analyse the material and conduct evidence management. Additionally, international prosecutors were drawn upon to write the initial case briefs that would meet the standards of international criminal tribunals.

Like the two previous biographical case studies in this book, the CIJA was informed by the Nuremberg Tribunal as a model both in collecting linkage material produced by the perpetrators and in focussing (at least initially) on a small group of those most responsible. It also drew upon the knowledge and experience of a number of international criminal tribunals – such as the Criminal Tribunal for the former Yugoslavia (ICTY), the International Criminal Tribunal for Rwanda (ICTR), the International Criminal Court (ICC), and the Extraordinary Chambers in the Courts of Cambodia (ECCC), amongst others – including practices conducted at the offices of international prosecutors. The CIJA's strategy has been informed by multiple private non-State actors, with a broad array of knowledge and expertise. While

---

[4] To ensure the security of those analysts and investigators who continue to work or return to the field, the author is unable to disclose the location of CIJA's office and names of many of the staff or discuss the role of States that assist the investigators with the movement of documents. The SCJA (later renamed CIJA) was registered in May 2012. Initially, Wiley was secretary, with a Syrian lawyer formally serving as director. The formal structure was brought into line with the de facto structure in 2014, when the SCJA was renamed the CIJA.

documentary material and victims' statements are equally important, and complementary, it is often difficult in large-scale atrocity crimes to access documents that link senior leaders to underlying crimes. As Wiley maintained, at the heart of the CIJA is the willingness of local CIJA investigators, like Chief Investigator 1, who remain in the field to collect material, often under perilous conditions.

This case study also shows a different approach to the way private non-State actors interact with States and State legal officials. Unlike the previous two examples, the CIJA is supported financially by a number of States through their Foreign Affairs departments, although it is a not-for-profit agency with an independent mandate. Unlike Garcés and Guengueng, the CIJA does not submit criminal complaints to foreign courts. Rather, it increasingly cooperates with a number of war crimes units in Western states, including in Germany. The CIJA also cooperates with a number of other private non-State actors, such as Guernica 37, and international (State) institutions, such as the International, Impartial, and Independent Mechanism (IIIM) for Syria.

To date, the CIJA claims to have collected more than 1 million military and security-intelligence documents smuggled out of Syria. The CIJA also main-tains it has prepared ten case briefs against the top fifty leaders of the Syrian government, including the president of Syria, Bashar al Assad.[5] In 2014, it broadened its remit to include investigating Daesh (otherwise known as Islamic State (IS), the Islamic State of Iraq and Syria (ISIS), or the Islamic State of Iraq and the Levant (ISIL)) in Syria and Iraq. Between April 2019 and March 2020, it assisted thirty-two bodies from twelve states, including state law enforcement authorities. It has received 169 requests for assistance and pro-vided information on 451 suspects. By February 2021, it had completed twenty-four structural investigations and case briefs of those most responsible for core crimes in the Syrian government and Daesh and conducted 3,000 interviews, including with insider witnesses and victims.

The CIJA's material has also contributed to the arrest of a senior member of the Syrian government, Anwar R., as well as the conviction of a former Syrian secret service agent, Eyad A., in Germany. Considered to be a tertiary-level figure in the chain of command from President Assad, Anwar R. was arrested by German legal officials in 2019 for crimes against humanity, specifically in relation to the illegal detention and torture of Syrian demonstrators in the

---

[5] Melinda Rankin, 'The "Responsibility to Prosecute" Core International Crimes? The Case of German Universal Jurisdiction and the Syrian Government', *Global Responsibility to Protect* 11, no. 4 (2019): 394–410, https://doi.org/10.1163/1875984X-01104003.

early days of the Arab Spring.[6] On 23 April 2020, the combined trial of both Anwar R. and Eyad A. began in the Higher Regional Court in Koblenz, Germany; by early 2021, the trial of Anwar R. and Eyad A. was separated. On 24 February 2021, the Higher Regional Court in Koblenz issued a verdict against Eyad A., and he was convicted of aiding crimes against humanity in Syria, including the crime of torture.[7] While the CIJA's involvement in the arrest and the trial is discussed further in Chapter 5, it signifies the first conviction in the wake of the Arab Spring. In its decision, the court also described the context of atrocities perpetrated in Syria: it included recognising the large-scale and systematic attack on actual and alleged opposition by the Syrian government starting from early 2011, which was used to suppress civilians in the wake of the Arab Spring.[8] The verdict represents the first conviction of a former Syrian regime official for crimes against humanity in the wake of the Arab Spring. It is expected that the case of Anwar, which remains ongoing in the Higher Regional Court in Koblenz at the time of writing, will be decided in early 2022.

This chapter examines the evolution of the CIJA. As private non-State actors, it initially consisted of local Syrians but evolved to cooperate with a number of international practitioners, who formerly worked at an array of international criminal tribunals. This chapter argues the following. First, the creation of the CIJA was the result of four factors: the UK Foreign Office's desire to support human rights activists in Syria; lessons learned from previous international criminal tribunals, including the Nuremberg Trials; attempts by non-State actors to invent new ways to overcome the gaps and limitations of the international criminal justice system; and the willingness of Syrian civilians to risk their lives and use the law to hold those responsible for mass atrocities to account.

Second, the chapter argues that States played a larger role in laying the groundwork for accountability for atrocities committed in Syria. While China and Russia vetoed efforts to refer Syria to the ICC via the UN Security Council (UNSC), a number of private non-State actors and state legal officials in foreign courts have attempted to close the accountability gap left by the

---

[6] Rankin, 'The Future of International Criminal Evidence in New Wars?'
[7] Oberlandesgericht Koblenz, 'Urteil Gegen Einen Mutmaßlichen Mitarbeiter Des Syrischen Geheimdienstes Wegen Beihilfe Zu Einem Verbrechen Gegen Die Menschlichkeit', Landesregierung Rheinland-Pfalz, February 24, 2021, https://justiz.rlp.de/de/service-informationen/aktuelles/detail/news/News/detail/urteil-gegen-einen-mutmasslichen-mitarbeiter-des-syrischen-geheimdienstes-wegen-beihilfe-zu-einem-ver/.
[8] Koblenz, 'Urteil Gegen Einen Mutmaßlichen Mitarbeiter Des Syrischen Geheimdienstes Wegen Beihilfe Zu Einem Verbrechen Gegen Die Menschlichkeit'.

local Syrian judiciary, with the foreign ministries of a number of States playing a more active role. While members of the CIJA initiated their own investigations, States have financially supported their work. Moreover, unlike the case of Pinochet and Habré, German local officials also initiated their own investigation into Syrian leaders for crimes against humanity, without relying on a private non-State actors to submit a private complaint.

Third, this chapter argues that despite the cooperation of States and State legal officials, as private non-State actors, members of the CIJA were able to conduct the type in criminal investigations that were out of reach for State and international (State) institutions, including for the ICC, the Commission of Inquiry (CoI) for Syria and the IIIM. As private non-State actors, with a focus on evidence management, the CIJA's model may represent an innovative approach to investigating core international crimes, particularly for private non-State actors who wish to play a future role in evidence collection and management in response to core international crimes, including torture. The CIJA relies on the willingness of its Syrian (and later Iraqi) investigators to operate in the context of large-scale organized violence. This facilitated the preparation of a number of case briefs intended for a future prosecution, *while* the Syrian (and Iraq) war was in progress.

The chapter is organised as follows. First, it explores how and why Chief Investigator 1, as a witness to initial crimes, decided to adopt tasks and practices, ordinarily associated with the offices of international prosecutors, which would contribute to a future criminal prosecution for those most responsible. Given that Chief Investigator 1 remains anonymous, a detailed analysis of his biography and role in CIJA is limited. Second, it investigates the political and legal origins of the CIJA. It attempts to illuminate how the CIJA was formed and emerged as a formal institution, more so than previous case studies in this book. For this reason, it also focuses on William Wiley, director of CIJA, who informed how CIJA developed as a formal structure, largely inspired by his prior experience in several international criminal tribunals. This section includes the exploration of CIJA's wider historical and political context, key actors, governance model, operational decisions, training and capabilities. It also briefly considers what evidence the CIJA maintains it has prepared for a series of 'trial-ready' case briefs, which may show individual criminal liability for core international crimes. As torture and other international crimes are suspected of continuing in Syria by the Assad government at the time of writing this book, it may be too early to assess the CIJA's contribution. Indeed, it took almost a decade before Pinochet was indicted after he ceased being head of State, and almost two decades for Habré.

Nevertheless, the chapter assesses the early practices, innovations and contributions of the CIJA to date.

CHIEF INVESTIGATOR 1 AS A WITNESS

Like Garcés, CIJA's Chief Investigator 1 had earlier trained as a lawyer. But he never expected to be a criminal investigator for core international crimes. From the southern governorate of Dara'a in Syria, Chief Investigator 1 had left Syria and was working abroad as a civil lawyer. All of that changed with the rise of the Arab Spring.[9] In March 2011, inspired by the Arab Spring that swept across the Middle East, a number of schoolboys younger than age fifteen wrote anti-government graffiti across a wall in a public area in Dara'a. In response, Syrian intelligence arrested the schoolboys and tortured them. While Syrians had remained largely afraid to take to the streets following democratic protests in other Arab states, the arrest and torture of these schoolboys was considered by many Syrians a step too far – even for Syrian intelligence, known historically for its brutal suppression of opposition.[10] Many ordinary Syrians took to the street in largely peaceful protests across Syria. In response, the Syrian government attempted a range of ill-fit, often competing, strategies: first it lifted the emergency laws; however, it was purported, also began its violent crackdown on civilian demonstrators as they increased in number. Between March 2011 and November 2011, the UN Commission of Inquiry for Syria suspected that the Syrian government killed an estimated 3,500 civilians.[11] When Chief Investigator 1 returned to his hometown of Dara'a, shortly after the arrest of the fifteen schoolboys, he decided to get involved. Initially, he attempted to 'document' what he considered to be the high number of 'crimes', which, in his view, appeared to be committed with 'impunity'.[12] CIJA Chief Investigator 1 maintained that '[i]n the beginning when I heard about the incidents taking part in Dara'a, I returned and then I saw with my own eyes what was happening ... as a lawyer I could see a lot of crimes

---

[9]   CIJA Chief Investigator 1 (with translator CIJA Liaison Officer 1), interview with author; Julian Borger, 'Syria's Truth Smugglers', *The Guardian*, 12 May 2015, www.theguardian.com/world/2015/may/12/syria-truth-smugglers-bashar-al-assad-war-crimes.

[10] Dara Conduit, *The Muslim Brotherhood in Syria*, Cambridge Middle East Studies (Cambridge: Cambridge University Press, 2019), https://doi.org/10.1017/9781108758321.

[11] United Nations Human Rights Council, 'Resolution Adopted by the Human Rights Council at Its Seventeenth Special Session, Resolution, S-17/1, Situation of Human Rights in the Syrian Arab Republic. Office of Human Rights Commission, 22 August 2011'. (2011: Office of Human Rights Commission), ttp://www.ohchr.org/Documents/HRBodies/HRCouncil/CoISyria/Res S17_1.pdf.

[12] CIJA Chief Investigator 1 (with translator CIJA Liaison Officer 1), interview with author.

happening, but nobody was documenting them'.[13] As the level of violence increased, he and a number of other lawyers and journalists self-organised to document the violence. To broaden their skills in human rights documentation, they attended a number of human rights courses in late 2011.

A turning point came when Chief Investigator 1 attended one of five UK-funded 'Syria Investigation' courses, led by William Wiley during 2011 and 2012. At this point, he began to take a wholly different approach to investigating. The Syrian private non-State actors were provided with an unconventional training program. Chief Investigator 1 and others were trained on the type of material that would inform an international criminal prosecution for those *most* responsible. It included how material should follow a 'chain of custody', the importance of collecting *all* material identified (to include exculpatory evidence) in a particular location (such as a military intelligence office) and to ensure that a record was maintained of the times and places this material was moved, and by whom. They were also provided ongoing training that reflected Wiley's professional experiences and context. Wiley later argued that providing Syrians with the requisite training to investigate core international crimes to an international criminal law standard served to 'fill a gap'.[14] Moreover, from a practical perspective, he reasoned, conducting the training was the easy part. The more difficult task was investigating senior leaders for grave breaches of international law in the context of war and organized violence, a task that most intergovernment bodies were reticent to undertake even if provided the requisite UNSC mandate. Hence, he reasoned, if Syrians were *willing* to use the law and take the risk, the process of investigating could, practically speaking, begin.[15] Investigators were also trained on what constituted acceptable evidence in an international criminal prosecution at the international level, most particularly with regard to individual criminal liability for the most senior suspects of crimes against humanity. As in the Nuremberg Trials, Wiley emphasized efforts to 'secure documentation generated contemporaneously by the party which is suspected of involvement in the *prima facie* crimes under examination', namely because inculpatory materials and documentation produced by or attributed to suspects have at times proven the most important evidence in international criminal

---

[13] CIJA Chief Investigator 1 (with translator CIJA Liaison Officer 1), interview with author.
[14] William Wiley (CIJA director), interview with author, January 2017.
[15] William Wiley (CIJA director), interview with author; Ben Taub, 'The Assad Files: Capturing the Top-Secret Documents That Tie the Syrian Regime to Mass Torture and Killings', *The New Yorker*, 18 April 2016, www.newyorker.com/magazine/2016/04/18/bashar-al- assads-war-crimes-exposed.

prosecutions.[16] During the next nine years, training with Syrian investigators continued, not unlike an internship, whereby mentoring combined with formal training was furthered as war followed.[17]

Chief Investigator 1 believed that the Syria Investigation courses led by Wiley enabled him to think about how use the law differently.[18] He explained that although he was a lawyer, he was initially unaware of the concepts or processes pertaining to international criminal investigations and how they could or should function.[19] He believed that this lack of knowledge and awareness of international criminal law reflected a wider lack of awareness, not just in Syria but also in the Arab World more broadly – and most particularly amongst private non-State actors: 'We were not thinking this way at the beginning', but during the first investigative training course, 'we really realized that this is what *should* be done.'[20] Moreover, he stated that after the course, he, and many who attended, started to believe that unless they attempted to achieve justice in this way, to investigate suspected core international crimes to the standard the course instructors were advancing, any other approach could only ever serve to 'contribute to the chaos'.[21] It was only through an international rule of law that justice could truly be achieved. Chief Investigator 1 recalled that this training not only changed the way he viewed the law, and international law, but also the way to solve the problem of protecting fundamental rights from arbitrary power, not just in Syria but also across the broader Middle East.[22] Indeed, he believed that the process of criminal prosecution was critical, even if it meant that the president of Syria was acquitted – as long as it was a fair, impartial and independent trial for core international crimes. For him, the process of criminal prosecution itself was

---

[16] Just as importantly, the training notes underscored the value of civil society and non-State actors as playing an essential role collecting material concerning suspected senior leaders for a future war crimes or crimes against humanity prosecution, particular given their tolerance for risk. The training notes also emphasised the need for both inculpatory and exculpatory documents. It used some of the texts written or co-written by Wiley; Morten Bergsmo and William Wiley, 'Human Rights Professionals and the Criminal Investigation and Prosecution of Core International Crimes', in Siri Skare, Ingvild Burkey and Hege Mork, eds., *Manual on Human Rights Monitoring: An Introduction for Human Rights Field Officers*, University of Oslo (Oslo: Norwegian Centre for Human Rights, 2008), 9–10.

[17] William Wiley (CIJA director), interview with author; Chris Engels (CIJA deputy director), interview with author, January 2017.

[18] CIJA Chief Investigator 1 (with translator CIJA Liaison Officer 1), interview with author; Borger, 'Syria's Truth Smugglers'.

[19] CIJA Chief Investigator 1 (with translator CIJA Liaison Officer 1), interview with author.

[20] CIJA Chief Investigator 1 (with translator CIJA Liaison Officer 1).

[21] CIJA Chief Investigator 1 (with translator CIJA Liaison Officer 1).

[22] CIJA Chief Investigator 1 (with translator CIJA Liaison Officer 1).

important – namely to show that no one was above the law – Syria's domestic law, as well as international law – but also to establish the truth.[23] It was during this time that he first met Stephen Rapp.

Chief Investigator 1 said that upon their return to the field, his and the new investigative team's objectives were twofold: first, to investigate those suspected of being the most responsible for grave breaches of international criminal law perpetrated by the Syrian government and, second, his objectives were also normative and aspirational. The process of investigating senior suspects, with the purpose of preparing a case for individual criminal liability, was not just about bringing senior members of the Syrian government to account. They believed that using international criminal law was the *practical means* to end the violence in Syria and achieve long-term stability in the country – namely because, as Chief Investigator 1 argued, it attempted to solve a broader problem across the region: a 'culture of impunity'.[24] Across the Middle East, he maintained, the judicial system was often subordinated to the political elite and constrained by corruption.[25] For this reason, Chief Investigator 1 began to believe that more private non-State actors should develop both investigative and analytical capabilities and use international law to bring senior leaders to account.[26]

Nevertheless, without a UNSC mandate (or the assistance of domestic prosecutorial authorities, which was never an option), securing documentation generated by the Syrian government required some creative thinking on the part of the investigators. This included building rapport with armed opposition forces as they emerged in Syria, on the assumption that they may, at some point, gain significant territory from the Syrian Arab Armed Forces. Two such opportunities arose when opposition forces separately secured the cities of Raqqa and Deir ez-Zor,[27] where investigators negotiated access to critical military and security intelligence material which was left behind by the retreating government forces and then seized by the opposition. Thereafter, the material was smuggled across the Syrian border, adhering to CIJA chain-of-custody protocols put into place from the start of the

---

[23]   CIJA Chief Investigator 1 (with translator CIJA Liaison Officer 1).
[24]   CIJA Chief Investigator 1 (with translator CIJA Liaison Officer 1).
[25]   This is the view of Chief Investigator 1. This concern is reflected in Transparency International's Corruption Perception Index. In 2016, Transparency International's Corruption Perception Index (CPI) scored states in the middle east, as follows: Jordan 48; Saudi Arabia 46; Kuwait 41; Turkey 41; Egypt 34; Iran 29; Lebanon 28; Iraq 17 (100 = very clean; 0 = highly corrupt).
[26]   CIJA Chief Investigator 1 (with translator CIJA Liaison Officer 1), interview with author.
[27]   Borger, 'Syria's Truth Smugglers'; Taub, 'The Assad Files: Capturing the Top-Secret Documents That Tie the Syrian Regime to Mass Torture and Killings'.

document collection process.[28] According to senior analysts at CIJA, this material, and others like it, would later serve to form the basis for early analysis and to establish the facts about how the Syrian government and security apparatus were structured and behaved during the crisis from 2011 onwards. It was based on this evidence that CIJA began to develop a case concerning allegations of illegal detention and torture against senior leaders in the Syrian government.

Before I explore the role of Chief Investigator 1 in the context of the formation of CIJA and as part of a broader cooperative criminal accountability community, I first examine the allegations and challenges posed by other actors and institutions – including States, international (State) institutions (such as the ICC), and State legal officials – in investigating core international crimes in Syria. This will serve to contextualize the role that private non-State actors have played in Syrian criminal accountability and how they remain distinct from other actors. Moreover, it seeks to show that in contrast to the Pinochet and Habré governments, States have played a greater role in attempting to investigate grave breaches of international law in relation to the Assad government. Yet despite this, it illustrates how challenges remain, including the ability to access and collect potential evidence in Syria.

CLOSING THE CRIMINAL ACCOUNTABILITY GAP IN SYRIA

From the very early stages of the Arab Spring, the list of allegations against the Syrian government was long. They included large-scale arbitrary detention; persecution; enforced disappearances; and sometimes murder, of actual and perceived opposition to the regime.[29] A particular weapon of choice was the systematic and brutal use of torture. In 2017, then–United Nations High Commissioner for Human Rights Zeid Ra'ad Al Hussein described Syria as the worst human-made disaster since the Second World War, whereby 'the entire country had become a torture-chamber: a place of savage horror and

---

[28]   Borger, 'Syria's Truth Smugglers'; Taub, 'The Assad Files: Capturing the Top-Secret Documents That Tie the Syrian Regime to Mass Torture and Killings'.

[29]   United Nations Human Rights Council, 'Resolution Adopted by the Human Rights Council at Its Seventeenth Special Session, Resolution, S-17/1, Situation of Human Rights in the Syrian Arab Republic. Office of Human Rights Commission, 22 August 2011'; Zeid Ra'ad Al Hussein, 'Syria Worst Man-Made Disaster since World War II, Geneva, Text of a Statement by UN High Commissioner for Human Rights Zeid Ra'ad Al Hussein to a High-Level Panel Discussion at the Human Rights Council on the Situation of Human Rights in the Syrian Arab Republic', 14 March 2017, www.ohchr.org/EN/NewsEvents/Pages/DisplayNews.aspx?NewsID=21373&LangID=E.

absolute injustice.'[30] It is alleged that the aim of the violent crackdown was to impede the protest movement with the aid of the Syrian intelligence services as soon as possible, and to terrorize the population so as to maintain the regime in power.[31] Allegations of criminal responsibility have since been assigned to the very top of the Syrian government.[32]

Although Syrian intelligence played an essential role in the alleged crimes,[33] notable also was the role of the Syrian judiciary. Syria has been a State Party to the Convention Against Torture since August 2004. Torture was also explicitly prohibited in the Syrian constitution. However, not only did the Syrian judiciary fail to hold senior actors to account for allegations of torture (amongst other crimes), but the available evidence suggests that the judiciary aided Syrian government officials by providing purported justifications for mass arrests and detention of members of the opposition – thus giving the large-scale persecution of civilians a veneer of processes governed by the rule of law.[34]

To date, international (State) institutions have shown a very limited ability to collect evidence of atrocities in Syria (on Syrian territory), to prepare

---

[30]   Hussein, 'Syria Worst Man-Made Disaster since World War II, Geneva, Text of a Statement by UN High Commissioner for Human Rights Zeid Ra'ad Al Hussein to a High-Level Panel Discussion at the Human Rights Council on the Situation of Human Rights in the Syrian Arab Republic'.

[31]   Generalbundesanwalt (German Federal Public Prosecutor General's Office), 'Presse: Festnahme Eines Mutmaßlichen Mitarbeiters Des Syrischen Militärischen Geheimdienstes Wegen Des Dringenden Tatverdachts Eines Verbrechens Gegen Die Menschlichkeit (Press Statement: Arrest of a Suspected Syrian Military Intelligence Agent on Suspicion of a Crime against Humanity)', 22 June 2020, www.generalbundesanwalt.de/.

[32]   In June 2018, Germany was the first state to issue an arrest warrant against a senior member of the Syrian regime, Jamil Hassan, the director of the Air Force Intelligence Directorate, for 'crimes against humanity', including torture, later followed by France. See Jorg Diehl, Christoph Reuter, and Fidelius Schmid, 'Germany takes aim at Assad's torture boss.' *Der Spiegel*, 8 June 2018, www.spiegel.de/international/world/senior-assad-aid-charged-with-war-crimes-a-1211923.html, accessed 20 May 2019. Other investigations are underway in Sweden, France and Austria, amongst others. In November 2018, France issued an arrest warrant against three members of the Syrian government, including Ali Mamlouk, Jamil Hassan, and Abdel Salam Mahmoud; See Emmanuel Jarry, 'France issues arrest warrants for senior Syrian officials.' *Reuters*, 5 November 2018, https://www.reuters.com/article/us-syria-crisis-france/france-issues-arrest-warrants-for-senior-syrian-officials-idUSKCN1NA11L, accessed 20 May 2019.

[33]   Generalbundesanwalt (German Federal Public Prosecutor General's Office), 'Presse: Festnahme Eines Mutmaßlichen Mitarbeiters Des Syrischen Militärischen Geheimdienstes Wegen Des Dringenden Tatverdachts Eines Verbrechens Gegen Die Menschlichkeit (Press Statement: Arrest of a Suspected Syrian Military Intelligence Agent on Suspicion of a Crime against Humanity)'.

[34]   Taub, 'The Assad Files: Capturing the Top-Secret Documents That Tie the Syrian Regime to Mass Torture and Killings'.

criminal case briefs and to prosecute suspects. There are a number of reasons for this. As Syria is not a State Party to the Rome Statute, the ICC does not have jurisdiction over crimes committed in Syria (Rome Statute 1998/2002).[35] The Independent International Commission of Inquiry on the Syrian Arab Republic (CoI) was established in 2011 (United Nations Human Rights Council 2011, Resolution S-17/1) 'to investigate all alleged violations of international human rights law since March 2011 in the Syrian Arab Republic.' Nonetheless, the CoI has remained significantly stymied. For example, it was not granted permission by Syria (or the UNSC) to enter Syrian territory. This meant that collecting vital linkage material, such as documents produced by the alleged perpetrators, which could establish criminal linkages between the Syrian government and the underlying crimes, was significantly curtailed. Moreover, while the CoI's mandate was to preserve evidence and identify where possible those who may be criminally responsible, its mandate was never extended to preparing criminal case briefs.[36]

Similarly, those international (State) institutions that were *permitted* to enter Syria had limited impact. In 2012, a number of monitoring agencies were permitted to enter Syria, such as the United Nations Supervision Mission in Syria (UNSMIS).[37] However, its mandate remained restricted to monitoring the cessation of violence in Syria. Even with such a narrow mandate, the UNSMIS withdrew operations after three months, by July 2012, stating that the conditions were impossible and too dangerous for its personnel, as requirements of 'the cessation of the use of heavy weapons and a reduction in the level of violence sufficient by all sides' were not met.[38]

Lastly, both the UNSC and the UN General Assembly (UNGA) have remained paralyzed to address criminal accountability in significant ways. In 2014, Russia and China blocked efforts by States, led by France and co-sponsored by sixty-five member States, to refer Syria to the ICC through the UNSC.[39] This was an added blow, not only for the ICC but also for the

---

[35]   United Nations General Assembly, 'Rome Statute of the International Criminal Court', 17 July 1998.
[36]   Zeid Ra'ad Al Hussein, 'International, Impartial and Independent Mechanism on International Crimes Committed in the Syrian Arab Republic, 34th Session of the Human Rights Council, Remarks by Zeid Ra'ad Al Hussein, United Nations High Commissioner for Human Rights' (Office of the High Commissioner for Human Rights (OHCHR), 27 February 2017), https://www.ohchr.org/EN/NewsEvents/Pages/DisplayNews.aspx?NewsID=21241.
[37]   'United Nations Security Council (UNSC), Resolution 2043' (2012). It established a UN Supervision Mission in April 2012 to monitor the cessation of violence in Syria.
[38]   'United Nations Security Council (UNSC), Resolution 2059' (2012).
[39]   'United Nations Security Council (UNSC), Draft Resolution S/2014/348' (2014).

international criminal justice community more broadly.[40] As a means to fill the accountability gap, Lichtenstein and Qatar led a proposal to establish an International, Impartial and Independent Mechanism (IIIM) for Syria through the UNGA. In December 2016, the UNGA adopted the resolution creating the IIIM. The resolution was approved by 105 States, with 15 voting against, and 52 abstentions.[41] While the IIIM was an important innovation, it too remained limited in its impact. Unlike the CoI, the IIIM does have a mandate to investigate and prepare criminal case briefs for those most responsible for atrocity crimes.[42] Nonetheless, it has not been granted authorization by either the Syrian government or the UNSC under a Chapter VII resolution to enter Syria, nor is it an international criminal tribunal with the ability to prosecute individuals.

In conclusion, international (State) institutions have been unwilling or unable to first, *collect* material from within Syria for the purpose of preparing evidence that links those most responsible for atrocity crimes for the purpose of criminal prosecution and, second, to *prosecute* alleged atrocity crimes committed in Syria in either a domestic or international criminal court. In addition, even if an international (State) institution, such as the ICC, had obtained authority to enter Syria, the question remains: would it have stayed in Syria to collect material as large-scale conflict engulfed much of the country, or would it have left like the UNSMIS due to safety concerns? As the Assad government regains control over much of Syria, prospects for collecting probative documentation and forensic material appear to be diminishing. Relevant material within reach of the authorities may be destroyed.[43] While states have engaged international (State) institutions to play a larger role in criminal accountability in Syria, more so than Chile and Chad, they still face serious challenges in achieving criminal accountability.

---

[40] Ben Saul, 'Standing Up for Justice in War', Chatham House, 8 November 2016, www .chathamhouse.org/expert/comment/standing-justice-war.

[41] United Nations General Assembly, 'International, Impartial and Independent Mechanism to Assist in the Investigation and Prosecution of Those Responsible for the Most Serious Crimes under International Law Committed in the Syrian Arab Republic since March 2011, a/Res/71/ 248' (2016).

[42] United Nations General Assembly, 'International, Impartial and Independent Mechanism to Assist in the Investigation and Prosecution of Those Responsible for the Most Serious Crimes under International Law Committed in the Syrian Arab Republic since March 2011, a/Res/71/ 248' (2016).

[43] Louisa Loveluck, Asma Ajroudi, and Suzan Haidamous, 'Chemical Weapons Coverup Suspected in Syria as Inspectors Remain Blocked', *Chicago Tribune*, 20 April 2018, www .chicagotribune.com/nation-world/ct-chemical-weapons-coverup-syria-20180420-story.html.

The following section returns to the role of Chief Investigator 1 and the CIJA, and how they have attempted to solve many (although not all) of these challenges. It shows how they also cooperated with State legal officials in foreign courts to complete the criminal processes while the alleged core crimes, including torture, continue in Syria.

CIJA AND THE COOPERATIVE CRIMINAL ACCOUNTABILITY COMMUNITY

While private non-State actors, such as Chief Investigator 1, were essential in starting the criminal investigation in Syria, States also played a role in the training of Syrian activists. Arguably, documenting crimes would not be enough to establish criminal liability at the highest level of the Syrian government. The UK government funded the initial training that would enable Syrian investigators to know *how* and *what* material to collect to inform a future criminal prosecution, specifically for those most responsible.

The notion of training Syrian activists in investigating mass atrocities in the wake of the Arab Spring arose as organised violence increased and options to investigate human rights violations appeared limited in the broader international arena. In 2011, the United Kingdom's Foreign and Commonwealth Office's (FCO) accused the Syrian government of violently suppressing unarmed civilian protestors and wanted to show its support for human rights in Syria.[44] William Hague, then UK foreign secretary, attempted a number of initiatives, including lobbying the UNSC to commence sanctions against the Syrian government, as well as pressing the UNSC to provide the CoI for Syria the mandate 'to investigate all alleged violations of international human rights law since March 2011'.[45] Nonetheless, as stated earlier, the resolution was blocked by Russia and China. Through the course of the war, another ten UNSC resolutions were also vetoed by Russia and China,[46] including a draft

---

[44]   For example, *see,* William Hague, 'Announcement: Foreign Secretary appalled at violence in Syria', Foreign and Commonwealth Office, United Kingdom, 31 July 2011, www.gov.uk/gov ernment/news/foreign-secretary-appalled-at-violence-in-syria.

[45]   For example, *see,* Draft Resolution S/2011/612, 4 October 2011; also *see,* William Hague 'Announcement: Foreign Secretary meets Syrian opposition', Foreign and Commonwealth Office, United Kingdom, 21 November 2011b, www.gov.uk/government/news/foreign-secretary-meets-syrian-opposition; Draft Resolution S/2011/612, 9-2-4; Note that this was also considered in association with non-lethal measures to support armed 'moderate' opposition in Syria. The Arab League suspended their monitoring in Syria in January 2012, citing a deterioration of situation.

[46]   As at the 22 November 2017.

resolution to refer the situation in Syria to the ICC in 2014.[47] As Russia and China intervened to stop these processes, and top-down measures seemed limited, William Hague and the UK's FCO considered alternative options to support unarmed civilian protestors in Syria directly.[48]

While options for the FCO appeared limited, this was also an opportunity to attempt something different. Initially, the FCO considered training Syrian activists in human rights advocacy, with several hundred thousand pounds marked for the project. A former UK government consultant (referred hereafter as 'Former UK Government Consultant 1') maintained that the UK government 'didn't have a particularly large or in depth team' with expertise on Syria at that time and recalled that, for the most part, 'we were just working day-to-day, just reacting to the situation' as it unfolded:[49]

> The reason the FCO Syria team in London was pretty small in early 2011 to 2012 was due to the disruption caused by the evacuation of the UK Embassy from Damascus and the pressures of the Arab Spring. Some staff from Damascus joined us in London, some moved to the embassies in Istanbul or Beirut, some were moved on to other posts to cover other Arab Spring events. By 2014–15 the team was much stronger with many more Arabic speakers.[50]

Former UK Government Consultant 1 recalled that the program from which CIJA was born was quite limited in the beginning.[51] It included training Syrian activists as a type of citizen journalist,

> measuring the size of the shell craters and the angle, and assessing where it was fired from, what type of weapon was used, and therefore you could document the Syrian government is using this type of weapon, which [for example] is linked to this unit, against these areas. So it was quite basic at that time. That was just how it began. It was very much about giving local community, local human rights activists, lawyers, the ability to document use of heavy weapons against civilians.[52]

By chance, a different type of training was posed. One consultant who was asked to conduct training in relation to the Syrian activists was William Wiley,

---

[47] *See,* Draft Resolution S/2014/348, 22 May 2014; also *see,* Draft Resolution S/2012/77, 4 February 2012; and Draft Resolution S/2012/538, 19 July 2012.

[48] Jamal Abbasi (Former 'FCO Programme Manager', and former Chief of Staff, CIJA), interview with author, February 2017.

[49] Former UK Government Consultant 1, interview with author, November 2017.

[50] Former UK Government Consultant 1.

[51] Former UK Government Consultant 1.

[52] Former UK Government Consultant 1.

then the director of his own consultancy business, Tsamota Ltd.[53] Wiley maintained that although citizen journalists raised awareness of the violence occurring in Syria at both the domestic and international levels, this type of material was, for the most part, not able to sufficiently link the underlying crimes with those most responsible for core crimes in a criminal prosecution. Wiley proposed instead to train them on the types of evidence that informed individual criminal liability for those most responsible, specifically for the purpose of war crimes or crimes against humanity prosecution and, in so doing, to enable the Syrian activists to collect material that would be admissible in a future criminal prosecution. Given the limited options available to the FCO at the time, as well as the opportunities it presented, the FCO agreed to Wiley's proposal.[54] Over the course of the next several months, between the end of 2011 and late 2012, around sixty to seventy Syrian activists were trained in countries neighbouring Syria.[55]

The training of CIJA's first investigators reflected the lessons learned from previous international criminal tribunals, starting with the prosecution of Nazi war criminals and ending with the trial of Saddam Hussein in Bagdad: the training and initial direction of the group that would become CIJA was largely informed by Wiley's experiences, as the principal trainer and future director of CIJA. Early in his career, Wiley was an officer in the Canadian Armed Forces, and his interest in the role of military history and military law led him to complete a doctorate on German land forces and war crimes committed during the Second World War.[56] Wiley commenced his career in international criminal law as an analyst and investigator at the War Crimes Section of the Canadian Justice Department, prosecuting German war criminals. Thereafter, he moved to Europe to work as a war crimes analyst and investigator at the International Criminal Tribunal for the Former Yugoslavia (ICTY) and the International Criminal Tribunal for Rwanda (ICTR) in the Hague and Arusha, respectively. In 2003, he was appointed the first investigator to work with the newly established ICC, investigating the case of Thomas Lubanga Dyilo (referred to as the *Lubanga* case).[57]

[53] Borger, 'Syria's Truth Smugglers'.
[54] Jamal Abbasi (Former 'FCO Programme Manager', and former Chief of Staff, CIJA), interview with author.
[55] Borger, 'Syria's Truth Smugglers'.
[56] *See*, William Wiley, "Onwards and Upwards': The German Field Army and War Crimes during the Second World War', PhD thesis, York University, Canada, 1996; William Wiley (CIJA director), interview with author, January 2017.
[57] See *The Prosecutor v. Thomas Lubanga Dyilo*, International Criminal Court, The Hague, ICC-1/04-01/06.

Although the ICC was new and a significant step forward in international criminal justice, a lack of universal jurisdiction continued to stymie the court's reach.[58] Yet the greater difficulty, according to Wiley, was Luis Moreno Ocampo, the ICCs first prosecutor, who Wiley believed cut corners and acted unethically.[59] After two years at the ICC, Wiley moved to Bagdad, working first as a human rights officer for the United Nations Assistance Mission for Iraq, monitoring the Iraqi High Tribunal proceedings involving Saddam Hussein and later, as legal advisor in the Defence Office of the Iraqi High Tribunal (IHT) for two years, on the defence of a number of high-profile former Baathist leaders.[60]

Bagdad was nothing short of a challenge and the criminal proceedings were inherently political. Wiley believed that a key systemic failure of the IHT was the intervention into the judicial process by Bagdad's newly formed political leadership, largely motivated by sectarian revenge.[61] Nevertheless, Bagdad also provided Wiley with significant independence as legal advisor to the defence, as well as experience of the region. By the end of his tenure in Bagdad, Wiley begin to consider working independently, outside of a State or interstate structure.[62] In March 2008, he left Iraq and started Tsamota Ltd.[63] As Tsamota Ltd was established, he began a number of attempts to influence

---

[58] William Wiley (CIJA director), interview with author, January 2017; this view was shared by others, for example, on issues of ICC, *see* Antonio Cassese, 'Is the ICC Still Having Teething Problems', *Journal of International Criminal Justice* 4, no. 3 (2006): 434–41; on issues surrounding wider international criminal prosecution, for example, *also see* Carla Del Ponte, 'Investigation and Prosecution of Large-scale Crimes at the International Level', *Journal of International Criminal Justice* 4, no. 3 (2006): 539–58.

[59] Wiley, interview; also *see* Milan Markovic, 'The ICC Prosecutor's Missing Code of Conduct', *Texas International Law Journal* 27, no. 1 (2011): 201–36; Yet, he was also keen to see the ICC adapt and consider innovative investigative means that could lead to more effective prosecution; Wiley, interview; others practicing international criminal law have proposed similar arguments; *see for example*, Del Ponte, 'Investigation and Prosecution of Large-Scale Crimes at the International Level'.

[60] John Burns, 'Western Lawyers Say Iraq Discarded Due Process in Hussein Trial', *New York Times*, 24 September 2008, www.nytimes.com/2008/09/25/world/middleeast/25trial.html.

[61] For Wiley's role in Iraq, *see* Burns, 'Western Lawyers Say Iraq Discarded Due Process in Hussein Trial'; Wiley, interview; others also believed that IHT represented a missed opportunity for justice and was marred by political intervention, for example, *see* Miranda Sissons and Ari Bassin 'Was the Dujail Trial Fair?' *Journal for International Criminal Justice*, 5 (2007): 272–86.

[62] Wiley (CIJA director), interview with author.

[63] Tsamota Group Ltd consulted mainly for foreign governments and international businesses on subjects such as the rule of law, international criminal law, justice security reform projects and averting war crimes. Wiley explained that he could begin to decide with whom he was going to work; Jamal Abbasi, 'Introduction to Tsamota Group', 13 April 2013, https://prezi.com /wii-ka79kgjb/introduction-to-tsamota-group/.

how professionals and the public more broadly thought about investigative approaches to aid international criminal justice.[64] In particular, Wiley attempted to influence private non-State actors and those who might traditionally be involved in the area of human rights advocacy to adopt the tasks and practices related to international criminal law investigations. This included increasing their knowledge of investigative processes and identifying/collecting material that would be admissible in a future criminal prosecution.[65] It was in this context that Wiley was asked by the UK government, through a firm owned by a former colleague of Wiley at the ICTY, to train Syrians in the midst of the Arab Spring.[66]

The training of Syrians to become investigators, combined with the collection of government documents from Syria, posed a number of practical and conceptual questions. How would investigators, and the incoming material collected, be managed from an operational viewpoint? The Syrian investigators voiced these concerns during one of the initial training sessions. Wiley invited Ambassador Stephen Rapp, then US ambassador-at-large for Global Criminal Justice, to meet with investigators during their training in early 2012. As noted in the previous chapter, before his role as ambassador, Rapp was chief prosecutor for the Special Court of Sierra Leone, and also chief of prosecutions at the ICTR. Rapp and some of his colleagues had provided expertise in the establishment of the

---

[64] For example, Wiley attempted to show how best practice could be achieved using his professional experience in the case of Taha Yaseen Ramadan to illuminate the weaknesses of domestic criminal trials in Iraq and broader misunderstandings for the nature of international criminal prosecution. Drawing on his experiences as investigator in the case of Thomas Lubanga Dyilo, he also attempted to highlight misconceptions relating to the practical nature of investigative work, as well as what evidence informed a successful prosecution for crimes against humanity in relation to individual criminal liability of a senior leader. *See* William Wiley 'Taha Yaseen Ramadan before the Iraqi High Tribunal: An Insider's Perspective', in T. McCormack and J. Klefner, eds., *Yearbook of International Humanitarian Law 2006*, vol. 9 (Cambridge and New York: T.M.C. Asser Press 2008): 181–243; William Wiley, 'Societal Reconciliation, the Rule of Law and the Iraqi High Tribunal', FICHL Policy Brief Series, no. 35, 2015; *See* William Wiley, 'The Difficulties Inherent in the Investigation of Allegations of Rape before International Courts and Tribunals', in Morten Bergsmo, Alf Butenschon Skre and Elizabeth Wood, eds., *Understanding and Proving International Sex Crimes* (Beijing: Torkel Opsahl Academic EPublisher, 2012): 367–89.

[65] For example, *see* Morten Bergsmo and William Wiley, 'Human Rights Professionals and the Criminal Investigation and Prosecution of Core International Crimes', in Siri Skare, Ingvild Burkey and Hege Mork, eds., *Manual on Human Rights Monitoring: An Introduction for Human Rights Field Officers*, University of Oslo (Oslo: Norwegian Centre for Human Rights, 2008).

[66] By the end of 2011, the level of violence was suspected to have increased significantly in Syria but a court or UN agency was not appointed or permitted to investigate these allegations from an international criminal law perspective.

Extraordinary African Chambers in Senegal. When Habré was indicted, Rapp attended his prosecution in his new role as ambassador-at-large for Global Criminal Justice. Rapp recalled that one of the first issues articulated by the Syrian investigators, including by Chief Investigator 1, was the need for a 'commission' to manage the evidence.[67] The Syrian investigators envisaged the commission as a non-profit, independent organisation.

Increasingly, the Syrian investigators were developing their vision for how the group could work and what they could achieve. Moreover, according to Former UK Government Consultant 1, during the summer of 2012, the Syrian investigators 'started to capture huge amounts of documentation',[68] and this was further supported by financial contributions by the US government in late 2012. Former UK Government Consultant 1 says that the initiative to collect documentation at great personal risk was very much driven from the ground up, and that the UK government had not told the Syrian investigators how to approach the investigation.[69] As Former UK Government Consultant 1 argued, it was 'very much driven by what people were actually doing on the ground, and what they were able to find. When that came back to us, they started asking "Can you fund us to do this work? We think we can start delivering documentation, start building that towards case files."' He recalls that they presented a concept paper to the UK FCO with the idea of 'expanding the scope of the program to include storing, processing, and analyzing those documents'.[70] The UK government granted the additional funds. Former UK Government Consultant 1 also remembered that, at this point, the program began to move away from the idea of citizen journalists towards building cases for a future accountability processes.[71] From mid-2013, CIJA received the first large grant from the European Union, and thereafter other new donors such as Denmark came aboard. This enabled CIJA to establish analytical, administrative and (paid) leadership structures, additional to the collection capability and evidence management structure, which came onto the payroll during 2012.

OPERATIONALISING COOPERATIVE CRIMINAL ACCOUNTABILITY PRACTICES

Initially, as the group became more formalised, it was established as the Syrian Commission for Justice and Accountability (SCJA). Prior to receiving the

[67] Stephen Rapp (CIJA commissioner), interview with author, January 2017.
[68] Former UK Government Consultant 1, interview with author.
[69] Former UK Government Consultant 1, interview with author.
[70] Former UK Government Consultant 1, interview with author.
[71] Former UK Government Consultant 1, interview with author.

additional grants, Wiley and Rapp began the difficult task of raising the additional funding required to support such an operation. In this respect, Wiley maintained, Rapp was key: States were initially reticent to fund a group of private non-State actors to develop a type of commission ordinarily established by States or multilateral agencies.[72] In the interim, analysts were required to begin the task of reviewing the material collected and to ascertain if a potential criminal case could be prepared in response to events that had unfolded in the early days of the Arab Spring. While attempting to source additional funding, Wiley recruited SCJA/CIJA 's first two senior analysts, along with an Arabic translator,[73] who served on a *pro bono* basis until mid-2013. Both senior analysts had worked for more than ten years on a number of high-profile war crimes cases at the ICC and ICTY, and they viewed their roles as not only establishing the facts but also scrutinizing the narratives that had developed during the course of the war, particularly narratives produced by Western media. According to Senior Analyst 2, international justice was not only about showing there was no impunity but also braking down false or incorrect narratives of the underlying events.[74] Moreover, Senior Analyst 2 attempted to view the material collected through an impartial lens:

> [We viewed] the documents as critical contemporaneous references from a regime dealing with a significant and very complex security problem. What did this material tell us about the regime's response, the chronology of events, the political, military and security structures involved, the identification of commanders and senior figures and the actions of the opposition? Critically, what evidence was there of the decision making processes that had a 'cause and effect' on the events in Syria?[75]

To do this, Senior Analyst 1 and Senior Analyst 2 attempted to reconstruct the command structures of the Syrian government and, through them, to establish criminal linkages. A critical turning point in 2013 occurred when analysts discovered the existence of an entity called 'Central Crisis Management Cell' and associated structures pertaining to it.[76] Once command structures and key events were established, they began the task of identifying corresponding crime-based evidence, established by insider and/or victim statements and corroborating materials.[77] As Senior Analyst 1 maintained:

---

[72] William Wiley (CIJA director), interview with author.
[73] CIJA Senior Analyst 1, interview with author, January 2017; CIJA Senior Analyst 2, interview with author, January 2017; William Wiley (CIJA director), interview with author.
[74] CIJA Senior Analyst 2, interview with author.
[75] CIJA Senior Analyst 2, interview with author.
[76] CIJA Senior Analyst 1, interview with author.
[77] CIJA Senior Analyst 1; CIJA Senior Analyst 2, interview with author.

[It was not] until very late in the game (I think it took us over a year), before we dared to utter our first working hypothesis as to how things might have worked in Syria. It was the documentary evidence that led us to where we are now, not the other way round. And we duly noted the existence of exculpatory material and logged it at every corner in the process. It also formed part of the briefs that CIJA has produced since then.[78]

It took time to persuade other States to contribute financially to a non-profit, independent commission. Although SCJA/CIJA was a separate legal entity from Wiley's Tsamota Ltd, it was initially forced to rely on Tsamota for the crucial seed funding, along with the funding from the UK FCO, to enable SCJA/CIJA to commence its evidentiary analysis work. This included drawing on Tsamota's staff and office space,[79] until the funds and the staff to operate independently from Tsamota Ltd were secured.

Over time, SCJA/CIJA was funded by the European Union (EU), the US, Canada, Denmark, Norway, Switzerland, and Germany, with continued support from the UK.[80] In mid-2013, once SCJA/CIJA secured additional funding, it began to establish an operational and governance model in earnest.[81] This included the appointment of a project manager to act as chief of staff;[82] to establish structural, procedural and technological improvements to increase efficiency; and further to establish systems and procedures to safeguard the organisation against risk, most particularly for those in the field.[83] It also included appointing additional expertise. Alongside Wiley, two others would form a board of directors: Chris Engels, a US lawyer, and Nerma Jelacic, previously head of communications for the ICTY. SCJA/CIJA also established a *pro bono* advisory panel to provide advice and feedback on evidentiary and legal issues. The panel consisted of former senior practitioners, such as analysts and investigators, prosecutors, defence counsel and judicial advisors. As their geographical remit expanded in mid-2014, the organisation was renamed the Commission for International Justice and

---

[78] CIJA Senior Analyst 1, interview with author.
[79] In this respect, Wiley explained, 'the non-profit constituted a serious financial drain on my commercial operation'. William Wiley (CIJA director), correspondence with author, February 2017.
[80] Borger, 'Syria's Truth Smugglers'.
[81] William Wiley (CIJA director), correspondence with author, February 2017.
[82] The initial incumbent was an English solicitor with long service in operational positions in Iraq and Afghanistan; he returned to England in September 2015, whereupon he was replaced as chief of staff by Jamal Abbasi, a former programme manager at the FCO who had been responsible for, amongst other things, the SCJA/CIJA file; Wiley, correspondence; Abbasi, interview.
[83] Abbasi, interview.

Accountability (CIJA), and the non-profit foundation was registered in The Hague.[84]

As a cooperative criminal accountability community, CIJA continued to draw extensively on those with expertise in international criminal tribunals. For some practitioners who would later join CIJA's board of commissioners in 2016, part of the appeal was that it represented something different. Each advisor provided different skill sets and experiences. For example, Alex Whiting was a senior prosecutor at the ICTY before he became an investigation coordinator and later prosecutions coordinator at the ICC. Whiting was keen to be involved in the CIJA. In the realm of international criminal law, he explained, 'there are limited structures and political support to [investigate] these cases', particularly given the limitations placed on the ICC. Indeed, Whiting argued: 'so what this international criminal justice project requires is creativity and initiative'.[85] Similarly, Larry Johnson, another CIJA commissioner, was a keen supporter of the concept. Johnson's expertise lay in the establishment and management of international criminal tribunals, particularly from a diplomatic, policy and legal viewpoint, including his role as *Chef de Cabinet*, at the Office of the President for the ICTY. What appealed to Johnson was that the CIJA represented an 'innovative' approach to solving a key problem for international criminal justice: namely that one did not (and should not) need to wait until a particular tribunal was identified or established to start collecting evidence. One could prepare case briefs that were 'ready to go for a national, regional or international tribunal' as, and when, courts become available.[86] One other important commissioner was Stephen Rapp, who formally joined CIJA as an independent commissioner, once he resigned from his post as US ambassador. It was Wiley's emphasis on linkage, modes of liability and focus on senior perpetrators that appealed to Rapp, and he continued to work with Wiley to ensure CIJA was established and increased its capability.[87] In short, while establishing the operational and governance model was important, CIJA's key proposition appeared to be twofold: its expertise in establishing criminal linkage and the role of the local Syrian investigators who were willing to operate in the field as war continued in Syria.

---

[84]　Commission for International Justice and Accountability (CIJA), 'Conversion and amendment to the articles of association 'The Commission for International Justice and Accountability', The Hague, 2016; CIJA Senior Analyst 1, interview; 'CIJA Senior Analyst 2, interview; Wiley, interview.

[85]　Alex Whiting, (CIJA commissioner), interview with author, January 2017.

[86]　Larry Johnson (CIJA commissioner), interview with author, January 2017.

[87]　Stephen Rapp (CIJA commissioner), interview with author, January 2017.

Once a significant number of documents had been collected and the initial criminal linkage analysis was conducted by senior military and political analysts, CIJA asked international criminal prosecutors to begin the task of assessing the evidence against international criminal norms, identifying relevant crimes and modes of liability and drafting the first case briefs. In 2014, Tarik Abdulhak, who had worked as an international prosecutor at the Extraordinary Chambers in the Courts of Cambodia (ECCC) and previously as a legal advisor to the president of the War Crimes and Organised Crime Chamber in Bosnia Herzegovina, was the first international prosecutor recruited. Like the senior analysts, he was guided by the evidence, namely the documents which had either been gener- ated, used or received by alleged perpetrators. Increasingly, the first case emerged as the illegal detention, persecution and torture of Syrian demonstra- tors, starting in March 2011. According to Abdulhak, although CIJA's biggest challenge was balancing institutional capacity with being 'nimble', they worked to an international standard:[88] 'We were doing investigations of the kind you would be doing at an international tribunal ... the work is done to a very high degree of forensic analysis and attention to detail.'[89] In terms of his work in writing the first case brief, Abdulhak adhered to substantive and procedural standards of international criminal law: 'The level to which I tried to work was as if this was a filing to an international criminal tribunal.'[90]

The briefs provided a detailed analysis of the available evidence across a number of areas. They included the historical and institutional context; crime-based evidence (i.e. material proving the commission of specific acts of torture, murder, rape, enforced disappearance); the joint criminal enterprise through which the crimes were allegedly orchestrated; the relevant authority structures and communications systems through which the enterprise was coordinated; and the responsibility of particular individuals for the alleged crimes under international law. Of necessity, the briefs included an identifi- cation and analysis of any material that was exculpatory in nature. CIJA analysts and lawyers viewed this as an integral component of their work, and as an important ethical consideration in the drafting of the briefs. Once drafted, the CIJA commissioners would review the case brief, including accessing the underlying documents referenced in it.[91] The commissioners provided critical advice and feedback on the quality of the briefs.[92]

---

[88] Tarik Abdulhak (CIJA legal advisor), interview with author, December 2017.
[89] Tarik Abdulhak (CIJA legal advisor), interview with author, December 2017.
[90] Tarik Abdulhak (CIJA legal advisor), interview with author, December 2017.
[91] Tarik Abdulhak (CIJA legal advisor), interview with author, December 2017.
[92] For more on the independent committee, see, Rankin, 'The Future of International Criminal Evidence in New Wars?'

In writing the first case brief on the Syrian government, CIJA tested the outcomes of the investigation against the norms of international criminal law, and they also identified sources of international law. According to Abdulhak, the underlying investigative and analytical processes were the same, irrespective of in which legal regime the evidence would ultimately be presented: "The point is, whether you apply the ICC statute, customary international law or even a domestic [Syrian] statute definition of substantive crimes (murder, torture etc.), the forensic analysis of the material is essentially the same.'[93] Although a court was yet to be available to prosecute, CIJA also began identifying the hierarchy of the sources of international criminal law in the process of writing its briefs. Abdulhak explained that

> Back in 2014, I think the view was that the ICC statute provided the most convenient starting point because all the offences are defined in one place . . . [However] customary international law would be of higher authority than the ICC statute because customary international law (which was the law applied by ICTY, ICTR, ECCC etc), is technically universal, while the ICC's Rome Statute isn't.[94]

In this way, CIJA had identified the sources of law as customary international law but had defined the offenses as per the Rome Statute as an interim measure.

OPERATIONAL OPPORTUNITIES AND LIMITATIONS TO PRACTICE

Since its inception, the CIJA has had to make a number of important decisions. As violence ensued across Syria, a number of armed non-State actors emerged, and its State funders asked the CIJA if it would consider extending its focus to other armed actors in Syria. While little known at the time, an emerging force, growing rapidly in numbers, and suspected of directly targeting civilians, was a group then called the Islamic State of Iraq and the Levant (ISIL). The group was later referred to as the Islamic State of Iraq and Syria (ISIS), and Islamic State (IS) (hereafter referred to by its Arabic acronym, Daesh).[95] As CIJA began to investigate Daesh's activities, its remit extended into Iraq to reflect its strategic reach, particularly in relation to allegations of the sexual slavery of Yazidi women and children in 2014. CIJA recruited and

---

[93] Tarik Abdulhak (CIJA legal advisor), correspondence with author, May 2018.
[94] Tarik Abdulhak (CIJA legal advisor), correspondence with author, May 2018.
[95] Fawaz A. Gerges, *ISIS: A History* (Princeton, NJ: Princeton University Press, 2016).

trained additional Syrian and Iraqi investigators to conduct this part of the investigation across the two theatres.[96]

Up to this point, the CIJA had limited its investigative remit by not focusing on other armed actors who might be suspected of war crimes in Syria or Iraq. There were a number of practical factors that informed this decision. First, from an operational perspective, the CIJA was concerned not to overextend its remit in the two theatres. Keen to prove its worth, it prized quality over the quantity of senior actors or groups it could investigate. Second, the directors at the CIJA believed that there were already a number of inherent risks for investigators who continued to operate in the theatre of war without a UN mandate. It was envisaged that these risks increased significantly should opposition groups become a part of the CIJA's remit, namely because there would be no incentive to assist the CIJA with its investigations – or to keep CIJA personnel alive – which would serve to compromise its initial objectives.[97] Moreover, to add to the challenge of investigating armed opposition groups, these groups have, broadly speaking, remained structurally very fluid.

Yet, these limitations also reflect the difficulties of conducting criminal investigations in the theatre of war, particularly in view of international laws that govern proportionality.[98] Given that Daesh had attempted to show itself as a proto-state, it was more likely that the CIJA could build a case or series of cases briefs of suspected war crimes, crimes against humanity and/or genocide. For example, Daesh was, like the Syrian government, a centralized hierarchical organization. It produced documentation, albeit far less than the Syrian government, and senior leaders gave orders through a chain of command,[99] which could be interpreted in some instances as endorsing or directing gross mistreatment of civilians.[100]

Added to this, the CIJA made a number of other important decisions. Like Garcés and Guengueng, it could not and did not make arrests or attempt private prosecution. Yet, unlike Garcés and Guengueng, it did not submit private criminal complaints to foreign courts. Nonetheless, like Garcés and

---

[96] William Wiley (CIJA director), interview with author; Frank Gardner, 'Iraq's Sinjar Yazidis: Bringing IS Slavers to Justice', *BBC News*, 2 August 2016, sec. Middle East, www.bbc.com /news/world-middle-east-36960657.

[97] William Wiley (CIJA director), interview with author.

[98] *See* Article 51 para. 5b of the Geneva Conventions of 1977, which prohibits '[a]n attack which may be expected to cause incidental loss of civilian life, injury to civilians, damage to civilian objects, or a combination thereof, which would be excessive in relation to the concrete and direct military advantage anticipated'; *see* International Committee of the Red Cross (1977), 'Protocols additional to the Geneva Conventions of 12 August 1949', Geneva: ICRC.

[99] William Wiley (CIJA director), interview with author.

[100] Gardner, 'Iraq's Sinjar Yazidis'.

Guengueng, it adopted the practices or tasks of the offices of international prosecutors, with the intention of handing the material over to a public domestic or international criminal tribunal.

There are a number of important criticisms of the CIJA. They include that it operated outside a UN mandate. Some observers have raised questions concerning the legitimacy of private non-State actors conducting investigations and preparing briefs for breaches of international criminal and humanitarian law against senior leaders of State and non-State armed actors.[101] Another criticism is that CIJA's investigative focus is restricted to two groups, the Syrian government and Daesh. Lastly, to access the material collected, the CIJA must, at least in the evidence-gathering process, interact with groups that may, during the course of the war, also be suspected of committing war crimes.[102] In principle, the CIJA's remit should extend to all State and non-State actors, operating in both theatres. For example, the remit should potentially include Hezbollah, Russia, Britain, Kurdish armed forces, Qatar, the United Kingdom, Turkey, the United States, Iran, Saudi Arabia and Australia.[103] Or, indeed other State actors involved in Syria. Moreover, it is estimated that, at one point, more than 1,000 armed opposition groups operated within Syria alone, and that these groups remained characteristically fluid.[104] Should the CIJA want to set for itself the aim of ending impunity for *all* senior leaders suspected of atrocities in Syria and Iraq, it would surely fail.[105]

These are important limitations acknowledged by the CIJA.[106] In response, the CIJA is keen to note there is nothing preventing other private actors from investigating belligerent parties which are not the focus of CIJA investigations. Indeed, the CIJA would like to see other private non-State actors take on this role, and have recently partnered with the International Nuremberg Principles Academy to draft guidelines for private investigative bodies, titled 'Nuremberg Guidelines for Non-Public Investigative Bodies in the Field of International Criminal and Humanitarian Law'.[107]

---

[101]   Rankin, 'The Future of International Criminal Evidence in New Wars?'
[102]   Rankin, 'The Future of International Criminal Evidence in New Wars?'
[103]   Zachary Laub, 'Who's Who in Syria's Civil War', Council on Foreign Relations, 28 April 2017, www.cfr.org/site-api/cfr-wrapper.
[104]   'Guide to the Syrian Rebels – BBC News', *BBC News*, 13 December 2013, www.bbc.com/n ews/world-middle-east-24403003.
[105]   Melinda Rankin, 'Investigating Crimes against Humanity in Syria and Iraq: The Commission for International Justice and Accountability', *Global Responsibility to Protect* 9, no. 4 (2017): 395–421, https://doi.org/10.1163/1875984X-00904004.
[106]   William Wiley (CIJA director), interview with author.
[107]   Internationale Akademie Nürnberger Prinzipien, 'Private Investigations in International Criminal Justice', International Nuremberg Principles Academy, 2020, www.nurembergacad

Nevertheless, if the CIJA was attempting to show that one small group of private non-State actors, not supported by a UNSC resolution or Chapter 7 mandate, could, in principle, conduct investigation and evidentiary analysis focusing on the involvement of senior leaders in humanity's gravest crimes; while the alleged crimes were continuing, it may mark an important advancement in how we view de facto international prosecutors. The CIJA had the opportunity to test if its investigative and analytical approach adheres to international standards in German courts, particularly in relation to the conviction of Eyad A. (see Chapter 5). Evidence gathered may also contribute to prosecutions in future domestic or international criminal tribunals.[108]

CIJA'S OUTPUTS TO DATE

At the time of writing in 2021, Chief Investigator 1 and CIJA are continuing to investigate war crimes and crimes against humanity in Syria and elsewhere. The CIJA also continues to investigate war crimes, crimes against humanity and allegations of genocide in Iraq, amongst other places. It maintains that it has prepared ten case briefs against fifty of the most senior leaders in the Syrian government and security/military apparatus, including President Bashar al-Assad.[109] Thus far, more than 1 million pages of governmental, security, intelligence and military documentation have been collected,[110] and several thousand interviews with witnesses conducted (including those who worked inside the Syrian and Daesh regimes).[111] Since broadening its scope to include the collection and development of evidence against Daesh in 2014, CIJA claims that it had prepared eight case briefs against forty of the most senior members of Daesh.[112] It has also provided material to the UN's Investigative Team in Iraq additional to the IIIM.

CIJA's material has contributed to a number of initiatives and cases. As discussed earlier in this chapter, CIJA was a major contributor of material to

emy.org/projects/detail/9c75eeaeeobd858dfdaeacaiead42e55/private-investigations-in-international-criminal-justice-24/.

[108]   Rankin, 'Investigating Crimes against Humanity in Syria and Iraq'.

[109]   *See* Chris Engels, Written Testimony before the Tom Lantos Human Rights Commission, United States Congress, HVC-210 U.S. Capitol Visitor Center, Washington, 23 September 2016, www.congress.gov/114/bills/hr5732/BILLS-114hr5732rfs.pdf.

[110]   William Wiley (CIJA director), interview with author.

[111]   CIJA Senior analyst 2, interview with author; William Wiley (CIJA director), interview with author; Alex Whiting, 'The UN General Assembly's Historic Resolution on Accountability for Syria: What It Means and What Are Its Limits', *Just Security*, 22 December 2016, www .justsecurity.org/35795/syria-general-assembly-sidesteps-security-council/.

[112]   William Wiley (CIJA director), communication with author, February 2021.

the IIIM for Syria.[113] In 2016, Christian Wenaweser, permanent representative of Liechtenstein to the UN in New York, and CIJA explored various means for how the UN could contribute to international criminal accountability in relation to the situation in Syria.[114] According to Wenaweser, informal consultations took place, with CIJA and others, such as the Syrian Accountability Project, which helped inform the drafting of a resolution for the UNGA to establish the IIIM. Wenaweser imagined that the material collected by these actors should be made accessible to a UN 'mechanism'.[115] In December 2016, Wenaweser proposed a draft resolution (71/248) to the UNGA, entitled 'International, Impartial and Independent Mechanism to Assist in the Investigation and Prosecution of Persons Responsible for the Most Serious Crimes under International Law Committed in the Syrian Arab Republic since March 2011' (hereafter 'IIIM' or 'Mechanism'). It defined the mandate of the Mechanism: namely to 'collect, consolidate, preserve and analyze evidence of such crimes'. The resolution (A/RES/71/248) was adopted by the UNGA on 21 December 2016. It included the investigation of core international crimes (war crimes, crimes against humanity and genocide) with the intention of preparing 'files in order to facilitate and expedite fair and independent criminal proceedings in accordance with international standards, in national, regional or international courts or tribunals that have or may in the future have jurisdiction over these crimes'.[116] As Wenaweser later maintained, CIJA would 'be one of the primary suppliers of evidence and material to the mechanism'.[117]

CIJA's material also contributed to a civil case concerning the targeted killing of Marie Colvin, an international journalist, by the Syrian government in *Colvin* v. *Syrian Arab Republic*.[118] In the US district court for the District of

---

[113]   Christian Wenaweser (2017), 'UN Press Briefing: Christian Wenaweser (Liechtenstein) and Alya Ahmed Saif Al-Thani (Qatar) on International, Impartial and Independent Mechanism concerning serious crimes in Syria, 27 January, http://webtv.un.org.

[114]   'Liechtenstein GA Draft on Accountability in Syria: International investigation', UN Report (Documents) Monday 19 December, http://un-report.blogspot.com.au/2016/12/liechtenstein-unga-draft-resolution-on.html

[115]   Christian Wenaweser (permanent representative of Liechtenstein to the United Nations), interview with author, 2017.

[116]   'Liechtenstein GA Draft on Accountability in Syria: International investigation'.

[117]   Christian Wenaweser (2017), 'UN Press Briefing: Christian Wenaweser (Liechtenstein) and Alya Ahmed Saif Al-Thani (Qatar) on International, Impartial and Independent Mechanism concerning Serious Crimes in Syria.

[118]   *Colvin* v. *Syrian Arab Republic No.* 1: 2016cv 01423 – Document 59 (DDC 2019), https://law.justia.com/cases/federal/district-courts/district-of-columbia/dcdce/1:2016cv01423/180335/59/; *also see* 'Ewan Brown Exhibits.' The Center for Justice and Accountability, 26 March 2018. https://cja.org/what-we-do/litigation/colvin-v-syria/pleadings/ewan-brown-exhibits/

Columbia, Judge Amy Jackson decided that Marie Colvin was 'specifically targeted' by the responsible State 'because of her profession, for the purpose of silencing those reporting on the growing opposition movement in the country'.[119]

More recently, CIJA's material has been drawn upon in relation to a number of ongoing criminal cases. For example, CIJA's material was submitted to the Madrid courts under universal jurisdiction. The sister of a Syrian truck driver who was allegedly kidnapped, tortured and murdered by the Syrian government submitted the complaint.[120] Acting on behalf of the sister was Guernica 37, an emerging group of international lawyers. Toby Cadman, one of the co-founders of Guernica 37, also sits on the Advisory Panel of the CIJA. Cadman viewed the Pinochet case as a 'benchmark' standard in international criminal law, and to a lesser extent the Habré case as well, and more recently he worked alongside Juan Garcés on a different case.[121] At the time of writing, the case in the Madrid courts remains ongoing.

Nonetheless, the case against Anwar R. and Eyad A. in the Higher Regional Court in Koblenz in Germany presents the greatest test case for the CIJA's investigative and analytical approach. In the next chapter, I detail the case further and also explain how the CIJA and other private non-State actors played a key role in the prosecution in Germany.

CONCLUSION

This chapter showed how Chief Investigator 1, as an early witness to Syrian government crimes, worked with local and later international actors to emerge as de facto international prosecutors. This group evolved to become a formal institution, CIJA, which was (and continues to be) financially supported by a small number of States. In this way, the cooperative criminal accountability community widened from very early on and later included State legal officials in foreign courts. CIJA based its approach on lessons learned at Nuremberg, and also the jurisprudence of international criminal tribunals that emerged in the 1990s.

Despite all this, the role of the local investigators who remain in the field and are willing to collect material under arduous and insecure conditions

---

[119] *Colvin v. Syrian Arab Republic No. 1*: 35. https://law.justia.com/cases/federal/district-courts/district-of-columbia/dcdce/1:2016cv01423/180335/59/.

[120] Sara Afshar, *Syria's Disappeared: The Case Against Assad*, documentary film, directed by Sara Afshar (aired 23 March 2017 (UK), Afshar Films)

[121] Toby Cadman (international lawyer and co-founder of Guernica 37), interview with author, November 2020.

remains an essential feature of CIJA and to extending the reaches of international criminal law to those most responsible.

While CIJA does not provide for a complete investigative solution, as a private non-State actor, CIJA's model represents an innovative and adaptive approach to investigating core international crimes, *while* they are occurring. This is particularly so if the evidence it has collected helps establish individual criminal liability in other future domestic or international criminal tribunal, including the case against Anwar R. in the German courts. It shows how the CIJA could complement other international (State) institutions, such as the ICC, as well as States that have a legal obligation to prosecute or extradite those suspected of core crimes, including the *jus cogens* crime of torture. In this way, the CIJA demonstrated the ability to access linkage material that states could not, given limits to access Syria jurisdiction. Chief Investigator 1 and CIJA support State legal officials, such as German federal legal authorities, who have accepted their legal obligations to prosecute or extradite, but who cannot otherwise access important linkage material.

The next chapter shows how Germany played a role in criminal accountability in Syria, including with private non-State actors, such as CIJA and European Centre for Constitutional and Human Right (ECCHR). Unlike the previous three chapters, which focused on the role of private non-State actors, the next chapter focuses on the role of State legal officials in a foreign court – as de facto international prosecutors. It also seeks to show a broader understanding of the role of States, including the role of Foreign Affairs departments, in widening the exercise of universal jurisdiction for core crimes in their domestic legal systems. Lastly, it shows how German state legal officials of a foreign court played an essential role as de facto international prosecutors working with other private non-State actors in the criminal accountability process for Syria. In short, it illuminates how private non-State actors and state legal officials of a foreign court rely upon each other to extend the reaches of international criminal law as de facto international prosecutors.

5

A Legal Obligation to Prosecute: From De Facto to *De Jure* International Prosecutors? (Germany/Syria)

The previous three chapters focused primarily on the role of private non-State actors who act as de facto international prosecutors, with particular emphasis on victims and witnesses of core crimes. This chapter directs our attention to the role of State legal officials in foreign courts who act as de facto international prosecutors and situates them in a particular historical, political and legal context. Specifically, it examines the evolution of German universal jurisdiction, in light of the atrocities committed by the German Third Reich and the legacy of the Nuremberg Trials. As noted earlier in Chapter 1, the Nuremberg Charter and Nuremberg Tribunal marked a turning point in international criminal law. While Germany continues to address past atrocities in various ways, one of them was to champion the role of international criminal law universally, which saw Germany emerge as one of the broadest universal jurisdictions in the world. One of the outcomes of this was, unlike the cases of Pinochet and Habré, State legal officials did not rely on private non-State actors to submit a criminal complaint to launch its investigations into alleged core crimes in Syria. Rather, it had a domestic legal obligation to do so.

This chapter also serves to extend our understanding of how government actors can play a delicate and nuanced role in providing the effective preconditions for accountability, including establishing a domestic legal system that empowers State legal officials to exercise universal jurisdiction. In doing this, we also better understand the role universal jurisdiction plays in criminal accountability for core crimes, particularly for those crimes accepted and recognised as peremptory norms (*jus cogens*) of international law, and when local efforts towards criminal accountability fail in the jurisdiction where the alleged crimes occur.

This chapter argues that Germany conceptually positioned international criminal law within a broader notion of the international rule of law.

Moreover, it demonstrated not only a willingness to use international criminal law but also a 'responsibility to prosecute' those most responsible for core international crimes, including senior members of the Syrian government. As the first in the world to convict a former member of the Syrian government for crimes against humanity, including torture, since 2011, Germany's current investigations into alleged crimes against humanity in Syria provides a unique and illuminating case study.

This chapter is organised as follows. First, it starts by comparing and contrasting the cases of Pinochet (Spain and the United Kingdom) and Habré (Senegal and Belgium) to reflect upon how government actors in these biographical case studies influenced the accountability process. Second, the chapter focuses directly on Germany as a unique case study and elucidates the evolution of German universal jurisdiction, which remains the broadest in the world, next to that of Norway. Third, it examines how German legal officials have investigated those suspected of core crimes in the senior leadership of the Syrian government, and how they worked with other private non-State actors, including the European Center for Constitutional and Human Rights (ECCHR) and the Commission for International Justice and Accountability (CIJA). It also provides a brief overview of the case against Anwar R. and Eyad A. in the Higher Regional Court of Koblenz in Germany. Lastly, it briefly examines how the Netherlands offers a unique example of a State that may be willing to take Syria to an international tribunal for the breach of its obligations under the Convention Against Torture (CAT), just as Belgium did in the case of *Questions relating to the Obligation to Prosecute or Extradite* with Senegal (*Belgium* v. *Senegal*), in relation to Hissène Habré.[1]

BEYOND LEGAL INTERPRETATIONS: THE PINOCHET AND HABRÉ CASES

While de facto international prosecutors played an essential role in the cases outlined in this study, they also relied on other actors to pursue criminal accountability in a multiplicity of ways. The role of State actors, such as heads of State, foreign ministers, heads of government and parliaments also contributed to establishing important processes for international accountability. As the three biographical case studies illuminated, the ability of private non-State actors and State legal officials in foreign courts, as de facto international actors, to pursue criminal accountability for international crimes was enabled by the

---

[1]   Questions relating to the Obligation to Prosecute or Extradite (*Belgium* v. *Senegal*), Judgment, ICJ Reports (2012).

way national governments had conferred them with particular powers. Criminal accountability for core international crimes hinges on a multiplicity of complex factors. Yet, as observed in this study, States, particularly government actors, play a key role in several ways.

First, government actors must permit the judiciary independence and refrain from intervening in its ability to perform vital tasks, including criminal accountability for former heads of State and senior leaders suspected of core crimes. In the case of Pinochet, both the UK and Spanish governments refrained from intervening in judicial activities. Similarly, in the case of Habré, Belgium also respected judicial independence; when forced to limit universal jurisdiction under US pressure, government actors permitted the Habré case to continue as an exception (as a 'grandfather' clause).

Second, and following on from this, the three biographical case studies reveal the role governments can play in limiting or constraining the exercise of universal jurisdiction. For example, more recently, government legislation in Spain, the United Kingdom and Belgium has seen restrictions placed on how their judiciaries exercise universal jurisdiction for core crimes. In contrast, Germany has set a different trend. Not only has it established one of the broadest universal jurisdictions in the world, it has also enshrined judicial independence in its constitution ('Basic Law for the Federal Republic of Germany', *Grundgesetz für die Bundesrepublik Deutschland*),[2] including from core international crimes.

Third, an important feature of the Pinochet and Habré cases was that governments granted powers to private non-State actors to submit private criminal complaints to foreign courts exercising universal jurisdiction for international crimes, which triggered the official investigation in the Spanish, Senegalese and Belgium courts.

Fourth, the three biographical case studies also show how government actors must be willing to use international law and accept their international obligations, particularly for *jus cogens* crimes such as torture, and as State Parties to the CAT. For example, in the case of Habré, on the advice of the Belgium judiciary and victims of Habré, the Belgium government submitted its ongoing dispute with Senegal to the International Court of Justice (ICJ), when Senegal refrained from its obligation to prosecute or extradite under the CAT. In contrast, while powerful States, such as the United States, championed the CAT, the

---

[2] 'Grundgesetz Für Die Bundesrepublik Deutschland (Basic Law for the Federal Republic of Germany) in the Revised Version Published in the Federal Law Gazette Part III, Classification Number 100–1, as Last Amended by Article 1 of the Act of 28 March 2019 (Federal Law Gazette I, 404)' (n.d.), www.gesetze-im-internet.de/englisch_gg/englisch_gg.html.

biographical case studies outlined in this book illustrated how several US administrations played a fundamental role in supporting heads of State who were suspected of core international crimes, such as Pinochet in Chile, and Habré in Chad. In addition, although the United States is a State Party to the CAT, it played a role in pressuring the Belgium government to limit its universal jurisdiction, because it shared concerns that US senior government actors, including Donald Rumsfeld, might be subject to indictment for the US intervention into Iraq in 2003, and alleged crimes committed thereafter.

Lastly, the biographical case studies illuminate the importance of a range of organisations, tribunals and conventions created and maintained by States, which, among other things, enable criminal accountability, including INTERPOL, the ICJ, the Vienna Convention on the Law of Treaties, the CAT and customary international law, amongst others.

I now turn to explore in further detail the German judicial system, which offers a unique trend in the exercise of universal jurisdiction. I survey the key characteristics that explain why Germany has established one of the broadest universal jurisdictions in the world. I then investigate how Germany has evolved as a global leader in the investigation and prosecution of those most responsible for core international crimes in the Syrian government since 2011.

GERMAN UNIVERSAL JURISDICTION: THE UNLIKELY INTERNATIONAL PROSECUTOR

Today, one could argue that Germany reflects a 'responsibility to prosecute' breaches of international criminal and humanitarian law. It was under these conditions that Germany was seen as one of the first to issue an arrest warrant for a senior member of the Syrian government, Jamil Hassan, the director of the Air Force Intelligence Directorate, for core international crimes in June 2018. More recently, the German Federal Criminal Police Office (*Bundeskriminalamt*) was the first in the world to arrest and prosecute a senior member of the Syrian government in 2019, for alleged crimes against humanity, Anwar R. and his co-defendant Eyad A.

Before we discuss these cases, we first explore the evolution of Germany's unique legal system with regard to universal jurisdiction. Between 1996 and 1998, Germany began to play a central role in championing the development of the International Criminal Court (ICC) and the Rome Statute.[3] During

---

[3]   Markus Eikel, '"Germany's Global Responsibility" and the Creation of the International Criminal Court, 1993–1998', *Journal of International Criminal Justice* 16, no. 3 (1 July 2018): 543–70, https://doi.org/10.1093/jicj/mqy022.

this process, German negotiators were often equally involved in meetings with representatives of the Permanent Members (P-5) of the United Nations Security Council (UNSC) but were often opposed to them, advocating instead for the universal application of the future ICC. Amongst other things, a key motivation was to address past atrocities of Nazi Germany and the legacy of Nuremberg. This in large part motivated Germany's aspirations to engage more fully in the growing body of public international law and a 'willingness to act globally'.[4]

Moreover, key German government actors, who were involved in the early discussions concerning the ICC, voiced a desire for an international legal order, whereby force and coercion were displaced by the international rule of law. When negotiations for an ICC were at their most difficult in 1997, Klaus Kinkel, then German minister for foreign affairs, stated: 'We need an International Criminal Court. The law of the strongest must be replaced by the rule of law. Our goal is the establishment of a global legal order and the promotion of civil societies.'[5]

Although the ICC was never adopted as a universal project, Germany remained committed to the notion of international criminal law as a 'standard'[6] applied universally and equally to everyone. The German government continued to introduce this principle into its domestic jurisdiction. This included introducing the Rome Statute – as well as other international human rights and humanitarian laws, which were enshrined in customary international law – into the domestic judiciary, through the adoption of the Code of Crimes against International Law (*Völkerstrafgesetzbuch* or VStGB).[7] Next to Norway, Germany had adopted the broadest and most liberal universal jurisdiction laws in the system of international criminal law. When the VStGB was ratified by the German Parliament (*Bundestag and Bundesrat*), it also involved amending the German constitution ('Basic Law for the Federal Republic of Germany',

---

[4] Eikel, '"Germany's Global Responsibility" and the Creation of the International Criminal Court, 1993–1998', 26.

[5] Kinkel quoted in, Eikel, '"Germany's Global Responsibility" and the Creation of the International Criminal Court, 1993–1998', 26.

[6] H. L. A. Hart, *The Concept of Law*, ed. Joseph Raz and Penelope A. Bulloch, 3rd ed., Clarendon Law Series (Oxford: Oxford University Press, 2012).

[7] 'Völkerstrafgesetzbuch (VStGB) (Code of Crimes Against International Law), Entered into Force on June 30, 2002', Pub. L. No. Federal Law Gazette I, 2254 (n.d.), www.gesetze-im-internet.de/vstgb/BJNR225410002.html; www.iuscomp.org/gla/statutes/VoeStGB.pdf; Melinda Rankin, '"Responsibility to Prosecute?" The Case of German Universal Jurisdiction, CIJA and the Arrest of Syrian Perpetrators', *LawLog, Center for Global Constitutionalism, WZB* (blog), 13 March 2019, https://lawlog.blog.wzb.eu/2019/03/13/responsibility-to-prosecute-the-case-of-german-universal-jurisdiction-cija-and-the-arrest-of-syrian-perpetrators/.

Grundgesetz für die Bundesrepublik Deutschland).[8] As much as defining domestic law, the German constitution also played a significant role in defining Germany's engagement with the system of international law. For example, the German constitution allows for the 'transfer of sovereign powers to international organisations' under Article 24, 'Transfer of sovereign powers – System of collective security'[9][10] and stipulates that the general rules of international law are integral to Germany federal law under Article 25, 'Primacy of international law'.[11] More particularly, Article 96, 'Other federal courts', explicitly outlined Germany's obligations in relation to core international crimes. In this respect, the courts in each *Land* (province or State) exercise federal powers, as follows:

> 5) With the consent of the Bundesrat, a federal law may provide that courts of the *Länder* shall exercise federal jurisdiction over criminal proceedings in the following matters:

> 1. genocide;
> 2. crimes against humanity under international criminal law;
> 3. war crimes;
> 4. other acts tending to and undertaken with the intent to disturb the peaceful relations between nations (paragraph (1) of Article 26);
> 5. State security.

The German constitution also stipulates that each *Land* has federal powers, vested in the Federal Criminal Police Office (*Bundeskriminalamt*), to investigate,[12] in addition to the Office of the German Federal Public Prosecutor

---

[8] 'Grundgesetz Für Die Bundesrepublik Deutschland (Basic Law for the Federal Republic of Germany) in the Revised Version Published in the Federal Law Gazette Part III, Classification Number 100–1, as Last Amended by Article 1 of the Act of 28 March 2019 (Federal Law Gazette I, 404)' (n.d.), www.gesetze-im-internet.de/englisch_gg/englisch_gg.html.

[9] 'Völkerstrafgesetzbuch (VStGB) (Code of Crimes Against International Law)'; www.iuscomp.org/gla/statutes/VoeStGB.pdf; Rankin, "'Responsibility to Prosecute?'".

[10] Article 24, 'Transfer of sovereign powers – System of collective security', para 1, states: 'The Federation may, by a law, transfer sovereign powers to international organisations.'

[11] Article 25, 'Primacy of international law' states: 'The general rules of international law shall be an integral part of federal law. They shall take precedence over the laws and directly create rights and duties for the inhabitants of the federal territory.'

[12] Article 73, 'Matters under exclusive legislative power of the Federation' para 10, states: 'cooperation between the Federation and the *Länder* concerning

> a) criminal police work,
> b) protection of the free democratic basic order, existence and security of the Federation or of a *Land* (protection of the constitution), and
> c) protection against activities within the federal territory which, by the use of force or preparations for the use of force, endanger the external interests of the Federal Republic of Germany, as well as the establishment of a Federal Criminal Police Office and international action to combat crime;'

(*Generalbundesanwaltschaft*, GBA). In other words, if a suspect of core international crimes is identified to be within the jurisdiction of any *Land*, including crimes committed abroad by foreign nationals, the Federal Criminal Police Office is obliged to investigate. This legal obligation is also strengthened with public policy. For instance, the War Crimes Unit of the Federal Criminal Police Office has a policy that supports the notion of addressing impunity for atrocity crimes: 'No safe haven for the perpetrators and no impunity'.[13] Similarly, should the Federal Criminal Police Office have sufficient evidence against suspects within their *Land*, the German constitution obliges the Higher Regional Court (*Oberlandesgericht*) in the respective *Land* to exercise federal jurisdiction over the prosecution of core crimes.

In addition to the powers exercised by each *Land* is the role of the Federal Public Prosecutor General (*Generalbundesanwalt*), who has a legal obligation to investigate and prosecute core international crimes, which also includes crimes committed abroad by foreign nationals. In addition to changes to the German Basic Law, the VStGB[14] also required amendments to *inter alia* the German Code of Criminal Procedure (*Strafprozessordnung*, StPO).[15] This included that the Office of the German Federal Public Prosecutor has the power to prosecute an individual for core international crimes, regardless of the citizenship of the suspect or victim, and irrespective of where the crime occurred, including core crimes that are perpetrated abroad, independently of political considerations.[16]

---

[13] "'The BKA'. Bundeskriminalamt (Federal Criminal Police Office)', n.d. 2018, www.bka.de/EN/Home/home_node.html;jsessionid=8D4B493C1B288EC3EF2E0280AB5EAD9E.live2301.

[14] Article 3, 'Amendment to the Code of Criminal Procedure'.

[15] 'Strafprozessordnung (StPO) (German Code of Criminal Procedure), Entered into Force April 7, 1987, Sections 230 and 231a' (n.d.), www.gesetze-im-internet.de/stpo/. (Federal Law Gazette (*Bundesgesetzblatt*) Part I pp. 1074, 1319), as most recently amended by Article 3 of the Act of 23 April 2014 (Federal Law Gazette Part I p. 410).

[16] The Criminal Code Procedure States in Section 153f, 'Dispensing with Prosecution of Criminal Offences under the Code of Crimes against International Law': '(1) The public prosecution office may dispense with prosecuting a criminal offence for which there is criminal liability pursuant to sections 6 to 14 of the Code of Crimes against International Law in the cases referred to in Section 153c subsection (1), numbers 1 and 2, if the accused is not resident in Germany and is not expected to so reside. If, in the cases referred to in Section 153c subsection (1), number 1, the accused is a German, however, this shall only apply if the offence is being prosecuted before an international court of justice or by a State on whose territory the offence was committed or a citizen of which was injured by the offence.

(2) The public prosecution office may dispense with prosecuting an offence for which there is criminal liability pursuant to sections 6 to 14 of the Code of Crimes against International Law in the cases referred to in Section 153c subsection (1), numbers 1 and 2, in particular if

1. no German is suspected of having committed the crime;
2. the offence was not committed against a German;
3. no suspect is, or is expected to be, resident in Germany;

The Criminal Code Procedure States in Section 153f 'Dispensing with Prosecution of Criminal Offences under the Code of Crimes against International Law':

> (1) The public prosecution office may dispense with prosecuting a criminal offence for which there is criminal liability pursuant to sections 6 to 14 of the Code of Crimes against International Law in the cases referred to in Section 153c subsection (1), numbers 1 and 2, if the accused is not resident in Germany and is not expected to so reside.

In other words, the Federal Public Prosecutor General has discretion to monitor and choose to pursue a formal investigation of those suspected of atrocity crimes abroad. The investigation does not require a legal relationship with the German State. As stated earlier, it does not require the victim or perpetrator related to the alleged crime to be a German citizen or that the alleged crime be committed within German jurisdiction. Having said this, a trial will not be conducted in absentia (if the suspect is not within German jurisdiction, they may investigate but not conduct a trial). The only limitation relates to direct concerns about German national security, such as terrorist-related activity (directly perpetrated against the German State, in which case a different body has investigative responsibility). Combined with this, Section 152, 'Indicting Authority; Principle of Mandatory Prosecution', stipulates that the Federal Public Prosecutor General is *obliged* to investigate and prosecute, including core international crimes:

> (2) Except as otherwise provided by law, the public prosecution office shall be obliged to take action in relation to all prosecutable criminal offences, provided there are sufficient factual indications.

To add to investigative and judicial independence, the Federal Public Prosecutor General is legally obliged to operate independently of German government intervention, as per the general principle of its judiciary.[17] As two

---

4. the offence is being prosecuted by an international court of justice or by a country on whose territory the offence was committed, a citizen of which is either suspected of the offence, or suffered injury as a result of the offence. The same shall apply if a foreigner who is accused of a criminal offence that was committed abroad is resident in Germany but the requirements of the first sentence, numbers 2 and 4, are met and transfer to an international court of justice or extradition to the prosecuting State is admissible and intended.

(3) If, in the cases referred to in subsections (1) or (2) public charges have already been preferred, the public prosecution office may, at any stage of the proceedings, withdraw the charges and terminate the proceedings'.

[17]   Christian Ritscher, 'Panel Discussion "Universal Jurisdiction Revisited: German Prosecutions of International Crimes Committed in Syria"'. (Current Debates in International Criminal

State legal officials in the German federal justice system, Thomas Beck, federal public prosecutor at the German Federal Court of Justice, and Christian Ritscher, federal public prosecutor at the German Federal Court of Justice and head of the War Crimes Unit S4 at the Office of the Federal Public Prosecutor, have stated:

> For the same reasons, the German legislator has decided to ensure that the investigation of international crimes does not depend upon political considerations. It is, for example, not possible to refrain from prosecuting due to foreign policy reasons – contrary to the situation of crimes against the State, where refraining from prosecution is possible according to section 153d German Code of Criminal Procedure (*Strafprozessordnung, StPO*) if the proceedings pose a risk of serious detriment to the Federal Republic of Germany. It is only in cases of offences committed abroad without any link to Germany whatsoever that the German Federal Prosecutor General (*Generalbundesanwalt*), responsible for the prosecution of international crimes, is enabled to exercise his/her discretion to dispense with prosecution.[18]

In 2011, the first trial conducted under the VStGB in Germany was for two Rwandan suspects in relation to the Rwandan genocide who were later sentenced.[19] Since then, German State legal officials have adapted lessons learned while their role as de facto international prosecutors has increased.

Justice Conference, Humboldt University, Berlin, 2018); Christian Ritscher (head of the War Crimes Unit S4, Federal Public Prosecutor, the Office of the German Federal Public Prosecutor General), communication with author, August 2018; Rankin, '"Responsibility to Prosecute?"'

[18] Thomas Beck and Christian Ritscher, 'Do Criminal Complaints Make Sense in (German) International Criminal Law? A Prosecutor's Perspective', *Journal of International Criminal Justice* 13, no. 2 (1 May 2015): 230, https://doi.org/10.1093/jicj/mqv010. Beck and Ritscher state: 'Section 153d StPO reads: [Dispensing with Court Action on Political Grounds] (1) The Federal Public Prosecutor General may dispense with prosecuting criminal offences of the nature designated under section 74a subsection 1, numbers 2–6, and under section 120 subsection (1), numbers 2–7, of the Courts Constitution Act (i.e. crimes against the State), if the conduct of proceedings poses a risk of serious detriment to the Federal Republic of Germany, or if other overriding public interests present an obstacle to prosecution. (2) If charges have already been preferred, the Federal Public Prosecutor General may withdraw the charges under the conditions listed in subsection 1 at any stage of the proceedings and terminate the proceedings. Translations of this, and other provisions of the German Code of Criminal Procedure, by Brian Duffett and Monika Ebinger (updated by Kathleen Muller-Rostin and Iyamide Mahdi), www.gesetze-im-internet.de/englisch_stpo/englisch_stpo.html).

[19] AFP, 'Rwandan Rebel Leaders Jailed in Germany for War Crimes', *The Guardian*, 28 September 2015, www.theguardian.com/global-development/2015/sep/28/rwandan-rebel-leaders-jailed-in-germany-for-war-crimes.

WHO HAS THE 'RESPONSIBILITY TO PROSECUTE' IN GERMANY'S UNIVERSAL JURISDICTION?

Within German jurisdiction, victims are legally permitted to raise international criminal complaints to the German Federal Prosecutor General. They can also act as private accessory prosecutors during the trial, alongside a public prosecutor. Yet, there is a view that victims should not be *expected* to bear the responsibility for initiating investigations. Moreover, victims of core international crimes are not required to be in German jurisdiction or be German residents for an investigation to commence. As Beck and Ritscher argued, victims should not carry the burden for initiating a complaint: 'As such, [victims] do not have to bear the responsibility of being the cause of a criminal prosecution or of creating the substantive preconditions for ensuring that international crimes do not go unpunished.'[20] Rather, the responsibility sits firmly with the German Federal Prosecutor General, who is, in fact, legally obligated under German law to initiate an investigation of suspected atrocity crimes. Indeed, this is an interpretation shared by members of the Office of the German Federal Public Prosecutor, including Beck and Ritscher:

> International crimes – the most serious crimes of concern to the international community as a whole – are categorized as offences absolutely requiring public prosecution (*Offizialdelikte*). Thus, a criminal investigation is to be commenced in all cases where the procedural and substantial preconditions are met. ... Due to the principle of legality as provided in section 152 subparagraph 2 German Code of Criminal Procedure, the German Federal Prosecutor General is obliged to officially take action in all cases of sufficient factual indications as to the commission of a criminal offence according to sections 6–14 German Code of Crimes against International Law.[21]

To fulfil their responsibility to international criminal law, the German Federal Prosecutor General also has the capacity and resources within its team[22] to (1) monitor international events as they unfold and (2) begin formal

---

[20]   Beck and Ritscher, 'Do Criminal Complaints Make Sense in (German) International Criminal Law?' 230.

[21]   Beck and Ritscher, 'Do Criminal Complaints Make Sense in (German) International Criminal Law?' 230–32. As quoted in Beck and Ritscher: 'Section 152 subsection 2 StPO reads: Except as otherwise provided by law, the public prosecution office shall be obliged to take action in relation to all prosecutable criminal offences, provided there are sufficient factual indications.'

[22]   German Federal Public Prosecutors Office has finite resources, and cases are investigated at the discretion of the prosecutor, who has come under criticism from victims. Nevertheless, it

criminal investigations, as per its remit.[23] Although, needless to say, if the number and/or complexity of investigations increased, resources would also need to adapt as well.

All of this is not to say that witnesses and victims of core international crimes do not play an active role in accountability in German jurisdiction. They do so in several important ways. Witnesses' and victims' statements that lead or contribute to the development of an investigation are considered by the German Federal Prosecutor General to have investigative value.[24] In the case of Syria, this point is particularly salient. Not only does Germany have a broad universal jurisdiction to investigate core international crimes, it also experienced a significant inflow of asylum seekers from Syria after 2011, which further increased when the German government welcomed Syrians to stay in Germany.[25] This not only increased the number of witnesses and victims of Syrian core crimes migrating to Germany but also alleged perpetrators. Moreover, other private non-State actors, such as Chief Investigator 1 and the CIJA, have played a role in criminal accountability in Germany, as will be further explored later in the chapter. But before I do that, I further explore how State legal officials in Germany have emerged as de facto international prosecutors as a means to close the accountability gap for core crimes left by the local legal officials in Syria.

IN PRACTICE: HOW TO FILL A GAP IN SYRIA

A key actor pursing criminal accountability for core crime in Syria is the War Crimes Unit of the Office of the German Federal Public Prosecutor. Since 2011, as the Arab Spring swept across Syria, the Office of the German Federal Public Prosecutor began monitoring and then investigating the large-scale detention and torture of Syrian demonstrators, as reports emerged from UN agencies, the media, and the many Syrians who relocated to Germany. Despite its ongoing investigation, the Office of the German Federal Public Prosecutor highlighted that it never intended to act as the international Office

---

has recently been further supported by an increase in resources particularly at the *Land* level. See Benjamin Duerr, 'International Crimes: Spotlight on Germany's War Crimes Unit', JusticeInfo.Net, 10 January 2019, www.justiceinfo.net/en/tribunals/national-tribunals/39936-international-crimes-spotlight-on-germany-s-war-crimes-unit.html, accessed 20 May 2019.

[23] Beck and Ritscher, 'Do Criminal Complaints Make Sense in (German) International Criminal Law?' 232–33.

[24] Beck and Ritscher, 'Do Criminal Complaints Make Sense in (German) International Criminal Law?' 233.

[25] Beck and Ritscher, 'Do Criminal Complaints Make Sense in (German) International Criminal Law?' 233.

of the Prosecutor. That is to say, it never meant to replace the ICC or other interstate bodies. Rather it intended to complement pre-existing international bodies. The absence of an international agency or criminal prosecutor, such as the ICC, with the authority to investigate in Syria, meant that it persisted in investigating core international crimes, as per its remit.[26] Since then, a number of important developments can be observed.

Arrest Warrant for Jamil Hassan

In June 2018, Germany issued an arrest warrant for a senior member of the Syrian regime, Jamil Hassan, then incumbent director of the Air Force Intelligence Directorate, for 'crimes against humanity'; France later did the same.[27] The competent pretrial judge at the German Federal Court of Justice issued the German arrest warrant on 8 June 2018, as per a respective motion by the Office of the German Federal Public Prosecutor. The charges filed claimed that Hassan commanded (or at least knew) that officials under his authority in Air Force Intelligence were perpetrating acts of torture, and that they resulted in the deaths of hundreds of protestors detained illegally across a number of official detention centres in Syria between 2011 and 2013.[28] Information that led to the arrest warrant was based on the 'Caesar photographs': the 55,000 photos which were smuggled out of Syria by a former forensic military photographer, code-named 'Caesar'. They show that more than 6,700 people died in Syrian government custody. The arrest was also based on Syrians who were tortured, many of whom are now based in Germany and who provided witness statements to public prosecutors.[29] Although the opportunity to arrest and prosecute Jamil Hassan, who remains outside German jurisdiction, appears slight at this stage, the warrant sent

---

[26] Christian Ritscher, 'Panel Discussion "Universal Jurisdiction Revisited: German Prosecutions of International Crimes Committed in Syria"'; Christian Ritscher (head of the War Crimes Unit S4, Federal Public Prosecutor, the Office of the German Federal Public Prosecutor General), Communication with author; Rankin, '"Responsibility to Prosecute?"'

[27] Jorg Diehl, Christoph Reuter and Fidelius Schmid, 'Germany Takes Aim at Assad's Torture Boss', *Der Spiegel*, www.spiegel.de/international/world/senior-assad-aid-charged-with-war-crimes-a-1211923.html; Emmanuel Jarry, 'France Issues Arrest Warrants for Senior Syrian Officials', *Reuters*, 5 November 2018, www.reuters.com/article/us-syria-crisis-france/france-issues-arrest-warrants-for-senior-syrian-officials-idUSKCN1NA11L. Other investigations are underway in Sweden, France and Austria, amongst others. In November 2018, France issued an arrest warrant for three members of the Syrian government – Ali Mamlouk, Jamil Hassan and Abdel Salam Mahmoud

[28] Diehl, Reuter and Schmid, 'Germany Takes Aim at Assad's Torture Boss'.

[29] Reuters Staff, 'Germany Issues International Arrest Warrant for Top Assad Officer', *Reuters*, 8 June 2018, www.reuters.com/article/us-syria-crisis-germany-idUSKCN1J41VQ.

a powerful message to the Syrian government and the international community.

The German Prosecution of Anwar R. and Eyad A.

German federal police and public prosecutors have also played an active role in the accountability process for two former members of the Syrian government suspected of perpetrating crimes against humanity in the early days of the Arab Spring, and who had resided in Germany. In February 2019, the German Federal Criminal Police Office (*Bundeskriminalamt, BKA*) arrested Anwar R. in Germany on suspicion of perpetrating acts of torture against detainees while working for Syria's General Intelligence Directorate.[30] Anwar R. is considered to have been a tertiary-level figure in the chain of command down from President Assad. It is alleged that in the early days of the Arab Spring, Anwar R. headed the investigations section at two detention centres (Branch 251 and Branch 285) in Damascus, between 2011 and 2012, before leaving Syria and arriving in Germany.[31] Specifically, Anwar R. was 'sufficiently suspected to have committed a complicity in a crime against humanity (Section 7 (1) No. 1, No. 5 and No. 9 VStGB, Section 25 StGB)'.[32] Under Section 7 'crimes against humanity' of the VStGB, they relate to

[30] Generalbundesanwalt (German Federal Public Prosecutor General's Office), 'Presse: Festnahme Zweier Mitarbeiter Des Allgemeinen Syrischen Geheimdienstes Wegen Des Verdachts Der Begehung von Verbrechen Gegen Die Menschlichkeit (Press Statement: Arrest of Two Members of the General Syrian Intelligence Servive on Suspicion of Committing Crimes against Humanity)', 2019a, www.generalbundesanwalt.de/; Generalbundesanwalt (German Federal Public Prosecutor General's Office), 'Presse: Anklage Gegen Zwei Mutmaßliche Mitarbeiter Des Syrischen Geheimdienstes Wegen Der Begehung von Verbrechen Gegen Die Menschlichkeit Ua Erhoben (Press Statement: Charges Have Been Brought against Two Alleged Employees of the Syrian Intelligence Service for Committing Crimes against Humanity) 29 October', 2019b, www .generalbundesanwalt.de/; Generalbundesanwalt (German Federal Public Prosecutor General's Office), 'Presse: Festnahme Eines Mutmaßlichen Mitarbeiters Des Syrischen Militärischen Geheimdienstes Wegen Des Dringenden Tatverdachts Eines Verbrechens Gegen Die Menschlichkeit (Press Statement: Arrest of a Suspected Syrian Military Intelligence Agent on Suspicion of a Crime against Humanity)', 22 June 2020, www .generalbundesanwalt.de/.
[31] Thomson Reuters, 'High-Ranking Syrian Suspected of Torturing Prisoners Arrested in Germany | CBC News', CBC, 14 February 2019, www.cbc.ca/news/world/syrian-arrested-germany-suspected-torture-1.5017799.
[32] Generalbundesanwalt (German Federal Public Prosecutor General's Office), 'Presse: Anklage Gegen Zwei Mutmaßliche Mitarbeiter Des Syrischen Geheimdienstes Wegen Der Begehung von Verbrechen Gegen Die Menschlichkeit Ua Erhoben (Press Statement: Charges Have Been Brought against Two Alleged Employees of the Syrian Intelligence Service for Committing Crimes against Humanity) 29 October'.

(1) Anyone in the context of a widespread or systematic attack against a civilian population:

1. kills a person . . .
5. tortures a person who is in his custody or in any other way under his control by causing him significant physical or mental harm or suffering that is not merely the result of sanctions permissible under international law . . .
9. seriously deprives a person of physical freedom in violation of a general rule of international law.[33]

In connection with this, Anwar R. is also accused of murder in fifty-eight cases (Section 211 StGB) and rape and serious sexual coercion (Section 177 Paragraph 1 No. 1, Paragraph 2 No. 1, Paragraph 3 No. 1 StGB in the up to November 9, 2016 version).[34]

At the same time as the arrest of Anwar R., German authorities arrested another Syrian man for related atrocity crimes. Eyad A. was a low-ranking officer in the Sub-Division 40, part of Branch 251, which was believed to operate independently under the control of Hafez Makhlouf, a cousin of Al-Assad. Eyad A. was accused of 'aiding and abetting a crime against humanity', again pertaining to sections 1, 7 (1) No. 5 and No. 9 of the VStGB, as well as § 27 German Criminal Code (StGB), which outlines separate criminal liability of parties to the offence.[35] As a joint investigation between German and French legal officials, French authorities arrested a third man.[36] Providing greater details surrounding the alleged offences, the Office of the German Federal Public Prosecutor also stated the following:

> Since the end of April 2011 at the latest, the Syrian regime has been using brutal force to suppress all activities by the opposition that are critical of the government across the board. The Syrian secret services played an essential role in this. The aim was, with the help of the secret services, to stop the protest movement as early as possible and to intimidate the population. The two accused belonged to the Syrian General Secret Service, specifically Department 251 responsible for security in the Damascus area.
>
> Anwar R. headed their so-called investigation unit with an attached prison. In the period from the end of April 2011 to the beginning of September 2012, at least 4,000 prisoners were subjected to brutal and massive torture by employees of the accused when they were interrogated. At least 58 people died as

---

[33] Völkerstrafgesetzbuch (VStGB) (Code of Crimes Against International Law), entered into force on 30 June 2002.
[34] Generalbundesanwalt (German Federal Public Prosecutor General's Office).
[35] Generalbundesanwalt (German Federal Public Prosecutor General's Office).
[36] Rankin, "'Responsibility to Prosecute?'"

a result of the mistreatment. A variety of torture methods were used during the interrogations: ... The accused Anwar R., as head of the investigative unit, determined and monitored the work processes in the prison, including the use of systematic and brutal torture. He was also aware that prisoners were dying as a result of the massive violence.[37]

On 23 April 2020, the trial of both Anwar R. and Eyad A. began in the Higher Regional Court in Koblenz, Germany. In early 2021, the trial was seperated. While the trial of Anwar R. continues at the time of writing with a decision expected in early 2022, on the 24 February 2021 the Higher Regional Court in Koblenz issued a verdict against Eyad A. He was convicted of aiding and abetting thirty counts of crimes against humanity, including torture, in the early days of the Arab Spring. Eyad A. was sentenced to four years and six months in prison. In the judgment by the German court, Eyad A. was convicted for crimes against humanity committed as part of the extensive and systematic attack on the civilian population by the Syrian government that took place starting from April 2011, which was determined to be a means to suppress actual or alleged opposition movements.[38]

As reflected in the previous chapter, a multiplicity of actors worked together as a cooperative criminal accountability community to extend the system of international criminal law to Syria. In this respect, German State legal officials did not work alone as de facto international prosecutors.

CIJA's Contribution

While the main credit for the arrests should go to the German authorities, material collected by the CIJA in Syria played a key role in contributing to the arrests, including supporting the German Federal Police investigation since 2017. For example, the CIJA's material related to written government documentation smuggled out of Syria, which provided broader context for the inner workings and organisation of the detention facilities. Some documents also referred to Anwar R. directly. Witness and expert testimony was also provided to the Federal Criminal Police Office.

During the trial, the CIJA also provided a number of contributions. In November 2020, a member of CIJA was an expert witness during the trial over the course of two days. The expert testimony included analysis of the Syrian government's security-intelligence organisation, as well as the nature of the large-scale and systematic use of torture in Syrian detention facilities,

---

[37]   Generalbundesanwalt (German Federal Public Prosecutor General's Office).
[38]   Oberlandesgericht Koblenz.

including Branch 251 and Sub-division 40. The CIJA expert witness presented more than sixty slides briefly summarising CIJA's evidence. A cache of documents was also entered into evidence at the request of the judges after the testimony. The documents were also read into record in the following days of the trials, including the last day of the trial.

During the trial, the CIJA's expert witness testimony and documents also aided in directly linking and identifying individuals in the Caesar Files. As stated earlier, the photos depict the bodies of thousands of detainees who had been processed through military intelligence and other security organs and who appeared to have been brutally tortured.

ECCHR's Contribution

As noted, local German private non-State actors, such as ECCHR, along with other Syrian civil society actors based in Europe and the Middle East, have worked closely with the Office of the German Federal Public Prosecutor to distribute information and identify potential insider witnesses and victims of crimes against humanity allegedly perpetrated by the Syrian government. For instance, the Office of the German Federal Public Prosecutor and ECCHR worked in partnership to identify and record witnesses' statements for future criminal prosecutions.[39]

Specifically in relation to the trial of Anwar R. and Eyad A., ECCHR and one other Syrian NGO did a great deal to find crime-based witnesses, in direct cooperation with the German authorities. Moreover, Patrick Kroker, a lawyer at ECCHR, represented nine Syrian victims during the Al Khatib trial, involving Anwar R. and Eyad A.

THE NETHERLANDS AND SYRIAN OBLIGATIONS UNDER THE CAT

As stated in the Introduction and Chapter 1, while Germany has played a lead role in Syrian accountability, it is not the only State pursing accountability for Syria. On 18 September 2020, the Netherlands government released a public statement announcing its decision to hold Syria to account for grave breaches to international human rights law. Entitled 'The Netherlands Decides to Hold

---

[39] Ritscher, 'Panel Discussion "Universal Jurisdiction Revisited: German Prosecutions of International Crimes Committed in Syria"'; Ritscher (head of the War Crimes Unit S4, Federal Public Prosecutor, the Office of the German Federal Public Prosecutor General), communication with author.

Syria Responsible for Gross Human Rights Violations',[40] the public statement maintained that the Netherlands had informed the Syrian government of its decision by diplomatic note. In his statement, Stef Blok, the Netherlands minister for foreign affairs, also focused on the role of victims. As Blok maintained, 'The victims of these serious crimes must obtain justice, and we are pursuing that end by calling the perpetrators to account.'[41] Just as crucially, a path for the Netherlands has been carved out by the past efforts of de facto international prosecutors, supported by a cooperative criminal accountability community. In particular, the jurisprudence stemming from the Pinochet case in the British House of Lords and the case of *Belgium v. Senegal* in the ICJ could inform the case. Moreover, according to Blok, 'The Assad regime has committed horrific crimes time after time. The evidence is overwhelming.'[42] In drafting the note, the Netherlands did not work alone. As advisors to the Netherlands on the drafting of the diplomatic note, Toby Cadman and Guernica 37 have been working with a number of Syrian civil society groups to support the Foreign Ministry of the Netherlands. As stated earlier, Cadman also sits on the Advisory Panel of the CIJA, which has collected more than 1million pages of government documents from Syria. Crucially the Netherlands will be in a position to draw upon the evidence collected by a number of de facto international prosecutors, including CIJA, the Office of the German Federal Public Prosecutor and ECCHR, amongst others. As is evident from previous chapters, it takes a multiplicity of actors to extend the reach of international criminal law.

CONCLUSION

Both CIJA and the Office of the German Federal Public Prosecutor are keen to point out that they never intended to replace the role of the ICC or any other international (State) institution. For instance, William Wiley, director of CIJA, maintained that training Syrians to collect material that would be admissible to a future criminal prosecution was a means to fill the gap'[43] Similarly, Christian Ritscher, head of the War Crimes Unit and Federal

---

[40] Ministry of Foreign Affairs, 'The Netherlands Holds Syria Responsible for Gross Human Rights Violations', Government of the Netherlands, 19 September 2020, www.government.nl/latest/news/2020/09/18/the-netherlands-holds-syria-responsible-for-gross-human-rights-violations.

[41] Ministry of Foreign Affairs, 'The Netherlands Holds Syria Responsible for Gross Human Rights Violations'.

[42] Ministry of Foreign Affairs, 'The Netherlands Holds Syria Responsible for Gross Human Rights Violations'.

[43] Wiley (director of CIJA), interview with author, 3 January 2017.

Public Prosecutor in the Office of the German Federal Public Prosecutor, said that they never intended to be an international Office of the Prosecutor (OTP), or to replace the ICC or any other international (State) institution.[44] Rather, in this instance, as in the two previous case studies outlined earlier, the CIJA and the German prosecutors adopted the role of de facto international prosecutors in an effort to close the accountability gap when other institutions, including the local judiciary and other international criminal tribunals, could not.

This chapter raises a number of important questions: to what extent have State legal officials surpassed their role as de facto international prosecutors to become *de jure* international prosecutors, as may be the case in the German context? Moreover, to what extent are State legal officials in foreign courts increasingly obliged to prosecute or extradite those in their jurisdiction, for *jus cogens* crimes, such as torture, as an obligation *erga omnes*? To what extent does this include pursuing suspects of these core crimes, irrespective if the perpetrator is in the jurisdiction of the State as a legal obligation of State Parties to the CAT? Does this extend to those State actors who are not State Parties to the CAT? An interpretation of the Vienna Convention on the Law of Treaties would suggest that given the number of State Parties to the CAT, combined with the *jus cogens* nature of the crime of torture, it has accordingly been established by the 'international community as a whole as a norm from which no derogation is permitted'.[45] One could argue that the obligation increasingly extends to all in the international system of law. Moreover, the study raises questions in relation to the role of international tribunals, such as the ICJ, as not only playing a role as a dispute settlement mechanism but also upholding the norms governing *jus cogens* crimes, as reflected in the case of *Belgium* v. *Senegal*. As noted earlier, States such as Belgium and perhaps the Netherlands also view the ICJ as playing such as role.

I now turn to Part III of this book. In Chapter 6, I outline a theoretical framework for how de facto international prosecutors may implicitly or explicitly conceptualise international criminal law.

---

[44] Ritscher (head of the War Crimes Unit S4, Federal Public Prosecutor, the Office of the German Federal Public Prosecutor), communication with author, 18 August 2018. Ritscher, 'Panel discussion "Universal Jurisdiction Revisited"'.

[45] Article 53, United Nations, 'Vienna Convention on the Law of Treaties (VCLT)', 23 May 1969.

PART III

FRAMEWORK II: HOW DE FACTO INTERNATIONAL PROSECUTORS CONCEPTUALISE INTERNATIONAL CRIMINAL LAW

6

A Basic Law for International Criminal Law?

This chapter outlines a conceptual framework for how de facto international prosecutors implicitly or explicitly conceptualise international criminal law. As reflected in the previous chapters, de facto international prosecutors represent a broad array of experiences, knowledge and expertise. They include private non-State actors, particularly witnesses and victims of core crimes, but also human rights advocates, investigators, analysts and international prosecutors with previous experience on international criminal tribunals, amongst others. Indeed, as described in Chapter 1, they can also share more than one identity: they can be a witness and victim of core international crimes, as well as a practitioner of international criminal justice. De facto international prosecutors also include State legal officials in foreign courts, such as police, public prosecutors, and judges. All have adopted some or all of the practices or tasks of the offices of international prosecutors (Chapter 1). In all three biographical case studies – Chile, Chad and Syria – de facto international prosecutors close the accountability gap initially left by the local judiciary in the geographical location/jurisdiction where the alleged core international crimes were committed. In all three biographical case studies, amongst others crimes, torture was an essential means of suppressing actual and alleged opposition. In each of the three case studies, respective foreign courts involved in the cases were in States that were State Parties to the Convention Against Torture (CAT).

While narrowing down a conceptual framework that reflects all the views of de facto international prosecutors detailed in the three biographical case studies is an ambitious goal, I nonetheless attempt to begin the process, with the expectation that greater debate and insight will contribute to future theoretical insights. Specifically, the theoretical frameworks draws on the practices, statements and behaviours of de facto international prosecutors explored in this study and seeks to explain and interpret how they may implicitly or explicitly conceptualise international criminal law.

As an emerging phenomenon, de facto international prosecutors play a vital role in maintaining key tenets of the UN-System and the international rule of law – particularly in the realm of international justice for core crimes. How they conceptualise international criminal law (and the actors, institutions and mechanisms that support it) is important to our understanding of these actors. At the least, it goes some way to highlighting and understanding their efficacy, as well as how we may assist them better in the future.

This chapter aims to identify some characteristics of how de facto international prosecutors conceive of international criminal law and the practices they adopt to pursue accountability. Therefore, this conceptual framework attempts to draw on their practices, statements and behaviour to reflect how they implicitly or explicitly conceptualise the evolving system of international criminal law. To that end, I argue that the conceptual framework outlined here consists of six interrelated components. To elucidate the model, I draw mostly on H. L. A. Hart's concept of law.[1] First, a conceptual framework starts with the notion that private non-State actors implicitly view the 'system' of international criminal justice as *not* being located in specific institutions, such as the International Criminal Court (ICC), but rather the system *is the law*: in this case, international criminal law. Thus private non-State actors adopt a number of practical tasks ordinarily associated with the offices of international prosecutors, but not restricted to them. These include collecting linkage material that will inform evidence in a future public prosecution, recording witnesses' and victims' statements, submitting private complaints or writing case briefs, and, just as importantly, identifying the sources of international law.

Second, and following on from this, although private non-State actors identify sources of international criminal law, they implicitly or explicitly do so on an interim or 'probationary' basis,[2] with the intention of having those practices and acts 'validated' by State and interstate legal officials[3] in a future criminal prosecution. Third, private non-State actors implicitly view and apply international criminal law, as a legal 'standard', in the way that Hart described it: that is, as law that applies equally to all. In other words, *all* are subject to international criminal law equally, irrespective of where the crimes

---

[1] H. L. A. Hart, *The Concept of Law*, ed. Joseph Raz and Penelope A. Bulloch, 3rd ed., Clarendon Law Series (Oxford: Oxford University Press, 2012).

[2] Keith Culver and Michael Giudice, *Legality's Borders: An Essay in General Jurisprudence* (Oxford: Oxford University Press, 2010).

[3] Hart, *The Concept of Law*; Culver and Giudice, *Legality's Borders*.

occurred and by whom. Furthermore, private non-State actors implicitly view the role of foreign criminal courts in third States as supporting the international rule of law. In other words, they view foreign courts exercising universal jurisdiction as serving the international rule of law by their obligation to prosecute or extradite for core crimes, such as torture, as per the CAT.

Fourth, private non-State actors implicitly view the sources of international criminal law as not only governed by State conventions and statutes between States but also regulated by customary international law, which constitutes a unique area of public international law. Fifth, it reflects the importance of how international criminal law practices are governed, and the importance of the interplay between capacity and autonomy. Lastly, with these five components in mind, I argue that private non-State actors implicitly refer to the body of international criminal law, particularly crimes deemed peremptory norms (*jus cogens*) of international laws, such as torture and genocide, as the beginnings of a type of 'international unwritten constitution', which obliges States and individuals, respectively. In this way, the *willingness* to use and practice the law is key. I now turn to outline the proposed theoretical framework in further detail.

I 'RULES OF RECOGNITION' AND GENERAL PRINCIPLES OF LAW

Historically, Western legal and International Relations (IR) traditions have conceptualised international law[4] in a way that positions the nature of authority as wielded by the sovereign, prince or ruler in a top-down, hierarchical institutional fashion, and primarily through orders backed by the use of force and coercion. In this traditional view of international law, States are the primary actors and subjects of international law.[5] More recently, while key IR thinkers, such as E. H. Carr and Hans Morgenthau, acknowledged the role of international law, they believed international law to be less important than the role of power in international relations.[6] Similarly, Colin Wight has argued that 'International law is shot through with purposeful ambiguity and powerful states will manipulate it to follow the course of action they feel necessary to protect

---

[4] Thomas Hobbes, *Leviathan* (Oxford: Oxford University Press, 2014); Jeremy Bentham, *Of Laws in General*, ed. H. L. A. Hart (London: The Athlone Press, 1970); John Austin, *The Province of Jurisprudence Determined*, ed. H. L. A. Hart (New York: The Noonday Press, 1954).

[5] Arthur Watts, "The Importance of International Law," in *The Role of Law in International Politics: Essays in International Relations and International Law*, ed. Michael Byers (Oxford: Oxford University Press, 2001), 5–16.

[6] Edward Carr, *The Twenty Years' Crisis*, 2nd ed. (London: Macmillan, 1946); Hans Morgenthau, *Politics Among Nations*, 2nd ed. (New York: Alfred Knopf, 1954).

their national interests (however defined).'[7] Other IR scholars have argued that the absence of a centralised legislature and police force to enforce the law explains why international law is limited or less effective.[8]

Nevertheless, drawing on the three biographical case studies – Chile, Chad and Syria – private non-State actors who act as de facto international prosecutors implicitly conceptualise and use the law in a way that more closely aligns with a Hartian conceptualisation of the modern municipal legal system.[9] Rather than being contingent on specific State or international (State) institutions in a top-down, hierarchical institutional manner, the ability to identify the sources of law and the 'rule of recognition' are key. In other words, the emphasis is on international criminal law as the basis of the system, rather than international (State) institutions (although they are still important). In the biographical case studies, this enabled de facto international prosecutors, including witnesses and victims of core international crimes, to collect evidence, write private complaints and case briefs and identify primary sources to pose complex legal arguments concerning international criminal law.[10] When private non-State actors have the expertise to identify the sources of law, the *willingness* to use the law,[11] as well as adopt the practical tasks of the offices of international prosecutors, they become essential actors ensuring the system of international criminal law applies to powerful actors, including former heads of State. They then draw and depend upon institutions and important bodies, such as foreign courts, to officially *decide* the case.

Added to this, although Hart argued that a modern municipal legal system relies on a system of law, he argued that it did not need to be *centralised*. With this in mind one may question: *if* the system of international criminal law has sufficiently developed as a system of law at all, and, if so, has it evolved in the same way as the modern municipal legal system? During the Nuremberg Trials, the system of international criminal law appeared somewhat unformed. Since then, however, one could argue that international criminal law has evolved as a system of law that exhibits

[7]   Colin Wight, "Violence in International Relations: The First and the Last Word," *International Relations* 33, no. 2 (1 June 2019): 183, 184, https://doi.org/10.1177/0047117819851168.
[8]   Shirley V. Scott, *International Law in World Politics: An Introduction/ Shirley V. Scott.*, 3rd ed. (Boulder, CO: Lynne Rienner Publishers, 2017); George Nolte, "The Limits of the Security Council's Powers and Its Function in the International Legal System: Some Reflections," in *The Role of Law in International Politics*, 317–26.
[9]   Hart, *The Concept of Law*.
[10] Hart, *The Concept of Law*, 100.
[11] Leslie Green and H. L. A. Hart, "Introduction," in *The Concept of Law*, ed. Joseph Raz and Penelope A. Bulloch, 4th ed., n.d., xv–lv.

both primary and secondary rules as Hart envisaged.[12] As Cassese argued, since the 1940s, the sources of international criminal law are derived from the relevant rules which are regarded as those proper to international law.[13] Further still, Crawford and Brownlie argued that international criminal law has emerged to 'form a more robust body of jurisprudence'.[14] For example, international criminal law practitioners must borrow from primary sources (such as customary international law and treaties); secondary sources (such as law-making processes envisioned by customary international law rules as well as treaty provisions, including United Nations Security Council (UNSC) binding resolutions); and general principles of law that are shared by national legal systems.[15] Some may argue that for realists, '[J]udicial decisions could not simply be derived from rules and, therefore, had to be largely the result of idiosyncratic factors.'[16] While decisions varied in each case, what underpinned judgments in the three biographical case studies were rules in relation to the sources of law, particularly in relation to torture, which were a mix of codified law (such as the CAT) and customary international law (*jus cogens* nature of torture). To that end, Hart did not believe in a top-down view of the law based on force, and therefore it is not contingent on one or two international (State) institutions. It is this decentralised effect that acts as an enabler for de facto international prosecutors in this study, in that they can pursue justice in foreign courts, even though the perpetrator is not located (and the crime not perpetrated) in the respective jurisdiction.

Nevertheless, Hart did insist that *sources* of law be composed of a structure or hierarchy. In a similar way, peremptory norms (*jus cogens*) of international law invoke a type of hierarchy that serves to void or override other domestic and international laws, including the laws governing immunity (with the exception of incumbent heads of State, foreign ministers and heads of government). Hart also viewed private non-State and State legal officials with the capacity to identify primary rules, although unlike officials, private actors were not obliged to do so:

---

12 Hart, *The Concept of Law.*
13 Antonio Cassese, *Cassese's International Criminal Law*, 3rd ed./revised by Antonio Cassese et al. (Oxford: Oxford University Press, 2013).
14 Ian Brownlie and James Crawford, *Brownlie's Principles of Public International Law*, 8th ed., Principles of Public International Law (Oxford: Oxford University Press, 2012), 271.
15 Cassese, *Cassese's International Criminal Law.*
16 Michael V. Kratchowil, "How Do Norms Matter?" in *The Role of Law in International Politics*, 43.

> Wherever such a rule of recognition is accepted, both private persons and officials are provided with authoritative criteria for identifying the primary rules of obligation. . . . In a modern legal system where there are a variety of 'sources' of law, the rule of recognition is correspondingly more complex: the criteria for identifying the law are multiple and commonly include a written constitution, enactment by legislature, and judicial precedents.[17]

As demonstrated in the biographical case studies, private non-State actors, as practitioners of international criminal law, made use of the rule of recognition to identify the primary sources of domestic and international criminal law. While the CAT could be described as a primary rule, it was increasingly applied under customary international law. This is not to say that international criminal law has developed to the level of a modern municipal legal system. Rather, international criminal law has developed as a system to the extent that officials (State and interstate) and private (non-State) actors regularly conduct acts of recognition (identification) in relation to the sources of international criminal law (ICL), as demonstrated in the cases of Pinochet and Habré. While some de facto international prosecutors, including skilled practitioners (such as domestic public prosecutors and dispute lawyers), may not have the depth of knowledge initially, they draw upon broader cooperative criminal accountability community to aid them.

II PRIVATE NON-STATE ACTORS AS CONDUCTING PROBATIONARY ACTS OF RECOGNITION

Second, and following on from the previous discussion, private non-State actors, such as Juan Garcés, Souleymane Guengueng, Reed Brody, Chief Investigator 1, and the Commission for International Justice and Accountability (CIJA), amongst others, implicitly view the practices they adopt as de facto international prosecutors as being conducted on a provisional or probationary basis. While private non-State actors may carry out tasks and practices that suggest they can competently understand the 'authoritative criteria for identifying the primary rules of obligation', as Hart argued earlier,[18] they do so to fill what is perceived to be an accountability gap left by States. Moreover, they do so with the intention of having State legal officials – such as judges who decide law in the Spanish, English, Senegalese, Belgium or German courts – validate their actions at a later date. As Culver and Guidice proposed:

---

[17] Hart, *The Concept of Law*, 100.
[18] Hart, *The Concept of Law*, 100.

For a rule to count among the rules of a legal system, it must be recognised. Yet recognised by whom? Private citizens may conduct what appear to be acts of recognition, but those acts have at most probationary status, awaiting review by officials. This scenario might occur in a situation in which private citizens apply legal norms as best they can in the absence of relevant officials. So recognition *may* come from citizens, but such recognition is not sufficient for validation, which is necessarily conferred by the officials of the legal system.[19]

In short, private non-State actors, including witnesses and victims of core international crimes, do not intend to act alone to close the accountability gap. Instead, they implicitly view international criminal law as being necessarily facilitated by a broader community of practice that includes State legal officials in foreign courts.

Nevertheless, it suggests that a multiplicity of actors, including private non-State actors and legal officials (State and/or interstate), are required to use the law to conduct probationary (non-State) and official (State and interstate) acts of recognition, respectively, to fulfil the various practices that lead to successful prosecution – particularly for those most responsible for core international crimes in a foreign or international tribunal. As Andrew Hurrell has argued, 'Many legal rules are constitutive of actors.'[20] The three biographical case studies reveal the value private non-State actors place on the role of official judges in foreign courts acting under universal jurisdiction. While they do not seek to replace them, they support and complement them in the global accountability process.

III INTERNATIONAL CRIMINAL LAW RESEMBLES A TYPE OF CASE LAW OR COMMON LAW SYSTEM

Third, de facto international prosecutors implicitly and explicitly view international criminal law as increasingly shaped by how codified law increasingly interacts[21] with the unique nature of customary international law. While the Nuremburg Charter and the Nuremberg Trials established the basis for modern international criminal law,[22] the 'changing nature of customary

---

[19] Culver and Giudice, *Legality's Borders*, 10.
[20] Andrew Hurrell and Michael Byers, "International Law and the Changing Constitution of International Society," in *The Role of Law in International Politics: Essays in International Relations and International Law* (Oxford: Oxford University Press, 2001), 346.
[21] Lon Fuller, "Human Interaction and the Law," in *The Principles of Social Order*, ed. Kenneth J. Winston (Oxford and Portland, OR: Hart Publishing, 2001).
[22] Guénaël Mettraux, "Trial at Nuremberg," in *Routledge Handbook of International Criminal Law*, ed. William Schabas and Nadia Bernaz (Oxford: Routledge, 2013), 5–16.

international law',[23] particularly rules governing ICL mean that many rules are not written in treaties or a single document but rather have evolved largely as what I argue resemble a case law or common law system.[24] Moreover, as Noora Arajärvi argued,[25] State acceptance of the formation of international criminal law under customary international law has increasingly evolved as *tacit* acceptance by States, in that they accept the various decisions of judges in foreign courts or practices of States.[26] While codified laws, such as the CAT or the Genocide Conventions, are important and contribute to positivist notions of international law, these codified laws have further evolved in customary international law, through court judgments in foreign and international tribunals, including the Pinochet case in the British House of Lords, as well as international tribunals, such as *Belgium v. Senegal* at the ICJ.[27] That is not to say that private non-State actors believe codified laws and conventions ratified by States, such as the CAT, are not important. They are. For example, both the United Kingdom and Spain signed the CAT, which played a vital role in establishing the obligations of the State to prosecute or extradite Pinochet for the alleged crimes in Chile. Nonetheless, as torture was deemed a *jus cogens* according to customary international law, this had the effect of voiding or overriding laws that governed immunity. States, one could argue, *tacitly* accepted this decision by the British House of Lords.

In short, private non-State actors implicitly view the system of ICL as having *universal* application for *jus cogens* crimes such as torture. Nevertheless, there remain areas of contention. As stated earlier, immunity still applies to incumbent heads of State, foreign ministers and heads of government under customary international law. Moreover, the role of the ICC is also contentious because the ICC relies upon States that are *willing* to ratify the Rome Statute to be subject to ICC jurisdiction.[28] In other words, for the ICC to have jurisdiction over core international crimes in a State suspected of

---

[23]   Noora Arajärvi, *The Changing Nature of Customary International Law: Methods of Interpreting the Concept of Custom in International Criminal Tribunals* (London and New York: Routledge, 2014).

[24]   Cassese, *Cassese's International Criminal Law*; Arajärvi, *The Changing Nature of Customary International Law*.

[25]   Arajärvi, *The Changing Nature of Customary International Law*.

[26]   Cassese, *Cassese's International Criminal Law*; Arajärvi, *The Changing Nature of Customary International Law*.

[27]   Cassese, *Cassese's International Criminal Law*; Arajärvi, *The Changing Nature of Customary International Law*.

[28]   James Crawford, "The Drafting of the Rome Statute," in *From Nuremberg to The Hague: The Future of International Criminal Justice*, ed. Philippe Sands (Cambridge: Cambridge University Press, 2003), 109–56.

breaching core international crimes, the State in question must become a State Party to the Rome Statute. As Cassese stated:

> Many criminal lawyers ... believe that the major source of ICL can be found in the Statute of the ICC, or at least that such Statute is a sort of 'code of international criminal law'. This is the wrong assumption, although admittedly the Statute is the only international written instrument laying down international rules on both the 'general part' of ICL and a fairly comprehensive definition of international crimes. The truth of the matter is, however, that the ICC Statute embraces a set of rules only applicable by the ICC itself ... some of the Statutes provisions may gradually turn into customary international law as a result of other international criminal courts broadly accepting and applying these provisions as encapsulating the world society's *opinio juris* on the matter.[29,30]

IV THE LAW AS A 'STANDARD' AND INTERNATIONAL RULE OF LAW (*RECHTSSTAAT*)

Fourth, de facto international prosecutors implicitly and explicitly view and apply the international criminal law as a Hartian 'standard'.[31] This means that laws are applied consistently to everyone, everywhere, irrespective of an individual's role, including those who make domestic and international laws. As new standards of behaviour in relation to core international crimes have been introduced into the system of international criminal law, via treaties, statutes and/or customary international law, the concern is increasingly with standards rather than orders. Like in the modern municipal legal system, private non-State actors implicitly and explicitly apply ICL as a standard, in that individual responsibility for alleged core international crimes applies to *all* actors, *equally*. A notion of a standard according to Hart is that *the law applies to all, and those who legislate or set rules are bound by the same rules/laws, equally.*[32] As Garcés stated in relation to the appeals case in the British House of Lords, the Pinochet case had become 'a normal legal case' whereby a former head of State would not have immunity for crimes such as torture. With a vertical view of the law rather than the institutions or actors within the system of law, as Noora Arajarvi argued, the responsibility shifts

---

[29] Cassese, *Cassese's International Criminal Law*, 10.
[30] Cassese, *International Criminal Law*; Arajarvi, *The Changing Nature of Customary International Law*, 10.
[31] Hart, *The Concept of Law*, 57–58.
[32] Hart, *The Concept of Law*, 58.

away from 'the state to the individual' to form a 'horizontal relationship between the perpetrator and the victim'.[33]

Notably, in all three biographical case studies outlined, the constitutions of the respective States – Chile, Chad and Syria – also specified a notion of a standard to the effect that all were equal before the law – even during the times core international crimes were alleged. In other words, private non-State actors disregard any claims of immunity for those suspected of core international crimes, even at the most senior level. For example, even though immunity in international law may apply to incumbent heads of State, such as Syria's President Bashar al-Assad, this does not stop de facto international prosecutors, such as Chief Investigator 1 and the CIJA, from investigating him.

Added to the notion of international criminal law as a standard, private non-State actors implicitly view the role of *domestic* and foreign courts exercising universal jurisdiction as supporting the principle of the international rule of law (*Rechtsstaat*) for crimes deemed as *jus cogens* by the international community as a whole. Perhaps one of the most influential interpretations of the principle of the international *Rechtstaat* is informed by Germany's historical experience, which remains a legacy of the Nuremberg Trials. Within the German domestic context, the notion of *Rechtstaat* has experienced a number of iterations,[34] but in the post–World War II era, it has been adapted in the German *Basic Law* as a response to arbitrary State power and tyranny. Today, one could argue, the *Rechtstaat* is referenced in '*the Basic Law as shorthand for the concept*', and the protection, '*of fundamental rights, which is complemented by the ... strong*' and independent '*role of the judiciary*' to protect individual rights against arbitrary power.[35] And, I would add, to ensure accountability through an independent, impartial criminal prosecution for those most responsible when the protection of those rights fail and core international crimes are suspected. One could argue that this was the intention of the Nuremberg Trials,[36] which established the international rule of law as a central principle of international criminal law.[37] As noted in the

---

[33]   Arajärvi, *The Changing Nature of Customary International Law*, 34.

[34]   Michel Rosenfeld, 'The Rule of Law and the Legitimacy of Constitutional Democracy', *Southern California Law Review* 74, no. 5 (2001): 1307–52.

[35]   Rainer Grote, 'Rule of Law, Rechtsstaat and Etat de Droit', in *Constitutionalism, Universalism and Democracy – Comparative Analysis*, ed. Christian Starck (Baden-Baden: Nomos Verlagsgesllschaft, 1999), 286.

[36]   R. H. Roberts. 1945. Second Day, Wednesday, Part 04. Opening Statement before the International Military Tribunal. 21 November. In Trial of the Major War Criminals before the International Military Tribunal. Volume II. Proceedings: 11/14/1945–11/30/1945. [Official text in the English language.] Nuremberg: IMT: 98–102.

[37]   Cassese, *Cassese's International Criminal Law*.

Introduction and Chapter 1, the Nuremberg Charter and Number Trials were integral to the UN-System and post–World War II order. Moreover, in the post-Nuremberg era, universal jurisdiction has played (i.e. *Attorney General of the Government of Israel* v. *Adolf Eichmann*, *The Prosecutor* v. *Klaus Barbie*) and continues to play (*Pinochet 3* and Eyad A.) an important role in the accountability of *jus cogens* crimes. The notion of an international rule of law positions the accountability for torture and genocide[38] as an obligation assigned to domestic and foreign courts under international criminal law, and more broadly as an obligations *erga omnes*.

In the three biographical case studies, de facto international prosecutors implicitly conceptualised an international rule of law within the context of universal jurisdiction. When local courts – such as those in Chile, Chad and Syria – were unwilling or unable to serve this function, de facto international prosecutors, including witnesses and victims of core crimes, adopted the practices of offices of international prosecutors on an interim basis with the view that a public criminal court in a third State should and would be obliged to complete the accountability process within a broader system of international criminal law. Or in the case of the CIJA, have been asked by State legal officials to contribute vital linkage material to assist with the arrest of known suspects within its jurisdiction. In this way, State legal officials who enjoy universal jurisdiction can and do play an important role in closing the accountability gap for atrocity crimes, alongside their private counterparts.

V GOVERNING THE CRIMINAL ACCOUNTABILITY IN THE GLOBAL LEGAL ORDER

Fifth, the three biographical case studies reflect the importance of how international criminal law practices are governed, and the importance of the interplay between capacity and autonomy.[39] What is important to each of the biographical case studies is that the cooperative criminal accountability community was able to operate autonomously and independently from State actors but still adhered to the rules and practices that govern international criminal law. For example, the CIJA's operational model raises the question of how we understand governance within the context of the international justice system. If we rely upon more traditional notions of the State,[40] and top-down notions

---

[38] Brian Z. Tamanah, *On the Rule of Law* (Cambridge: Cambridge University Press, 2012), 109.

[39] Francis Fukuyama, 'What Is Governance?' *Governance* 26, no. 3 (2013): 347–68, https://doi.org /10.1111/gove.12035.

[40] Hobbes, *Leviathan*; Bentham, *Of Laws in General*; Austin, *The Province of Jurisprudence Determined*.

of governance, then the role of private non-State actors, including CIJA's approach, fails to adhere. However, if we apply a governance model advanced by Francis Fukuyama,[41] for instance, the CIJA's model illuminates the importance of the interaction between capacity *and* autonomy in addressing international criminal justice, as well as the importance of self-organisation.[42]

On the one hand, if we use Fukuyama's notion of *capacity*, it could be argued that Juan Garcés, Souleymane Guengueng, Reed Broady, Chief Investigator 1 and the CIJA, amongst others, were compelled to work to high standards of ethical conduct recognized by previous and existing domestic and international tribunals. For example, they operated within established rules of how to collect evidence (that could potentially show individual criminal liability for senior leaders) at professional industry standards. In the case of Chad and Syria, the Extraordinary African Chambers and the Higher Regional Court of Koblenz in Germany accepted material collected by private non-State actors. In Chile, while the case against Pinochet was unable to proceed, the investigating judge accepted the material collected by private non-State actors. Moreover, in all three biographical cases, de facto international prosecutors operated within a high level of discipline[43] and in a cooperative manner.

On the other hand, one could argue that Juan Garcés, Souleymane Guengueng and Chief Investigator 1's (and the CIJA's) uniqueness, within the international criminal justice system, is that it also reflects the importance of *autonomy*. In all three instances, private non-State actors required a high degree of individual responsibility at all levels of the organization. For example, many Syrian investigators and analysts felt a personal sense of responsibility and public duty to investigate and prepare evidence.[44] Combined with this is the flexibility that allows them to experiment and seek to innovate or adapt to the complex environment experienced in the theatre of war and/or to find additional inputs for evidence as gaps became apparent or the need to strengthen a particular case arose.[45] For instance, Souleymane Guengueng and Chief Investigator 1 acted as investigators in

[41]   Francis Fukuyama, 'What Is Governance?'
[42]   Melinda Rankin, 'Investigating Crimes against Humanity in Syria and Iraq: The Commission for International Justice and Accountability', *Global Responsibility to Protect* 9, no. 4 (2017): 395–421, https://doi.org/10.1163/1875984X-00904004.
[43]   Jamal Abbasi (Former FCO programme manager, and former chief of staff, CIJA), interview with author, February 2017; Manuel Castells, *The Rise of the Network Society* (Oxford: Wiley-Blackwell, 2009); Rankin, 'Investigating Crimes against Humanity in Syria and Iraq'.
[44]   CIJA Chief Investigator 1 (with translator CIJA Liaison Officer 1), interview with author, January 2017.
[45]   Chris Engels (CIJA deputy director), interview with author, January 2017.

difficult and insecure environments. Given the ICC's limitations in terms of jurisdiction or the inability of State legal officials in Germany to physically investigate in Syrian jurisdiction, private non-State actors, particularly those who are witnesses and victims to core crimes, showed that they could act with greater autonomy. In this way, they could provide a necessary counter-balance to State power and serve to complement and enhance the ICC's and other foreign courts' roles in the broader legal system.[46] Similarly, autonomy can be important in domestic and foreign courts in holding those suspected of core international crimes to account. State legal officials in Spain, Belgium and Germany, as outlined in the three biographical case studies, reflected the ability to pursue justice autonomously and unrestricted from State intervention.

VI ICL AS AN 'INTERNATIONAL UNWRITTEN CONSTITUTION', WHICH IMPOSES LIMITS ON SOVEREIGNS

Lastly, and to conclude the theoretical framework, while de facto international prosecutors do not explicitly view the sources of ICL as an 'international unwritten constitution', I argue that the five components combined imply that they defer to the body of ICL, particularly for crimes deemed as *jus cogens* of international law, as a type of 'international unwritten constitution' or unwritten international Basic Law. Unlike Klabber, Peter and Ulfstein, who argue the UN Charter could act as a constitutional form as the basis of international law,[47] I argue that a single overarching document is not necessary. Rather an international unwritten constitution could potentially consist of a range of sources, such as codified, customary law and case law. If, as Bardo Fassbender argued, 'we content ourselves with an international constitutional law limited to a few meta-rules similar to H. L. A. Hart's rule of recognition, we may well do without a written constitution'.[48] Indeed, international criminal law is located in a mix of codified law (such as the Convention Against Torture) but, as stated earlier, also relies upon on customary international law, which is tacitly accepted by States.[49] Furthermore, if understood as increasingly resembling a type of case law or common law system, like the

---

[46] Rankin, 'Investigating Crimes against Humanity in Syria and Iraq'.

[47] Jan Klabbers, Anne Peters and Geir Ulfstein, *The Constitutionalization of International Law* (Oxford: Oxford University Press, 2009).

[48] Bardo Fassbender, 'Written Versus Unwritten: Two Views on the Form of International Constitution', in *Handbook on Global Constitutionalism*, ed. Anthony Lang and Antje Wiener (Cheltenham, UK: Edward Elgar Publishing, 197AD), 204.

[49] Arajärvi, *The Changing Nature of Customary International Law*.

British legal system, constitutions do not require a written document.[50] And with it one could argue, as Klabber, Peter and Ulfstein do, that an international unwritten constitution also suggests a notion of a public order: 'Verticalization, by definition, carries a sense of hierarchy with it. . . . This is symbolized not least by the emergence of international criminal law as a branch of international law – criminal law, after all, in presupposing the existence of a public order and someone to speak for that public order, presupposes a strong notion of hierarchy to begin with.'[51]

De facto international prosecutors do not necessarily or explicitly point to the emergence of an international unwritten constitution. Yet the emergence of peremptory norms (*jus cogens*) of international law placed hierarchically above all other laws raises the possibility of an international unwritten constitution, at least conceptually. This is not to infer, as Hans Kelsen would argue, that de facto international prosecutors view the system of international law as one, single global legal system. Rather, the international unwritten constitution implies one system of law that coexists and/or overlaps with a myriad of other legal systems. Or, as Culver and Guidice crisply explained, as 'clusters' between legal orders.[52] In this way, private non-State actors draw upon a mix of local, foreign and international law to bring senior actors suspected of torture and genocide to account. Indeed, the notion of a multiplicity of legal systems coexisting and/or overlapping is not uncommon in the modern municipal legal system. For example, the United Kingdom could be described as several legal systems coexisting and overlapping (England and Wales, Scotland and Northern Ireland).[53] Nor is it uncommon that regional or international systems of law coexist and/or overlap with domestic laws of a modern municipal legal system, such as trade and human rights laws of the European Union.[54]

As a unique area of public international law, the unusual development of international criminal law provides an opportunity to contribute to the early emergence of an international unwritten constitution. Nonetheless, some

---

[50] Andrew Hurrell, *On Global Order: Power, Values, and the Constitution of International Society* (Oxford: Oxford University, 2007); Christian Tomuschat, *Obligations Arising for States without or against Their Will*, vol. 241, Collected Courses of The Hague Academy of International Law (The Hague: Martinus Nijhoff, 1993), https://referenceworks-brillonline-com.ezproxy.library.uq.edu.au/entries/the-hague-academy-collected-courses /*A9780792329541_02.

[51] Klabbers, Peters and Ulfstein, *The Constitutionalization of International Law*, 15.

[52] Culver and Giudice, *Legality's Borders.*

[53] John Gardner, *Law as a Leap of Faith: Essays on Law in General* (Oxford: Oxford University Press, 2012), https://oxford-universitypressscholarship-com.ezproxy.library.uq.edu.au/view/10 .1093/acprof:oso/9780199695553.001.0001/acprof-9780199695553.

[54] Culver and Giudice, *Legality's Borders.*

have argued, such as Fassbender, that there are 'no empirically recordable acknowledgement by states' of 'customary constitutional rules of international law', which outlines *jus cogens* as a type of constitutional obligation,[55] either in written or unwritten form.[56] Yet, if we adopt Hart's approach to a system of primary and secondary rules, then, as Jeremy Waldron argued, the constitution or statute of 'the International Court of Justice as a court is definitely an instance of a secondary rule as Hart understands this category of rule'.[57] Indeed, Article 38 of the ICJ statute[58] also serves to outline the formally recognised sources of public international law more broadly[59] and includes customary international law which contributes to international criminal law.[60] In other areas of public international law, we could accept Fassbender's notion that states do not record obligations as *jus cogens* as such. Yet, one could argue that the case of Pinochet in the British House of Lords and Habré in *Belgium v. Senegal* at the ICJ, as outlined earlier in the Chile and Chad cases, respectively, held that torture was a *jus cogens*. Moreover, the British House of Lords and ICJ recognised the respective States were *obliged* to 'prosecute or extradite'. For instance, even conservative members of the House of Lords in the *R v. Bow Street Metropolitan Stipendiary Magistrate*, ex parte Pinochet Ugarte (No 3) held that torture

---

[55] Anne Peters, 'Are We Moving towards Constitutionalization of the World Community?' in *Realizing Utopia: The Future of International Law*, ed. Antonio Cassese (Oxford: Oxford University Press, 2012), 119.

[56] Fassbender, 'Written Versus Unwritten', 204.

[57] Jeremy Waldron, 'International Law: "A Relatively Small and Unimportant" Part of Jurisprudence?' in *Reading HLA Hart's The Concept of Law*, ed. Andrea Dolcetti and James Edwards (Oxford and Portland, OR.: Hart Publishing, 2013), 216.

[58] For example, Article 38 of the ICJ Statute states:

   1. The Court, whose function is to decide in accordance with international law such disputes as are submitted to it, shall apply:
      a. international conventions, whether general or particular, establishing rules expressly recognized by the contesting states;
      b. international custom, as evidence of a general practice accepted as law;
      c. the general principles of law recognized by civilized nations;
      d. subject to the provisions of Article 59, judicial decisions and the teachings of the most highly qualified publicists of the various nations, as subsidiary means for the determination of rules of law.

   2. This provision shall not prejudice the power of the Court to decide a case *ex aequo et bono*, if the parties agree thereto.' United Nations. 1945. Statute of the International Court of Justice. San Francisco, 24 October.

[59] Brownlie and Crawford, *Brownlie's Principles of Public International Law*, 20–47.

[60] Cassese, *Cassese's International Criminal Law*, 3–21.

was an international crime against humanity and *jus cogens*, and that after the Convention Against Torture came into effect, there had been a universal jurisdiction to 'either extradite or punish a public official who committed torture.'[61]

Indeed, the three biographical case studies show that international and foreign courts operating according to a notion of universal jurisdiction for *jus cogens* crimes, based on codified and customary international law, tacitly accepted by States were norms that States and the ICJ were obliged to uphold. In this way, de facto international prosecutors implicitly conceptualise the evolving nature of the international criminal law system as a type of common law governed by an unwritten international constitution for crimes accepted and recognised as *jus cogens* of international law. If we accept that State leaders act as '*qua* proxies' on behalf of their subjects,[62] as Samantha Besson argues, this approach further serves to lift the veil on States. While this type of international unwritten constitution does not follow faithfully with how the British legal system has evolved, one could argue that it serves as an early prototype or basis of a type of common law system that has emerged uniquely and is underpinned by the acceptance and recognition that torture is a *jus cogens* under customary international law and obligation *erga omnes partes* by State Parties.

In short, the unwritten international constitution imposes limits on all actors,[63] including State, interstate and non-State actors, to both legislate to permit acts, *inter alia*, of torture and genocide, and to a lesser extent other crimes against humanity. As Hart argued, a constitution 'not only imposes legal duties' but also legal limits. By 'limits' Hart implied 'not the presence of duty but the absence of legal power'.[64] In other words, even if, hypothetically speaking, senior members of the Syrian government or Deash (as a proto-State or non-State actors) were to legislate to legalise torture, customary international law supersedes these laws, as per, *inter alia* Nuremberg, ICTY, ICTR, Bow Street Magistrate, and ICJ, amongst others. While an international unwritten constitution does not oblige private non-State actors to investigate and prosecute those suspected of core international crimes, it confers judicial powers to State legal officials in various modern courts.

---

[61]   R v. *Bow Street Metropolitan Stipendiary Magistrate*, ex parte Pinochet Ugarte (No 3) (Pinochet 3) [2000] (House of Lords, Great Britain (UK) 24 March 1999).

[62]   Samantha Besson, 'The Authority of International Law: Lifting the State Veil', ed. Gianna Sergi, *Sydney Law Review* 31, no. 3 (2009): 343–80.

[63]   Hart, *The Concept of Law*, 67–69; T. R. S. Allan, *The Sovereignty of Law: Freedom, Constitution and Common Law* (Oxford: Oxford University Press, 2013), 3.

[64]   Hart, *The Concept of Law*, 69.

Furthermore, should an alleged perpetrator find their way into a jurisdiction that does not permit universal jurisdiction, it nevertheless obliges foreign courts to investigate and prosecute *jus cogens* crimes such as torture. In this way, as TRS Allan would argue, private non-State actors, like legal constitutionalists 'concentrate on the legal framework of the constitution, treating the judiciary as the ultimate guardians of a system of law designed to regulate the exercise of power and protect individual liberty'.[65] Here, I also add, to establish accountability when the protection from torture or other core international crime is suspected of being needed.

Returning to the first component of this framework, private non-State actors implicitly and explicitly view the sources of international criminal law as possessing a legal hierarchy, whereby the international unwritten constitution for *jus cogens* crimes are placed above other laws regulating the global order – including the systems of law that govern immunity. Some scholars have referred to 'new constitutionalism' as a means for private transnational authority to overshadow States.[66] I take the notion of an international unwritten constitution to share similarities with the term 'global constitutionalism'. According to Mattias Kumm, global constitutionalism is then understood in 'international law as the law of an international community constituted by law'.[67] Enabled by this, de facto international prosecutors seek to adopt the practices of the offices of international prosecutors as a means to close the accountability gap when local options fail to hold senior leaders to account. The notion of an international unwritten constitution therefore serves as the beginnings of how to govern the international rule of law. As Klabber, Peter Ulfstein argued, 'constitutionalization and the rule of law are intimately linked ideas'.[68]

> Constitutionalism promises to settle the score once and for all, by giving either *jus cogens* priority, or trade, or human rights, or *erga omnes* principles. Here, then, constitutionalization comes in armed with a clear set of normative commitments, which displays that at least in this guise, constitutionalization is an intensely political process.[69]

---

[65] Allan, *The Sovereignty of Law*, 1.

[66] A. Claire Cutler, 'The Judicialization of Private Transnational Power and Authority', *Indiana Journal of Global Legal Studies* 25, no. 1 (2018): 61–95, https://doi.org/10.2979/indjglolegstu .25.1.0061.

[67] Mattias Kumm, 'Global Constitutionalism and the Rule of Law', in *Handbook on Global Constitutionalism*, ed. Anthony Lang and Antje Wiener (Cheltenham, UK: Edward Elgar Publishing, 2017), 204.

[68] Klabbers, Peters and Ulfstein, *The Constitutionalization of International Law*, 3.

[69] Klabbers, Peters and Ulfstein, *The Constitutionalization of International Law*, 18.

CONCLUSION

Arguably the notions of an unwritten international constitution that underpins international order is a contested one. What is less contested is that accountability for those responsible for humanities' greatest crimes, particularly crimes accepted and recognised as *jus cogens* of international law, is a means to maintain the UN-System and the international order – one that is also upheld by the practices of de facto international prosecutors. Indeed, at the heart of the post–World War II era and the UN-System are the notions of criminal accountability for core international crimes, as well as justice and human rights. As quoted earlier in this book, Brownlie and Crawford aptly argued, 'It is not too much of an exaggeration to say that the United Nations era began with a trial and a promise.'[70] The Nuremberg Tribunal and the promise that the principles underpinning the Nuremberg Charter were treated as international law underscores the current international system of law in ways that are often overlooked when the focus remains firmly on State behaviours and compliance. A focus on the role of de facto international prosecutors shines light on how criminal accountability can and is pursued in practice, when local efforts for accountability fail. It also illuminates how the promise of Nuremberg is not just a normative vision. Indeed, de facto international prosecutors have drawn upon the evolving body of international laws governing core international crimes and applied them successfully in what are considered some of the most important cases in international criminal law to date. In doing so, de facto international prosecutors have become an essential feature of the international legal order.

[70]   Brownlie and Crawford, *Brownlie's Principles of Public International Law*, 671.

Conclusion

This book illuminated the role of de facto international prosecutors as an emerging phenomenon. To that end, this study had two objectives.

First, and foremost, the primary aim was to explain how and why de facto international prosecutors, particularly private non-State actors, attempt to extend the reach of international criminal law. To do that, it brought together three biographical case studies to investigate how and why de facto international prosecutors adopt the tasks and practices of the offices of international prosecutors, particularly when the local judiciary is unable or unwilling to hold senior leaders suspected of core crimes to account. In particular, the book examined how witnesses and victims of core crimes – both historically and more recently – have played an essential role in closing the accountability gap. The study shows that rather than isolated incidents, de facto international prosecutors are an emerging phenomenon and an essential feature of the UN-System and global legal order.

Second, and to a lesser extent, the book endeavoured to develop two theoretical frameworks. The first theoretical framework outlined the conceptual and theoretical arguments for defining and explaining de facto international prosecutors. The second framework explained how de facto international prosecutors, particularly, private non-State actors, implicitly or explicitly conceptualise international criminal law. These theoretical frameworks aim to contribute to the debate concerning the actors, institutions and means by which we maintain the international system of justice and accountability.

On a broader level, this project illuminates one of the most important questions for international relations and international law, today: how do we hold those most responsible for humanity's greatest crimes to account?

A number of lessoned learned can be drawn from the three biographical case studies outlined in this study. While understanding compliance in relation to core crimes such as torture is useful in the study of international relations and international law, it does not provide the whole picture. It fails to capture the complexities of the system of international criminal law, the role of a multiplicity of actors in adopting the practices of the offices of international prosecutor and the importance of judicial decisions. For example, scholars, such as Brunnee and Toope, have focused on the compliance aspect of international criminal and humanitarian law, including for torture. For example, Brunnee and Toope maintained the following:

> The anti-torture norm is also undermined by contrary practice . . . an analysis that focuses on shared understandings as the foundation of legal obligation does not necessarily paint a positive picture of international law. Whereas the conventional approach would say that the existence of formal law banning torture is definitive, we show that the normative understandings are fragile.[1]

This view of compliance is understandable and important. But an examination of a broader range of actors, institutions and means in the accountability process also opens up our understanding to the range of possibilities available to maintain the system of international criminal law. In this way Juan Garcés, Souleymane Guengueng, and Chief Investigator 1 demonstrated imagination and innovation in the ways they extended the reach of international criminal law.

Furthermore, the biographical case studies reveal the importance of language when critiquing international law. Indeed, some international relations and international law scholars and practitioners view international law as a rather perilous system or are reticent to consider international law a real system of law at all. This pessimism can extend to international criminal law. As stated in the Introduction, one scholar and former chief prosecutor referred to the International Criminal Court (ICC) as a 'bruised and battered court', which is 'languishing', and suggested the 'age' of criminal accountability was in decline.[2] While we may perhaps feel disappointed with the ICC in some respects, what is also clear is that modern municipal legal systems often have an unfair advantage over the way that international law is recognised. As Rosalyn Higgins argued:

> The language of supplicant victims is often applied to international law and international judicial institutions. We read of actions 'supporting'

---

[1] Jutta Brunnée and Stephen J. Toope, *Legitimacy and Legality in International Law: An Interactional Account* (Cambridge and New York: Cambridge University Press, 2010), 17.

[2] David Crane, '"Not Perfect Candidates" to Be the Next Prosecutor of the International Criminal Court', *Jurist* (blog), 10 July 2020, www.jurist.org/commentary/2020/07/david-crane-icc-prosecutor/.

international law or the international Court of Justice. Current events put international law 'in danger'. We do not speak of 'supporting' or damaging' contract or tort law. Such language suggests a lack of confidence in the reality of international law, which like other fields of law, objectively exists and is sometimes complied with and sometimes not.[3]

While international criminal law is a fledging 'system' of law, the three biographical case studies reflect the extent that de facto international prosecutors held confidence in the reality of international law. In each of the three cases, the witness and victims of core crimes, Juan Garcés, Souleymane Guengueng, and Chief Investigator 1, exhibited confidence that international law would prevail, and that senior leaders should and could be held accountable. In fact, accountability could only be achieved through international law. In this way, de facto international prosecutors ensured that one of the key tenets of the Convention Against Torture, providing no safe harbour for those suspected of torture, was enforced.

Lastly, although the legacy of Nuremberg radically reshaped laws on immunity, and the biographical studies showed how international criminal law applied to Pinochet and Habré, immunity for incumbent heads of State remains. As Cassese maintained, an incumbent head of State, or foreign minister reflects *personal* immunity *(ratione materiae)*,[4] as per the *Arrest Warrant* Congo v. *Belgium* case (57–61). Nevertheless, increasingly the question remains to what extent do incumbent heads of State have immunity for *jus cogens* crimes?[5] Notwithstanding this, as Chief Investigator 1 and the Commission for International Justice and Accountability (CIJA) have demonstrated, there is nothing stopping de facto international prosecutions from investigating incumbent heads of State in preparation for when they leave office and are then subjects of international criminal law.

THE FUTURE OF DE FACTO INTERNATIONAL PROSECUTORS

As at the time of writing at the end on 2021, all three – Juan Garcés, Souleymane Guengueng, and Chief Investigator 1 – continue to work in the field of international criminal justice. Recently, Juan Garcés has assisted the President Allende Foundation in an ongoing case in the Madrid courts against

---

[3] Higgins quoted in 'Reimagining the Law', British Institute of International and Comparative Law, 23 June 2020, www.biicl.org/reimagining/20/reimagining-the-law-23-june-2020.

[4] Antonio Cassese, *Cassese's International Criminal Law*, 3rd ed./revised by Antonio Cassese et al.. (Oxford: Oxford University Press, 2013), 21.

[5] Rain Liivoja, *Criminal Jurisdiction over Armed Forces Abroad* (Cambridge: Cambridge University Press, 2017), https://doi.org/10.1017/9781139600392.

those civilians who aided the Pinochet regime. As stated in Chapter 2, in recent years Chile has pursued accountability for members of the military junta who committed crimes against humanity. Nevertheless, Chile has yet to prosecute civilians. In January 2021, the appeals court in Madrid decided that a case against Chilean civilians could be prosecuted in Spanish courts exercising universal jurisdiction.[6] Similarly, Guengueng continues to work with witnesses and victims of core crimes in other African states and elsewhere through his foundation, in an effort to pursue criminal accountability for those most responsible.[7] Chief Investigator 1 continues to investigate in the field in Syria.

This begs an important question: what basic tools are available to future de facto international prosecutors who wish to pursue criminal accountability for those most responsible for core crimes – particularly when local options are not available? Both Garcés and Guengueng continue to guide future de facto international prosecutors on an ongoing basis. Similarly, the CIJA has also attempted to share its knowledge and expertise more formally with other private non-State actors keen to adopt the practices of de facto international prosecutors. In consultation with state actors and NGOs, the CIJA and the International Nuremberg Principles Academy have prepared a code of conduct for private investigative bodies, titled 'Nuremberg Guidelines for Non-Public Investigative Bodies in the Field of International Criminal and Humanitarian Law'.[8] Indeed, there are now a number of basic tools available to de facto international prosecutors to aid their practices and sharpen their ability to investigate and prosecute (web link details are provided in the footnote).[9]

Juan Garcés, Souleymane Guengueng and Chief Investigator 1, as well as the broader cooperative criminal accountability community, were not the first and are unlikely to be the last de facto international prosecutors to fight for justice. For this reason, reconsidering the ways we might extend the reach of international criminal law remains central to the UN-System and the international legal order they strive to uphold.

---

[6] Audiencia Nacional Sala de lo Penal Sección Cuarta Rollo 206/20 Juzgado Central de Instrucción No 5 Diligencias Previas 40/50, Auto n 15/2021.

[7] See Souleymanu Guengueng Foundation, https://sggfblog.com/

[8] Internationale Akademie Nürnberger Prinzipien, 'Private Investigations in International Criminal Justice', International Nuremberg Principles Academy, 2020, projects/detail/9c75ee aeeobd858dfdaeacaiead42e55/private-investigations-in-international-criminal-justice-24/.

[9] For example, see the 'Basic Toolbox' for de facto international prosecutors at www.defactointernationalprosecutors.org.

References

Abakar, Mahamat Hassan. 'The Making of Chad's Truth Commission'. In *The President on Trial: Prosecuting Hissene Habre*, edited by Sharon Weill, Kim Thuy Seelinger and Kerstin Bree Carlson, 24–30. Oxford: Oxford University Press, 2020.

Abbasi, Jamal (Former FCO Programme Manager and former Chief of Staff, CIJA). Interview with author, February 2017.

Abers, Rebecca Neaera, and Margaret E. Keck. *Practical Authority: Agency and Institutional Change in Brazilian Water Politics*. Oxford: Oxford University Press, 2013.

Adler, Emanuel. *Communitarian International Relations: The Epistemic Foundations of International Relations*. London: Taylor & Francis Group, 2005. http://ebook central.proquest.com/lib/uql/detail.action?docID=214749.

'The Spread of Security Communities: Communities of Practice, Self-Restraint, and NATO's Post–Cold War Transformation'. *European Journal of International Relations* 14, no. 2 (2008): 195–230. https://doi.org/10.1177/1354066108089241.

Adler, Emanuel, and Michael Barnett, eds. *Security Communities*. Cambridge Studies in International Relations. Cambridge: Cambridge University Press, 1998. https://doi.org/10.1017/CBO9780511598661.

Adler, Emanuel, and Vincent Pouliot. 'International Practices'. *International Theory* 3, no. 1 (2011): 1–36. https://doi.org/10.1017/S175297191000031X.

eds. *International Practices*. Cambridge: Cambridge University Press, 2012.

Agence France-Presse (AFP). 'Rwandan Rebel Leaders Jailed in Germany for War Crimes'. *The Guardian*, 28 September 2015. www.theguardian.com/global-devel opment/2015/sep/28/rwandan-rebel-leaders-jailed-in-germany-for-war-crimes

African Union. *Report of the Committee of Eminent African Jurists on the Case of Hissene Habre*. Addis Ababa, Ethiopia: African Union, 2006.

Ainley, Kirsten. 'From Atrocity Crimes to Human Rights: Expanding the Focus of the Responsibility to Protect'. *Global Responsibility to Protect* 9, no. 3 (2017): 243–66. https://doi.org/10.1163/1875984X-00903003.

'The International Criminal Court on Trial'. *Cambridge Review of International Affairs* 24, no. 3 (2011): 309–33. https://doi.org/10.1080/09557571.2011.558051.

'The Responsibility to Protect and the International Criminal Court: Counteracting the Crisis'. *International Affairs* 91, no. 1 (2015): 37–54. https://doi.org/10.1111/1468-2346.12185.

Alexander, Larry. *Constitutionalism: Philosophical Foundations.* 1st ed. Cambridge, UK and New York: Cambridge University Press, 1998.

Allan, T. R. S. *The Sovereignty of Law: Freedom, Constitution and Common Law.* Oxford: Oxford University Press, 2013.

Allen, Tim, and David Styan. 'A Right to Interfere? Bernard Kouchner and the New Humanitarianism'. *Journal of International Development* 12, no. 6 (August 2000): 825–42.

Anheier, Helmut K., Marlies Glasius, Mary Kaldor and Fiona Holland. *Global Civil Society Yearbook 2004/05.* London: SAGE, 2005.

Application of the Convention on the Prevention and Punishment of the Crime of Genocide (The Gambia v. Myanmar) (n.d.). www.icj-cij.org/en/case/178.

Arajärvi, Noora. 'Between Lex Lata and Lex Ferenda? Customary International (Criminal) Law and the Principle of Legality'. *Tilburg Law Review* 15, no. 2 (2010). https://brill-com.ezproxy.library.uq.edu.au/view/journals/tilr/15/2/article-p163_4.xml.

'Is There a Need for a New Sources Theory in International Law? A Proposal for an Inclusive Positivist Model'. *ASIL Annual Meeting Proceedings* 106 (2012): 370–3. https://doi.org/10.5305/procannmeetasil.106.0370.

The Changing Nature of Customary International Law: Methods of Interpreting the Concept of Custom in International Criminal Tribunals. London and New York: Routledge, 2014.

Arendt, Hannah. *Eichmann in Jerusalem: A Report on the Banality of Evil.* New York: Penguin Books, 2006.

Arrest Warrant of 11 April 2000 (*Democratic Republic of the Congo* v. *Belgium*), Judgment, I.C.J. Reports. (2002). www.icj-cij.org/en/case/121.

Assembly of the African Union. 'Decision On The Hissène Habré Case and The African Union, Seventh Ordinary Session, Doc. Assembly/Au/3(VII)', 1 July 2006. www.africa-union.org/root/au/Conferences/Past/2006/July/summit/doc/Decisions_and_Declarations/Assembly-AU-Dec.pdf.

'Decision On The Hissène Habré Case and The African Union, Sixth Ordinary Session, Doc. Assembly/AU/Dec.103(VI)',23 January 2006. www.au.int/en/sites/default/files/ASSEMBLY_EN_23_24_JANUARY_2006_AUC_%20SIXTH%20_ORDINARY_SESSION_DECISIONS_DECLARATIONS.pdf.

Attorney General of Israel v. *Eichmann*, Supreme Court of Israel 36 ILR 277 (1962).

Austin, John. *The Province of Jurisprudence Determined.* Edited by H. L. A. Hart. New York: The Noonday Press, 1954.

Australian Government. 'Royal Commission into Institutional Responses to Child Sexual Abuse – Final Report'. Royal Commissions, 15 December 2017. www.royalcommission.gov.au/royal-commission-institutional-responses-child-sexual-abuse/final-report.

Barnett, Michael, and Raymond Duvall. *Power in Global Governance.* Cambridge and New York: Cambridge University Press, 2005.

Barnett, Michael, and Martha Finnemore. *Rules for the World: International Organizations in Global Politics.* Ithaca, NY: Cornell University Press, 2004.

Barnett, Michael, and Martha Finnemore. 'The Politics, Power, and Pathologies of International Organizations'. *International Organization* 53, no. 4 (1999): 699–732. https://doi.org/10.1162/002081899551048.

Bassiouni, M. Cherif. *Crimes against Humanity: Historical Evolution and Contemporary Application*. Cambridge: Cambridge University Press, 2011. https://doi.org/10.1017/CBO9780511976537.

   Crimes against Humanity in International Criminal Law. 2nd rev. ed. The Hague, London and Boston: Kluwer Law International, 1999.

   'International Crimes: Jus Cogens and Obligations Erga Omnes'. *Law and Contemporary Problems* 59, no. 4 (1996): 63–74.

   Post-Conflict Justice. Ardsley, NY: Transnational Publishers, 2002.

   'Statement at the Ceremony for the Opening for Signature of the Convention on the Establishment of an International Criminal Court', Rome, 18 July 1998. http://m cherifbassiouni.com/wp-content/uploads/MCB-Rome-Speech-18_July_1998.pdf.

Bassiouni, M. Cherif, and William Schabas. *The Legislative History of the International Criminal Court*, 2nd rev. and exp. ed. Leiden and Boston: Brill Nijhoff, 2016.

Bassiouni, M. Cherif, and Edward M. Wise. *Aut Dedere Aut Judicare: The Duty to Extradite or Prosecute in International Law*. Dordrecht: Martinus Nijhoff, 1995.

Batros, Ben. 'A Confusing ICC Appeals Judgment on Head of State Immunity'. Just Security, 7 May 2019. www.justsecurity.org/63962/a-confusing-icc-appeals-judg ment-on-head-of-state-immunity/.

BBC. 'Guide to the Syrian Rebels – BBC News', 13 December 2013. www.bbc.com/ news/world-middle-east-24403003.

Beck, Thomas, and Christian Ritscher. 'Do Criminal Complaints Make Sense in (German) International Criminal Law? A Prosecutor's Perspective'. *Journal of International Criminal Justice* 13, no. 2 (May 1, 2015): 229–35. https://doi.org/10.1 093/jicj/mqv010.

Bell, Duncan S. A. 'International Relations: The Dawn of a Historiographical Turn?' *British Journal of Politics & International Relations* 3, no. 1 (2001): 115–26. https:// doi.org/10.1111/1467-856X.00053.

Bentham, Jeremy. *Of Laws in General*. Edited by H. L. A. Hart. London: The Athlone Press, 1970.

Bercault, Olivier. 'The 'Archives of Terror'. In *The President on Trial: Prosecuting Hissene Habre*, edited by Sharon Weill, Kim Thuy Seelinger and Kerstin Bree Carlson, 17–23. Oxford: Oxford University Press, 2020.

Besson, Samantha. 'How to Theorise Law in a Transnational Context'. *Transnational Legal Theory* 2, no. 4 (2011): 573–79. https://doi.org/10.5235/TLT.2.4.573.

   'Law Beyond the State: A Reply to Liam Murphy'. *European Journal of International Law* 28, no. 1 (2017): 233–40. https://doi.org/10.1093/ejil/chx005.

   'Sovereignty, International Law and Democracy'. *European Journal of International Law* 22, no. 2 (2011): 373–87. https://doi.org/10.1093/ejil/chr029.

   'State Consent and Disagreement in International Law-Making. Dissolving the Paradox', *Leiden Journal of International Law* 29, no. 2 (2016): 289–316. https://d oi.org/10.1017/S0922156516000030.

   'The Authority of International Law: Lifting the State Veil'. Edited by Gianna Sergi. *Sydney Law Review* 31, no. 3 (2009): 343–80.

'The Extraterritoriality of the European Convention on Human Rights: Why Human Rights Depend on Jurisdiction and What Jurisdiction Amounts To', *Leiden Journal of International Law* 25, no. 4 (2012): 857–84. https://doi.org/10.10 17/S0922156512000489.

The Legitimacy of International Human Rights Regimes: Legal, Political and Philosophical Perspectives. Cambridge: Cambridge University Press, 2013.

Besson, Samantha, and Jean d Aspremont. *The Oxford Handbook of the Sources of International Law.* Oxford: Oxford University Press, 2017. https://doi.org/10.1093/law/9780198745365.001.0001.

Besson, Samantha, and José Luis Martí. 'Legitimate Actors of International Law-Making: Towards a Theory of International Democratic Representation'. *Jurisprudence* 9, no. 3 (2018): 504–40. https://doi.org/10.1080/20403313.2018 .1442256.

Besson, Samantha, and John Tasioulas, eds. *The Philosophy of International Law.* Oxford and New York: Oxford University Press, 2010.

Black, Ian, and Ewen MacAskill. 'US Threatens Nato Boycott over Belgian War Crimes Law'. *The Guardian*, 13 June 2003. www.theguardian.com/world/2003/jun/13/nato.warcrimes.

Boas, Gideon, and William Schabas. *International Criminal Law Developments in the Case Law of the ICTY.* Leiden and Boston: Martinus Nijhoff Publishers, 2003.

Boas, Gideon, William Schabas and Michael P. Scharf. *International Criminal Justice Legitimacy and Coherence.* Cheltenham, UK and Northampton, MA: Edward Elgar, 2012.

Boli, John, and George M. Thomas. *Constructing World Culture: International Nongovernmental Organizations since 1875.* Stanford, CA: Stanford University Press, 1999.

Borger, Julian. 'Syria's Truth Smugglers'. *The Guardian*, 12 May 2015. www.theguardian.com/world/2015/may/12/syria-truth-smugglers-bashar-al-assad-war-crimes.

British Institute of International and Comparative Law. 'Reimagining the Law', 23 June 2020. www.biicl.org/reimagining/20/reimagining-the-law-23-june-2020.

Brody, Reed. 'Bringing a Dictator to Justice: The Case of Hissène Habré'. *Journal of International Criminal Justice* 13, no. 2 (1 May 2015): 209–17. https://doi.org/10.10 93/jicj/mqv005.

'Chad: The Victims of Hissène Habré Still Awaiting Justice'. *Human Rights Watch* 17, no. 10 (A) (July 2005): 1–43.

'Enabling a Dictator'. Human Rights Watch, 28 June 2016. www.hrw.org/report/201 6/06/28/enabling-dictator/united-states-and-chads-hissene-habre-1982-1990.

'Inside a Dictator's Secret Police'. *Foreign Policy* (blog), 9 March 2010. https://foreignpolicy.com/2010/03/09/inside-a-dictators-secret-police/.

'Tenacity, Perseverance, and Imagination in the "Private International Prosecution" of Hissene Habre'. In *The President on Trial: Prosecuting Hissene Habre*, edited by Sharon Weill, Kim Thuy Seelinger, and Kerstin Bree Carlson, 39–37. Oxford: Oxford University Press, 2020.

'The Prosecution of Hissene Habre – An "African Pinochet"'. *New England Law Review* 35, no. 2 (2001 2000): 321–36.

Brown, Chester. *A Common Law of International Adjudication.* Oxford: Oxford University Press, 2007.

Browne-Wilkinson, Nicolas. *R v. Bow Street Metropolitan Stipendiary Magistrate*, ex parte Pinochet Ugarte (No 3) (Pinochet 3) [2000] (1999).

Brownlie, Ian. *State Responsibility*. Oxford: Clarendon Press, 1983.

Brownlie, Ian, and James Crawford. *Brownlie's Principles of Public International Law*. 8th ed. Oxford: Oxford University Press, 2012.

Brunnée, Jutta, and Stephen J. Toope. 'Interactional International Law: An Introduction'. *International Theory* 3, no. 2 (2011): 307–18. https://doi.org/10.1017/S1752971911000030.

'Interactional International Law and the Practice of Legality'. In *International Practices*, edited by Emanuel Adler and Vincent Pouliot, 108–35. Cambridge: Cambridge University Press, 2012.

'International Law and the Practice of Legality: Stability and Change'. *Law Review (Wellington)* 49, no. 4 (2018): 429–45. https://doi.org/10.26686/vuwlr.v49i4.5334.

Legitimacy and Legality in International Law: An Interactional Account. Cambridge and New York: Cambridge University Press, 2010.

'The Sovereignty of International Law?' *University of Toronto Law Journal* 67, no. 4 (2017). https://doi.org/10.3138/utlj.67.2.

Bukovansky, Mlada, Ian Clark, Robyn Eckersley, Richard M. Price, Christian Reus-Smit and Nicholas J. Wheeler. *Special Responsibilities Global Problems and American Power*. Cambridge: Cambridge University Press, 2012.

Burgers, J. Herman, and Hans Danelius. *The United Nations Convention against Torture: A Handbook on the Convention against Torture and Other Cruel, Inhuman, or Degrading Treatment or Punishment*. Dordrecht and Boston: Nijhoff, 1988.

Burke, Roland. *Decolonization and the Evolution of International Human Rights*. Philadelphia: University of Pennsylvania Press, 2010. http://muse.jhu.edu/book/924.

Byers, Michael. *Custom, Power and the Power of Rules: International Relations and Customary International Law*. Cambridge, UK and New York: Cambridge University Press, 1999.

Cai, Weiyi, Alicia Parlapiano, Lauren Leatherby, Blacki Migliozzi and Jeremy White. 'Trump Impeachment Results: How Democrats and Republicans Voted'. *New York Times*, 5 February 2020, sec. U.S. www.nytimes.com/interactive/2020/02/05/us/politics/impeachment-vote-results.html,.

Carr, Edward. *The Twenty Years' Crisis*. 2nd ed. London: Macmillan, 1946.

Carroll, Matt, Sacha Pfeiffer, Michael Rezendes and Walter V. Robinson. 'Church Allowed Abuse by Priest for Years'. BostonGlobe.com, 6 January 2002. www.bostonglobe.com/news/special-reports/2002/01/06/church-allowed-abuse-priest-for-years/cSHfGkTIrAT25qKGvBuDNM/story.html.

Case Concerning Oil Platforms (*Islamic Republic of Iran v. United States of America*), Judgment, merits, ICJ Reports (separate opinion of Judge Simma). (2003).

Cassese, Antonio. 'Amicus Curiae Brief of Professor Antonio Cassese and Members of the *Journal of International Criminal Justice* on Joint Criminal Enterprise Doctrine'. *Criminal Law Forum* 20, no. 2–3 (2009): 289–330. https://doi.org/10.1007/s10609-009-9099-8.

'Are International Human Rights Treaties and Customary Rules on Torture Binding upon US Troops in Iraq?' *Journal of International Criminal Justice* 2, no. 3 (2004): 872–78. https://doi.org/10.1093/jicj/2.3.872.

'Balancing the Prosecution of Crimes against Humanity and Non-Retroactivity of Criminal Law'. *Journal of International Criminal Justice* 4, no. 2 (2006): 410–18. https://doi.org/10.1093/jicj/mql016.

Cassese's International Criminal Law. 3rd ed./revised by Antonio Cassese et al. Oxford: Oxford University Press, 2013.

'Eichmann: Is Evil So Banal?' *Journal of International Criminal Justice* 7, no. 3 (2009): 645–52. https://doi.org/10.1093/jicj/mqp028.

Human Rights in a Changing World. Philadelphia, PA: Temple University Press, 1990.

Inhuman States: Imprisonment, Detention and Torture in Europe Today. Oxford, UK and Cambridge, MA: Polity Press Blackwell Publishers, 1996.

International Criminal Law: Cases and Commentary. Oxford and New York: Oxford University Press, 2011.

International Law. 2nd ed. Oxford and New York: Oxford University Press, 2005.

International Law in a Divided World. Oxford: Clarendon Press; New York: Oxford University Press, 1986.

'Is the ICC Still Having Teething Problems?' *Journal of International Criminal Justice* 4, no. 3 (2006): 434–41. https://doi.org/10.1093/jicj/mql033.

Realizing Utopia. Oxford: Oxford University Press, 2012.

'Reflections on International Criminal Justice'. *Modern Law Review* 61, no. 1 (1998): 1–10. https://doi.org/10.1111/1468-2230.00124.

'Remarks given at the Old State House, Hartford CT, 18 October 1996. (International Criminal Courts)(Law, War and Human Rights International Courts and the Legacy of Nuremberg)'. *Connecticut Journal of International Law* 12, no. 2 (1997): 208.

'The Belgian Court of Cassation v. The International Court of Justice: The *Sharon and Others* Case'. *Journal of International Criminal Justice* 1, no. 2 (2003): 437–52. https://doi.org/10.1093/jicj/1.2.437.

The Human Dimension of International Law: Selected Papers. New York and Oxford: Oxford University Press, 2008.

'The ICTY: A Living and Vital Reality'. *Journal of International Criminal Justice* 2, no. 2 (2004): 585–97. https://doi.org/10.1093/jicj/2.2.585.

'The Legitimacy of International Criminal Tribunals and the Current Prospects of International Criminal Justice'. *Leiden Journal of International Law* 25, no. 2 (2012): 491–501. https://doi.org/10.1017/S0922156512000167.

'The Nexus Requirement for War Crimes'. *Journal of International Criminal Justice* 10, no. 5 (2012): 1395–417. https://doi.org/10.1093/jicj/mqs082.

'The Nicaragua and Tadic Tests Revisited in Light of the ICJ Judgment on Genocide in Bosnia'. *European Journal of International Law* 18, no. 4 (2007): 649–68. https://doi.org/10.1093/ejil/chm034.

The Oxford Companion to International Criminal Justice. Oxford and New York: Oxford University Press, 2009.

The Oxford Handbook of the History of International Law. Oxford: Oxford University Press, 2012.

'The Role of Legal Advisers in Ensuring That Foreign Policy Conforms to International Legal Standards'. *Michigan Journal of International Law* 14, no. 1 (1992): 170.

The Rome Statute of the International Criminal Court: A Commentary. Oxford and New York: Oxford University Press, 2002.

Violence and Law in the Modern Age. Cambridge: Polity Press, 1988.

Cassese, Antonio, Andrew Clapham and Joseph Weiler. *Human Rights and the European Community: The Substantive Law*. Baden-Baden: Nomos Verlagsgesellschaft, 1991.

Cassese, Antonio, Marina Spinedi and Joseph H. Weiler. *International Crimes of State: A Critical Analysis of the ILC's Draft Article 19 on State Responsibility*. Reprint 2011. Berlin and Boston: De Gruyter, 2011.

Cassese, Antonio, and Lal Chand Vohrah. *Man's Inhumanity to Man: Essays on International Law in Honour of Antonio Cassese*. The Hague: Kluwer Law International, 2003.

Cassese, Antonio, and Joseph H. H. Weiler. *Change and Stability in International Law-Making*. Reprint 2010. Berlin Boston: De Gruyter, 2010.

Castells, Manuel. *The Rise of the Network Society*. Oxford: Wiley-Blackwell, 2009.

'Chad-Report.Pdf'. www.usip.org/sites/default/files/file/resources/collections/commissions/Chad-Report.pdf.

Charter of the International Military Tribunal – Annex to the Agreement for the Prosecution and Punishment of the Major War Criminals of the European Axis (Referred to as the Nuremberg Charter or London Charter), II Jurisdiction and General Principles (1945).

Chinkin, Christine, and Alan Boyle. *The Making of International Law*. Oxford: Oxford University Press, 2007.

Chinkin, Christine, and Mary Kaldor. *International Law and New Wars*. Cambridge: Cambridge University Press, 2017.

Chowdhury, Abdul Quader. 'Trial of Former Chilean Dictator General Pinochet'. *The Independent*, 10 September 2000. www.independent.co.uk.

Engels, Chris (CIJA deputy director). Interview with author, January 2017.

Christensen, Mikkel Jarle. 'Crafting and Promoting International Crimes: A Controversy among Professionals of Core-Crimes and Anti-Corruption'. *Leiden Journal of International Law* 30, no. 2 (2017): 501–21. https://doi.org/10.1017/S0922156517000036.

'From Symbolic Surge to Closing Courts: The Transformation of International Criminal Justice and Its Professional Practices'. *International Journal of Law, Crime and Justice* 43, no. 4 (2015): 609–25. https://doi.org/10.1016/j.ijlcj.2015.02.001.

'From Symbolic Surge to Closing Courts: The Transformation of International Criminal Justice and Its Professional Practices'. *International Journal of Law, Crime and Justice* 43, no. 4 (1 December 2015): 609–25. https://doi.org/10.1016/j.ijlcj.2015.02.001.

'The Emerging Sociology of International Criminal Courts: Between Global Restructurings and Scientific Innovations'. *Current Sociology* 63, no. 6 (2015): 825–49. https://doi.org/10.1177/0011392115588963.

'The Judiciary of International Criminal Law'. *Journal of International Criminal Justice* 17, no. 3 (2019): 537–55. https://doi.org/10.1093/jicj/mqz033.

Church, Rosemary, Richard Palo, Ralitsa Vassileva, Al Goodman, Paula Hancocks, Jonathan Mann and Juan Garcés. 'The Death of Augusto Pinochet'. CNN Insight, 11 December 2006.

CIJA Chief Investigator 1 (with translator CIJA Liaison Officer 1). Interview with author, January 2017.

CIJA Senior Analyst 1. Interview with author, January 2017.

CIJA Senior Analyst 2. Interview with author, January 2017.

Clark, Ann Marie, and Kathryn Sikkink. 'Information Effects and Human Rights Data: Is the Good News about Increased Human Rights Information Bad News for Human Rights Measures?' *Human Rights Quarterly* 35, no. 3 (2013): 539–68. https://doi.org/10.1353/hrq.2013.0046.

Clark, Ian, Sebastian Kaempf, Christian Reus-Smit and Emily Tannock. 'Crisis in the Laws of War? Beyond Compliance and Effectiveness'. *European Journal of International Relations* 24, no. 2 (1 June 2018): 319–43. https://doi.org/10.1177/1354066117714528.

Combs, Nancy A. *Fact-Finding without Facts: The Uncertain Evidentiary Foundations of International Criminal Convictions.* New York and Cambridge: Cambridge University Press, 2010.

   Guilty Pleas in International Criminal Law: Constructing a Restorative Justice Approach. Stanford, CA: Stanford University Press, 2007.

Combs, Nancy Amoury. 'A New Look at Fact-Finding at the ICTR: Advances in Judicial Acknowledgement. (Symposium: Evidence and Proof in the Practice of the International Criminal Tribunal for Rwanda)'. *Criminal Law Forum* 26, no. 3–4 (2015): 387–401. https://doi.org/10.1007/s10609-015-9263-2.

   'Deconstructing the Epistemic Challenges to Mass Atrocity Prosecutions'. *Washington and Lee Law Review* 75, no. 1 (2018): 223–300.

   'Evidence'. In *Routledge Handbook of International Criminal Law*, edited by William Schabas and Nadia Bernaz, 323–34. Oxford and New York: Routledge Publishing, 2013.

   'Grave Crimes and Weak Evidence: A Fact-Finding Evolution in International Criminal Law'. *Harvard International Law Journal* 47–58, no. 1 (2017): 125.

   'Unequal Enforcement of the Law: Targeting Aggressors for Mass Atrocity Prosecutions'. *Arizona Law Review* 61, no. 1 (2019): 155–204.

Commissions of Inquiry (Chad). 'Chad: Report of the Commission of Inquiry into the Crimes and Misappropriations Committed by Ex-President Habre, His Accomplices and/or Accessories – Investigation of Crimes Against the Physical and Mental Integrity of Persons and Their Possessions'. N'DJamena, 7 May 1992. www.usip.org/sites/default/files/file/resources/collections/commissions/Chad-Report.pdf.

Condorelli, Luigi. 'Customary International Law: The Yesterday, Today, and Tomorrow of General International Law'. In *Realizing Utopia: The Future of International Law*, edited by Antonio Cassese, 147–57. Oxford: Oxford University Press, 2012.

Conduit, Dara. *The Muslim Brotherhood in Syria*. Cambridge Middle East Studies. Cambridge: Cambridge University Press, 2019. https://doi.org/10.1017/9781108758321.

Council on Foreign Relations. 'Who's Who in Syria's Civil War'. 2020. www.cfr.org/site-api/cfr-wrapper.

Crane, David. '"Not Perfect Candidates" to Be the Next Prosecutor of the International Criminal Court'. *Jurist* (blog), 10 July 2020. www.jurist.org/commentary/2020/07/david-crane-icc-prosecutor/.

Crawford, James. *Brownlie's Principles of Public International Law.* 9th ed. Oxford and New York: Oxford University Press, 2019.

'Execution of Judgments and Foreign Sovereign Immunity'. *The American Journal of International Law* 75, no. 4 (1981): 820–69. https://doi.org/10.2307/2201355.

'The Drafting of the Rome Statute'. In *From Nuremberg to The Hague: The Future of International Criminal Justice,* edited by Philippe Sands, 109–56. Cambridge: Cambridge University Press, 2003.

Culver, Keith, and Michael Giudice. *Legality's Borders: An Essay in General Jurisprudence.* Oxford: Oxford University Press, 2010.

Cupido, Marjolein, Manuel J. Ventura and Lachezar Yanev, eds. *Modes of Liability in International Criminal Law.* Cambridge: Cambridge University Press, 2019. http s://doi.org/10.1017/9781108678957.

Cutler, A. Claire. *Private Power and Global Authority: Transnational Merchant Law in the Global Political Economy.* Cambridge: Cambridge University Press, 2003.

'The Judicialization of Private Transnational Power and Authority'. *Indiana Journal of Global Legal Studies* 25, no. 1 (2018): 61–95. https://doi.org/10.2979/ indjglolegstu.25.1.0061.

'The Legitimacy of Private Transnational Governance: Experts and the Transnational Market for Force'. *Socio-Economic Review* 8, no. 1 (2010): 157–85. https://doi.org/10.1093/ser/mwp027.

Cutler, A. Claire, Virginia Haufler, and Tony Porter. *Private Authority and International Affairs.* Albany: State University of New York Press, 1999.

D'Amato, Anthony A. *The Concept of Custom in International Law.* Ithaca, NY: Cornell University Press, 1971.

'The Concept of Special Custom in International Law'. *American Journal of International Law* 63 (1969): 211–23.

Dancy, Geoff, Bridget E. Marchesi, Tricia D. Olsen, Leigh A. Payne, Andrew G. Reiter and Kathryn Sikkink. 'Behind Bars and Bargains: New Findings on Transitional Justice in Emerging Democracies'. *International Studies Quarterly* 63, no. 1 (2019): 99–110. https://doi.org/10.1093/isq/sqy053.

Day, Adam. 'Crimes against Humanity as a Nexus of Individual and State Responsibility: Why the ICJ Got *Belgium* v. *Congo* Wrong'. *Berkeley Journal of International Law* 22, no. 3 (2004): 489–512. https://doi.org/10.15779/Z38GH1Z.

De Letelier v. *Republic of Chile,* 567 F. Supp. 1490 (S.D.N.Y.) U.S. District Court for the Southern District of New York – 567 F. Supp. 1490 (S.D.N.Y. 1983) (28 July 1983).

Del Ponte, Carla. 'Prosecuting the Individuals Bearing the Highest Level of Responsibility'. *Journal of International Criminal Justice* 2, no. 2 (1 June 2004): 516–19. https://doi.org/10.1093/jicj/2.2.516.

Department of Defence. '2016 Defence White Paper'. Canberra: Commonwealth of Australia, 2016. www.defence.gov.au/WhitePaper/.

'2020 *Defence Strategic Update.*' Canberra: Commonwealth of Australia, 2020.

Der Spiegal – International. 'SPIEGEL Interview With War Crimes Prosecutor Carla Del Ponte: "Politics Have Interfered With Our Work"', 18 October 2007. www .spiegel.de/international/world/spiegel-interview-with-war-crimes-prosecutor-carl a-del-ponte-politics-have-interfered-with-our-work-a-512188.html.

Deutsch, Karl, Sidney A. Burrell, Robert A. Kann, Maurice Lee Jr., Martin Lichterman, Raymond E. Lindgren, Francis L. Loewenheim and Richard W. Van Wagenen.

Political Community and the North American Area. Princeton, NJ: Princeton University Press, 2015. www-degruyter-com.ezproxy.library.uq.edu.au/prince tonup/view/title/522395.

DeYoung, Karen. 'The Prosecutor Who Never Rested'. *Washington Post*, 8 October 1999. www.washingtonpost.com/archive/lifestyle/1999/10/08/the-prosecutor-who-never-rested/64047db5-0991-4b43-8907-38251ff16bf7/.

Diehl, Jorg, Christoph Reuter and Fidelius Schmid. 'Germany Takes Aim at Assad's Torture Boss'. *Der Spiegel*. 2018. www.spiegel.de/international/world/senior-assad-aid-charged-with-war-crimes-a-1211923.html.

Diehl, Jorg, Christoph Reuter, and Fidellus Schmid. 'Internatioanl Arrest Warrent: Germany Takes Aim at Assad's Torture Boss'. Der Spiegal – International, 8 June 2018. www.spiegel.de/international/world/senior-assad-aid-charged-with-war-crim es-a-1211923.html.

Di Sarsina, Roberti, William Schabas Jacopo and Augusto Barbera. *Transitional Justice and a State's Response to Mass Atrocity: Reassessing the Obligations to Investigate and Prosecute.* The Hague and Berlin: Springer: T.M.C. Asser Press, 2019.

Doherty, Ben. 'Aung San Suu Kyi Cannot Be Prosecuted in Australia, Christian Porter Says'. *The Guardian*, 17 March 2018. www.theguardian.com/world/2018/mar/17/a ung-san-suu-kyi-cannot-be-prosecuted-in-australia-christian-porter-says.

Donelan, Michael D. *The Reason of States: A Study in International Political Theory.* London and Boston: Allen & Unwin, 1978.

Drescher, Seymour. *Abolition: A History of Slavery and Antislavery.* Cambridge and New York: Cambridge University Press, 2009.

Duerr, Benjamin. 'International Crimes: Spotlight on Germany's War Crimes Unit'. JusticeInfo.Net, 10 January 2019. www.justiceinfo.net/en/tribunals/national-tribu nals/39936-international-crimes-spotlight-on-germany-s-war-crimes-unit.html.

Dunne, Timothy, and Christian Reus-Smit. *The Globalization of International Society.* Oxford: Oxford University Press, 2017.

Bilder, Richard, and Nico Krisch,. 'Legitimacy and Legality in International Law: An International Account'. *American Journal of International Law* 106 (2012): 203+.

Eikel, Markus. '"Germany's Global Responsibility" and the Creation of the International Criminal Court, 1993–1998'. *Journal of International Criminal Justice* 16, no. 3 (1 July 2018): 543–70. https://doi.org/10.1093/jicj/mqy022.

Fall, Mbacké. 'Prosecuting International Crimes in Senegal'. In *The President on Trial: Prosecuting Hissène Habré,* edited by Sharon Weill, Kim Thuy Seelinger and Kerstin Bree Carlson, 103–10. Oxford: Oxford University Press, 2020.

Fassbender, Bardo. 'Written Versus Unwritten: Two Views on the Form of International Constitution'. In *Handbook on Global Constitutionalism,* edited by Anthony Lang and Antje Wiener. Cheltenham, UK: Edward Elgar Publishing.

Finnemore, Martha. 'Are Legal Norms Distinctive? (Response to Article by Steven R. Ratner in This Issue, p. 591) (Minority Disputes in Europe: Toward New Roles for International Law)'. *New York University Journal of International Law and Politics* 32, no. 3 (2000): 705.

'Fights about Rules: The Role of Efficacy and Power in Changing Multilateralism'. *Review of International Studies* 31, no. S1 (2005): 187–206. https://doi.org/10.1017/S0260210505006856.

'Rules of War and Wars of Rules: The International Red Cross and the Restraint of State Violence'. In *Constructing World Culture: International Nongovernmental Organisations Since 1873*, 149–65. Standford, CA: Stanford University Press, 1999.

The Purpose of Intervention. Ithaca, NY: Cornell University Press, 2013.

Finnemore, Martha, and Judith Goldstein. *Back to Basics: State Power in a Contemporary World*. Oxford: Oxford University Press, 2013.

Finnemore, Martha, and Michelle Jurkovich. 'Getting a Seat at the Table: The Origins of Universal Participation and Modern Multilateral Conferences'. *Global Governance: A Review of Multilateralism and International Organizations* 20, no. 3 (2014): 361–73. https://doi.org/10.1163/19426720-02003003.

Finnemore, Martha, and Kathryn Sikkink. 'International Norm Dynamics and Political Change'. *International Organization* 52, no. 4 (1998): 887–917. https://doi.org/10.1162/002081898550789.

Finnemore, Martha, and Stephen Toope. 'Alternatives to "Legalization": Richer Views of Law and Politics'. *International Organization* 55, no. 3 (2001): 743–58. https://doi.org/10.1162/00208180152507614.

El Clarin.cl. 'Fondo de Ayuda a Las Víctimas Del Alzamiento de Bienes y Blanqueo de Capitales de Augusto Pinochet', 12 February 2008. www.elclarin.cl/fpa/indemni zaciones.html?phpMyAdmin=cf9bcaoef760364025bbda1263ac199 f.

The Independent. 'Former Pinochet Officials on Trial', 9 December 2010. www.inde pendent.co.uk/news/world/europe/former-pinochet-officials-on-trial-2154922. html.

Former UK Government Consultant 1. Interview with author, November 2017.

France 24 News. 'France Investigates Crown Prince of Abu Dhabi on Torture Charges', 17 July 2020. www.fr24news.com/a/2020/07/france-investigates-crown-prince-of-a bu-dhabi-on-torture-charges.html.

Fransen, Daniel. 'The Belgian Investigation of the Habré Regime'. In *The President on Trial: Prosecuting Hissene Habre*, edited by Sharon Weill, Kim Thuy Seelinger and Kerstin Bree Carlson, 54–59. Oxford: Oxford University Press, 2020.

Fukuyama, Francis. 'What Is Governance?' *Governance* 26, no. 3 (2013): 347–68. https://doi.org/10.1111/gove.12035.

Fuller, Lon. 'Human Interaction and the Law'. In *The Principles of Social Order*, edited by Kenneth J. Winston. Oxford, UK and Portland, OR.: Hart Publishing, 2001.

The Morality of Law. New Haven, CT: Yale University Press, 1969.

Gardner, Frank. 'Iraq's Sinjar Yazidis: Bringing IS Slavers to Justice'. *BBC News*, 2 August 2016, sec. Middle East. www.bbc.com/news/world-middle-east-36960657.

Gardner, John. *Law as a Leap of Faith: Essays on Law in General. Law as a Leap of Faith*. Oxford: Oxford University Press, 2012. https://oxford-universitypressscholar ship-com.ezproxy.library.uq.edu.au/view/10.1093/acprof:oso/9780199695553.001. 0001/acprof-9780199695553.

Garzon, Baltasar. 'Spanish Judge Baltasar Garzón Tells the Story of the Arrest of Chile's Augusto Pinochet (Transcript)'. Democracy Now! 11 September 2013. www.dem ocracynow.org/blog/2013/9/11/spanish_judge_baltasar_garzn_tells_the_stor y_of_the_arrest_of_chiles_augusto_pinochet.

'Garzón Solicita Interrogar a Kissinger El 24 de Abril En Londres Por El Caso Pinochet'. *Europa Press*, 17 April 2002, Factiva edition.

Generalbundesanwalt (German Federal Public Prosecutor General's Office). 'Presse: Anklage Gegen Zwei Mutmaßliche Mitarbeiter Des Syrischen Geheimdienstes Wegen Der Begehung von Verbrechen Gegen Die Menschlichkeit Ua Erhoben (Press Statement: Charges Have Been Brought against Two Alleged Employees of the Syrian Intelligence Service for Committing Crimes against Humanity) 29 October', 2019b. www.generalbundesanwalt.de/.

'Presse: Festnahme Eines Mutmaßlichen Mitarbeiters Des Syrischen Militärischen Geheimdienstes Wegen Des Dringenden Tatverdachts Eines Verbrechens Gegen Die Menschlichkeit (Press Statement: Arrest of a Suspected Syrian Military Intelligence Agent on Suspicion of a Crime against Humanity)', 22 June 2020. www.generalbundesanwalt.de/.

'Presse: Festnahme Zweier Mitarbeiter Des Allgemeinen Syrischen Geheimdienstes Wegen Des Verdachts Der Begehung von Verbrechen Gegen Die Menschlichkeit (Press Statement: Arrest of Two Members of the General Syrian Intelligence Serive on Suspicion of Committing Crimes against Humanity)', 2019a. www.generalbundesanwalt.de/.

Gerges, Fawaz A. *ISIS: A History*. Princeton, NJ: Princeton University Press, 2016.

Gill, Stephen, and A. Claire Cutler. *New Constitutionalism and World Order*. Cambridge, UK and New York: Cambridge University Press, 2014.

Glasius, Marlies. 'Do International Courts Require Democratic Legitimacy?' *European Journal of International Law* 23, no. 1 (2012): 66.

'Extraterritorial Authoritarian Practices: A Framework'. *Globalizations: The Authoritarian Rule of Populations Abroad* 15, no. 2 (2018): 179–97. https://doi.org/10.1080/14747731.2017.1403781.

'"It Sends a Message"'. *Journal of International Criminal Justice* 13, no. 3 (2015): 419–47. https://doi.org/10.1093/jicj/mqv023.

The International Criminal Court: A Global Civil Society Achievement. 1st ed. New York and London: Routledge, 2006.

Glasius, Marlies, Meta De Lange, Jos Bartman, Emanuela Dalmasso, Aofei Lv, Adele Del Sordi, Marcus Michaelsen, and Kris Ruijgrok. *Research, Ethics and Risk in the Authoritarian Field*. Cham, Switzerland: Palgrave Macmillan and Springer International Publishing, 2018.

Glasius, Marlies, and Mary Kaldor. *A Human Security Doctrine for Europe Project, Principles, Practicalities*. Abingdon, UK and New York: Routledge, 2006.

Goldoni, Marco, and Christopher McCorkindale. *Hannah Arendt and the Law*, edited by Marco Goldoni and Christopher McCorkindale. *Law and Practical Reason*, v. 4. Oxford and Portland, OR: Hart, 2012.

Gooch, Adela. 'The Lawyer Who Wouldn't Forget'. *The Guardian*, 2 February 1999. www.theguardian.com/world/1999/feb/02/law.theguardian.

Goodman, Al. 'Pinochet: U.S. Urged to Charge Bank'. CNN.com, 16 September 2004. https://edition.cnn.com/2004/WORLD/europe/09/16/spain.riggs/.

Goodman, Amy, and Juan Garcés. '40 Years After Chilean Coup, Allende Aide Juan Garcés on How He Brought Pinochet to Justice (Transcript)'. Democracy Now! 10 September 2013. www.democracynow.org/2013/9/10/40_years_after_chilean_coup_allende.

Green, Leslie. *The Authority of the State*. Oxford: Clarendon Press, 1990.

Green, Leslie, and H. L. A. Hart. 'Introduction'. In *The Concept of Law*, edited by Joseph Raz and Penelope A. Bulloch, xv–1. Oxford: Oxford University Press.

Grossman, Nienke, Harlan Grant Cohen, Andreas Follesdal and Geir Ulfstein, eds. *Legitimacy and International Courts*. Studies on International Courts and Tribunals. Cambridge: Cambridge University Press, 2018. https://doi.org/10.1017/9781108529570.

Grote, Rainer. 'Rule of Law, Rechtsstaat and Etat de Droit'. In *Constitutionalism, Universalism and Democracy – Comparative Analysis*, edited by Christian Starck, 269–306. Baden-Baden: Nomos Verlagsgesllschaft, 1999.

Grundgesetz für die Bundesrepublik Deutschland (Basic Law for the Federal Republic of Germany) in the revised version published in the Federal Law Gazette Part III, classification number 100–1, as last amended by Article 1 of the Act of 28 March 2019 (Federal Law Gazette I, 404). (n.d.). www.gesetze-im-internet.de/englisch_gg/englisch_gg.html.

Guénaël, Mettraux. *Research Handbook on International Law and Terrorism*. Cheltenham, UK: Edward Elgar Publishing, 2014.

Guengueng, Souleymane. 'Documenting Crimes and Organizing Victims in Chad'. In *The President on Trial: Prosecuting Hissene Habre*, edited by Sharon Weill, Kim Thuy Seelinger and Kerstin Bree Carlson, 31–38. Oxford: Oxford University Press, 2020.

'Send Habré to Belgium for Trial'. *New York Times*, 16 January 2006. www.nytimes.com/2006/01/16/opinion/send-habr-to-belgium-for-trial.html.

Hakimi, Monica. 'Making Sense of Customary International Law'. *Michigan Law Review*, 118 no. 8 (2020): 1487–538. https://doi.org/10.36644/mlr.118.8.making.

Hale, Kip, and Melinda Rankin. 'Extending the "System" of International Criminal Law? The ICC's Decision on Jurisdiction over Alleged Deportations of Rohingya People'. *Australian Journal of International Affairs* 73, no. 1 (2 January 2019): 22–28. https://doi.org/10.1080/10357718.2018.1548565.

Hall, Allan, and John Lichfield. 'Germany Opens Its Gates: Berlin Says All Syrian Asylum-Seekers Are Welcome to Remain, as Britain Is Urged to Make a "Similar Statement"'. *The Independent*, 24 August 2015. www.independent.co.uk/news/world/europe/germany-opens-its-gates-berlin-says-all-syrian-asylum-seekers-are-welcome-to-remain-as-britain-is-10470062.html.

Harris, Whitney R. *Tyranny on Trial: The Evidence at Nuremberg*. New York: Barnes and Noble Books, 1954.

Hart, H. L. A. *The Concept of Law*, edited by Joseph Raz and Penelope A. Bulloch. 3rd ed. Clarendon Law Series. Oxford: Oxford University Press, 2012.

Heartfield, James. *The British and Foreign Anti-Slavery Society, 1838–1956: A History*. Oxford: Oxford University Press, 2017.

Henckaerts, Jean-Marie, and Louise Doswald-Beck. *Customary International Humanitarian Law*. Cambridge and New York: Cambridge University Press, 2005.

Herik, Larissa van Den. 'The Decline of Customary International Law as a Source of International Criminal Law'. In *Custom's Future: International Law in a Changing World*, edited by Curtis A. Bradley, 230–52. Cambridge: Cambridge University Press, 2016.

Herz, John H. 'Idealist Internationalism and the Security Dilemma'. *World Politics* 2, no. 2 (January 1950): 157–80. https://doi.org/10.2307/2009187.

Hicks, Celeste. *The Trial of Hissène Habré: How the People of Chad Brought a Tyrant to Justice*. London: Zed Books Ltd, 2018.

Higgott, Richard A., and Kim Richard Nossal. 'Australia and the Search for a Security Community in the 1990s'. In *Security Communities*, edited by Emanuel Adler and Michael Barnett, 1st ed., 265–94. Cambridge: Cambridge University Press, 1998. https://doi.org/10.1017/CBO9780511598661.008.

Hilton, Isabel, Geoffrey Bindman, and Juan Garcés. 'Justice in the World's Light'. openDemocracy, 15 June 2001. www.opendemocracy.net/en/justice-in-worlds-light/.

Hobbes, Thomas. *Leviathan*. Oxford: Oxford University Press, 2014.

Hoogh, Andre de. *Obligations Erga Omnes and International Crimes: A Theoretical Inquiry into the Implementation and Enforcement of the International Responsibility of States*. The Hague and Boston: Kluwer International Law, 1996.

Hughes, Edel, William Schabas, and Ramesh Thakur. *Atrocities and International Accountability beyond Transitional Justice*. New York: United Nations University Press, 2007.

Human Rights Watch (HRW). 'The Pinochet Precedent: How Victims Can Pursue Human Rights Criminals Abroad', March 2000. www.hrw.org/legacy/campaigns/chile98/precedent.htm.

Hurrell, Andrew. *On Global Order: Power, Values, and the Constitution of International Society*. Oxford: Oxford University, 2007.

Hurrell, Andrew, and Michael Byers. 'International Law and the Changing Constitution of International Society'. In *The Role of Law in International Politics: Essays in International Relations and International Law*, 328–48. Oxford: Oxford University Press, 2001.

Hussein, Zeid Ra'ad Al. 'International, Impartial and Independent Mechanism on International Crimes Committed in the Syrian Arab Republic, 34th Session of the Human Rights Council, Remarks by Zeid Ra'ad Al Hussein, United Nations High Commissioner for Human Rights'. Office of the High Commissioner for Human Rights (OHCHR), 27 February 2017. www.ohchr.org/EN/NewsEvents/Pages/DisplayNews.aspx?NewsID=21241.

'Syria Worst Man-Made Disaster since World War II, Geneva, Text of a Statement by UN High Commissioner for Human Rights Zeid Ra'ad Al Hussein to a High-Level Panel Discussion at the Human Rights Council on the Situation of Human Rights in the Syrian Arab Republic', 14 March 2017. www.ohchr.org/EN/NewsEvents/Pages/DisplayNews.aspx?NewsID=21373&LangID=E.

Inazumi, Mitsue. *Universal Jurisdiction in Modern International Law: Expansion of National Jurisdiction for Prosecuting Serious Crimes under International Law*. School of Human Rights Research Series, v. 19. Antwerpen: Intersentia, 2005.

Innes, John. 'Permission Sought to Question Kissinger'. *The Scotsman (Factiva)*, 18 April 2002.

International Committee of the Red Cross (ICRC). 'Convention for the Amelioration of the Condition of the Wounded in Armies in the Field', 22 August 1864.

International Criminal Court (ICC). 'Judgment on the Appeal against the Decision on the Authorisation of an Investigation into the Situation in the Islamic Republic of Afghanistan, Appeals Chamber, Decision', 5 March 2020. www.icc-cpi.int/Pages/record.aspx?docNo=ICC-02/17-138.

International Law Commission. '*Fragmentation of International Law: Difficulties Arising from the Diversification and Expansion of International Law: Report of the Study Group of the International Law Commission, Fifty-Eighth Session, A/CN.4/L.682*'. New York: United National General Assembly, 2006.

'Report of the International Law Commission on the Work of Its Sixty-Ninth Session U.N. Doc. A/74/10'. New York: Office of Legal Affairs, United Nations, 2019.

'Report of the International Law Commission on the Work of Its Sixty-Sixth Session, UN GAOR, 69th Sess, Supp No 10, UN Doc A/69/10'. New York: Office of Legal Affairs, United Nations, 5 August 2014.

'Report on the Work of the Fifty-Fourth Session (2002)'. New York: Office of Legal Affairs, United Nations, 2002.

Internationale Akademie Nürnberger Prinzipien. 'Private Investigations in International Criminal Justice'. International Nuremberg Principles Academy, 2020. projects/de tail/9c75eeaeeobd858dfdaeaca1ead42e55/private-investigations-in-international-cri minal-justice-24/.

'It Takes a Community; Informal Groups Known as Communities of Practice Are the Latest Technique for Getting Employees to Share What They Know. Here Are Seven Ways to Encourage Such Communities in Your Company. – ProQuest'. https://search-proquest-com.ezproxy.library.uq.edu.au/docview/205944743?Open UrlRefId=info:xri/sid:primo&accountid=14723.

Jackson, Robert. 'Nuremberg in Retrospect: Legal Answer to International Lawlessness'. *American Bar Association Journal* 35 (1949): 813.

Jackson, Robert H. *Report of Robert H. Jackson, United States Representative to the International Conference on Military Trials, London, 1945: A Documentary Record of Negotiations of the Representatives of the United States of America, the Provisional Government of the French Republic, the United Kingdom of Great Britain and Northern Ireland, and the Union of the Soviet Socialist Republics, Culminating in the Agreement and Charter of the International Military Tribunal.* Washington: United States Government Printing Office, 1949.

Second Day, Wednesday, 11/21/1945, Part 04, in Trial of the Major War Criminals before the International Military Tribunal. Volume II. Proceedings: 11/14/1945–11/ 30/1945.[Official Text in the English Language.] Nuremberg: International Military Tribunal (IMT), 1945.

The Nurnberg Case. New York: Cooper Square Publishers, 1971.

Jarry, Emmanuel. 'France Issues Arrest Warrants for Senior Syrian Officials'. *Reuters*, 5 November 2018. www.reuters.com/article/us-syria-crisis-france/france-issues-arr est-warrants-for-senior-syrian-officials-idUSKCN1NA11 L.

Jervis, Robert. 'Cooperation under the Security Dilemma'. *World Politics* 30, no. 2 (January 1978): 167–214. https://doi.org/10.2307/2009958.

Johnson, Larry (CIJA commissioner). Interview with author, January 2017.

Jung, Danielle F., and Dara Kay Cohen. *Lynching and Local Justice: Legitimacy and Accountability in Weak States.* Cambridge: Cambridge University Press, 2020. https://doi.org/10.1017/9781108885591.

Jutta, Brunnée, and J. Toope Stephen. 'Interactional Legal Theory, the International Rule of Law and Global Constitutionalism'. In *Handbook on Global Constitutionalism*, edited by Anthony F. Lang and Antje Wiener, 170–82. Cheltenham, UK: Edward Elgar Publishing Limited, 2017.

Kaldor, Mary. *Global Civil Society: An Answer to War*. 1st ed., Cambridge: Polity Press, 2003.

New and Old Wars: Organized Violence in a Global Era. 3rd ed. Cambridge and Malden, MA: Polity Press, 2012.

'The Idea of Global Civil Society'. *International Affairs* 79, no. 3 (2003): 583–93. https://doi.org/10.1111/1468-2346.00324.

Kaldor, Mary, and Anna Leander. 'Global Civil Society: An Answer to War'. Edited by Mary Kaldor and Anna Leander. *Journal of International Relations and Development* 7, no. 4 (2004): 444–47. https://doi.org/10.1057/palgrave.jird.1800025.

Kaldor, Mary, Henrietta L. Moore, Sabine Selchow, and Tamsin Murray-Leach. *Global Civil Society 2012 Ten Years of Critical Reflection*. London: Palgrave Macmillan, 2012.

Kaldor, Mary, and Saskia Sassen. *Cities at War: Global Insecurity and Urban Resistance*. New York: Columbia University Press, 2020.

Kaldor, Mary, and Sabine Selchow. 'The "Bubbling Up" of Subterranean Politics in Europe'. *Journal of Civil Society* 9, no. 1 (2013): 78–99. https://doi.org/10.1080/17448689.2013.784501.

Kandé, Jean. 'Investigations in Senegal and Chad: Cooperation and Challenges'. In *The President on Trial: Prosecuting Hissene Habre*, edited by Sharon Weill, Kim Thuy Seelinger, and Kerstin Bree Carlson, 82–89. Oxford: Oxford University Press, 2020.

Kebe, Mouhamed. 'State and Universal Jurisdiction: Assessing an Uneasy Relationship'. In *Rule of Law through Human Rights and International Criminal Justice: Essays in Honour of Adama Dieng*, edited by Charles Riziki Majinge. Newcastle-upon-Tyne, UK: Cambridge Scholars Publisher, 2015.

Keck, Margaret E., and Kathryn Sikkink. *Activists beyond Borders: Advocacy Networks in International Politics*. Ithaca, NY: Cornell University Press, 2014.

'Transnational Advocacy Networks in International and Regional Politics'. *International Social Science Journal* 68, no. 227–28 (2018): 65–76. https://doi.org/10.1111/issj.12187.

Kelton, Maryanne, Michael Sullivan, Emily Bienvenue, and Zac Rogers. 'Australia, the Utility of Force and the Society-Centric Battlespace'. *International Affairs* 95, no. 4 (July 1, 2019): 859–76. https://doi.org/10.1093/ia/iiz080.

Khan, Karim A., Caroline Buisman, and Christopher Gosnell. *Principles of Evidence in International Criminal Justice*. Oxford: Oxford University Press, 2015.

Klabbers, Jan, Anne Peters, and Geir Ulfstein. *The Constitutionalization of International Law*. Oxford: Oxford University Press, 2009.

Kornbluh, Peter. *The Pinochet File: A Declassified Dossier on Atrocity and Accountability*. New York: The New Press, 2013.

Kratchowil, Michael V. 'How Do Norms Matter?' In *The Role of Law in International Politics: Essays in International Relations and International Law*, edited by Michael Byers, 35–67. Oxford: Oxford University Press, 2001.

Kumm, Mattias. 'Global Constitutionalism and the Rule of Law'. In *Handbook on Global Constitutionalism*, edited by Anthony Lang and Antje Wiener, 197–221. Cheltenham, UK: Edward Elgar Publishing, 2017.

Langer, Máximo. 'Universal Jurisdiction Is Not Disappearing: The Shift from "Global Enforcer" to "No Safe Haven" Universal Jurisdiction". *Journal of International Criminal Justice* 13, no. 2 (1 May 2015): 245–56. https://doi.org/10.1093/jicj/mqv009.

Larson, Sarah. '"Spotlight" and Its Revelations'. *The New Yorker*, 8 December 2015. www.newyorker.com/culture/sarah-larson/spotlight-and-its-revelations.

Laub, Zachary. 'Who's Who in Syria's Civil War'. Council on Foreign Relations, 28 April 2017. www.cfr.org/site-api/cfr-wrapper.

Lave, Jean, and Etienne Wenger. *Situated Learning: Legitimate Peripheral Participation*. Cambridge: Cambridge University Press, 1991.

'Law as a Leap of Faith: Essays on Law in General – Oxford Scholarship'. https://oxford-universitypressscholarship-com.ezproxy.library.uq.edu.au/view/10.1093/acprof:os o/9780199695553.001.0001/acprof-9780199695553.

'Law Journal Library Southern California Law Review – HeinOnline.Org'. https://heinon line-org.ezproxy.library.uq.edu.au/HOL/Index?index=journals%2Fscal&collection =journals.

Lepard, Brian D., ed. *Reexamining Customary International Law*. ASIL Studies in International Legal Theory. Cambridge: Cambridge University Press, 2017. http s://doi.org/10.1017/9781316544624.

Liivoja, Rain. *Criminal Jurisdiction over Armed Forces Abroad*. Cambridge: Cambridge University Press, 2017. https://doi.org/10.1017/9781139600392.

Long, Jackie. 'Syria's Disappeared: New Evidence That Military Leaders Knew of Torture'. Channel 4 News, UK, 9 August 2018. www.channel4.com/news/syrias-disappeared-new-evidence-that-military-leaders-knew-of-torture.

Loveluck, Louisa, Asma Ajroudi, and Suzan Haidamous. 'Chemical Weapons Coverup Suspected in Syria as Inspectors Remain Blocked'. *Chicago Tribune*, 20 April 2018. www.chicagotribune.com/nation-world/ct-chemical-weapons-cov erup-syria-20180420-story.html.

Mallet, Victor. 'France Follows US to Set up Military Space Command'. *Financial Times*, 14 July 2019. www.ft.com/content/a479bcb6-a628-11e9-984 c-fac8325aaa04.

Meierhenrich, Jens. *Genocide: A Reader*. Oxford: Oxford University Press, 2014.

Mettraux, Guénaël. 'Crimes against Humanity in the Jurisprudence of the International Criminal Tribunals for the Former Yugoslavia and for Rwanda'. *Harvard International Law Journal* 43, no. 1 (2002): 316.

Perspectives on the Nuremberg Trial. Oxford and New York: Oxford University Press, 2008.

The Law of Command Responsibility. Oxford: Oxford University Press, 2016.

'Trial at Nuremberg'. In *Routledge Handbook of International Criminal Law*, edited by William Schabas and Nadia Bernaz, 5–16. Oxford: Routledge, 2013.

Mettraux, Guénaël, John Dugard, and Max Du Plessis. 'Heads of State Immunities, International Crimes and President Bashir's Visit to South Africa'. *International Criminal Law Review* 18, no. 4 (2018): 577–622. https://doi.org/10.1163/15718123-01804005.

Michel-Luviano, Veronica. 'Access to Justice, Victims' Rights, and Private Prosecution in Latin America: The Cases of Chile, Guatemala, and Mexico'. Dissertation, University of Minnesota, 2012.

Miles, Tom. 'German Arrest Is First Big Catch for Syria Investigators'. *Reuters*, 14 February 2019. https://uk.reuters.com/article/uk-germany-syria-investigators-idUKKCN1Q22FP.

Military and Paramilitary Activities in and against Nicaragua (*Nicaragua* v. *United States of America*). Merits, Judgment. ICJ Reports (1986).

Ministère Public v. *Hissein Habré, Extraordinary African Chambers*, Judgment of 30 May 2016.

Ministry of Foreign Affairs. 'The Netherlands Holds Syria Responsible for Gross Human Rights Violations'. Government of the Netherlands, 19 September 2020. www.government.nl/latest/news/2020/09/18/the-netherlands-holds-syria-responsible-for-gross-human-rights-violations.

Minority Staff of the Permanent Subcommittee on Investigations. 'Money Laundering and Foreign Corruption: Enforcement and Effectiveness of the Patriot Act – Case Study Involving Riggs Bank Report'. Washington, DC: US Senate, Permanent Subcommittee on Investigations, Committee on Government Affairs, 15 July 2004.

Morgenthau, Hans. *Politics Among Nations*. 2nd ed. New York: Alfred Knopf, 1954.

Moses, A. Dirk, Marco Duranti, and Roland Burke. *Decolonization, Self-Determination, and the Rise of Global Human Rights Politics*. Edited by A. Dirk Moses, Marco Duranti and Roland Burke. Human Rights in History. Cambridge: Cambridge University Press, 2020.

Moudeïna, Jaqueline. 'From Victim to Witness and the Challenges of Sexual Violence Testimony'. In *The President on Trial: Prosecuting Hissene Habre*, edited by Sharon Weill, Kim Thuy Seelinger and Kerstin Bree Carlson, 118–24. Oxford: Oxford University Press, 2020.

Nadler, Jerrold. 'Text – H.Res.755 – 116th Congress (2019–2020): Impeaching Donald John Trump, President of the United States, for High Crimes and Misdemeanors'. Webpage. Congress.gov., 5 February 2020. www.congress.gov/bill/116th-congress/house-resolution/755/text.

Nako, Madjiasra, and Emma Farge. 'Chad Security Agents Face First Trial over 1980s Killings, Torture'. *Reuters*, 14 November 2014. https://in.reuters.com/article/us-chad-trial-idUSKCN0IY1YO20141114.

Nicholson, Joanna. 'The Role Played by External Case Law in Promoting the Legitimacy of International Criminal Court Decisions'. *Nordic Journal of International Law* 87, no. 2 (2018): 189. https://doi.org/10.1163/15718107-08702005.

Nikoghosyan, Hovhannes. 'Government Failure, Atrocity Crimes and the Role of the International Criminal Court: Why Not Syria, but Libya'. *The International Journal of Human Rights: R2P: Perspectives on the Concept's Meaning, Proper Application and Value* 19, no. 8 (2015): 1240–56. https://doi.org/10.1080/13642987.2015.1082838.

Nolte, George. 'The Limits of the Security Council's Powers and Its Function in the International Legal System: Some Reflections'. In *The Role of Law in International Politics: Essays in International Relations and International Law*, edited by Michael Byers, 317–26. Oxford: Oxford University Press, 2001.

Noortmann, Math, August Reinisch, Cedric Ryngaert and Barrie Axford. *Non-State Actors in International Law*. Oxford and Portland, OR: Hart Publishing, 2015.

Oberlandesgericht Koblenz. 'Urteil Gegen Einen Mutmaßlichen Mitarbeiter Des Syrischen Geheimdienstes Wegen Beihilfe Zu Einem Verbrechen Gegen Die Menschlichkeit'. Landesregierung Rheinland-Pfalz, 24 February 2021. https://jus tiz.rlp.de/de/service-informationen/aktuelles/detail/news/News/detail/urteil-gege n-einen-mutmasslichen-mitarbeiter-des-syrischen-geheimdienstes-wegen-bei hilfe-zu-einem-ver/.

'Obligations Arising for States without or against Their Will (Volume 241) – Brill'. https://referenceworks-brillonline-com.ezproxy.library.uq.edu.au/entries/the-hag ue-academy-collected-courses/*A9780792329541_02.

Obregon, Edgardo Sobenes, and Benjamin Samson Ashtamkar. *Nicaragua before the International Court of Justice Impacts on International Law*. Cham, Switzerland: Springer Verlag, 2017.

Office of the Prosecutor (OTP) of the International Criminal Court (ICC). 'International Criminal Court Prosecutor Recommends Investigation of Potential War Crimes in Afghanistan, Including Actions by U.S. Military and Central Intelligence Agency'. *American Journal of International Law* 111, no. 2 (April 2017): 517–23. https://doi.org/10.1017/ajil.2017.4.

Onishi, Norimitsu. 'He Bore Up Under Torture. Now He Bears Witness'. *New York Times*, 31 March 2001. www.nytimes.com/2001/03/31/world/he-bore-up-under-tor ture-now-he-bears-witness.html.

Ostrander, Jeremy. 'The Last Bastion of Sovereign Immunity: A Comparative Look at Immunity from Execution of Judgments'. *Berkeley Journal of International Law* 22, no. 3 (2004): 541–82. https://doi.org/10.15779/Z38706X.

Payne, Leigh A., and Kathryn Sikkink. *Transitional Justice in the Asia-Pacific*. Cambridge: Cambridge University Press, 2013.

Peel, Michael. 'Russia Presses EU to Pay for Rebuilding Syria'. *Financial Times*, 10 January 2018. www.ft.com/content/21483e5c-f22a-11e7-b220-857e26d1aca4.

Pennington, Kenneth. *The Prince and the Law, 1200–1600: Sovereignty and Rights in the Western Legal Tradition*. Berkeley: University of California Press, 1993.

Pennington, Kenneth, and Melodie Harris Eichbauer. *Law as Profession and Practice in Medieval Europe: Essays in Honor of James A. Brundage*. London and New York: Routledge, 2016.

Pennington, Kenneth, and Wilfried Hartmann. *The History of Courts and Procedure in Medieval Canon Law*. Washington, DC: Catholic University of America Press, 2016.

Peters, Anne. 'Are We Moving towards Constitutionalization of the World Community?' In *Realizing Utopia: The Future of International Law*, edited by Antonio Cassese. Oxford: Oxford University Press, 2012.

Phillips, Andrew, and Christian Reus-Smit. 'Culture and Order in World Politics'. In *Culture and Order in World Politics*, edited by Andrew Phillips and Christian Reus-Smit, 23–46. Cambridge: Cambridge University Press, 2019.

Pinheiro, Paulo Sérgio (Former head of the CoI for Syria). Interview with author, December 2018.

Porter, Brian. *The Aberystwyth Papers: International Politics, 1919–1969*. London: Oxford University Press for the University College of Wales, 1972.

'Profile: Chad's Hissene Habre'. *BBC News*, 30 May 2016, sec. Africa. www.bbc.com/ news/world-africa-18927845.

Prosecutor v. *Furundžija*, Judgment, International Criminal Tribunal for the Former Yugoslavia, Trial Chamber, Case No IT-95–17/1-T (10 December 1998).

Prouvèze, Rémy. 'Immunities'. In *Routledge Handbook of International Criminal Law*, edited by William A. Schabas and Nadia Bernaz, 355–68. London and New York: Routledge, 2011.

'Questions relating to the Obligation to Prosecute or Extradite' (*Belgium* v. *Senegal*), Judgment, ICJ Reports (2012).

R v. *Bow Street Metropolitan Stipendiary Magistrate*, ex parte Pinochet Ugarte (No 3) (Pinochet 3) [2000] (House of Lords, Great Britain (UK) 24 March 1999).

Rankin, Melinda. 'A Road Map for Germany: Negotiating a Path to Accountability with Assad'. PeaceLab, Global Public Policy Institute (GPPI), 18 December 2018. https://peacelab.blog/2018/12/negotiating-a-path-to-accountability-with-assad.

'Australia's Responsibility to Prosecute? Bridging the Gap of International Criminal Law in Syria and Iraq'. *Australian Journal of International Affairs* 72, no. 4 (2018): 322–28. https://doi.org/10.1080/10357718.2017.1414772.

'Investigating Crimes against Humanity in Syria and Iraq: The Commission for International Justice and Accountability'. *Global Responsibility to Protect* 9, no. 4 (2017): 395–421. https://doi.org/10.1163/1875984X-00904004.

'"Responsibility to Prosecute"? The Case of German Universal Jurisdiction, CIJA and the Arrest of Syrian Perpetrators'. *LawLog, Center for Global Constitutionalism, WZB* (blog), 13 March 2019. https://lawlog.blog.wzb.eu/2019/03/13/responsibility-to-prosecute-the-case-of-german-universal-jurisdiction-cija-and-the-arrest-of-syrian-perpetrators/.

'The Future of International Criminal Evidence in New Wars? The Evolution of the Commission for International Justice and Accountability (CIJA)'. *Journal of Genocide Research* 20, no. 3 (2018): 392–411. https://doi.org/10.1080/14623528.2018.1445435.

The Political Life of Mary Kaldor: Ideas and Action in International Relations. Boulder, CO: Lynne Rienner Publishers, 2017.

'The "Responsibility to Prosecute" Core International Crimes? The Case of German Universal Jurisdiction and the Syrian Government'. *Global Responsibility to Protect* 11, no. 4 (2019): 394–410. https://doi.org/10.1163/1875984X-01104003.

Rapp, Stephen (CIJA commissioner),. Interview with author, January 2017.

Raz, Joseph. *The Authority of Law: Essays on Law and Morality*. Oxford: Oxford University Press, 2012.

Sputnik International. 'Rebuilding Syria After War to Cost Up to $400Bln – Assad', 10 May 2018. https://sputniknews.com/middleeast/201805101064319713-rebuilding-syria-assad-cost/.

Relea, Francesc. 'Un Grupo Especial Del FBI Colabora Con El Juez García Castellón Para Investigar a Pinochet (An FBI Special Group Collaborates with Judge Garcia Castellon to Investigate Pinochet)'. *El Pais*, 19 October 1997. http://www.elpais.es.

'ResS17_1.Pdf'. www.ohchr.org/Documents/HRBodies/HRCouncil/CoISyria/Res S17_1.pdf.

Reus-Smit, Christian. *Individual Rights and the Making of the International System*. Cambridge and New York: Cambridge University Press, 2013.

The Moral Purpose of the State: Culture, Social Identity, and Institutional Rationality in International Relations. Princeton, NJ: Princeton University Press, 1999.

The Politics of International Law. Cambridge and New York: Cambridge University Press, 2004.

Reus-Smit, Christian, and Duncan Snidal. *The Oxford Handbook of International Relations*. Oxford: Oxford University Press, 2008.

Reydams, Luc. 'The Rise and Fall of Universal Jurisdiction'. In *Routledge Handbook of International Criminal Law*, edited by William Schabas and Nadia Bernaz, 337–54. Oxford: Routledge, 2013.

Universal Jurisdiction: International and Municipal Legal Perspectives. Universal Jurisdiction. Oxford: Oxford University Press, 2015. https://oxford-universitypress scholarship-com.ezproxy.library.uq.edu.au/view/10.1093/acprof:oso/97801992742 60.001.0001/acprof-9780199274260.

Reydams, Luc, Jan Wouters and Cedric Ryngaert. *International Prosecutors*. Oxford: Oxford University Press, 2012.

'Introduction'. In *International Prosecutors*, edited by Luc Reydams, Jan Wouters and Cedric Ryngaert, 1–5. Oxford: Oxford University Press, 2012.

Transnational Institute (TNI). 'Riggs Bank to Pay Millions to Pinochet Victims: Press Release from Spanish Legal Team', 25 February 2005. https://www.tni.org/es/no de/13586.

Ritscher, Christian (Head of the War Crimes Unit S4, Federal Public Prosecutor, the Office of the German Federal Public Prosecutor General). Communication with author, August 2018.

Ritscher, Christian. 'Panel Discussion "Universal Jurisdiction Revisited: German Prosecutions of International Crimes Committed in Syria"'. At the Current Debates in International Criminal Justice Conference. Humboldt University, Berlin, 21–22 June 2018.

Roht-Arriaza, Naomi. *Prosecuting Heads of State*. Cambridge: Cambridge University Press, 2009.

The Pinochet Effect: Transnational Justice in the Age of Human Rights. Philadelphia: University of Pennsylvania Press, 2005.

Roling, B. V. A., and Antonio Cassese. *The Tokyo Trial and beyond: Reflections of a Peacemonger*. Cambridge: Polity Press, 1993.

Roman, Mar. 'Spanish Judge Seeks Permission from Britain to Question Kissinger over South American Dictatorship Links'. *Associated Press Newswires (Factiva)*, 17 April 2002.

Rosenfeld, Michel. 'The Rule of Law and the Legitimacy of Constitutional Democracy'. *Southern California Law Review* 74, no. 5 (2001): 1307–52.

Ruffert, Matthias. 'Pinochet Follow Up: The End of Sovereign Immunity?' *Netherlands International Law Review* 48, no. 2 (August 2001): 171–95. https://do i.org/10.1017/S0165070X00001248.

Sadat, Leila Nadya. *Forging a Convention for Crimes against Humanity*. Cambridge and New York: Cambridge University Press, 2011.

'Why the ICC's Judgment in the Al-Bashir Case Wasn't So Surprising'. *Just Security*, 12 July 2019. www.justsecurity.org/64896/why-the-iccs-judgment-in-the-al-bashir-case-wasnt-so-surprising/.

Sands, Philippe. *East West Street: On the Origins of "Genocide" and "Crimes Against Humanity"'*. London: Knopf Doubleday Publishing Group, 2016.

Torture Team: Deception, Cruelty and the Compromise of Law. London and New York: Allen Lane, 2008.

Sassen, Saskia. 'New Frontiers Facing Urban Sociology at the Millennium'. *The British Journal of Sociology* 51, no. 1 (2000): 143–59. https://doi.org/10.1111/j.1468-4446.2000.00143.x.

Saul, Ben. 'Standing Up for Justice in War'. Chatham House, 8 November 2016. www.chathamhouse.org/expert/comment/standing-justice-war.

Schabas, William. 'Crimes Against Humanity as a Paradigm for International Atrocity Crimes'. *Middle East Critique: New Scholarship on the Relocation of Ottoman Armenians from Eastern Anatolia in 1915–16* 20, no. 3 (2011): 253–69. https://doi.org/10.1080/19436149.2011.619762.

Genocide in International Law: The Crime of Crimes, 2nd ed. Cambridge and New York: Cambridge University Press, 2009.

'Introductory Remarks by William Schabas. (Annual Ben Ferencz Session: Africa and the International Criminal Court)'. *Proceedings of the Annual Meeting-American Society of International Law* 106 (2012): 305.

'Prevention of Crimes Against Humanity'. *Journal of International Criminal Justice* 16, no. 4 (2018): 705–28. https://doi.org/10.1093/jicj/mqy033.

'Prosecuting Dr Strangelove, Goldfinger, and the Joker at the International Criminal Court: Closing the Loopholes'. *Leiden Journal of International Law* 23, no. 4 (2010): 847–53. https://doi.org/10.1017/S0922156510000403.

'The Banality of International Justice'. *Journal of International Criminal Justice* 11, no. 3 (2013): 545–51. https://doi.org/10.1093/jicj/mqt027.

The Cambridge Companion to International Criminal Law. Cambridge: Cambridge University Press, 2016.

'The Contribution of the Eichmann Trial to International Law'. *Leiden Journal of International Law* 26, no. 3 (2013): 667–99. https://doi.org/10.1017/S0922156513000290.

'The International Court of Justice and Non-Party States'. *Windsor Yearbook of Access to Justice* 28, no. 1 (2010): 21.

'The International Criminal Court and Non-Party States'. *The Windsor Yearbook of Access to Justice* 28, no. 1 (2010): 1–22. https://doi.org/10.22329/wyaj.v28i1.4488.

The UN International Criminal Tribunals: The Former Yugoslavia, Rwanda and Sierra Leone. Cambridge: Cambridge University Press, 2006.

Unimaginable Atrocities Justice, Politics, and Rights at the War Crimes Tribunals. Oxford: Oxford University Press, 2012.

Schabas, William, and Nadia Bernaz. *Routledge Handbook of International Criminal Law*. London and New York: Routledge, 2011.

Scharf, Michael P. *Aut Dedere Aut Iudicare: Max Planck Encyclopedia of Public International Law* [MPEPIL]. Oxford Public International Law. Oxford: Oxford University Press, 2008.

Scheffer, David. *All the Missing Souls: A Personal History of the War Crimes Tribunals*. Course Book. Princeton, NJ: Princeton University Press, 2012.

'Blueprint for Legal Reforms at the United Nations and the International Criminal Court'. *Georgetown Journal of International Law* 36, no. 3 (2005): 683–701.

'Proposal for an International Criminal Court Arrest Procedures Protocol'. *Northwestern Journal of International Human Rights* 12, no. 3 (2014): 229–52.

'Reflections on Contemporary Responses to Atrocity Crimes'. *Genocide Studies International* 10, no. 1 (2016): 105. https://doi.org/10.3138/gsi.10.1.10.

'Staying the Course with the International Criminal Court'. *Cornell International Law Journal* 35, no. 1 (2002): 47, 69–87.

'The Complex Crime of Aggression under the Rome Statute'. *Leiden Journal of International Law* 23, no. 4 (2010): 897–904. https://doi.org/10.1017/S0922156510000452.

'The United States and the International Criminal Court. (Developments in International Criminal Law)'. *American Journal of International Law* 93, no. 1 (1999): 12–22. https://doi.org/10.2307/2997953.

'War Crimes and the Clinton Administration'. Edited by David Scheffer. *Social Research* 69, no. 4 (2002): 1109–17.

'Whose Lawfare Is It, Anyway? (Symposium: Lawfare)'. *Case Western Reserve Journal of International Law* 43, no. 1 (2010): 215.

Scott, Shirley V. *International Law in World Politics: An Introduction*, 3rd ed. Boulder, CO: Lynne Rienner Publishers, 2017.

'Second Day, Wednesday, 11/21/1945, Part 04', in Trial of the Major War Criminals before the International Military Tribunal. Volume II. Proceedings: 11/14/1945–11/30/1945.[Official text in the English language.] Nuremberg: International Military Tribunal (IMT) (1945).

Der Spiegal – International. 'Serbia's Difficult Choices: Belgrade Boxed in Over War Criminals, Kosovo and EU Membership', 27 December 2007. www.spiegel.de/international/europe/serbia-s-difficult-choices-belgrade-boxed-in-over-war-criminals-kosovo-and-eu-membership-a-525502.html.

Shenon, Philip. 'U.S. Releases Files on Abuses in Pinochet Era'. *New York Times*, 1 July 1999. https://archive.nytimes.com/www.nytimes.com/library/world/americas/070199chile-us-rights.html.

Shklar, Judith N. *Legalism*. Cambridge, MA: Harvard University Press, 1964.

Sikkink, Kathryn. *Amnesty in the Age of Human Rights Accountability: Comparative and International Perspectives*. Cambridge: Cambridge University Press, 2012.

'Human Rights: Advancing the Frontier of Emancipation'. *Development* 61, no. 1–4 (2018): 14–20. https://doi.org/10.1057/s41301-018-0186-1.

The Justice Cascade: How Human Rights Prosecutions Are Changing World Politics. 1st ed. New York: W. W. Norton, 2011.

The Persistent Power of Human Rights: From Commitment to Compliance. Cambridge University Press, 2013, https://doi.org/10.1017/CBO9781139237161.

'Situation in the Islamic Republic of Afghanistan, ICC-02/17, Investigation'. www.icc-cpi.int/afghanistan.

Skidelsky, Robert. 'Essay: Confessions of a Long-Distance Biographer'. *Independent on Sunday*, 29 November 2003. www.skidelskyr.com/site/article/a-writer-at-large-confessions-of-a-long-distance-biographer/.

Souleymane Guengueng et Autres C/Sénégal. 'Communication Presentée Au Comite Contre La Torture (Article 22 de La Convention), Pour Violation Des Articles 5 et 7 de La Convention', n.d. www.hrw.org/en/news/2010/10/14/legal-documents.

Staff, Reuters. 'Germany Issues International Arrest Warrant for Top Assad Officer'. *Reuters*, 8 June 2018. www.reuters.com/article/us-syria-crisis-germany-idUSKCN1J41VQ.

Strafprozessordnung (StPO) (German Code of Criminal Procedure), entered into force 7 April 1987, sections 230 and 231a (n.d.). www.gesetze-im-internet.de/stpo/.

Swart, Mia. 'The African Pinochet? Universal Jurisdiction and the Habré Case'. In *The President on Trial: Prosecuting Hissène Habré*, edited by Sharon Weill, Kim Thuy Seelinger, and Kerstin Bree Carlson, 406–14. Oxford: Oxford University Press, 2020.

'Sweden and Germany "at the Forefront" in Prosecuting Syria War Crimes'. *Sveriges Radio*, 5 October 2017, sec. Radio Sweden. https://sverigesradio.se/artikel/6791935.

Tamanah, Brian Z. *On the Rule of Law*. Cambridge: Cambridge University Press, 2012.

Tasioulas, John. 'Customary International Law: A Moral Judgment-Based Account | AJIL Unbound | Cambridge Core'. *American Journal of International Law (Unbound)* 108 (2014): 328–33.

'Human Rights, Legitimacy, and International Law'. *The American Journal of Jurisprudence* 58, no. 1 (June 1, 2013): 1–25. https://doi.org/10.1093/ajj/aut001.

Taub, Ben. 'The Assad Files: Capturing the Top-Secret Documents That Tie the Syrian Regime to Mass Torture and Killings'. *The New Yorker*, 18 April 2016. www.newyorker.com/magazine/2016/04/18/bashar-al-assads-war-crimes-exposed.

'Tenacity, Perseverance, and Imagination in the "Private International Prosecution" of Hissène Habré – Oxford Scholarship'. https://oxford-universitypressscholarship-com.ezproxy.library.uq.edu.au/view/10.1093/oso/9780198858621.001.0001/oso-9780198858621-chapter-6.

'"The BKA". Bundeskriminalamt (Federal Criminal Police Office)', 2018. www.bka.de/EN/Home/home_node.html;jsessionid=8D4B493C1B288EC3EF2E0280AB5EAD9E.live2301.

'The Muslim Brotherhood in Syria by Dara Conduit'. www-cambridge-org.ezproxy.library.uq.edu.au/core/books/muslim-brotherhood-in-syria/25B0E21E959D6F92C2BE88B58E357DF6.

The National Security Archive. 'Chile: 16,000 Secret Documents Declassified'. George Washinton University, 13 November 2000. https://nsarchive2.gwu.edu/news/2000 1113/.

The Right Livelihood Foundation. 'Juan Garcés – The Right Livelihood Award', 1999. www.rightlivelihoodaward.org/laureates/juan-garcs/.

Thirlway, H. W. A. *The Sources of International Law*. 2nd ed. Oxford Public International Law. Oxford: Oxford University Press, 2019.

Thomson Reuters. 'High-Ranking Syrian Suspected of Torturing Prisoners Arrested in Germany | CBC News'. CBC, 14 February 2019. www.cbc.ca/news/world/syrian-arrested-germany-suspected-torture-1.5017799.

Thouvenin, Jean-Marc, and Christian Tomuschat. *The Fundamental Rules of the International Legal Order: Jus Cogens and Obligations Erga Omnes*. Leiden and Boston: Martinus Nijhoff Publishers, 2006.

Tomuschat, Christian. 'International Law as a Coherent System: Unity or Fragmentation?' In *Looking to the Future*, edited by Mahnounsh H. Arsanjani, Jacob Cogan, Robert Sloane and Siegfried Wiessner, 323–54. Leiden and Boston: Brill Publishing, 2011.

Obligations Arising for States without or against Their Will Vol. 241. Collected Courses of The Hague Academy of International Law. The Hague: Martinus Nijhoff, 1993. https://referenceworks-brillonline-com.ezproxy.library.uq.edu.au/e ntries/the-hague-academy-collected-courses/*A9780792329541_02.

Trial of the Major War Criminals before the International Military Tribunal. Nuremberg: International Military Tribunal (IMT) (1945).

United Nations. 'Charter of the International Military Tribunal – Annex to the Agreement for the Prosecution and Punishment of the Major War Criminals of the European Axis ('London Agreement')', 8 August 1945.

Convention against Torture and Other Cruel, Inhuman or Degrading Treatment or Punishment (CAT), Treaty Series, 1465 § (1984).

'Convention on the Prevention and Punishment of the Crime of Genocide (Genocide Convention)', 9 December 1948.

'Statute of the International Court of Justice', 18 April 1945.

The Charter of the United Nations (1945).

'Vienna Convention on the Law of Treaties (VCLT)', 23 May 1969.

Yearbook of the International Law Commission 2002: Report of the Commission to the General Assembly on the Work of Its Fifty-Fourth Session. Vol. 2, Part 2. New York and Geneva: United Nations, 2009.

United Nations Committee Against Torture. 'Decisions of the Committee Against Torture under Article 22 of the Convention against Torture and Other Cruel, Inhuman or Degrading Treatment or Punishment, Communication No. 181/2001, CAT/C/36/D/181/2001', 19 May 2006. http://tbinternet.ohchr.org/_layouts/treaty bodyexternal/Download.aspx?symbolno=CAT%2fC%2f36%2fD%2f181% 2f2001&Lang=en.

United Nations General Assembly. General Assembly Resolution 95 (1), Affirmation of the Principles of International Law Recognised by the Charter of the Nurnberg Tribunal (1946). https://search-proquest-com.ezproxy.library.uq.edu.au/docview/ 1679073021?accountid=14723.

International, Impartial and Independent Mechanism to Assist in the Investigation and Prosecution of Those Responsible for the Most Serious Crimes under International Law Committed in the Syrian Arab Republic since March 2011, a/ res/71/248 (2016).

Resolution 56 (82), Report of the International Law Commission on the Work of Its Fifty-third Session (2002).

Resolution 96 (1), The Crime of Genocide (1946).

Resolution 217, The Universal Declaration of Human Rights (UDHR) (1948).

Resolution 2200A (XXI), International Covenants on Civil and Political Rights (1966).

'Rome Statute of the International Criminal Court', 17 July 1998.

'Terms of Reference of the International, Impartial and Independent Mechanism to Assist in the Investigation and Prosecution of Persons Responsible for the Most Serious Crimes under International Law Committed in the Syrian Arab Republic since March 2011'. 2017. https://iiim.un.org/terms-of-reference-of-iiim/.

United Nations Human Rights Council. 'Resolution Adopted by the Human Rights Council at Its Seventeenth Special Session, Resolution, S-17/1, Situation of Human Rights in the Syrian Arab Republic. Office of Human Rights Commission, 22 August 2011'. 2011: Office of Human Rights Commission, 2017. www.ohchr.org/Documents/HRBodies/HRCouncil/CoISyria/ResS17_1.pdf.

United Nations Security Council (UNSC), Draft Resolution S/2014/348 (2014).

Resolution 2043 (2012).

Resolution 2059 (2012).

United States. Executive Office of the President. 'U.S. Interests and Policy in Chad [Attached to Cover Memorandum] Secret, National Security Decision Directive. DNSA Collection: Presidential Directives, Part II. Signator: Reagan, Ronald W. PR01643. NSDD 322', 14 December 1988.

'Universal Jurisdiction: International and Municipal Legal Perspectives – Oxford Scholarship'. https://oxford-universitypressscholarship-com.ezproxy.library.uq.ed u.au/view/10.1093/acprof:oso/9780199274260.001.0001/acprof-9780199274260.

'Universal Jurisdiction Is Not Disappearing | Journal of International Criminal Justice | Oxford Academic'. https://academic-oup-com.ezproxy.library.uq.edu.au/jicj/art icle/13/2/245/896503.

Office of the High Commissioner for Human Rights OHCHR. 'Victim to Victor: The Story of Souleymane Guengueng', 19 January 2017. www.ohchr.org/EN/NewsEv ents/Pages/VictimToVictor.aspx.

Völkerstrafgesetzbuch (VStGB) (Code of Crimes Against International Law), entered into force on 30 June 2002, Pub. L. No. Federal Law Gazette I, 2254 (n.d.). www .gesetze-im-internet.de/vstgb/BJNR225410002.html; www.iuscomp.org/gla/stat utes/VoeStGB.pdf.

Waldron, Jeremy. 'International Law: "A Relatively Small and Unimportant" Part of Jurisprudence?' In *Reading HLA Hart's The Concept of Law*, edited by Andrea Dolcetti and James Edwards, 209–23. Oxford, UK and Portland, OR: Hart Publishing, 2013.

Watts, Arthur. 'The Importance of International Law'. In *The Role of Law in International Politics: Essays in International Relations and International Law*, edited by Michael Byers, 5–16. Oxford: Oxford University Press, 2001.

Weill, Sharon, Kim Thuy Seelinger, and Kerstin Bree Carlson, eds. *The President on Trial: Prosecuting Hissene Habre*. Oxford: Oxford University Press, 2020.

Weiner, Tim. 'U.S. Will Release Files on Crimes Under Pinochet'. *New York Times*, 2 December 1998. https://archive.nytimes.com/www.nytimes.com/library/world/ americas/120298pinochet-us.html.

Wenger, Etienne. 'A Social Theory of Learning'. In *Contemporary Theories of Learning: Learning Theorists … in Their Own Words*, edited by Knud Illeris, 219–28. London: Taylor & Francis Group, 2018.

'Communities of Practice and Social Learning Systems'. *Organization* 7, no. 2 (1 May 2000): 225–46. https://doi.org/10.1177/135050840072002.

Wenger, Etienne, Richard A. McDermott and William Snyder. *Cultivating Communities of Practice: A Guide to Managing Knowledge*. Boston, MA: Harvard Business Review Press, 2002.

Werner, Alain, and Emmanuelle Marchand. 'Supporting Victims at Trial: Civil Parties' Perspective'. In *The President on Trial: Prosecuting Hissene Habre*, edited by Sharon Weill, Kim Thuy Seelinger and Kerstin Bree Carlson, 125–33. Oxford: Oxford University Press, 2020.

Wessel, Ramses A., Math Noortmann, August Reinisch and Cedric Ryngaert. *International Governmental Organizations as Non-State Actors*. Oxford: Hart Publishing, 2015.

Whitaker, Raymond. 'Pinochet Denounces "Show Trial"'. *The Independent*, 18 November 1998. www.independent.co.uk/news/uk/crime/pinochet-denounce s-show-trial-739580.html.

Whiting, Alex. 'The UN General Assembly's Historic Resolution on Accountability for Syria: What It Means and What Are Its Limits'. Just Security, 22 December 2016. https://www.justsecurity.org/35795/syria-general-assembly-sidesteps-security-coun cil/.

(CIJA Commissioner). Interview with author, January 2017.

Wight, Colin. 'Violence in International Relations: The First and the Last Word'. *International Relations* 33, no. 2 (1 June 2019): 172–94. https://doi.org/10.1177/ 0047117819851168.

Wiley, William (CIJA director). Correspondence with author, February 2017.

Interview with author, January 2017.

Williams, Sarah, Hannah Woolaver, and Emma Palmer. *The Amicus Curiae in International Criminal Justice*. 1st ed. Oxford: Hart Publishing, 2020.

Wirth, Steffen. 'Immunity for Core Crimes? The ICJ's Judgment in the *Congo v. Belgium* Case'. *European Journal of International Law* 13, no. 4 (1 September 2002): 877–93. https://doi.org/10.1093/ejil/13.4.877.

Woetzel, Robert K. *The Nuremberg Trials in International Law*. London: Stevens; New York: Praeger, 1960.

Woodhouse, Diana. *The Pinochet Case: A Legal and Constitutional Analysis*. Oxford, UK and Portland, OR: Hart Publishing, 2000.

Zahar, Alexander. *International Criminal Law: A Critical Introduction*. Oxford, UK and New York: Oxford University Press, 2008.

Zeidy, Mohamed M. El. 'Admissibility in Intranational Criminal Law'. In *Routledge Handbook of International Criminal Law*, edited by William Schabas and Nadia Bernaz, 111–30. London and New York: Routledge, 2011.

Index

Abaifouta, Clement, 147
Abakar, Mahamat Hassan, 122
Abdulhak, Tarik, 171–2
accountability, 133–7, 182, 219
  Crane on, 80
  local, 122–4
  preconditions for, 179
  See also cooperative criminal accountability
    communities; criminal liability
accountability gap, 14, 21
  Syria and, 152, 158–62, 189–94, 196
Adler, Emanuel, 19, 41
  on cooperative criminal accountability
    communities, 43
  on innovation, 46
African Assembly for the Defense of Human
    Rights (RADDHO), 145
African Union, 137–40, 142, 143, 210
Allende, Salvador, 87, 88–9, 90, 101
  memorial foundation for, 94, 112, 219
Alsina, Joan, 95
Amnesty International
  Habré case and, 44
  Pinochet case and, 47, 55, 101, 103, 104,
    105
Andreu, Federico, 101
Annan, Kofi, 135
Anwar R. (Syrian defendant), 192
  arrest of, 67, 151
  prosecution of, 37, 177, 191–3
  trial of, 152
Arab Spring, 148, 149, 154
Arajärvi, Noora, 20, 76, 207
Argentine military case, 44, 93, 94
  cross-border kidnappings in, 97
Assad, Bashar al, 151, 175, 195, 208

Association for the Promotion and Defence of
    Human Right (APTDH), 118, 127
Association of the Relatives of the Disappeared
    Detainees, 104
Association of the Victims of Political
    Repression and Crime (AVCRP), 118, 124,
    125, 132, 145
Association of the Victims of the Crimes of the
    Regime of Hissène Habré
    (AVCRHH), 145
aut dedere aut judicare (duty to prosecute), 3,
    16, 61, 67
  erga omnes and, 28, 63
  Geneva Convention and, 38
aut dedere aut punire, 62, 63
autonomy, 210

Barbie, Klaus, 209
Barcella, Larry, 91
Barcelona Traction case, 62, 64
Bartle, Ronald, 108
Bassiouni, M. Cherif, 20, 62, 71
Beck, Thomas, 187, 188
Belgium v. Senegal, 44, 57, 63, 65–6, 141
  African Union and, 139
  ICJ and, 181
  Syria and, 68
Belgium v. Spain, 62, 64
Bell, Duncan, 17
Benetech Initiative, 132
Bercault, Oliver, 131
Besson, Samantha, 20, 214
Bindman, Geoffrey, 98, 104
Blok, Stef, 67, 68, 195
Brazil, 97
Brody, Reed, 35, 132

CPSIA information can be obtained
at www.ICGtesting.com
Printed in the USA
LVHW082254130123
737115LV00006B/520

9 781108 498166